Pedagogy and Power is a volume of interdisciplinary essays which explore the political dimensions of Greco-Roman education and of its subsequent models. Seeking to make the various structures and discourses of intellectual authority more apparent, the essays argue that there is a social context for the knowledge imparted by classical models of pedagogy: knowledge is always implicated in the processes, structures and articulations of power and their critiques. They examine how such pedagogies instruct their pupils to function as citizens who rule or are ruled, privileging certain knowledges over others, and including some individuals while excluding others. Overall the book proposes that classical education is an idea that has the capacity to be endlessly created and recreated, granted or denied authority, interrogated, and restructured in the service of the political community. It shows that the complex and plural authorities and power that have been associated with classical learning and knowledge are not part of a legacy to be unproblematically inherited or reproduced.

IDEAS IN CONTEXT 50

PEDAGOGY AND POWER

IDEAS IN CONTEXT

Edited by QUENTIN SKINNER (*General Editor*)
LORRAINE DASTON, WOLF LEPENIES,
J. B. SCHNEEWIND and JAMES TULLY

The books in this series will discuss the emergence of intellectual traditions
and of related new disciplines. The procedures, aims and vocabularies
that were generated will be set in the context of the alternatives available
within the contemporary frameworks of ideas and institutions. Through
detailed studies of the evolution of such traditions, and their modification
by different audiences, it is hoped that a new picture will form of the
development of ideas in their concrete contexts. By this means, artificial
distinctions between the history of philosophy, of the various sciences, of
society and politics, and of literature may be seen to dissolve.

The series is published with the support of the Exxon Foundation.

A list of books in the series will be found at the end of the volume.

PEDAGOGY AND POWER

Rhetorics of classical learning

EDITED BY

YUN LEE TOO

Assistant Professor of Classics, Columbia University

and

NIALL LIVINGSTONE

Teaching and Research Fellow in Greek, University of St Andrews

CAMBRIDGE
UNIVERSITY PRESS

PUBLISHED BY THE PRESS SYNDICATE OF THE UNIVERSITY OF CAMBRIDGE
The Pitt Building, Trumpington Street, Cambridge CB2 1RP, United Kingdom

CAMBRIDGE UNIVERSITY PRESS
The Edinburgh Building, Cambridge CB2 2RU, United Kingdom
40 West 20th Street, New York, NY 10011–4211, USA
10 Stamford Road, Oakleigh, Melbourne 3166, Australia

First published 1998

Printed in the United Kingdom at the University Press, Cambridge

Typeset in 11/12½ pt Baskerville No. 2 [GT]

A catalogue record for this book is available from the British Library

Library of Congress cataloguing in publication data

Pedagogy and power: rhetorics of classical learning / edited by Yun
Lee Too and Niall Livingstone.
p.   cm. — (Ideas in context)
Includes bibliographical references and index.
ISBN 0 521 59435 9 (hardback)
1. Classical education – Political aspects.   2. Classical
education – Social aspects.   I. Too, Yun Lee.   II. Livingstone,
Niall.   III. Series.
LC1021.P43   1998
370.11′2–dc21   97–29632 CIP

ISBN 0 521 59435 9 hardback

Contents

Contributors

PANAGIOTIS A. AGAPITOS is Associate Professor of Byzantine Language and Literature at the University of Cyprus. He has published *Narrative Structure in the Byzantine Vernacular Romances* (Munich, 1991) and *The Study of Medieval Greek Romance* (Copenhagen, 1992), and articles on Byzantine rhetoric and philosophy, Greek palaeography, and modern Greek poetry. His current project is a critical edition of the thirteenth-century verse romance *Livistros and Rhodamne*.

CATHERINE ATHERTON is Fellow in Classical Philosophy at New College, Oxford. She is the author of *The Stoics on Ambiguity* (Cambridge, 1993) and articles on ancient rhetoric and grammar. She is currently working on the papyrus fragments of a logical work by the Stoic scholarch Chrysippus of Soli.

WARREN BOUTCHER is Lecturer in English at Queen Mary and Westfield College, University of London. He has published articles on Montaigne and on English vernacular humanism, and is working on a book on the modern intellectual history of the humanists.

CLARE BRANT is Lecturer in English at King's College London. She is the co-editor of *Women, Texts and Histories 1575–1760* (London, 1992), has published various articles on eighteenth-century and Romantic literature, and is writing a book about eighteenth-century letters.

PAUL CARTLEDGE is Director of Studies of Classics and Fellow of Clare College, Cambridge and Reader in Greek History, University of Cambridge. He is the author, editor, and co-editor of ten books, including most recently *The Greeks* (Oxford, rev. edn., 1997), and *The Cambridge Illustrated History of Ancient Greece* (Cambridge, 1997). He is currently writing a book on political thought in ancient Greece.

SARAH COLVIN is Lecturer in German at the University of Edinburgh. Her research interests are in the fields of women's writing, rhetoric and irony, drama and film. Her current project is a major study of women and the drama in Germany and Austria 1871–1990. Her doctoral thesis will shortly be published by Oxford University Press as *The Rhetorical Feminine: Gender and Orient on the German Stage 1647–1742*.

NIALL LIVINGSTONE is Teaching and Research Fellow in Greek at the University of St Andrews. His principal research interests are in the intellectual history of the fourth century BC, Greek oratory and rhetorical instruction, declamation and prose fiction in antiquity, and the history of the reception and translation of classical texts. Current projects include a commentary on Isocrates' *Busiris* and a book on the persuasive techniques of classical rhetoric.

TERESA MORGAN is Research Fellow at St John's College, Cambridge. Her book *Literate Education in the Hellenistic and Roman Worlds* will be published by Cambridge University Press.

DAVID RUNDLE is College Lecturer in early modern history at Mansfield College, Oxford. He researches both humanist political thought and the circulation of humanist manuscripts in fifteenth- and early sixteenth-century England. He has published articles on Thomas More and on the early reception of 'humanism' in England.

JANE STEVENSON is Research Fellow in the Humanities at the University of Warwick. Her interests include post-classical Latin and women's writing. Her most recent book is *The Laterculus Malalianus and the School of Archbishop Theodore* (Cambridge, 1995), and she is now principally engaged on two projects, *The Oxford Book of Early Modern Women Poets* and a book on women's poetry in Latin.

CHRISTOPHER STRAY is Honorary Research Fellow in the Department of Classics and Ancient History at the University College of Wales, Swansea; he is also currently a Visiting Fellow of Wolfson College, Cambridge, where he is working on the history of the Classical Tripos 1822–1914. He has published on the reception of Victorian Latin grammars (*Grinders and Grammars*, Reading, 1995) and on public-school slang and idiolect (*The Mushri-English Pronouncing Dictionary*, Berkeley/Swansea/Wellington, privately printed, 1996). His book *Classics Transformed: Schools, Universities, and Society 1830–1960* will by published by Oxford University Press in 1998.

YUN LEE TOO is Assistant Professor of Classics at Columbia University. Her publications include *The Rhetoric of Identity in Isocrates: Text, Power,*

Pedagogy (Cambridge, 1995) and *The Idea of Ancient Literary Criticism* (Oxford, forthcoming). Her current projects include an edited collection of essays on the history of education in antiquity (to be published by E. J. Brill), and a commentary on Isocrates' *Antidosis*.

TIM WHITMARSH is Junior Research Fellow at St John's College, Cambridge. He has published articles on Heliodorus, and is working on a translation of Achilles Tatius.

Acknowledgements

An interdisciplinary project has the potential to afford opportunities for establishing links and contacts across different fields. *Pedagogy and Power* has not disappointed. The project has been most productive in bringing together individuals from various disciplines, with distinct approaches within the same disciplines, and at different stages in their careers, and we would like to express our appreciation to our contributors for their extraordinary enthusiasm and effort in helping us bring this volume to completion.

Moreover, the editors of this volume would both like to express their gratitude to Ewen Bowie, Terence Cave, Anthony Grafton, Edith Hall, and David Norbrook for their advice at early stages of the project, and to Susan Bassnett for her suggestions and warm encouragement. We would in particular like to thank Quentin Skinner, the editor of the Ideas in Context series, for his faith in the book, in the editors and contributors, and for his unfailing support and assistance over the project's three years (1994–7).

Introduction

Yun Lee Too[1]

At the end of the twentieth century telling people that you are a classicist – we mean someone who studies and/or teaches ancient Greek and Latin, and their cultures – is likely to produce a variety of responses. For one of the editors of this volume, being a 'classicist' can serve as a form of social camouflage, if a rather odd one. At one end of the spectrum, incomprehension and embarrassed amusement ('I do Greek' can be an effective conversation-stopper); at the other extreme, there is the (imagined) recognition of a fellow-member of the club dedicated to preserving ancient (where 'ancient' means nineteenth-century) values, traditions and privileges: 'keep up the good work!' Different but related is the reaction of the wife of an older (non-classicist) male academic: 'a Greats man! You must be clever!' The other editor of this volume has provoked puzzlement, incredulity, discomfort. She has been asked if 'classics' is to be understood in its 'normal' sense (*she wonders what they regard as 'normal'*); if she does 'classics' in an 'extended' sense (*she wonders in turn if 'extended' denotes Penguin Classics, and the classics of English literature*[2]); or if she does ballet or music. She has also been told on more than one occasion that it is a pity that she does not do her own languages (*but she asks herself* to whom *can Greek and Latin actually belong*).[3]

What makes one of us more readily accepted as a classicist than the other? The answer is one that raises issues much larger than the question of what sort of people each of us as individuals might be or appear to be. A response to the term 'classicist' is to some degree a response

[1] I would like to thank Niall Livingstone for his meticulous editorial attention to the Introduction, and for his discussion with me of its arguments and points.

[2] See P. Cartledge, 'So different and so long ago', *New Statesman and Society* (1 March, 1996), pp. 36–7 and his chapter in this volume.

[3] In his excellent undergraduate dissertation, *'Laughter and Grief '? The Portrayal of Classics in School Fiction* (Part II Classical Tripos Dissertation), pp. 30–2, Jonathan Cooper points out that the Chinese pirate of Arthur Ransome's *Missee Lee* (published 1941) is an unlikely classicist who forces the children of the book into learning Latin grammar on the high seas of South East Asia.

to a perception, or perhaps the assumptions and presumptions that
underlie a perception, of what classical learning and knowledge entail.
It is a response to the perception of who might or should be expected to
have classical learning and knowledge, and about the value of classical
learning and knowledge. It is perhaps also a response to the understanding of what sort of community classics might be thought either to
construct or to have validity within. *Pedagogy and Power* is a volume which
turns to history for some of the explanations for these understandings,
stereotypes and prejudices, precisely because history plays an important part in the pedagogical imaginary. In particular, it is classical
antiquity which has provided us with ideals of how and what we teach,
and how and what we learn, and it is the idea of classical education
that is the concern of this volume.

In the contemporary academy, the study of classical education has a
formidable genealogy. Where the classicist is concerned, the history of
ancient education is a discourse that has been occupied in the latter half
of the twentieth century almost solely by Henri Marrou's influential and
much revered *Histoire de l'éducation dans l'antiquité* (Paris, 1948).[4] This
history concerned itself with what might be taught and learned in the
ancient 'classroom', often drawing anachronistic analogies between the
scholar's understanding of twentieth-century education and of ancient
education. Education, its nature, functions, and discourses were never
interrogated from first principles: for instance, what might it mean to
pass on knowledge? What might 'knowledge' be? Typically, the history of education, and particularly of education in distant antiquity,
can provide an insulating, because distant, set of images and ideals, an
iconography of which we are not fully aware because we do not interrog-
ate it. This history is liable to be rendered a static, perfect paradigm
or reverentially studied as a closed text. When either of these situations
happens, it becomes part of an *unconscious*, which creates our hopes
and desires for pedagogy and which has authority and power precisely
because it is not always noticed for what it is.

The historical unconscious conventionally dreams itself into an unproblematic 'esprit de corps' with its revered teacher and his descendants,
into recreations of the Platonic Academy (of course, without its homo-
erotics and its oligarchic politics), Aristotle's Lyceum, the medieval
monastic communities of scholar-priests, the Florentine circle of the

[4] Cf. H. I. Marrou, *De la connaissance historique* (Paris, 1954), p. 209. E. J. Brill will be publishing *A New History of Education in Antiquity* (ed. Y. L. Too) to replace Marrou's *Histoire* in 2000.

Renaissance tyrant Lorenzo de' Medici, the coffee house cliques of the eighteenth century, the untroubled quadrangles of Oxbridge of a few decades ago perhaps as misremembered in Evelyn Waugh's *Brideshead Revisited*. It has provided paradigms untroubled by questions of context, of explicit ideology (for its ideology is too often an implicit one), of interpretive method. Accordingly, existing accounts of (ancient) education often and largely implicitly propose its subject matter to be a discourse of reproduction, one which minimises change and individuality not just among teachers and students, but across historical eras.[5] Marrou totalised ancient pedagogy as a largely static process from archaic Greece to the Byzantine Period and beyond this to the mid-twentieth century (as his constant contemporary analogies, and indeed anachronisms, insinuate). It is worth pointing out that the shape of this narrative owes its origins to a particular historiographical ideology, in which social and economic structures were studied in preference to political events, and accordingly in which vast epochs and eras (so 'la longue durée') rather than short periods were studied in order to trace historical change and development.

On the other hand, the glorifying tradition likes to insist upon the possibility of a seamless line of descent from ancient Greece – most often the Athens of Plato – to the present. As Henry Louis Gates discerned, a rhetoric of lineage and inheritance, which has been most visible in apologies for the canon, especially in its form as 'Great Books', tends to insist upon the sameness of past and present, and in the process, creates a sense of Otherness for those who have no claims on this 'inheritance'.[6] As Pierre Bourdieu has observed, academic communities tend to appoint sucessors who are homogenised, or easily homogenised.[7] So histories of ancient education appoint the present as the inheritors of the past, demonstrating the likeness of then and now and closing ranks with the imperfectly distinguished past. Hence Marrou accorded little importance to specificities of method, of culture, or of individuals to the extent that Byzantine education was still essentially 'Hellenistic' insofar as it retained traces of Greek antiquity.[8]

[5] See M. W. Apple, *Education and Power* (Boston, London, etc., 1982), esp. pp. 54ff. and P. Bourdieu and J.-C. Passeron, *Reproduction in Education, Society and Culture*, tr. Richard Nice (London and Beverley Hills, 1977). That reproduction is the aim of pedagogy continues to underlie the recent collection of essays edited by J. Gallop, *Pedagogy: The Question of Impersonation* (Bloomington and Indianapolis, 1995), see especially pp. 4–5.
[6] H. L. Gates, *Loose Canons: Notes on the Culture Wars* (Oxford and New York, 1992), pp. 109–10.
[7] P. Bourdieu, *Homo Academicus* (Oxford, 1988), pp. 143–4.
[8] Marrou, *A History of Education*, p. 452.

The idea that classical education might be inherited as a legacy also lends itself to less than plural accounts. In some (very influential) quarters classical learning is regarded as the basis for what makes the West what it is – namely, democratic, inquiring, original, creative: in fact, now as then, the antitype of the barbarian. Knowledge of classical texts has thus been lauded and reverentially celebrated by scholars and intellectuals both inside and outside of the field of classics.[9] In the United States, classical literature is most frequently celebrated in the context of the 'Great Books', the canon of literature that was thought to be essential to every *gentleman*'s education. (That the gentleman's education is the concern is evident from the attacks on feminism, deconstruction, post-modernism, and minority literature and criticism which often accompany defence of the canon.) Mary Louise Pratt points out that the establishment of the Western civilisation course at Columbia in 1919, which scholars trace as the origin of 'Great Books', actually grew out of War Issues courses held in 1918 at various universities to instruct US soldiers in the European culture and heritage that they were to defend.[10] W. B. Carnochan offers an alternative, but complementary explanation that the historical programmes of study were in part originally established in response to a sense of the need to integrate and homogenise a growing immigrant population.[11] But more to the point they offered a recuperation of the Arnoldian programme of classical and European literature as a civilising force.

The ideal of classical education has had a wide influence from antiquity up to the present day, and not just as a socialising force. It has also asserted its influence in a variety of different disciplines and discourses, especially in modern literary and cultural studies. Where the posture has been defensive, the homogenising potential of classics has been deployed as part of a response to anxieties about the fragmentation of cultural ideals and icons under the influence of problematising

[9] See S. Lawall (ed.), *Reading World Literature: Theory, History, Practice* (Austin, 1994), pp. 21–2 on the responses to this question produced by the National Endowment for the Humanities in the United States. The concern is above all that the contemporary academy is rejecting the 'Great Books', which are viewed as a means of constructing community. Cf. also P. du Bois, *Sappho is Burning* (Chicago and London, 1995), p. 32 on the need for feminist perspectives and presences to make themselves felt in classical scholarship.
[10] See Pratt in D. J. Gless and B. Herrnstein Smith, *The Politics of Liberal Education* (Durham, NC, 1992), pp. 13–31.
[11] W. B. Carnochan, *The Battleground of the Curriculum. Liberal Education and American Experience* (Stanford, 1993), p. 69.

discourses and realities (among them multiculturalism, feminism, deconstruction, postmodernism, gay and queer studies).[12]

The present volume, *Pedagogy and Power*, is not a history of ancient education in any conventional sense. Here the editors want to draw attention to the fact that they consciously use the term 'pedagogy' as one that
is distinct from 'education' (from Latin *educare*, 'to raise up', 'to lead out').
'Pedagogy' (from Greek *paid-* + *agōgē*, 'the leading of the child/slave')
might quite literally, and in its original usage and sense, propose an
exclusive process, one that is concerned with the training of pre-adult
males. In the late twentieth century, however, it has very different connotations in that it seeks to include rather than to exclude. Contemporary pedagogy is an enterprise often associated with social change
and left-leaning agendas – hence 'radical pedagogy'.[13] Pedagogy is not
really a discipline in its own right, and when one tries to constitute it as
such, this may lead to embarrassment. Scholars, such as Jane Tompkins
and Susan Miller, observe that pedagogy was not so long ago a 'dirty
little secret, the fearsome and demeaned professional impropriety'.
Pedagogy is personal; it is a bit like sex. It involves talking about yourself, especially if you regard yourself as a teacher whose teaching is an
activity with a significant impact.[14] Nonetheless, it has of late become a

[12] Camille Paglia is quoted as saying, 'When we hear all this nonsense about how we should be
teaching poor students about the peasants of Guatemala in Marxist rhetoric, I say, excuse me,
the factory workers I have had contact with, black and white, they don't want to read about
the peasants of Guatemala. They want Sophocles and Shakespeare' (*THES* (3 March, 1995),
p. 17). Paglia advocates a core curriculum based mainly on the classics, and dislikes gay studies,
women's studies, African-American studies, and so on (p. 18).
[13] See P. Freire, *Pedagogy of the Oppressed* (Harmondsworth, 1972; originally published New York,
1970); and more recently, also L. Davis and M. B. Mirabella, *Left Politics and the Literary
Profession* (New York and Oxford, 1990); Gallop, *Pedagogy*; Gless and Herrnstein Smith, *The
Politics*; G. Graff, *Beyond the Culture Wars. How Teaching the Conflicts Can Revitalize American Education* (New York and London, 1992); B. Johnson, *The Pedagogical Imperative. Teaching as a Literary
Genre*, Yale French Studies 63 (1982); M. Le Doeuff, *Hipparchia's Choice: An Essay Concerning
Women, Philosophy, etc* (Oxford, 1991) [*L'Etude et le rouet* (Paris, 1989)].
[14] See J. Tompkins, 'The Pedagogy of the Distressed', *College English* 52 (1990) 653–60, esp. p. 655
and S. Miller, '*In Loco Parentis*: Addressing (the) Class', in Gallop, *Pedagogy*, p. 155. For William
Armstrong Pearcy III, talking about 'pedagogy' does indeed involve talking about sex; see his
celebration of archaic and classical Greek pedagogy as a site of homoeroticism and homosexual
relations, *Pederasty and Pedagogy in Archaic Greece* (Urbana and Chicago, 1996). Also cf. D. Lusted,
'Why Pedagogy?', *Screen* 27 (1986), pp. 2–4 (I would like to thank David Hamilton and Erica
McWilliam for this reference). The uncomfortable affinity of the words 'pedagogy' and 'pederasty', which both share the '*pais*' (Greek for 'child' or 'slave') root may explain the embarrassing
association between pedagogy and sex, one supported by the traditional stereotype of teaching
and learning as a site of male homosocial and -sexual interaction.

major topic and theme in contemporary work in the fields of literature, feminism, cultural studies, philosophy, and political theory.

Without a distinct disciplinary locale, pedagogy has even less any obvious genealogy. Pedagogy lacks the venerable history that has accrued to education, even though history might serve to ensure the critical and theoretical dimensions of pedagogical inquiry. Radical pedagogy, as Henry Giroux defines it, must *understand* the world in order to change it for the better. Understanding means coming to terms with what we perceive to be the privileged past, and those who consider transforming the contemporary scenario will not reject but reread and reclaim what is deemed canonical.[15] An underlying axiom of this book is that our defining images are always inlaid with a set of other less familar and less visible dynamics and their discourses. Where some might envisage a conservative agenda for 'tradition', history might alternatively serve as a possible 'other', as a site from which the present may wish to differentiate itself. With the project of revisionism in mind, one might explore the ways in which prior pedagogies might signify in different ways or help us to make pedagogy signify alternatively, if only by supplying models that we must reject as unpalatable.

Such an enterprise necessarily involves intertextualities revealed by juxtapositions between the ancient and the more contemporary, between the pedagogic and the less obviously pedagogic. Situations depicted by earlier authors serve as valuable sub-texts for analysis of subsequent scenes, even if they are ultimately to be rejected as models for the latter. The privileged and authoritative pedagogical traditions and histories offer a genealogy for some of the long-held perceptions, sometimes mistaken, sometimes overidealised, sometimes unconscious, sometimes unarticulated, about what the 'pedagogical' might be. Indeed, one notes the almost obligatory reference to 'Socrates' – and not necessarily Plato's – in contemporary writing on pedagogy, and particularly in writing which attempts to wrest teaching and learning from its more conventional constituencies.[16] We reread the pedagogical past in the belief

---

[15] See L. Robinson's chapter in Davis and Mirabella, *Left Politics*.
[16] See e.g. S. Felman, 'Psychoanalysis and Education: Teaching Terminable and Interminable', in Johnson, *The Pedagogical Imperative*, pp. 21–44; Le Doeuff, *Hipparchia's*, pp. 9–10 and passim; L. Irigaray, *Speculum of the Other Woman*, tr. G. Gill (Ithaca, 1985) [*Speculum de l'autre femme* (Paris, 1974)]; D. Purkis, 'The Lecherous Professor Revisited' in C. Brant and Y. L. Too (eds.), *Rethinking Sexual Harassment* (London, 1994), esp. pp. 198ff.; for Socrates as aporetic teacher, see S. Kofman, 'Beyond Aporia?', in A. Benjamin (ed.), *Poststructuralist Classics* (London, 1988), pp. 7–44. Eve Sedgwick merely cites Socrates in a title of an essay on queer pedagogy and performativity to signal its concern with teaching, 'Socratic Raptures, Socratic Ruptures: Notes Toward Queer Performativity', in S. Gubar and J. Kamholtz (eds.), *English Inside and Out: The Places of Literary*

that it has become an imaginary zone both well imaged and rehearsed in and by subsequent academies and their pedagogies, and also a zone in need of demystification by the present.

This much said, where classics and pedagogy are concerned, the inkling of history might perhaps be claimed in Jacques Barzun's attempt in 1959 to dislodge antiquity from the ideas of 'legacy' and 'inheritance' by showing that 'classics' resists precisely the pull towards reproduction. For Barzun, studying 'classics', perhaps because of its association with the elite and with high 'standards', was what permitted individualism in contrast to the uniformity imposed by contemporary systems of mass education.[17] But individualism is an emphasis that risks obscuring the ideas of intellectual community and of social process which are inevitably aspects of the pedagogical scenario. By contrast with Barzun's approach, this is not a book about individual and great teachers, as, for instance, Gilbert Highet's *The Immortal Profession: The Joys of Teaching and Learning* is.[18] Distinctively, it is a pedagogical history which ventures the claim that pedagogy can have a past without re-inscribing tradition, a history which establishes a break from the history of writing about education. Despite, or possibly because of, this background of scholarship on classical education, *Pedagogy and Power* stands both in a vacuum and against a hegemonic discourse. It does not reject the canonical or privileged, and offers rereadings of them.

The essays in this volume seek to expand the issues we might address and the texts we might read in constructing histories of classical education. As a result, the present volume does not produce a familiar or predictable narrative. Contributors look at different, but no less significant, moments in the history of classical pedagogy, with the result that the volume establishes different continuities and discontinuities between ancient and post-antique models of classical learning and education. While insisting upon the relationship between classical pedagogy and power, this volume calls into question assumptions that this relationship is a straightforward or static one. It recognises that the discourses which represent and constitute classical teaching may both, and sometimes simultaneously, affirm and undermine the authorities of teacher, ruler, state, and even of the pedagogy itself. Pedagogy is a

---

Criticism (New York and London, 1993), pp. 122–36; see also M. Nussbaum, 'The Softness of Reason: A Classical Case for Gay Studies', *New Republic* (July 13 and 20, 1992), pp. 26–35.

[17] J. Barzun, *The House of Intellect* (London, 1959), pp. 88ff.

[18] (New York, 1976). Highet offers encomia of Gilbert Murray, Albert Schweizer and Jesus amongst others as teachers who exemplify 'the immortal profession'.

far more diffuse set of activities than what is most obviously recognised
as the technique of imparting a knowledge. Insofar as pedagogy is a
socially framed and socially constructed activity, it thus has the power
to transform and to redefine social institutions. Accordingly, the political effect of education – and any education, for that matter – is always
open to reinterpretation, for elites and their authorising/authorised
knowledges may be defined and redefined, their boundaries shifted
and problematised. This volume demonstrates that classical pedagogies
have been and continue to be complex and plural in their significations.
Prior pedagogies can be subsumed within and reinterpreted by later
models through, for example, imitation or counter-definition, or they
can be fictionalised/travestied and acquire mythical status.

Against a background of singulars and of absolutes, *Pedagogy and Power*
deliberately and significantly addresses itself to plurals. The volume
locates classical model*s* of pedagogy, their *knowledges*, and the ideal*s*
which formed them or were formed on the basis of them within the
social and intellectual context*s* which generated them, in which they
have subsequently been invoked and specially privileged. It proposes
that 'education in antiquity' is not necessarily 'classical education':
pedagogy in the ancient world is not to be treated as a unity, and there
exists a diversity of pedagogies that are classical, are influenced by the
classics or give classics a central role. It demonstrates that it is not
possible to uphold an unproblematic or simple paradigm of ancient
education, arguing that classical pedagogy is complex and plural in its
constitution and in its significations. A further premiss of this volume
is that the 'knowledges' imparted by classical models of education and
their rhetorics are never disinterested; such 'knowledges' are always
necessarily implicated in the structures, processes, and articulations of
power (political, social, cultural, and so on), and their critiques. *Pedagogy
and Power* rejects the writing of a history of classical pedagogy which
seeks to reclaim tradition or assert the legacy of classical education's
past from a perspective of rose-tinted nostalgia. Rather it aspires to
show that the authority and power that have been associated with
classical learning and knowledge, and that we might associate with
them, are far more complex (because varied and broadly disseminated)
than has previously been recognised. So chapters in the volume disclose the various modes of political involvement in which classical
models of pedagogy engage. They examine how in antiquity education
instructs students to function as citizens and/or to rule and be ruled,
how it constructs elites and trains subjects, in short how it produces

and reproduces its particular state. Other essays show that when post-classical pedagogies trace their genealogy back to antiquity they have constructed ideal pedagogies variously. Contributors demonstrate that these pedagogies engage in nostalgic retrospection towards the 'classics', taking from antiquity models of the Great Teacher, or alternatively violently reject the 'classics', arguing for a displacement of the pedagogical authority of the ancients.

This understanding of knowledge as a political structure is not unfamiliar in the late twentieth century. Concentrating for the most part on the post-Enlightenment, Michel Foucault's work has demonstrated the link between knowledge and power, namely that knowing – and 'knowing' is a complex condition – is linked to political structures and their economies, both creating and reflecting the structure of power within a community. Where classical antiquity is concerned, the assertions that knowledge is related to power have their own histories. In his study of Greek education and culture, *Paideia*, Werner Jaeger insisted upon the necessarily aristocratic nature of Greek education, insisting that 'all higher civilisation springs from the differentiation of social classes – a differentiation which is created by natural variations in physical and mental capacity between man and man.'[19] With Jaeger, one suspects that the recognition of the elite politics of Greek education is a reflection of a personal agenda involving advocacy of an intellectual meritocracy. Marrou highlighted the elitist origins of ancient education – and how could it be otherwise given the nature of the material he studies? He located the beginnings of Greek education in aristocratic, Homeric culture as depicted in the *Iliad* and *Odyssey*, where fathers educated their sons to rule.[20] In an article entitled 'The Training of Elites in Greek Education' Robert Bolgar attempts to offer a more carefully and sensitively inflected account, arguing that the rise of city-states produced groups of elites with diverse interests who together constituted and ruled the community.[21] Declarations of the power of ancient education and its latter-day counterparts have also sometimes been deliberately oblique, if only because they are regarded as self-evident truth.

Furthermore, the agents of classical pedagogies have been individuals who directly participate in the production and maintenance of power. The anthropologist Sally Humphreys has suggested that the intellectual

---

[19] W. Jaeger, *Paideia: the Ideals of Greek Culture*, vol. 1, tr. Gilbert Highet (Oxford, 1939), p. 2.
[20] See Marrou, *A History of Education*, pp. 24ff.
[21] R. Bolgar in Rupert Wilkinson, *Governing Elites: Studies in Training and Selection* (New York, 1969) pp. 23–49.

– the poet, the wise man, the teacher, the adviser, and so on – is a figure who occupies a special place in his community, an 'interstitial' position, inasmuch as through language 'he necessarily had the ability to recreate social relationships and manipulate them in thought'.[22] Frank Vatai, following in particular the work of Werner Jaeger, has amongst others drawn attention to the way in which the philosopher in the ancient Greek world might be a man of action or a contemplative.[23] But there is a sense in which the dichotomy between an active and a contemplative intellectual is a misleading one, and perhaps one which owes more to Christian models of identity. The contemplative is the individual who has wisdom; he is the wise adviser or counsellor, perhaps like Herodotus' Solon (cf. *Histories* 1.29ff.),[24] Themistocles' adviser, the sophist Mnesiphilus,[25] or the future ruler's teacher, perhaps as Aristotle was to the young Alexander. It is also the case, however, that in such a capacity, this figure is no less a man of action in that his discourse may determine political actions and decisions, and thus is no less a bearer of political authority. The ruler is after all someone who has been trained by a man of wisdom and intellect, if not ideally to become such a person himself, and the figure who best proposes the invalidity of the distinction between pragmatic and theoretical man is the Platonic philosopher-king. This is the individual who has had experience of Truth and Beauty and would like to continue in this detached condition, but whose very enlightened condition leads him or her to undertake the government of the state.

The editors and contributors to this volume are of course no less implicated in structures of authority, representing forms of institutional power as lecturers, teachers, writers, and researchers. But we also often call them into question, if only as individuals who wish to make some of the structures and discourses of power more apparent. For against a

---

[22] S. Humphreys, '"Transcendence" and Intellectual Roles: the Ancient Greek Case' in *Anthropology and the Greeks* (London, 1978), p. 238.

[23] F. L. Vatai, *Intellectuals in Politics in the Greek World* (London, Sydney, Dover, 1984), p. 31; also cf. W. Jaeger, *Aristotle. Fundamentals of the History of his Development* (Oxford, 1948), pp. 426–61. Vatai's study ignores cultural specificities in its attempt to draw analogies between the ancient Greek and modern world (cf. p. 11).

[24] On the figure of the 'wise adviser' in Herodotus, see R. Lattimore, 'The Wise Adviser in Herodotus', *CP* 34 (1939), pp. 24–35; for Xenophon's use of this motif, see V. Gray, 'Xenophon's *Hiero* and the Meeting of the Wise Man and Tyrant in Greek Literature', *CQ* 36 (1986), pp. 115–23.

[25] Cf. Herodotus 8.57, Thucydides 1.138.3 and Xenophon *Memorabilia* 4.2.2; also J. S. Morrison, 'An Introductory Chapter in the History of Greek Education', *Durham University Journal* (1949) pp. 55–63.

particular backdrop which regards education and privilege as necessary concomitants, *Pedagogy and Power* is a critical history, which to a considerable degree seeks to consider the authorities of classical education itself, both in Greek and Roman antiquity and in post-antiquity. That the volume is a strongly interdisciplinary one speaks to the fact that even if pedagogy has no strongly defined disciplinary authority, it nevertheless has authority in and across numerous disciplines. The contributors to *Pedagogy and Power* are classicists and non-classicists, who may all mean different things by 'classics' – they are literary scholars, historians, philosophers, and cultural critics, although even these designations are somewhat arbitrary as a number of us might also describe our work in terms which defy traditional disciplinary boundaries.

Pedagogy and Power resists the idea that it can, or should, be a narrative purporting to completeness. This volume makes no claims to total coverage, as no cultural or literary history with such a broad coverage as the present book could with sincerity, nor does it seek simply to reinscribe what might be regarded as the privileged topics of the discourse of classical pedagogy. Rather it looks to *other* less obvious texts and structures for classical pedagogy in order to supplement the existing narratives of classical education. So, for instance, contributors read texts by Isocrates and Xenophon rather than by Plato or Aristotle in considering what classical Greek education is; German classical learning is not just that of Wilamowitz or Nietzsche but schooling as regards the exclusion of women; while the Victorian gentleman's 'classics' is the eccentric classroom schooling of a grammarian. Furthermore, the thematic and topical recurrences in chapters dealing with very different periods suggest that analogies and affinities between the various models of classical pedagogy do not necessarily arise from temporal proximity, as they do not. Having in common the aim of demonstrating the authority and power of classical pedagogies, each of the individual chapters offers an account of pedagogies, specific with regard to their historical, cultural, ideological, and textual contexts.

The volume is structured from back-to-front, with essays addressing the more contemporary invocations and uses of classical pedagogy coming first, and those treating the representation of pedagogy and power in classical antiquity coming last. This ordering is designed to reject the idea that what we might describe as education in antiquity is the cause or the paradigm for what subsequent communities might understand as 'classical' or as classicising education. Paul Cartledge

foregrounds the idea of transformation in 'classical education' when he
calls for pedagogical *renovatio* where classics is concerned at the end of
the twentieth century, proposing a model of classical education which
emphasises the cultural dimension of the study of Greek and Roman
antiquity – classical studies – rather than just philology. Following
chapters show the different forms that classical pedagogy might take,
and in particular, examine its varying relationships to political, social
and cultural power.

Christopher Stray places the reader *en scène* in the Victorian classroom of the famous Winchester classics teacher, Edmund Moreshead
('Mushri'), where the teacher's peculiar and sometimes transgressive
Latin pronunciations both enforce and undermine the authority of the
pedagogue and his students as far as the classroom and the larger world
are concerned. Sarah Colvin examines how German classical training
from the early modern period to the beginning of the twentieth century,
ecclesiastical institutions, educational and political systems valorise Greek
and especially Latin as prerequisites for advancement. She shows that
through their exclusion from classical learning women were traditionally
confined to the domestic sphere in German society. Clare Brant considers the use of classical dialogue form in political debate and teaching
in eighteenth-century England. Dialogue becomes an important political
medium for conservatives and radicals alike since it masks the teacher's
authority while enabling the student to be painlessly persuaded.

Jane Stevenson looks at the roles available to women in classical culture of early modern Europe. Classically trained women in a number of
countries were active writers and thinkers, but their intellectual enfranchisement was one which occurred often as a result of the involvement
of men as mediators, sponsors, and indeed as the fathers who permitted
their daughter's education. Next, Warren Boutcher argues that humanistic education in sixteenth-century England involved complex move-
ments between the regions and the centres of intellectual and political
power as young men were recruited from the country to Oxbridge and
the Court, together the latter-day 'Parnassus'. He looks at how schooling
either gave emphasis to the classical paradigms over the often brutal
Latin schoolmaster (as in Roger Ascham's preparatory pedagogy), or else
placed vernacular models alongside ancient authors (as in John Hoskyns'
rhetorical treatise.) David Rundle explores the use of panegyric in the
instruction of the prince in the Renaissance to suggest that in this period
classical paradigms might be put to specific political uses. He examines
the way in which, beginning with Erasmus, the teacher both circulated

and mimicked examples of this genre from Greek and Roman antiquity in order to instruct his political pupil through artful encomium such that 'praise is precept'. Panagiotis Agapitos traces the changing political climate after late antiquity which made possible the use of pagan learning in eleventh-century Byzantium. The study and teaching of pagan (Platonic and Neoplatonic) philosophy by Christian intellectuals such as Michael Psellus provoked a crisis which was resolved by the affirmation of antiquity's *paideia* as an 'inalienable possession' of even a Christian society.

The last five chapters examine the variety of ancient models of education which have been historically characterised as the monolith 'classical education' or 'education in antiquity'. In his chapter, Tim Whitmarsh looks at how Second Sophistic culture required 'reading power' to unpack the complex relations between intellectual and ruler, in the case he studies, between Dio Chrysostom and Trajan. He demonstrates that Dio's own account of cultural renaissance under Trajan is to be qualified by the former's biographer, Philostratus, who suggests a gap between the intellectual's superior *paideia* and the ruler's limited one. Then Catherine Atherton argues that the teaching of literacy and literary/oratorical skills were implicated in and indeed part of the social and political system from the Hellenistic period onwards. She explores how the inculcation of literate and oral skills by rote repetition, by rules and regulations, and by physical punishment served as a means of socialising the pupil to obedience and order in addition to and sometimes beyond the community's own structures.

Teresa Morgan adds another dimension to this narrative of rhetorical pedagogy by considering how Quintilian's grammatical and linguistic teaching is to be regarded as the basis for political authority in imperial Rome. The ideal of the 'good man skilled in speech' (*bonus vir dicendi peritus*) is the *sine qua non* of Quintilian's ideal state, while the ideal orator is someone who inhabits and leads a state which stands apart from any historical entity. In his study of the Athenian rhetorician Isocrates, Niall Livingstone examines how this teacher's *paideia* serves to project 'Greekness' onto its pupils in the service of a panhellenic project. Isocratean discourse is quite literally the voice of the master, uniform and uniformly Hellenic, despite a host of fictional speakers and identities. The volume closes with Yun Lee Too's chapter, which reiterates the point made by Cartledge, namely that the existence of a stable paradigm which we might describe as 'classical education' must be called into question. It reinforces the idea that classical education is a construction liable to change and transformation, when the Persia of Xenophon's *Cyropaedia* is read as a community which deliberately problematises pedagogy as both biological and social reproduction.

Classical education is an idea that is endlessly created and recreated, granted or denied authority, interrogated, and restructured. Read synchronically, the chapters offer a series of other narratives, which together portray the varying ways in which pedagogical and political structures might be configured and understood as speaking to other accounts of similarity, difference, non-analogy, and rupture. The word 'pedagogy' suggests that it is the child (*pais*) who is the primary subject of education, and indeed, a number of the chapters show the centrality of the child and notions of childhood in ancient models of pedagogy (see e.g. Too for analogies between father/ruler/teacher and son/subject; Atherton on the (problematic) humanity of children; Stray on the Victorian schoolboy). Other chapters suggest that pedagogy's subject is one included or excluded on the basis of sex and gender (Colvin on the exclusion of women; Stevenson on their inclusion), of religious belief (Agapitos), of ethnic or national identity (Livingstone), or of social status (see e.g. Too, Livingstone, and Rundle on associations between pedagogy and kingship, Stevenson on classics and the aristocracy, Brant on dialogue as a discourse which both transgresses and reinforces class distinctions).

Chapters in the book draw attention to the variety of genres that participate in the construction of ancient models of pedagogy: rhetorical discourse (Livingstone, Whitmarsh, Rundle, Boutcher), poetry and translation (Stevenson), prose fiction (Too), dialogue (Brant), textbook/treatise (Atherton, Morgan, Boutcher, Stray), drama (Colvin), ideological polemic (Cartledge, Agapitos). Moreover, if some classical pedagogies (e.g. Atherton, Morgan, Stevenson and Stray) empower their participants but perhaps at some cost, it is also the case that classical learning may provide the tools for subversion of the hegemonic political structure and its discourses: classics provides the oblique rhetorics of critique, disguised as instruction or panegyric, to the ruling classes (Whitmarsh, Rundle, Stray). In other cases, pedagogy and its discourses are the means by which cultural and/or political conflict are conducted (Brant, Cartledge).

We want this book to make a significant and provocative contribution to discussions, current and past, on the role of education in society – why we teach and learn what we do. Many of the contributors engage with recent debate on education and the canon/curriculum, and they underpin their interpretations with their own experiences as teachers and students. As a whole, this book offers an optimistic argument for the possibility of revising the position of classics in the modern academy. It proposes that classics can be displaced from its position as an 'elite' subject that excludes many groups (women, minorities, older students) and reinstated as a more democratic and plural subject which may help to authorise less empowered groups. It also makes a case for seeing the cultural and political value of a subject that is often perceived as standing in opposition to the various projects of social and intellectual transformation.

CHAPTER I

Classics: from discipline in crisis to (multi-)cultural capital

Paul Cartledge

The unexamined curriculum is not worth teaching[1]

I

Some thirty years ago, the distinguished early modern historian and acclaimed popularizer, J. H. (now Sir Jack) Plumb, responded to what he perceived to be a 'crisis in the humanities' by editing a volume of essays under that title. Somewhat paradoxically, perhaps, he included therein a typically astringent and comparative but also firmly optimistic essay on 'Classics' by his Cambridge colleague Moses (later Sir Moses) Finley, a no less distinguished pedagogue. Finley's optimism stemmed chiefly from his belief that Classics would survive by being transformed, into non-philological (or not primarily philological) 'Classical Studies' or 'Classical Civilization'.[2] A quarter of a century later, despite – or because of? – the immense growth in the popularity and influence of non-linguistic Classical Civilization (or Classical Studies, Classics in Translation) courses in both schools and universities, not to mention among the wider public, a group of leading academics on the other side of the Atlantic combined to produce *Classics: a Discipline and a Profession in Crisis?*, the terminal interrogative neatly encapsulating the ambiguity both of 'Classics' and of 'crisis' (everything going wrong – or moment of decision).[3]

Besides our extraordinarily conscientious and vigilant editors, I am especially indebted for all sorts of help and guidance to Pat Easterling and Chris Stray.

[1] E. R. Wolfe, 'The Brooklyn College Core Curriculum' *Arethusa* 27 (1994) 10.
[2] J. H. Plumb (ed.), *Crisis in the Humanities* (Harmondsworth, 1964); M. I. Finley, 'Crisis in the Classics', in Plumb, *Crisis*, pp. 11–23; also Finley's 1972 Encyclopaedia Britannica lecture 'The Heritage of Isocrates', repr. in Finley's *The Use and Abuse of History* (2nd edn, London, 1986), 193–214, 242–6.
[3] P. Culham and L. Edmunds (eds.), *Classics: a Discipline and a Profession in Crisis?* (Lanham, MD and London, 1989); cf. G. K. Galinsky, 'Classics beyond Crisis', *Classical World* 84 (1991), 441–53.

Since 1989, the situation of Classics, and the Humanities more generally, may be thought to have become if anything yet more politically fraught. No longer is the talk merely of 'crisis'. The word is rather of outright 'culture wars' being waged across and within North American university campuses, yet potentially of much wider significance: when Cambridge, Mass., sneezes, sooner or later Cambridge, England, catches a cold. With the end of the Cold War there has developed in the West, to use anthropological parlance, a pronounced fetishizing of culture as a religion-substitute, a sort of fundamentalism by other means. Culture in the relevant sense may be construed, again anthropologically, as the set of symbolic systems and social practices through which different groups make sense of their individual and collective selves.[4] These wars are being fought over (in particular) three fuzzily defined and not necessarily but certainly contingently interconnected phenomena: the 'core curriculum' or 'great books' in 'Western Civilization' courses;[5] multiculturalism;[6] and 'political correctness'.[7] Typically, the encounters in this latest battle of the books have pitted traditionalist defenders of canonical texts and objectively transcendent values against adherents of one or other variant of Postmodernist theory (sometimes arrogantly labelled Theory *tout court*), the latter united at least in their postulate

---

[4] On the culture wars, see H. L. Gates, *Loose Canons. Notes on the Culture Wars* (New York, 1993); J. Annette, 'The Culture Wars on the American Campus', in S. Dunant (ed.), *The War of the Words. The Political Correctness Debate* (London, 1994), 1–14; Wolfe, 'Brooklyn Core Curriculum'; J. H. Weiss, 'Interpreting Cultural Crisis: Social History Confronts Humanities Education' *Journal of the History of Ideas* 26.3 (1996), 459–74. Culture: M. Carrithers, *Why Humans Have Cultures* (Oxford, 1992); E. S. Gruen, 'Cultural Fictions and Cultural Identity', *Transactions of the American Philological Association* 123 (1993), 1–14. Fundamentalism: W. Steiner, *The Scandal of Pleasure: Art in an Age of Fundamentalism* (Chicago and London, 1995).

[5] On the curriculum/Great Books, see W. B. Carnochan, *The Battleground of the Curriculum. Liberal Education and American Experience* (Stanford, 1993); and his 'Where Did Great Books Come From Anyway?' (forthcoming). See also n. 13.

[6] H. Goulborne, *Ethnicity and Nationalism in Post-imperial Britain* (Cambridge, 1991); C. Taylor, *Multiculturalism and 'the Politics of Recognition'*, ed. A. Gutmann (Princeton, 1992); J. Appleby, L. Hunt and M. Jacob, *Telling the Truth about History* (New York, 1994); R. Bernstein, *Dictatorship of Virtue. Multiculturalism and the Battle for America's Future* (New York, 1994); D. Goldberg (ed.), *Multiculturalism: a Critical Reader* (Oxford, 1994); M. N. S. Sellers (ed.), *An Ethical Education: Community and Morality in the Multicultural University* (Oxford, 1994); C. Bernheimer (ed.), *Comparative Literature in the Age of Multiculturalism* (Baltimore, 1995); D. A. Hollinger, *Postethnic America. Beyond Multiculturalism* (New York, 1995); H. Maier 'Eine Kultur oder viele? Die Zukunft der Kulturen' *Gymnasium* 102 (1995), 11–30; D. D'Souza, *The End of Racism. Principles for a Multi-Cultural Society* (New York, 1995); K. A. Appiah and H. L. Gates, jr. (eds.), *Identities* (Chicago, 1996); N. Glazer, *We Are All Multiculturalists Now* (Cambridge, MA, 1997).

[7] P. Berman (ed.), *Debating P.C. The Controversy over Political Correctness on College Campuses* (New York, 1992); R. Hughes, *The Culture of Complaint. The Fraying of America* (New York, 1993); Dunant (ed.), *War of the Words*; P. R. Loeb, *Generation at the Crossroads. Apathy and Action on the American Campus* (New Brunswick, 1994); J. K. Wilson, *The Myth of Political Correctness. The Conservative Attack on Higher Education* (Durham, NC, 1995).

that, since meaning is inherently arbitrary, unstable and contestable, the idea of an authoritative canon is merely another name for social hegemony.[8]

So far as Classics or Classical Studies are concerned, Martin Bernal's *Black Athena* project, despite – or rather to some extent because of – its scholarly inadequacies, has served as a convenient focus (or whipping boy, as it were) in these antagonistic debates and has generated quite exceptional publicity, not all of it welcome.[9] It is therefore on this indubitably, if at times also misguidedly, scholarly project that the present paper will concentrate as a case-study, attempting, firstly, to give a brief characterization of the continuing curricular 'culture wars' (sec. II); then, secondly, to situate Classics today both in terms of its own disciplinary antecedents and concomitants and in relation to the aforementioned wars (sec. III); and, thirdly, to assess its potential contribution to future pedagogical theory and practice (sec. IV–V).

II

From time to time ripples of a major political and cultural or politico-cultural debate frothing on the other side of the Atlantic wash rather

[8] For 'theory' (including critical theory, cultural studies, deconstruction, feminism, neomarxism, neopragmatism, New Historicism, poststructuralism, and Postmodernism, all now consumingly concerned with language, discourse, and codes of representation) see variously R. Rorty, *Contingency, Irony and Solidarity* (Cambridge, 1989), with the reply of N. Geras, *Solidarity in the Conversation of Humankind: the Ungroundable Liberalism of Richard Rorty* (London, 1995); Z. Bauman, *Modernity and Ambivalence* (Oxford, 1991); B. Thomas, *The New Historicism and Other Old-fashioned Topics* (Princeton, 1991); A. Sinfield, *Cultural Materialism and the Politics of Dissident Reading* (Oxford, 1992); J. N. Cox and L. J. Reynolds (eds.), *New Historical Literary Study. Essays on Reproducing Texts, Representing History* (Princeton, 1993); T. Docherty (ed.), *Postmodernism. A Reader* (New York, 1993); A. Milner, *Contemporary Cultural Theory. An Introduction* (London, 1993); P. Stearns, *Meaning over Memory: Recasting the Teaching of Culture and History* (Chapel Hill, 1993); M. Bal and I. E. Boer (eds.), *The Point of Theory. Practices of Cultural Analysis* (Amsterdam, 1994); A. Easthope, *British Post-Structuralism* (London, 1994); F. Inglis, *Cultural Studies* (Oxford, 1994); L. Jackson, *The Dematerialisation of Karl Marx* (London, 1994); J. Docker, *Postmodernism and Popular Culture* (Cambridge, 1995); J. Margolis, *Interpretation Radical but not Unruly. The New Puzzle of the Arts and History* (Berkeley, 1995); L. Nicolson and S. Seidman (eds.), *Social Postmodernism. Beyond Identity Politics* (Cambridge, 1995); N. J. Rengger, *Political Theory, Modernity and Postmodernity: Beyond Enlightenment and Critique* (Oxford, 1995); E. M. Wood and J. B. Foster (eds.), *In Defense of History. Marxism and the Postmodern Agenda* (*Monthly Review* 47.3, 1995). An excellent overview, with special reference to Classics, in B. E. Goff (ed.), *History, Tragedy, Theory. Dialogues on Athenian Tragedy* (Austin, 1995) 1–37. Traditionalists prominently include A. Bloom, *The Closing of the American Mind. How Higher Education Has Failed Democracy and Impoverished the Souls of Today's Students* (New York, 1987); R. Kimball, *Tenured Radicals. How Politics has Corrupted our Higher Education* (New York, 1990); G. Himmelfarb, *On Looking into the Abyss. Untimely Thoughts on Culture and Society* (New York, 1995); and her *The De-Moralisation of Society: From Victorian Values to Modern Values* (London, 1995).
[9] M. Bernal, *Black Athena. The Afroasiatic Roots of Classical Civilization* 2 vols. (to date) (London and New Brunswick, 1987–91). See also n. 17.

feebly over these sceptred shores. For us, too, 'PC' no longer stands just for Police Constable, postcard, Privy Counsellor or even personal computer, but also and above all for political correctness – a term which, whatever its polemical use and abuse, concerns a cluster of issues around codes of civility and censorship both verbal and behavioural. Multiculturalism, institutionally a response to the growing diversity of the student body, intellectually a pluralist challenge to the assumptions about value underlying the canonization of certain writers and artists (chiefly dead, white, male, and of European origin or descent), is no longer just a term of the educational bureaucrat's art but has its practical analogues on the mean inner city streets of London and Bradford, as well as those of New York and Los Angeles. Nevertheless, it is in the States that the symbolic culture wars are waged most intensively and extensively, and it is the academy or university that forms the primary site of engagement (in both senses), since the debate about the teaching of the humanities to undergraduates (in literature and history above all) is as much about the idea of a university as it is about the idea of culture.

What then is the university, or rather, what is it for?[10] If the editors of a recent special issue of *The Oxford Literary Review* are right to speak of a 'delegitimation of academic life that is probably unstoppable', short of inventive and distracting ploys of curricular staging, then no idea of a university presumably can help, let alone save, us.[11] And there are always plenty of cynics eagerly claiming that academics are anxious to maintain their power within the academy in direct proportion as they lack it outside, or sneering that nowhere else are political passions so intense when the stakes are so low. But such claims and protestations are beside the point. Debates about education are rarely about education alone, and this one is no exception. What is at stake is not merely a discourse of power, but the power of a discourse, or rather a plenitude of competing discourses. It makes all the difference therefore whether one sees the university as, for example, the site of civic education, intended for the education of future citizens, or rather in class terms as a locus for the training of society's future ruling elites. For some Postmodern discourse theorists, like Charles Martindale (the Latin Professor

---

[10] Compare and contrast D. Bromwich, *Politics by Other Means. Higher Education and Group Thinking* (New Haven, 1992); T. Caesar, *Conspiring with Forms: Life in Academic Texts* (Athens, GA, 1993); F. Oakley, *Community of Learning. The American College and the Liberal Arts Tradition* (New York, 1993); R. Rand (ed.), *Logomachia. The Conflict of the Faculties* (Lincoln, NB, 1993); Sellers, *Ethical Education*; D. Damrosch, *We Scholars: Changing the Culture of the University* (Cambridge, MA, 1995).

[11] T. Clark and N. Royle (eds.), *The University in Ruins* (special issue of *The Oxford Literary Review*, 1995); B. Reedings, *The University in Ruins* (Cambridge, MA, 1997).

at Bristol) the university is 'a cultural ideological entity, having human meaning only within a field of discourse or discourses and of social "practices"'. Conservative traditionalists dispute the Postmodernists' epistemological premises but agree with the implied conclusion that ideas make history, so that to them too critical theory matters politically. The debate between the two sides is about cultural discrimination – who controls the culture, who decides what is good.[12]

Hence the special place occupied in the wars by the idea of the (or a) canon (not to mention the awful puns on can(n)on wars).[13] Traditionalists like to invoke the canon as 'the grand narrative' of literature, a supposedly transcendental and conflict-free zone of timeless purity. Against which the Postmodernists, the New Historicists among them to the fore, respond that so far from being timeless the canon is itself a historically contingent construct, and therefore necessarily changes in accordance with changed values and definitions of what is culturally 'good' – not 'the' canon but a succession of different canons, they contend, represents the historical reality, the reconfiguration of which is the order of the day. Certainly, those in the traditionalist camp who claim that the new discourses have abandoned the interest in pure knowledge that allegedly once characterized scholarship are being either naive or disingenuous. But canon reform does trigger a central anxiety about the coherence of the culture as a whole, and conservative traditionalists are right to fear curriculum reformers whose declared aim is to connect their radical or revolutionary understanding of epistemological and moral issues to the further democratisation of the American university along multiculturalist lines.[14] On the other hand, casting their

---

[12] The quotation is from C. Martindale, 'Professing Latin' *CUCD (Council of University Classical Departments) Bulletin* 23 (1994) 3–21, at p. 7. On value in criticism, see S. Connor, *Theory and Cultural Value* (Oxford, 1992); P. E. Frankel, F. D. Miller and J. Paul (eds.), *Cultural Pluralism and Moral Knowledge* (Cambridge, 1995); J. Frow, *Cultural Studies and Cultural Value* (Oxford, 1995); D. Parker, *Ethics, Theory and the Novel* (Cambridge, 1995). Power of discourses: P. Bourdieu and J.-C. Passeron, *Reproduction in Education, Society and Culture* (London and Beverley Hills, 1977 [1970]).

[13] Gates, *Loose Canons*; H. Bloom, *The Western Canon. The Books and School of the Ages* (New York, 1994); J. Guillory, *Cultural Capital. The Problem of Literary Canon Formation* (Chicago, 1993); Jackson, *Dematerialisation of Karl Marx*, esp. pp. 264–75; J. Guillory, 'Canon', in F. Lentricchia and T. McLaughlin (eds.), *Critical Terms for Literary Study* (2nd edn, Chicago, 1995). Classics and the canon: J. P. Hallett, 'Feminist Theory, Historical Periods, Literary Canons and the Study of Graeco-Roman Antiquity', in N. S. Rabinowitz and A. Richlin (eds.), *Feminist Theory and the Classics* (London and New York, 1993) 44–72; C. Segal, 'Classical Criticism and the Canon, or, Why Read the Ancient Critics?', in S. Lawall (ed.), *Reading World Literature. Theory, History, Practice* (Austin, 1994) 87–112; D. Tompkins, '"What Has This to do With the Praetor's Edict?": Classical Studies and Contemporary Society', *Arethusa* 27 (1994) 11–40; see also n. 43.

[14] Compare and contrast, e.g., Bernstein, *Dictatorship of Virtue* (conservative) with Hunt, Appleby and Jacob, *Telling the Truth about History* (radical).

position as a defence of Western Civilization against a supposedly subversive, barbarian multiculturalism is little but a polarizing rhetorical trope with a thoroughly Classical Greek pedigree going right back to 'the invention of the barbarian' by the Greeks as a cultural antitype in the fifth century BCE.[15]

To date, as noted above, only relatively faint echoes of the battles on the far side of the Atlantic have carried to these benighted shores, for institutional as well as cultural and political reasons. Or rather, such public political debate as there has been over the curriculum in the UK has been concentrated more on the secondary level of education, with special reference to the 'Englishness' (or otherwise) of the History syllabus in the so-called 'National Curriculum'. The reception over here of the inaugural volume of Bernal's *Black Athena*, which was actually first published on this side of the pond, was thus revealing. Although quite widely noticed in the serious daily or weekly press, it was in the main ignored by the academic Classics journals, for various reasons, some of them good ones. The author was not a specialist ancient historian. Few scholars were anyway competent across all Bernal's vast chronological and thematic range. His frankly political message ('to lessen European cultural arrogance') was found either uncomfortable or downright rebarbative.

In the United States they have managed these things very differently, partly because of the peculiar charge of race and ethnicity in American cultural debate, to which Bernal's Egyptianizing, quasi-Afrocentrist thesis spoke.[16] Entire special issues of two American learned journals and part of another have been devoted to the host of contentious issues raised or rather stirred up by *Black Athena*; so too a further edited collection and even a whole book, the very title of which constitutes it as a

---

[15] E. Hall, *The Invention of the Barbarian. Greek Self-Definition through Tragedy* (Oxford, 1989).

[16] D. D'Souza, *Illiberal Education. The Politics of Race and Sex on Campus* (New York, 1991); and his *The End of Racism*; P. Berman (ed.), *Blacks and Jews. Alliances and Arguments* (Delacorte, 1994) – it is worth adding that it is only a little over a generation since Jews began to gain due recognition in American universities: S. Klingenstein (ed.), *Jews in the American Academy, 1900–1940* (New Haven, 1992); P. Gilroy, *The Black Atlantic: Modernity and Double Consciousness* (London, 1993); T. Sowell, *Race and Culture. A World View* (New York, 1994); H. L. Gates jr. *et al.*, *Speaking of Race, Speaking of Sex: Hate Speech, Civil Rights and Civil Liberties* (New York, 1995); M. Marable, *Beyond Black and White. Transforming African-American Politics* (London, 1995). The attack on this aspect of Bernal's *Black Athena* project has been led by M. Lefkowitz, who particularly resents and rejects the charge, levelled notably by G. G. M. James, *Stolen Legacy* (New York, 1954) and warmly endorsed by some of Bernal's Afrocentrist supporters, that the Greeks somehow purloined their philosophy and other high culture from Egypt: Lefkowitz 'Ethnocentric History from Aristobulus to Bernal', *Academic Questions* 62 (1993) 12–20; and 'The Deconstruction of Ancient Greece', in A. Avramides (ed.), *Women of Ideas* (London, 1995) 103–26; see also next note.

defiantly explicit antilogy.[17] Any summary of Bernal's long and complex argument must necessarily be somehow inadequate, but space forbids more than a very brief synopsis and critique.

Bernal claims not to have coined the catchy oxymoron 'Black Athena', but he could hardly have hit upon a title better calculated to deliver the desired shock-effect. For it is his declared view that Greek Athena, goddess of wisdom and cunning intelligence, was not merely the functional equivalent but the lineal descendant of the Egyptian goddess Neit, introduced to Greece in prehistoric times by colonists from the Nile delta, and that the Egyptians who created and worshipped the original model were black in the sense of possessing negroid bodily characteristics of skin and hair, and so on. The remainder of the project's full title, *The Afroasiatic Roots of Classical Civilization*, is no whit less deliberately challenging. 'Afroasiatic' is designed to counter the 'orientalist' discourse that has supposedly dominated Western culture for the past two centuries, to de-emphasize or suppress any lingering Eurocentric connection or dimension of the Classical Greek achievement, and to recuperate and re-emphasize Greece's cultural debt to the black Egyptians of Africa and, secondarily, to the Semitic Phoenicians of Asia.[18] 'Roots' inescapably recalls Alex Haley and the African-American search for an African or Afrocentric narrative of origins to ground a sense of identity in authentically autonomous ethnicity.[19] 'Classical Civilization', lastly, does not here designate the entirety of ancient Graeco-Roman or Mediterranean civilization but specifically Classical Greek 'high' culture of the fifth and fourth centuries BCE, emblematized by the Athens of Pericles in which Bernal's not so secret hero Herodotus, originally from Halicarnassus in Asia Minor, was a welcome and honoured guest.[20]

---

[17] Responses, rejoinders and rebuttals include M. M. Levine (ed.), *The Challenge of 'Black Athena'* (special issue of *Arethusa*, 1989); *Journal of Mediterranean Archaeology* 3 (1990); *Isis*, 83.4 (December 1992); M. Lefkowitz, *Not Out of Africa: How Afrocentrism Became an Excuse to Teach Myth as History* (New York, 1996); Lefkowitz and G. M. Rogers (eds.), *Black Athena Revisited* (Durham, NC, 1996).

[18] On Orientalism, see E. Said, *Orientalism. Western Conceptions of the Orient* (1978, repr. with new Afterword, Harmondsworth, 1995) – now almost 'canonical' itself, but see the critiques by J. M. Mackenzie, *Orientalism: History, Theory and the Arts* (Manchester, 1995); and N. S. Thompson, *Herodotus and the Origins of the Political Community. Arion's Leap* (New Haven and London, 1996), pp. 130–41. A. S. Ahmed, *Postmodernism and Islam* (Cambridge, 1992) agrees with Bernal that the West has largely sold its Semitic inheritance for a mess of Greek pottage. V. Lambropoulos, *The Rise of Eurocentrism. Anatomy of Interpretation* (Princeton, 1993) reads the West's debt to (or construction of) Hellenism very differently; cf. A. Leontis, *Topographies of Hellenism. Mapping the Homeland* (Ithaca, 1995).

[19] The historicity of Haley's documentation has been rightly questioned, but that is not the be-all and end-all of such 'mythistory'. Berman, *Blacks and Jews*, is especially relevant here. See also n. 22.

[20] Note also Bernal, 'Phoenician politics and Egyptian justice in ancient Greece', in K. A. Raaflaub (ed.), *Anfänge politischen Denkens in der Antike: die nahöstlichen Kulturen und die Griechen* (Munich, 1993) 243–61.

Bernal clearly admires, indeed sees himself in some important sense as heir to, 'Classical Civilization', but it is the positive thrust of his thesis to aver that, had it not been for the genetic as well as cultural inputs from Africa and Asia, there would have been no 'Classical Civilization' in Greece and then Rome for scholars and others to worry themselves about today. This positive thesis is not without all merit, at least in so far as it properly reminds us of what the Greeks had to (and did) learn from their eastern neighbours.[21] But it is also deeply flawed, not least by inadequacy of historical method in point of source-criticism: Herodotus, for example, simply cannot bear the load imposed on him as the Atlas of Bernal's supposedly competitively plausible 'Ancient Model', and Bernal is prone to mistake myth, or at best 'mythistory', for actual matter of fact.[22] It is his negative thesis, however, that is of more relevance to our present concerns.

III

For in order to clear the way for his positive reconstruction, Bernal in effect contends that the prevailing construction of Western cultural identity and superiority is the outcome of a more or less deliberate and conscious process of 'fabricating' how it actually was in ancient Greece, and, conversely, of distorting or suppressing the genuine pioneering achievements of the Egyptians and Phoenicians. This is not quite a conspiracy theory of intellectual history, but it is very firmly an accusation of false consciousness on a fairly grand scale, and as such, if proven persuasively correct, would deliver a hammer blow to the authority, indeed the legitimacy, of some of the culturally and politically most important aspects of classical scholarship since the eighteenth century, and so by extension to the validity of the idea of the humanities itself.[23]

---

[21] W. Burkert, *The Orientalizing Revolution: Near Eastern Influence on Greek Culture in the Early Archaic Age* (Cambridge, MA, 1992; German original, 1984); S. P. Morris, *Daidalos and the Origins of Greek Art* (Princeton, 1992), with Bernal's review-article in *Arethusa* 28 (1995) 114–35; A. Bernand, *Leçon de Civilisation* (Paris, 1994); J. M. Sasson (ed.), *Civilizations of the Ancient Near East*, 4 vols. (Englewood Cliffs, 1995).

[22] On Herodotus, see recently Thompson, *Herodotus and the Origins of the Political Community*, pp. 113–21. On the use and abuse of myth, see E. Hall, 'When is a Myth not a Myth? Bernal's "Ancient Model"' *Arethusa* 25 (1992) 181–98.

[23] W. Den Boer (ed.), *Les études classiques aux XIXe et XXe siècles: leur place dans l'histoire des idées* (Entretiens Hardt 26, Vandoeuvres-Geneva, 1980); C. R. Phillips III, 'Classical Scholarship Against its History', *AJP* 110 (1989) 636–57; W. W. Briggs and W. M. Calder III (eds.), *Classical Scholarship. A Biographical Encyclopaedia* (New York, 1990); C. A. Stray, 'Ideology and Institution: English Classical Scholarship in Transition' *Annals of Scholarship* 10 (1993) 111–31; Martindale, 'Professing Latin'; I. M. Morris (ed.), *Classical Greece. Ancient Histories and Modern Archaeologies* (Cambridge, 1994). See also Christopher Stray's chapter in this collection.

For the latter reflected a kind of late-Victorian – it was mainly British in origin – consensus on the place and meaning of culture, including the place and significance of Greek and Roman antiquity both within and without the secondary and university curricula. Thanks particularly to the proselytising of Matthew Arnold, Classics became the sacred monster of the secondary curriculum, from roughly 1850 to perhaps as late as 1950; thanks likewise to Benjamin Jowett, Oxford pioneered a reformed university classical education, which proved eminently suitable for intending administrators of a vast colonial empire but long outlived its original pedagogical context.[24]

However, from late Victorian and more especially Edwardian times onwards in Britain and Ireland – much earlier in the States, though not Canada – Classics was gradually toppled from its pedestal of cultural hegemony both for internal reasons of increased disciplinarity (the divorce from English, for example, and from Anthropology, not to mention the curricular rise of the natural sciences), and more especially for external reasons of changing times and altered priorities.[25] By 1950, say, Classics could no longer claim either the power of the purse or the pride of place. With Classics went a certain sense of value, and it has been said, rightly, that the supersession of a classical value rooted in the past by the progressive search for a future truth 'marks the death of the "humanist lie of the identity of the true, the beautiful and the good"'.[26] But only partly rightly: for that search has not been found incompatible with, and indeed has hugely stimulated, a countervailing movement of 'classicizing', which in one sense is precisely 'looking back to an authoritative and exemplary past which can be used to make sense of the present' and to guide future policymaking and action.[27] On any properly balanced view, however, our century's history of genocide, colonialism and total warfare – as products of a rationalising, scientific vision of the world – must seriously challenge if it does not fatally undermine the classically based, civilising pretensions at the core of Euro-American self-understanding. A recent scholarly study of attitudes to deformity and disability in (mainly) ancient Greece is thus a perfect

[24] On Arnold, see F. M. Turner, *The Greek Heritage in Victorian Britain* (New Haven, 1981). On Jowett, see L. Dowling, *Hellenism and Homosexuality in Victorian Oxford* (Ithaca, 1994).

[25] Cambridge's nineteenth/twentieth-century experience of curriculum reform is instructive: G. Johnson, *F. M. Cornford's Cambridge and his Advice to the Young Academic Politician* (Cambridge, 1994) esp. pp. 38ff.; cf. P. Cartledge, 'The Greeks and Anthropology', *Anthropology Today* 10 (1994) 3–6.

[26] Stray, 'Ideology and Institution', p. 119 and n. 16, quoting U. Hölscher, *Die Chance des Unbehagens* (Göttingen, 1965) 64; cf. already Finley, 'Heritage of Isocrates,' p. 214 and n. 68.

[27] Stray, 'Ideology and Institution', p. 127. The title of B. M. W. Knox's *Backing into the Future. The Classical Tradition and Its Renewal* (New York, 1994) is eloquent.

sign and symbol of our disabused age: it does not confound only the pretensions of the ancient self-styled 'beautiful and good', but also those of their latterday avatars and nostalgic champions.[28]

In these circumstances, it hardly needs stating that 'no designer of the modern university assumes without question, as his predecessors did, that the study of classics is central to an Arts programme'.[29] Yet since the demise of traditional Classics, the humanities in general and especially perhaps English have seemed to yearn for a subject to underpin their enterprise, as maths, for example, does the physical sciences. Hence, in significant part, the claims or pretensions of (literary) Theory, with which we began our investigation of the culture wars. The pedagogical claims of Classics, though, at any rate of a renewed and revivified Classics, are surely not to be overlooked. Or so the remainder of this essay will seek to recommend. From the challenge *to* Classics we pass finally to the challenge *of* Classics.

IV

Classicizing, as we have seen, can be a way of 'backing into the future', but there is another, more positively fruitful sense of 'classical' according to which 'every reading of a classic is in fact a rereading'.[30] The ancients themselves not only invented the Western canon but constantly interrogated and reinvented it, and much of what we regard as modern literary theory traces its genealogies to ancient literary criticism and rhetorical theory. If a sign of Postmodernism is a self-conscious application of literary techniques, then the Hellenistic (post-Classical) poets are among the most 'postmodern' there are.[31] Re-readings, moreover, can and often should be made against as well as with the grain,

[28] R. S. J. Garland, *The Eye of the Beholder: Deformity and Disability in the Graeco-Roman World* (London, 1995).
[29] J. A. S. Evans, 'The Classics in English Canada' *Cahiers des études anciennes* 32 (1995) 33–43, at p. 43.
[30] Calvino, 'Why Read the Classics?' (Italian original 1981), in *The Literature Machine*, trs. P. Creagh (New York, 1982) 125–34, at p. 128. Compare T. S. Eliot, *What Is a Classic?* (London, 1944); F. Kermode, *The Classics. Literary Images of Permanence and Change* (Cambridge, 1977).
[31] On ancient literary criticism, see G. Nagy, 'Early Greek Views of Poets and Poetry', and G. Ferrari, 'Plato and Poetry', in G. A. Kennedy (ed.), *The Cambridge History of Literary Criticism* I. *Classical Criticism* (Cambridge, 1989), pp. 1–77, 92–148 respectively; C. Segal 'Cracks in the Marble of the Classic Form: the Problem of the Classical Today', *Annals of Scholarship* 10 (1993) 7–30; and S. Mailloux (ed.), *Rhetoric, Sophistry, Pragmatism* (Cambridge, 1996). (R. A. Lanham, *The Electronic Word: Democracy, Technology and the Arts* (Chicago, 1995) surprisingly couples his argument for a new, on-line concept of the university with a call for renewed attention to the rhetoric of Plato and Quintilian.) For theoretically freighted re-readings of Hellenistic poetry, see S. D. Goldhill, *The Poet's Voice. Essays on Poetics and Greek Literature* (Cambridge, 1991), pp. 223–83 (Theocritus), 284–333 (Apollonius Rhodius).

and Classicists have not been slow in availing themselves of the latest hermeneutic turns to produce readings even of the most seemingly impervious texts, such as tragedies, that are no less suspicious, dissident, or symptomatic than those of their fellows working in later literary epochs.[32] At the very least, such interrogative re-readings may and should lead to a broadening of the scope (and therefore weakening of the authority) of the canon. Other authors and genres besides Hellenistic poetry that have benefited from such canonical scope-broadening include especially the Greek novel or romance (Chariton's *Callirhoe* has been hailed, perhaps justly, as our first European novel) – it turns out that, with the rise of gender and cultural studies approaches, its sophisticated sexiness and self-consciousness have more to say to us than to earlier readers.[33]

Many of these re-readings depend, of course, on a quite intimate knowledge of ancient Greek or Latin, but if to read is to translate, then professional linguists no less than their Greek-less or Latin-less charges, for whom the Greek and Latin classics are most fully 'other', need to be *au courant* with the art – or is it science? – of translation: PC, it is worth adding, stands also for the Penguin Classics.[34] For the teachers as well as the taught, a comparative, interdisciplinary approach can offer classical pedagogy resources for renewal. The liberating effect of coming to see one's own culture and its wellsprings as but one possible form of life and sensibility is not the least of the potential gains.[35]

V

Culture, we know, can mean capital in the most brutally physical sense – in 1995 Yale lost $20m for not putting on a 'Western Civilization'

---

[32] On re-reading Homer, see the amusing essay by D. Denby, 'Does Homer have Legs?' *New Yorker*, 6 November (1993) 52–69. On Homer and tragedy, see more soberly P. W. Rose, *Sons of the Gods, Children of Earth. Ideology and Literary Form in Ancient Greece* (Ithaca, 1992). On tragedy, see J. Peradotto, 'Interrogating the Canon, Deposing the Tyrannus', *Annals of Scholarship* 10 (1993) 85–109; M. Katz, 'The Character of Tragedy: Women and the Greek Imagination', *Arethusa* 27 (1994) 81–103; Goff, *History, Tragedy, Theory*. On a variety of ancient texts, see A. Patterson, *Reading Between the Lines* (London and New York, 1993); D. Konstan, 'The Classics and Class Conflict', *Arethusa* 27 (1994) 47–70. See also n. 43.

[33] S. D. Goldhill, *Foucault's Virginity. Ancient Erotic Fiction and the History of Sexuality* (Cambridge, 1995); cf. E. Hall, 'The Ass with Double Vision: Politicising an Ancient Greek Novel', in D. Margolies and M. Joannou (eds.), *Heart of the Heartless World. Essays in Cultural Resistance in Memory of Margot Heinemann* (London and Boulder, CO, 1995) 47–59.

[34] P. Cartledge, 'So Different and So Long Ago' *New Statesman and Society*, 1 March (1996) 36–7; cf. the 'Prologue' to M. McDonald *Ancient Sun, Modern Light. Greek Drama on the Modern Stage* (New York, 1992).

[35] A. Szegedy-Maszak, 'Thales' Prayer', *Wesleyan* 74 (1992) 30–4 is salutary; cf. P. Cartledge, *The Greeks. A Portrait of Self and Others* (revised edn Oxford, 1997).

course in line with the donor's perhaps rather antiquated wishes. But it can also represent capital in a metaphysical sense, constituting an asset or liability according as it is used.[36] My concluding modest proposal is to view Classics as a form of cultural capital using a model drawn from New Historicist 'cultural poetics', a neo-marxist variant of cultural materialism that attempts to understand the material in terms of the mental and *vice versa*. The model I have specifically in mind is suggested by a notably sensitive treatment of the moral economy of *kudos* (a special charisma and prestige) in Pindar.[37] This has a special relevance today, since we, too, like Pindar, stand at a cultural crossroads, a crisis in the ancient etymological sense, that is, a moment of decision. What was at stake for Pindar was the persistence, transformation or extinction of aristocratic values in an increasingly democratic age. For us, as we approach the end of a millennium, the issue is how we are to (re)appropriate our cultural past and particularly our Classical heritage. Classics as a discipline, I would argue, despite or thanks to its technical difficulty and seeming practical irrelevance, has still a vital role to play. Indeed, it could even be usefully seen as conferring on its practitioners and consumers a plural, democratized form of *kudos*, which would of course depend on its *not* being identified pedagogically with a particular social milieu. The best way to prevent that form of stultification, I suggest, is by fostering the ongoing mutation of Classics into Classical Cultural Studies.[38]

When Birmingham University's Centre for Contemporary Cultural Studies was set up in 1964, under Richard Hoggart and then Stuart Hall, the Classics Department objected that Birmingham already had a centre for cultural studies – Classics. That was a remarkably prescient gesture, if also, alas, no more than that. Classics as a discipline, the Mother of all Canons, is still ripe for 'cultural studies' repositioning, as part of a culture and identity enmeshed in imperial history, a site of struggle and hybrid construction. Once the imagination has been thus decolonized, the new Classics will come to be more widely appreciated

[36] S. Cohen, *Academia and the Luster of Capital* (Minneapolis, 1993); for the Academy's preoccupation with prestige and hierarchy see also Caesar, *Conspiring with Forms*.
[37] L. Kurke, 'The Economy of *Kudos*', in C. Dougherty and L. Kurke (eds.), *Cultural Poetics in Archaic Greece. Cult, Performance, Politics* (Cambridge, 1993) 131–63.
[38] M. Beard and J. Henderson, *Classics. A Very Short Introduction* (Oxford, 1995) points a way forward; cf. Beard, 'What Classics has to Teach' *Times Literary Supplement*, 26 May (1995) 13–14. Classics, however, as Beard and Henderson forcefully remind us, is not only about written texts: cf. I. D. Jenkins, *Archaeologists and Aesthetes in the Sculpture Galleries of the British Museum* (London, 1993); Morris, *Classical Greece*; J. J. Tanner, 'Shifting Paradigms in Classical Art History', *Antiquity* 68 (1994) 650–5.

as good to think with as well as about. A genuinely non-oxymoronic Classical cultural studies programme would then be able to take its full part in the overall shift of attention in intercultural studies towards the contested edges of cultures, nations and identities.[39] Here perhaps lies the most unambiguously positive contribution of Bernal's *Black Athena* project towards the future of Classics.

Better such a repositioning, at any rate, than attempting to claim a place in the sun for Classics by alleging, misleadingly at best, that the ancient Graeco-Roman world was itself 'multicultural' *avant la lettre*.[40] That is to make the mistake of trying to use the Classics as conversation-stoppers, when, understood differently or otherwise, they are the great conversation openers. If the (ideal) ancient city has anything to teach us, it is above all that culture is a debate, not a monologue, and thrives on J. S. Mill's 'antagonism of opinion'.[41] Or, as Auden once epigrammatically remarked, it is not the 'Greek miracle' but the Greeks' self-reflexivity that is their most important cultural achievement.[42] Since the truly interdisciplinary departments are those which are critically reconstituting their own disciplines from the inside, the movement of reconstitution that has been initiated in Classics is at least a step in the right direction.[43] That is also a form of pedagogical re-empowerment. But, as the old Roman poet so sagely observed, 'Power, without good management, collapses under its own weight. Power, well managed, the gods advance to new heights'.[44]

---

[39] H. Bhaba, *The Location of Culture* (London and New York, 1994). At risk of a charge of ethnocentrism I might add that for more than a decade Part II of the Cambridge Classical Tripos has included a magic ingredient 'X' – signifying cross-over, interdisciplinary courses on such themes and topics as 'Classics: Nineteenth and Twentieth Century Perspectives' and 'Eros and Amor: Erotics and [not only *in*: PC] the Ancient World'.

[40] This is a ploy adopted by G. K. Galinsky, *Classical and Modern Interactions. Postmodern Architecture, Multiculturalism, Decline, and Other Issues* (Austin, TX, 1992); and B. M. W. Knox, *The Oldest Dead White European Males and Other Reflections on the Classics* (New York, 1993).

[41] This is the leitmotif of G. Graff, *Beyond the Culture Wars: How Teaching the Conflicts can Revitalize American Education* (New York, 1993); cf. Oakley, *Community of Learning*.

[42] W. H. Auden, *Forewords and Afterwords*, ed. E. Mendelsohn (New York, 1989) 8.

[43] C. A. Stray and R. A. Kaster (eds.), *Reinterpreting the Classics* (special issue of *Annals of Scholarship* 10.1, 1993); Rabinowitz and Richlin, *Feminist Theory and the Classics*; J. Peradotto and H. Hansen (eds.), *Rethinking the Classical Canon* (special issue of *Arethusa* 27, 1994); J. P. Euben, J. R. Wallach and J. Ober (eds.), *Athenian Political Thought and the Reconstruction of American Democracy* (Princeton, 1994); T. N. Mitchell, 'The Classics in an Age of Innovation and Technology' *Classics Ireland* 1 (1994) 1–17; Morris, *Classical Greece*; Goff, *History, Tragedy, Theory*, pp. 1–37.

[44] Horace, *Odes* 3.4.65–7, trans. J. Diggle, *Cambridge Orations 1982–1993* (Cambridge, 1994) 63.

CHAPTER 2

Schoolboys and gentlemen: classical pedagogy and authority in the English public school

Christopher Stray

By the end of the nineteenth century, the authority of classical education had been severely eroded. New areas of knowledge had invaded
an enlarged curriculum in the ancient universities (though much less
so in the public schools). A mature industrial economy faced increasing
competition from rivals abroad; the franchise was being extended to the
working classes and would soon also incorporate women. These challenges to the authority of classics and its bearers prompted a rearticula-
tion of ideas of classical knowledge and pedagogy in which the symbolic
centre of classics moved from 'culture' to 'discipline'. The compulsory
Greek requirement at Oxford and Cambridge, symbol both of the
dominance of Hellenism during the Victorian era and of the universities'
autonomy from the state, was repeatedly attacked, and finally was abolished in 1919–20. In turn, the study of Latin, previously subordinated
to Greek, came to be seen as an exemplary disciplinary subject within
the widened academic curriculum. In essence, it symbolised the intern-
alised self-control of the new voter, a bulwark against ochlocracy.

In learning grammar by rote in the lower forms of public schools,
boys (as they almost all were) were learning both to learn and to obey:
the two faces of *disciplina*. The same could be said of the 'nonsense
verses' with which many boys began their encounter with verse composition: metrically accurate, but not expected to make any sense.[1] Some
of those who went on past this stage, however, found that they were
creating poetry, and had found the key to a world of freedom and culture. The tension between order and freedom, discipline and culture,
echoed a wider tension between the stability of the social order and the
freedom of individual citizens: a structural dilemma characteristic of

---

[1] The progression from 'nonsense' to 'sense' (making verses which were semantically as well as
metrically well-formed) was embedded enough in some schools for two of the lowest forms to
be called by these names; as at Eton.

nineteenth-century liberal democratic states. The emergence in England of a society predicated on the autonomy of the individual is paralleled by the late eighteenth-century move from an Augustan classicism
focused on Rome to what became Victorian Hellenism. The shift from
the orderly imaginary of Rome to the wilder freedom of Greece represented, in effect, the adoption of a high-risk strategy oriented to free
individuals rather than to stable groups. The ordering of freedom was
accomplished, in the new era, by the finely modulated control mechan-
ism of the examination, whose institutional development accelerated
in this period.[2]

In this chapter, I want to look at the way social and intellectual styles
were reproduced and challenged in everyday institutional settings, concentrating in particular on pedagogic enounters in public-school classrooms. It is notoriously true that evidence of what actually happened
in classrooms in history is very difficult to find. A corpus of such evidence has, however, recently come to light in the form of transcripts of
classroom conversations in Winchester College in the 1880s and 1890s.
In the next section I give three excerpts from these texts, followed by a
commentary on the issues they raise. These issues are pursued in the
rest of the chapter.

HORAE MUSHRIANAE: A WINCHESTER CLASSICAL CLASSROOM IN THE 1880s

To cast a discussion in the form of text and commentary is of course to
opt for a rhetorical format deeply embedded in the history of classical
scholarship. There are, however, other reasons for adopting it here. One
is that it enables me to present the fine texture of classroom interaction,
and to show the use of language – vernacular and classical alike – in a
setting where most of the formal curriculum involved saturation in linguistic practice in English, Latin and Greek. But this format also helps
to redress the inequality of power between writer and reader by making
at least some of the former's evidence publicly available to the latter.

The photograph (Plate 1) was taken through the window of a classroom in Winchester College in 1898. Here Edmund Morshead, who
can be seen on the left, taught 'Junior Division Sixth Book' – that is,
the lower sixth form. Morshead's idiosyncratic speech mannerisms led
to his pupils' assembling a dictionary of 'Mushri' (his nickname was

[2] K. Hoskin, 'The Examination, Disciplinary Power and Rational Schooling', *History of Education*,
8 (1979), 135–46.

Plate 1. A powerfully peculiar pedagogue: Edmund Morshead, caught
in the act of teaching, *c.* 1898. (Reproduced from the frontispiece of
The Mushri-English Pronouncing Dictionary, 1996.)

'Mush', and his classroom, inevitably, was known as the Mushroom).
The picture shows Morshead with some of his pupils, and suggests an
engagement which adds an extra dimension to the conversations quoted
below, catching the nuances of stance and expression which we can so
rarely find in the printed record. The Winchester pupils redressed a
teacher/pupil imbalance of power by, as it were, writing and publishing their own minutes of their meetings. *Horae Mushrianae* ('Hours with
Mushri') forms part of a small corpus of material which Morshead's
pupils collected and printed between 1880 and 1901 as appendices to
their record of his speech mannerisms, *The Mushri-English Pronouncing
Dictionary.* I shall argue that paradoxically, this personal idiosyncrasy
(the display of which is the *raison d'être* of the *Dictionary*) is typical of
a widespread contemporary trend, one which is intimately linked to
nineteenth-century English discourses of authority and freedom.[3] The
first extract begins with remarks by Morshead.

[3] The Dictionary was first produced in manuscript early in 1880. It went into print later that
year, and further, enlarged editions appeared in 1888 and 1901. This last edition is reprinted
with an introduction and appendices in C. A. Stray, *The Mushri-English Pronouncing Dictionary. A
Chapter in 19th-century English Public School Lexicography* [*Dictionary*] (Berkeley/Swansea/Wellington:
privately printed, 1996). The theme of 'English freedom' is discussed in the introduction. See
also the essays collected in R. Colls and P. Dodd (eds.), *Englishness. Politics and Culture 1880–1920*
(London: Croom Helm, 1986).

I
Landor's sonnet to Ianthe, line 11,

> 'The conscious dove
> Bears in her breast the billet dear to love.'

In line 11 I have been a trifle too bold; I have not quite kept to the English; but I think the spirit of the passage quite requires some alteration, and this is just what a Latin would have said, –
'Pulchraque venustam portat rubecula florem.'
Well, T-lb-t, please keep your remarks till the end of the version; I really can't get on with the bidzness at this rate. – E in venustam short? Is it so? Why then, look it out, P-lt-r ('Short sir!') Formosam! there can be no objection to formosam. ('Please, sir, you said venustam!') I take it I said nothing of the sort. ('Yes you did, sir.') Is it so? so be it, then! I must have said it from the teeth outwards. ('Please, sir.') Why these interruptions? ('Sir, flos is masculine.') I am, I take it, quite aware of that: I said formosum. – I have put rubecula, redbreast, instead of pigeon, because it is so much more poetical, and the spirit of the passage seems to require it. Is it not so? – Mnyum-Mnyum! I take it, it is. (*Dictionary*, pp. 52–3)

This passage dates from the beginning of the 1880s. Morshead is taking a class in translation from English into Latin. The English text chosen is a poem by Walter Savage Landor, who was unusual in the nineteenth century in writing a large amount of original verse in Latin. The class would have been told to produce their own versions, after which – as here – the master would read out his own translation. This enabled him to display his own talents, but also offered a target to be attacked where errors or infelicities could be spotted by his pupils. In this case, they are able to point out that *venustam* will not scan, since its first syllable is not long but short. The passage shows Morshead attempting to cover his tracks by shifting to alternatives (first *formosam*, then *formosum*), either denying he had uttered an earlier word, or claiming he had spoken it but without meaning to. 'From the teeth outwards', a favourite phrase of his, seems to carry this meaning and is one of those listed in the *Dictionary*. Other idiosyncratic sayings in the passage – 'bidzness' [itself one of many variants] for 'business', 'Is it so? So be it then' and 'Mnyum-Mnyum' – are also listed. The second of these is noteworthy, since it is used as a formulaic utterance when deferring to a pupil's opinion – or rather, to the authority of a dictionary or grammar, as reported by a pupil. ('Rubecula' does not occur in classical Latin, and would have been found in an English-Latin dictionary used for verse composition. It is possible that Morshead is being teased for using late Latin – a revenge for his remarks about *regelatio* – see III below.)

II

Up to books. (Tacitus *Annals* ii. 54 § 3.)

Br-w-n construes: – 'Aquilones depulere, the eagles repulsed them.' Mush.
'Yes! that is, I take it, the Roman Standards!' T-lb-t. 'Sir, I read "aquilones."'
M. 'Yes, er! and what does "aquilones" mean?' T. 'Noθern. . . . winds.'
M. 'Well, er?' T. 'I thought you said "eagles." M. 'Well, er, and what is the
Latin for "eagles"?' T. 'Aquilae.' M. 'Yes, er?' T. 'Does your edition read
"aquilae"?' M. 'No, T-lb-t!' T. 'Then, sir, what edition does read "aquilae"?'
M. 'Br-w-n's, I presume, er!' (*Dictionary*, p. 53)

This scene comes from a lesson in which Tacitus is being read, the members of the class taking turns to analyse ('construe') each Latin sentence,
and then translate it into English. Morshead is represented as accepting,
at first, a mistranslation of *Aquilones* (northern winds) as *aquilae* (eagles,
hence the Roman legionary standards which bore an image of an
eagle). He then tries to throw his pupils off the track by suggesting that
the different translations reflect the readings in different editions of the
text. Mushric mannerisms in this scene are the use of 'I take it', and
the pronunciation of 'northern'. The *Dictionary* records that Morshead
pronounced 'northern clime' as 'noθern climm'. The pervasive influence of classical learning can be seen in the young authors' decision
to use the Greek letter theta (θ) to represent the unvoiced 'th' sound.
Morshead's speech is another strange language, following its own, often
mysterious, rules.

III

Another Version, 1881.
(Scene – The Peg's Class-room, 9 a.m. Enter Mush.)[4]

'We'll take the Latin prose first. I see that you have all used 'regelatio' for
'thaw.' Well, errumn! This 'regelatio' is an English word, first introduced into
Latin, I think, by Aggenus Urbicus. Just look it out, er! – (The Looker-out:
'Aggenus Urbicus.') – Yes! I thought so! he died, I take it, a few years before
I was born. Hush, please! The entray has been capitally done by everyone
except L-c-ck. Yes, L-c-ck, er, there is nothing to laugh at! Run through it,
Chittay, and show him how it should be done. Wait a minute. Cr-cksh-nk!
will you accentuate, please,* first? Yes, quite right, er; και is oxytone. I have
looked it out in my dictionaray! Hush, please! 'Now, Chittay, er! – (H. C. τίς
πότε κτλ) – Come, Chittay, do crawl a bit faster! Come, construe, construe!
– (H. C. τίς πότε 'Who in the world –') – Yes that is right! Or you might
bring out the meaning by repetition. – (H. C. 'Whŏ-whō) (Laughter). – Come,
Chittay, do not be an oaf!' – H. C. 'Sir, is that the language of one gentleman

<hr>

[4] 'The Peg' was George Ridding, headmaster 1866–84.

to another?' – 'No; but I take it, it is the language of a schoolmaster to a schoolboy!' (*Dictionary*, pp. 53–54)
*Rare

In this final scene, Morshead is going through Latin prose compositions and an 'entry' – an unseen translation, here from Greek into English, written in a previous lesson. The role of dictionaries as authoritative sources of knowledge looms large. Morshead's pupils have presumably used an English-Latin dictionary to find a word for 'thaw', and choosing to use a noun, found 'regelatio', a word cited only from the end of the 4th century AD in the works of an obscure writer on agriculture. Morshead has also checked in the dictionary, but chooses to demonstrate his learning by having the 'looker-out' investigate the word on the spot. This formal role of 'dictionary monitor' reflects the important part played by the Greek and Latin dictionaries in the life of this sixth-form classroom, in which pupils were assumed to have mastered the elements of grammar and syntax and to be on the verge of serious scholarship (in the photograph [Plate 1], the dictionaries can be seen on Morshead's desk). The *Dictionary* reveals that Morshead referred to Liddell and Scott's Greek-English dictionary, the standard work of reference on Greek, as 'Our two friends' (*Dictionary*, p. 45). This is the dictionary in which he will have checked the accentuation of και; and the public admission that he has done so, while it again points to the authority of the book, should also remind us that this whole account is written from a pupil's-eye view. (It is scarcely conceivable that Morshead would have needed to consult a dictionary to check on such a common word.) In this scene, Morshead's idiosyncratic pronunciation is again evident. He liked to pronounce final 'y' as 'ay' – here, in 'entray' and 'dictionaray'. But the issue of linguistic choice is also raised, not just by the whole nature of the translation exercises, but at a different level by his exchange with Chitty. This illuminates the uneasy relationship between a controlling adult and a group of boys who at the age of sixteen were on the verge of both adulthood and scholarship – potentially, but not actually, Morshead's peers. Chitty invokes the norms of gentlemanly politeness, to be rebuffed by Morshead's firm redefinition of the relationship, and hence of the relevant norms of interaction, as that of master and pupil.

The authority of the teacher is clearly a central issue in these scenes. It is asserted by Morshead with the help of standard reference works, the Greek and Latin dictionaries, which are nevertheless equally available, as we have seen, to his pupils. It is challenged in the classroom

largely through appeals to dictionary authority, but also by use of the
public evidence of Morshead's mistakes and self-contradictions. In the
Mushroom a triangular relationship obtained between teacher, pupils
and dictionaries ('our two friends' in the case of Greek). The role of
'looker out', which publicly legitimated the practice of reference to an
authority beyond Morshead's own, also acknowledged the status of his
pupils as apprentice sorcerers, potèntially masters of the mysteries of
Latin and Greek. In the Mushri *Dictionary*, the challenge is made retro-
spectively; but it should be remembered that Morshead was teaching
at Winchester throughout the publishing career of the *Dictionary*, and
that its subversive portrait of him will have been available to successive
generations of his pupils.[5] But he also had another claim to authority
(and another target for its subversion), through his published translations of classical and modern authors, including Aeschylus' *Agamemnon*
(1877) and of the whole Oresteian trilogy (1881). It is these which earned
him the sobriquet 'the G. T.' (the Great Translator: a title wickedly
described in the Mushri *Dictionary* as 'self-invented': *Dictionary*, p. 47).
The *Dictionary* contains several strange phrases from Morshead's translation of the *Oresteia*, which offered a rich quarry for evidence of his
idiosyncratic use of English, and also, by imputation, of misunder-
standings of the Greek original. Another title by which he is referred
to in the *Dictionary* is 'The Scribe'. This is prompted by his pupils' use
of Morshead's written comments on their work – another hostage to
fortune – which treats them as if they were recently-discovered papyrus
fragments demanding interpretation. The title 'The Scribe' neatly combines a mock-respect with gentle derision, since though the scribes who
transmitted manuscripts of classical authors had a crucial role in the
process, their work was mechanical, and they are known for their pro-
neness to error. Like the teacher's role, theirs is 'special but shadowed'.
The authority gained from their knowledge contrasts with their own
low status.[6]

It will be apparent that the conventions of classical learning have
been adopted, if only by way of parody, in Morshead's pupils' irrever-
ent account. His own comments on their work are treated as *scholia*:

[5] Morshead was flattered by the appearance of the early manuscript editions in the school, but
not at all pleased when later editions were printed outside Winchester, exposing these mannerisms to a wider world. (*Dictionary*, p. 32)

[6] See D. C. Lortie, *Schoolteacher* (Chicago: University of Chicago Press, 1975). A good account of
the role of copyists and editors in the transmission of classical texts is given by L. D. Reynolds
and N. G. Wilson, *Scribes and Scholars*, Oxford: Clarendon Press 1968 (note the disjunction in
their title).

the explanatory comments made by scribes on classical texts. The tables
are thus turned, the pupils' work becoming the text, the master's comments the subordinate annotation.[7] Comparable in some ways is the
first printed work of Max Beerbohm, written in July 1890 while he was
in the sixth form at Charterhouse School. The *Carmen Becceriense* is an
account of the mannerisms of the school music master, A. G. Becker,
presented as a Latin hexameter poem. The text is equipped with an
apparatus criticus which guys the conventions of the genre. In particular, it alludes to the school editions of classical authors produced by
T. E. Page, the sixth-form classical master at Charterhouse. Beerbohm's
notes which refer to 'my friend Professor Mayor' play on the authority of J. E. B. Mayor, author of a well-known edition of Juvenal, but
since Page and Mayor were friends (they had both been taught at
Shrewsbury by the famous Benjamin Kennedy), the phrase is probably a direct quote from Page's conversation.[8] The parallel with the
reference to Morshead as 'the G[reat] T[ranslator]' is obvious: the
status of a teacher as author of published works is deployed in his
pupils' interaction with him in school. And there are other parallels,
notably in Page's verbal mannerisms. The best known of these was his
habit of inserting 'please' in many of his sentences – a nice contrast
with Morshead, whose brusqueness is characterised in the final extract
quoted above by the comment 'Rare' on his use of the word.[9]

    The excerpts above come from classical lessons. How large a part
did these play in the total classroom experience of Junior Division
Sixth Book? By coincidence, the timetable of the form in 1898 – the
year in which the photograph of Morshead teaching the form was
taken – was printed in A. F. Leach's history of the school, published
in the following year. This was almost certainly provided by his eldest
son, T. A. Leach, who was in Morshead's form from January 1898
until July 1899.[10]

---

[7] In one case, a disparaging Morsheadic comment is itself treated as a classical text: 'Fragment
of a Mushric chorus' (*Dictionary*, p. 49). It begins thus:

      . . . Little, and stupid
      What there is of it.

[8] '*Carmen Becceriense*, cum prolegomenis et commentario critico, edidit H. M. B.', in J. G. Riewald
(ed.), *Max in Verse: Rhymes and Parodies* (London: Heinemann, 1964), pp. 1–3. See R. Viscusi,
Max Beerbohm, or the Dandy Dante. Rereading with Mirrors (Baltimore: Johns Hopkins University
Press, 1986), p. 24.

[9] For Page and his mannerisms, see W. J. N. Rudd, *Schoolmaster Extraordinary* (Bristol: Bristol
Classical Press, 1980), pp. 12–13.

[10] A. F. Leach, *A History of Winchester College* (London: Duckworth, 1899). My thanks to James
Sabben-Clare, headmaster of Winchester College, for information on T. A. Leach.

	7–7.45	10.15–11.15	11.15–12	4.15–5.15	5.15–6.15
Mon	Divinity	German	Livy	Mathematics [or substitute]	Aeschylus
Tues	Divinity	Mathematics [or substitute]	Horace		
Wed	Cicero Latin entry	Plato	Science (Sound)	German	Greek Entry
Thurs	Vergil	Mathematics [or substitute]	Livy		
Fri	Cicero	9.45–11.15 History and Horace	Prose version	Mathematics	Aeschylus
Sat	English	10–12 Plato and sundries		3.45–4.30 Science	

Young Leach also comments that 'Army Class substitute German for Greek, and cultivate Science and Mathematics at the expense of Plato and Aeschylus'. He explains that an 'entry' is an unseen translation written in class, and an 'entry version' is 'a don's idea of what a perfect version is' (Leach, History, p. 534). The phrases I have quoted nicely exemplify the resistant spirit we have already seen in *Horae Mushrianae*. T. A. Leach was in this case able to challenge authority in the public sphere by inserting his subversive statements in his father's book. Here he enters, however briefly, the realm of the 'G. T.' – he is at once within and without the classroom, both schoolboy and author.

In his *Athleticism in the Victorian and Edwardian Public School*, J. A. Mangan asserted that 'Inside the nineteenth-century public school classroom there was a blind belief in a classical prescription for all. Most found it irrelevant. It did nothing to train them for life; in consequence they had very little use for school work.'[11] Leach's timetable reveals that of the 24 lessons listed, 13 are classical. Science and modern languages have made some inroads into what fifty years earlier would have been an almost entirely classical curriculum, but Latin and Greek are still the staple, and the 'tasks' Leach goes on to list are almost all classical.[12] But though the domination of Victorian classrooms by classics can hardly be denied, it deserves a more nuanced account than Mangan gives. Leach's timetable, after all, comes from the very end of the century: is it representative beyond its time and place? Winchester had in fact concentrated more heavily on classics than many other public schools. This changed only in 1901, when, for the first time in the school's history,

[11] J. A. Mangan, *Athleticism in the Victorian and Edwardian Public School* (Cambridge: Cambridge University Press, 1986), p. 111. I am not here concerned with Mangan's denial of any 'training for life', but there is evidence in abundance to refute it.
[12] Leach, *History*, pp. 533–4.

a warden and a headmaster were appointed who were both non-Wykehamists.[13] From that point on, it became respectable to go through the school as something other than a classicist. That Mangan's assertion oversimplifies the situation, even in 1898, is shown by the existence of the Army Class. Even for Junior Division Sixth Book, a 13/24 classical curriculum hardly counts as a 'classical prescription'.[14] As for the 'blind belief' in classics for all, there were liberal, and classically-educated, masters who did not share this 'blind belief'.[15] Indeed, Morshead himself had some pungent things to say about the defenders of classical education in an address he gave in 1906, describing the challenges to classical dominance by scientists as 'an attack by Philistines upon Pharisees, of one sort of unreason upon another: impatience on the one side, bigotry on the other'.[16]

Mangan's reference to 'relevance' and 'training for life' raises the question of just what the concerns of pupils were in classrooms like Morshead's. Did they really think in these terms? 'Training for life' is surely more likely to have been something boomed from the pulpit in the school chapel. In the late Victorian decades, the thoughts of pupils are more likely to have been directed to performance at games – as Mangan himself has documented in detail. In any case, the schoolboys were not just passive puppets of a disciplinary regime. 'There was a blind belief' is unspecific and lacks a sense of agency, but this agency is certainly not lacking in the pupils quoted in *Horae Mushrianae*. Of course those in authority over them had the last word – usually – but the conversations quoted above suggest that pedagogic authority was subject to negotiation. Here the age of the pupils is crucial: these are adolescents on the edge of manhood, whom Morshead's idiosyncrasy will have encouraged to spread their own wings, especially as they were becoming interested in politics. In the early 1880s Gladstone's campaigns were leading to fierce local contests between his Liberal supporters and Conservative voters. Morshead was one of a minority of the Winchester staff who publicly proclaimed their Liberalism; and

[13] Like Eton, Winchester was a collegiate foundation in which authority was divided between a warden (at Eton 'provost') and a headmaster. Their appointments indicate that the governors were prepared to shake off the ancient ways.

[14] Unless the phrase means only that pupils did some classics, however little – in which case it loses most of its meaning.

[15] Examples include E. E. Bowen of Harrow (about whom Mangan has written) and E. A. Abbott, headmaster of the City of London School and author of *Flatland* (1884). Both men were members of a progressive discussion club known as the 'UU' (United Ushers).

[16] *Inaugural Address, delivered on 7th February 1906* (to the Birmingham and Midland Branch of the Classical Association), (Birmingham: Hall and English, 1906).

the election campaign of early 1880 was in fact one of the precipitating causes of the appearance of the *Mushri Dictionary*.[17]

THE STATE, MODERNITY AND THE MASSES:
CHANGE AND RESISTANCE

'Look at those big, isolated clumps of buildings arising up above the slates, like brick islands in a lead-coloured sea.'
'The board schools.'
'Light-houses, my boy! Beacons of the future! Capsules with hundreds of bright little seeds in each, out of which will spring the wiser, better England of the future.' (Arthur Conan Doyle, *The Naval Treaty*, 1893)

From the window of Morshead's classroom to the serried rows of windows in the board schools is a long journey; and not only because it takes us, in the 1890s, from the rural fastness of Winchester to the swarming life of the London suburbs. The school buildings are observed by Conan Doyle's Sherlock Holmes from the suburban railway line on which he and Dr Watson are travelling back into the capital from a case in the country. In the board schools, the children of the poor were taught a range of subjects which certainly did not include Latin or Greek. Yet these two very different worlds belonged to the same society, late-Victorian England. The contrast serves to remind us that classics was a major symbol of social distinction. The classical learning of the public schools did, in a sense, train for life, in providing public schoolboys with the shared knowledge of an elite social group; even if that knowledge was to be used in adulthood only to produce a few classical tags. The conversation between Holmes and Watson in the above passage reflects contemporary middle-class concerns with 'darkest England', the sprawling new world of the metropolis.[18] But it also hints at the appearance (much later in this country than on the continent) of mass schooling provided by the state; a development which gave rise to considerable unease. In a country which was home to a powerful ideological tradition celebrating individual and local autonomy (a

---

[17] *Dictionary*, pp. 16–22. For a survey of the scattered evidence for the subversive making of their own sense of classics by younger pupils, see C. A. Stray, 'The smell of Latin grammar: contrary imaginings in English classrooms', *Bulletin of the John Rylands University Library of Manchester* 76.3 (1994), pp. 201–220.

[18] Among the products of the social concerns of the 1880s is (General) William Booth's *In Darkest England and the Way Out*, published by the Salvation Army (which he had founded) in 1890. For a modern discussion see G. Stedman Jones, *Outcast London* (Oxford: Oxford University Press, 1971).

tradition to which the 'Mushri' phenomenon belonged), such central
intervention seemed to many an un-English solution to the problem
of securing the survival of England. The ideological campaign for
'national efficiency' conducted in the 1890s represented a compromise
formula: centralised intervention was justified if it would improve the
efficiency with which the state's human resources were used.[19] The
rhetoric of efficiency was used, for example, by Robert Morant, who
played a leading role in establishing the pattern of state schooling after
the 1902 Education Act. In a report on Swiss education written in 1898,
he warned that

Without control by 'knowledge' in the sphere of public education of all
grades ... a democratic state must be inevitably beaten in the international
struggle for existence, conquered from without by the concentrated brainpower
of competing nations, and shattered from within by the centrifugal forces of
her own people's unrestrained individualism.[20]

The idiosyncrasy which was celebrated, along with gloriously irrational tradition, in the myth of Englishness assembled in this period,
becomes problematic at the point when it spreads from elite sectors to
the mass of the population: from Winchester (where Morant himself
had been educated) to the Board Schools.

The intervention of the state in education led to a marked contrast
between different class-specific varieties of schooling. As free elementary schooling became the mark of the poor, cheap private schools aping
the public schools were set up, offering a curriculum which included
at least Latin, and sometimes Greek, and which thus marked out both
school and pupil as middle-class. To be able to send a child (still usually
a son) to such a school announced a social status above the world of the
board schools and their clientele. Conan Doyle was in a minority in
eulogising the future promise of the board schools, rather than denouncing their regimented routine or the 'cockney twang' of their pupils.[21]

Winchester sixth-form classics in the 1890s, then, was one of the peaks
of a dominant social and cultural formation, but one whose days were
numbered. The collapse of the grand Victorian alliance of classics and

[19] See G. R. Searle, *The Quest for National Efficiency* (Oxford: Blackwell, 1971); and on the relative
lateness of English state intervention, A. Green, *Education and State Formation. The Rise of Education Systems in England, France and the USA* (London: Macmillan, 1990).
[20] Quoted by Searle, *National Efficiency*, p. 210.
[21] J. Carey, *The Intellectuals and the Masses. Pride and Prejudice among the Literary Intelligentsia, 1880–1939*
(London: Faber, 1992), p. 16. For a more jaundiced view of the board schools, see S. Bullock,
'The Burden of the Middle Classes', *Fortnightly Review* 80 (ns) (1906), pp. 441–420.

class was symbolised by the abolition of the compulsory Greek requirement by Oxford and Cambridge after the First World War. 'Compulsory
Greek' had by then become a kind of Hindenburg Line of culture: a
last symbolic ditch to which the defenders of the classics had retreated.
Its abolition was followed by the expansion of science teaching in the
public schools in the 1920s. Classics retained a powerful hold over the
curricula of public schools, and of the grammar schools which aspired
to be like them, well into the 1950s. Alternative curricular tracks were
available, but it was common for top-stream pupils to be urged to
choose (e.g.) Greek rather than German.[22]

THE LANGUAGES OF GENTLEMEN: EXCLUSION, HIERARCHY AND SYMBOLIC MARKETS

At the heart of Morshead's teaching lay the making of delicate linguistic distinctions. The obscure and very late Latin agricultural writer
Aggenus Urbicus (sole user of 'regelatio' = thaw) is hardly a respectable
source. Morshead's remark about Aggenus' having 'died . . . just before
I was born' was surely intended to emphasis the weakness of Aggenus'
authority as a source of Latin usage. Elsewhere in the *Dictionary* we
are reminded that hierarchies of authorship also operated in English.
Expounding Tennyson's 'In Memoriam', Morshead quoted the cou-
plet 'And from his ashes may be made/The violet of his native land'
and asked the class for parallels. A pupil offered 'And the roses and
the posies/Fertilized by Clementine', and Morshead was ready to take
this seriously until he discovered that it was from 'a common music-
hall dittay', when he rejected it as beneath contempt.[23] The stratification of English in this period has been well documented, but the role
of Latin and Greek in social and linguistic hierarchies has been little
discussed.[24] The three languages constituted a market in which each
had different claims to distinction and different social and institutional
bases.[25] During the first half of the nineteenth century the introduction
of English notes in school editions of classical authors had been fiercely

---

[22] This was still a common practice in public schools in the early 1960s. [23] *Dictionary*, p. 55.
[24] See O. Smith, *The Politics of Language 1791–1819* (Oxford: Clarendon Press, 1984); T. Crowley,
The Politics of Discourse: the Standard Language Question in British Cultural Debates (London: Macmillan,
1989); and on class and accent, L. C. Mugglestone, '*Talking Proper*'. *The Rise of Accent as Social
Symbol* (Oxford: Clarendon Press, 1995).
[25] For a discussion of the symbolic market of languages, see E. Ben-Rafael, *Language, Identity and
Social Division. The Case of Israel* (Oxford: Clarendon Press, 1994), pp. 38–45.

resisted. Christopher Wordsworth, headmaster of Harrow, warned in 1838 that the practice 'will produce a general feebleness and indolence in the intellectual habits of the literary student . . . leading to . . . mental effeminacy.'[26] To counter the use of English, Wordsworth wrote a Latin grammar in Latin, *King Edward VI's Latin Grammar*, which became the market leader in the 1840s and 50s, and even urged his publisher to use Latin rather than English in advertising the book.[27]

In Morshead's classroom, language was both what was being learned (Latin and Greek) and the shared resource (English) with which ped-agogic authority was maintained and contested. To invoke 'the language of one gentleman to another' (Dictionary, p. 54) was to appeal to the etiquette of the adult male peer-group; to specify 'the language of a schoolmaster to a schoolboy' (*ibid.*) was to reject the claim to member-ship of that group implicit in the pupil's demand. Other 'languages', specific to social classes, regions and occupational groups, were being described in the late nineteenth century. The concern to record dia-lectal usage, in fact, formed part of the glorification of idiosyncrasy referred to above. The cultural status of such variant forms of English was ambiguous, for though they were to be respected as elements of organic folk life, yet they were clearly marginal to the 'standard English' which had consolidated its dominant position by this period. In the realm of pronunciation, what was called first 'Public School Pronunciation' and then, more neutrally, 'Received Pronunciation', constituted a standard which was in effect maintained by the socialisa-tion of the upper middle classes of the Home Counties.[28] It is easy to see that the assertion of gentlemanly idiosyncrasy might, if taken far enough, collide with the norms of standard usage. One of the most intriguing aspects of Morshead's speech mannerisms is that some of his pronunciations resemble Cockneyisms. For example, he pronounced 'There' as 'Theer' – the initial 'Th' being unvoiced (θeer). 'Theer' is, however, characteristic of Mrs Peggotty in Dickens' *David Copperfield*.[29] Morshead may thus have been deliberately employing 'vulgar' pro-nunciations to assert both his authority and individuality: using, that is, the language of a gentleman and of a schoolmaster.

---

[26] C. Wordsworth, 'On the Practice of Publishing Editions of Classical Authors with English Notes', *British Magazine* 13, (1 March 1838), pp. 243–6.

[27] See C. A. Stray, 'Paradigms of Social Order. The Politics of Latin Grammar in 19th-Century England', *Henry Sweet Society Newsletter* 13 (1989), pp. 13–23.

[28] See *Dictionary*, p. 29. [29] Mugglestone, '*Talking proper*', p. 242.

SUBJECTIVITIES

What role was the pupil expected to play in classical education? In the first half of the nineteenth century a progressive/developmental emphasis emerged to challenge the prevailing assumption that the pupil was there to be trained through rote learning and physical punishment. The word which summed up the sheer slog of learning, the discipline which combined the acquisition of knowledge with that of mental power, was 'grind'. The men who prepared small boys for public-school and university entrance examinations were familiarly known as 'gerund-grinders'.[30] What was at issue was not just pedagogic technique but the control of a developing intelligence: the formation of subjectivity. Well into the twentieth century we can trace a continuing tension between the search for pedagogic control and the aspiration to create independent thinkers. It is evident, for example, in the introductory essay 'Why learn Latin?' in G. M. Lyne's *Balbus. A Latin Reader for Junior Forms* (1934). Lyne explains that 'Latin is not dull, nor is it difficult . . . the most important part . . . is purely human' but goes on to stress that 'The grammar must be mastered: there must be some lack of firmness and determination in the character of the boy [sic] who cannot – or will not – master it'.[31] Here the disciplinary means (mastering the grammar) and the cultural end ('purely human') sit uneasily together.

By 1934, the need for independent yet disciplined thinkers had become a powerful ideological theme in English cultural debate. How else could a liberal democracy survive in a world inhabited by irrational extremisms of left (communism) and right (fascism)? The potential of Latin for the socialisation of self-controlled citizens – free voters who constituted bulwarks against ochlocracy – encouraged the continuation of 'grind' and militated against the exploration of literature in search of the 'purely human'. This tension between order and freedom, discipline and culture, can be seen as characteristic of liberal democratic regimes: driven by ideologies of individualism, yet nervous of the consequences of educating and enfranchising the masses. The result was the stultification of Latin teaching and learning.[32]

---

[30] See C. A. Stray, *Grinders and Grammars. A Victorian Controversy* (Reading: Textbook Colloquium, 1995).

[31] G. M. Lyne, *Balbus. A Latin Reader for Junior Forms* (London: Edward Arnold, 1934), pp. 9–10.

[32] Both the exemplary role of classics, and the more general emphasis on the learning of unquestioning obedience, are documented by Mary Evans in her *A Good School? Life in a Girls' Grammar School in the 1950s* (London: Women's Press, 1991).

In Victorian and Edwardian public schools, not only did a focus on grammar reflect a concern with control and the development of self-control, the emphasis on language deflected attention from the varieties of experience to be found in literature. When a literary text was studied, it was usually as a purely linguistic corpus. The classical expression of this strategy is the remark of the 'famous schoolmaster' who remarked to his class at the beginning of term that they were to study the *Oedipus Tyrannus* of Sophocles, 'a veritable treasure-house of grammatical peculiarities'.[33] The obsession with 'peculiarities' may seem to be the opposite of the constant focus on grammatical regularity, but both can be seen as ways of giving the power of classical language without opening the door to its dangers. To go through a literary text looking for linguistic minutiae, after all, is an effective way of diverting attention from the moral issues it may present – including questions of choice and fate, as in the *Oedipus Tyrannus*.[34] Nineteenth-century bourgeois morality had its own problems with the content of classical literature, nicely portrayed in Byron's account of the education of Don Juan. His mother, Donna Inez, was keen that he should learn Latin, but concerned that he might read of the 'filthy loves of gods and goddesses'.[35] Young Juan used an edition of Martial in which the improper lines were conscientiously excised, but were collected together in an appendix. The scholarly urge to completeness effectively subverted the pedagogic concern for propriety.[36] For instance, the widespread use of Caesar's *Bellum Gallicum* as an elementary Latin teaching text in the nineteenth and twentieth centuries may be due, in part, to its lack of sexually embarrassing subject matter. The combination of such a text

---

[33] The story first appeared in print in the preface to J. T. Sheppard's edition of the play: J. T. Sheppard, *The Oedipus Tyrannus of Sophocles* (Cambridge: Cambridge University Press, 1920). The 'schoolmaster' may be based on an eccentric Cambridge don, but it is just as likely that his fame is generated within (and subsequently by) the story itself.

[34] Such strategies had a long history, going back at least to the attempts made in early medieval Europe to control the potential of pagan classicism by focusing on grammatical features. See E. Durkheim, *L'Evolution Pédagogique en France* (Paris: Presses Universitaires de France, 1938), pp. 29, 42. Durkheim's analysis is summarised and systematised by M. S. Archer in *Culture and Agency. The Place of Culture in Social Theory* (Cambridge: Cambridge University Press, 1988), pp. 150–1, 162–5.

[35] J. J. McGann (ed.), *Lord Byron. The Complete Poetical Works* vol. 5 (Oxford: Oxford University Press, 1986) p. 21, line 322.

[36] Byron, *Don Juan*, canto I, stanzas 40–45. Byron himself had used such a book, an edition of Martial's epigrams (probably the Delphin edition of 1701) at Harrow. Cf. K. J. Dover, 'Expurgation of Greek literature', in his *The Greeks and their Legacy: Collected Papers II*, (Oxford: Blackwell 1988), pp. 270–91. The volume also contains Dover's essay 'Byron and the Ancient Greeks'.

and a relentless concentration on its linguistic features makes for a powerfully anodyne lesson in discipline.

In exploring the constitution of authority in Victorian classical ped-agogy we face two major difficulties. First, the paucity (not peculiar to this period) of evidence on what happened in classrooms. The conversa-tions in *Horae Mushrianae* give a rare opportunity to look at the way pedagogic authority is negotiated; the pupils who appear there were learning about both personal and textual authority. Second, the ideo-logical agenda which orients the analyst's gaze toward those oppressed by elites – women, workers, rebels – diminishes our understanding by ignoring the internal variety of elite culture, as well as the relationship between elite and non-elite groups.[37] The repression of the writing of American women, workers and blacks identified, and redressed, by Cary Nelson, has operated just as surely on elite groups.[38] The relationships recorded in *Horae Mushrianae* between teacher, pupils and texts may have been typical of the public-school classical classroom, but it is dangerous to generalise, as I have suggested above in commenting on Mangan's reference to 'blind belief in a classical prescription'. Henry Nevinson, who had been at Shrewsbury under H. W. Moss in the 1870s, recalled that 'To enter Headroom [the sixth-form classroom] was to become a scholar. I doubt if good Greek verse could be written any-where else. Winged iambics fluttered through the air; they hung like bats along the shelves, and the dust fell in Greek particles.' But Shrewsbury was not typical. Moss's predecessor Benjamin Kennedy had declared that 'My Sixth Form is the hardest Sixth Form in England, and I intend it to be so'.[39] Only by collecting and assessing the scanty evidence can

---

[37] See S. Collini, 'The Passionate Intensity of Cultural Studies', *Victorian Studies* 36 (1993), pp. 455–60.

[38] C. Nelson, *Repression and Recovery. Modern American Poetry and the Politics of Cultural Memory 1910–1945* (Madison: University of Wisconsin Press, 1989).

[39] H. W. Nevinson, *Between the Acts* (London: Duckworth, 1912), p. 17. Nevinson, it should be remembered, was a 'soured Salopian': see J. H. C. Leach, 'Dust and Greek particles', in P. Cowburn (ed.), *A Salopian Anthology. Some Impressions of Shrewsbury School during Four Centuries* (London: Macmillan, 1964), pp. 104–121. His portrait was, however, described by his contem-porary Graham Wallas as 'an extraordinarily accurate account of the intellectual atmosphere of the Shrewsbury Sixth at that time': G. Wallas, *The Art of Thought* (London: Jonathan Cape, 1926), p. 289. Kennedy's remark is quoted by D. S. Colman in his *Sabrinae Corolla: the Classics at Shrewsbury School under Dr Butler and Dr Kennedy* (Shrewsbury: Adnitt and Naunton, 1950), p. 8.

we hope to understand what was common and what was unusual in the classical pedagogy of these schools. Here the *Mushri Dictionary* provides an unusually rich source. Not only is its subject eccentric, its theme is eccentricity; but the embeddedness of idiosyncrasy in the late-Victorian ideology of Englishness means that the *Dictionary* is representative in its very uniqueness. It offers a glimpse, as does the photograph of Morshead himself, of a pedagogic process where pupils were learning, as a group, to be individuals.

CHAPTER 3

'Die Zung' ist dieses Schwert':[1] classical tongues and gendered curricula in German schooling to 1908

Sarah Colvin

When modern scholars trace the lives and achievements of educated women in Europe, two aspects of their accounts are consistently striking: first, that the most telling method of measuring learning before the twentieth century is by knowledge of the classical languages, and second, that women who command such knowledge are by definition *exceptional*. They are worthy of note in a way that the multitudes of classically-educated men cannot be. There is traditionally something *masculine* in the command of Latin or Greek, and this masculinity is reflected and perpetuated in the history of schooling: it finds expression in pedagogical notions of the need to silence and domesticate women while linguistically enabling men to participate in public life, as well as in anthropological ideas regarding women's non-intellectual nature. Valuable research has been done on the development of girls' schooling, and the intellectual education of women, often against the odds, has been charted in various periods;[2] nonetheless, there can be no question of educational equality until there is curricular equality in schools, and an effective yardstick is the availability of Latin and Greek.

The states of the Holy Roman Empire, which asserted their Germanic identity in the appendage *deutscher Nation* (of the German Nation) from 1474, provide an interesting location in which to observe the workings of classical pedagogues and their powerful perpetuation of gendered pedagogy. Sixteenth-century Reformers attacked the authority of the Church of Rome in every other respect, but they never cast aside the

---

[1] 'The tongue's a sword'. A. Gryphius, 'Leo Armenius oder Fürsten-Mord', in H. Powell and M. Szyrocki (eds.) *Gesamtausgabe der deutschsprachigen Werke* vol. v (Tübingen, 1965). p. 25.

[2] The most useful works in English on the education of German girls and women are P. Stock, *Better than Rubies: a History of Women's Education* (New York, 1978); C. Niekus Moore, *The Maiden's Mirror: Reading Material for German Girls in the Sixteenth and Seventeenth Centuries* (Wiesbaden, 1987); J. C. Albisetti, *Schooling German Girls and Women: Secondary and Higher Education in the Nineteenth Century* (New York, 1988); and P. Petschauer, *The Education of Women in Eighteenth-Century Germany: New Directions from the German Female Perspective* (Lewiston, NY, 1989).

classical learning which had long helped constitute Christian ecclesiastical authority. Martin Luther may have expostulated on the subject of
that 'blind heathen master, Aristotle, . . . that damned, arrogant rogue
of a heathen and his false words', but he still conceded that Aristotle's
works on logic, rhetoric and poetics were worthy of use, and that Cicero,
too, was acceptable.[3] Luther himself was a master of rhetoric, and we
can begin to understand his grudging tolerance of pagan wisdom when
he writes about language. For Luther, languages are the tool of the highest authority: 'when God wished to send the Gospel across the world
with the Apostles, he gave them the gift of tongues'.[4] Languages (he
mentions specifically Hebrew and Greek, and later Latin and German)
constitute the very humanity of humankind: without them we are beasts.
And like Gryphius (in the chapter title quotation) a century later, Luther
unwittingly betrays his conception of linguistic authority as masculine
in his choice of metaphor: 'languages are the sheaths into which the
knife of the spirit is thrust'.[5] Luther recognises the power of the spoken
word in both a secular and a religious context, and in his theory of
education – expressed in a sermon urging parents to send their sons to
school – the tongue is a young man's most important asset:

the best part (that is, the head) and the noblest appendage (that is, the tongue)
and the most exalted ability (that is, speech) of the human body must prove
themselves and work the hardest.[6]

For Luther this holds true for boys of all social backgrounds. They
must be taught to wield their noblest appendage through a classical
rhetorical training, and this remains a basic tenet of their education in
both Catholic and Protestant states.

From women, however, the sword is withheld. This chapter considers the position of those who were *not* to be armed with eloquence
by classical pedagogues. It explores first why, and then how girls and

[3] 'der blind heydnischer [*sic*] meyster Aristoteles . . . der vordampter, hochmütiger, schalckhafftiger heide mit seinen falschen worten'. M. Luther, 'An den Christlichen Adel deutscher Nation von des Christlichen standes besserung', in his *Werke: kritische Gesamtausgabe* (henceforth *WA*) vol. VI (Weimar, 1888), pp. 457–8.
[4] 'Denn gleich alls da Gott durch die Apostel wollt ynn alle wellt das Evangelion lassen komen [*sic*], gab er die zungen dazu'. See M. Luther, 'An die Burgermeyster und Radherrn allerley stedte ynn Deutschen landen', in *WA* XV (Weimar, 1899), p. 37.
[5] 'Die sprachen sind die scheyden, darynn dis messer des geysts stickt'. See ibid., p. 38.
[6] 'es mus gleich wol das beste stücke (als der kopff) und das edelste gelied (als die zunge) und das hohest werck (als die rede), so am menschen leibe sind, hie her halten und am meisten erbeiten [*sic*]'. M. Luther, 'Eine Predigt . . . das man kinder zur Schulen halten solle', in *WA* XXX/2 (1909), pp. 573–4.

women were denied access to Latin and Greek in German schools until this century, when the classics are losing their association with the sphere of power.

WITHHOLDING THE SWORD: THE PEDAGOGICAL DISARMING OF WOMEN

Latin . . . is a vehicle for our earliest learning and apprehension, a tool and preparation for scientific knowledge, and a powerful spur to the development of taste, the sparking of intelligence, and the successful presentation of independent thought. . . . we acquire diverse insights, judgements, historical and philosophical material, the foundations of morality and secular wisdom, and even a form of experience from the Ancients, and conserve these things for the systematic presentation of the philosophical disciplines in the future.[7]

This was Christian Heyne's appraisal in 1780, when German boys had been learning Latin for at least eight hundred years. Nowadays German universities are still among the most respected centres for classical studies, and many cities and towns are proud of their *humanistische Gymnasien*, selective secondary schools that teach the classical languages. These days they all admit girls. But even though Latin and Greek have been, in Heyne's words, a 'tool and preparation' for boys and men since the middle ages, organized classical schooling for girls has only been available for a century. We are confronted with a millenium of educational difference.

Male pedagogical theorists reveal a pronounced disinclination to equip girls and women with the tools of the intellect. The consensus has generally been that men require intellectual training, women moral training. Around 1210, the poet Gottfried von Straßburg created a version of the legendary Isolde in his *Tristan* epic. Gottfried's Isolde has been seen to exemplify educated upper-class womanhood in the high middle ages; she is accomplished in reading and writing, Irish,

---

[7] 'Latein . . . ist ein Vehikel der ersten gelehrten Kenntnisse, Werkzeug und Vorbereitung zu wissenschaftlichem Wissen, und kräftige Anleitung zu Bildung des Geschmacks, Erweckung des Witzes und eignem glücklichen Vortrag der Gedanken. . . . [Man muß nur die Sache so fassen, daß] . . . wir in den Alten zugleich mannigfaltige Einsichten, Urteile, Materialien historischer und philosophischer Art, Grundsätze der Moral und Weltklugheit und selbst eine Art von Erfahrung einsammeln und für den künftigen systematischen Vortrag der philosophischen Wissenschaften aufbewahren'. Chr. G. Heyne, 'Nachricht von der gegenwärtigen Einrichtung des Kgl. Pädagogii zu Ilfeld (1780)', in F. Paulsen, *Geschichte des gelehrten Unterrichts auf den deutschen Schulen und Universitäten vom Ausgang des Mittelalters bis zur Gegenwart. Mit besonderer Rücksicht auf den klassischen Unterricht* (Leipzig, 1885), p. 443.

French, Latin, music and singing. But the poet stresses most strongly
Isolde's education in *morâliteit*, moral behaviour. In the light of her
later affair with Tristan this may be an ironic touch, but it is certainly
gender-specific: the poet recommends that all young noblewomen
should receive *moral* instruction as a matter of priority.[8] The same
message, in a less elevated form, emerges from Marquard vom Stein's
Der Ritter vom Thurn (1485), in which the grotesque fates awaiting young
women who are not sufficiently virtuous are graphically depicted by an
apparently solicitous father figure.[9] Luther, too, saw morality or more
specifically Christian piety as the essential element in female education: he expressed the hope that each town should have a girls' school
'in which little girls might hear the Gospel read for one hour a day in
German or Latin'. He blithely passes over the problem of how they
are to understand the latter.[10] At a girls' school in Zwickau in 1526, the
(female) teachers were referred to as *Zuchtmeysterinnen*, or – literally –
mistresses of proper behaviour. Here again emphasis was on the moral
rather than the intellectual content of lessons; the girls were destined
to be submissive wives and capable mothers and housekeepers, not
articulate intellectuals.[11] Even the reforming pedagogues of the early
modern period, such as Wolfgang Ratke (Ratichius) (1570–1635) and
Johann Amos Comenius (1592–1670), who promoted elementary schooling for girls, show no sense that schooling might or ought to take girls
beyond that stage to the study of Latin, Greek and rhetoric. This stands
in distinct contrast to the Humanists' educational ideals for boys, succinctly expressed by Johann Sturm in 1538 as *sapiens atque eloquens pietas*:
piety that is not only wise but eloquent, linguistically able.[12]

Virtue and containment rather than wisdom and eloquence were the
constants in early pedagogical prescriptions for girls, and the same ideas
later influenced the theories of Jean-Jacques Rousseau. In his remarkably influential *Emile, ou de l'éducation* (1762), Rousseau transformed the

[8] G. von Straßburg, *Tristan* (Stuttgart, 1980), vv. 7966–8141. See also S. Barth, *Jungfrauenzucht: Literaturwissenschaftliche und pädagogische Studien zur Mädchenerziehungsliteratur zwischen 1200 und 1600* (Stuttgart, 1994), p. 45.

[9] This is a German translation of the Chevalier de la Tour de Landry's *Livre pour l'enseignement de ses filles*. I was made aware of the text by Anne Simon, of the University of Bristol.

[10] 'Und wolt got, ein yglich stadt het auch ein maydschulen, darynnen des tags die meydlin ein stund das Evangelium horetenn, es were zu deutsch odder latinisch!'. Luther, 'An den Christlichen Adel', p. 461.

[11] See S. Karant-Nunn, 'Continuity and Change: Some Effects of the Reformation on the Women of Zwickau', *Sixteenth-Century Journal* 13 (1982), pp. 18–24, esp. pp. 18–21.

[12] The quotation is from Sturm's educational manifesto for his own school in Straßburg, *De litterarum ludis recte aperiendis*. See Paulsen, *Geschichte des gelehrten Unterrichts*, p. 193.

traditional Christian idea of the sexually culpable women into an anthropological argument for gendered education:

in delivering him [= man] to immoderate passions, [the supreme Being]
joined reason to these passions that they might be governed; in delivering
woman to limitless desires, he joined modesty to these desires, that they might
be contained.[13]

Men's passions are thus naturally controlled by the intellect, women's
by (sexual) modesty (*pudeur*). Even Theodor Gottlieb von Hippel, whose
tract in the aftermath of the French Revolution *On the Improvement of
Women's Position as Citizens* (1792) is an unusually liberal consideration of
women's social position and rights,[14] saw a need to separate the sexes
at puberty. Hippel is worried by the development of the 'seeds of
sexuality' (*Geschlechtskeime*) in girls of this age, and therefore advocates
differentiation and segregation. The upshot of all this is not that women
should receive no education at all, but that their schooling should not
go beyond the level of what one might term intellectual and practical
socialisation, taking place as far as possible privately, within the sphere
of the family. The same sense of women's normal or natural place as
a *private* place (reflecting the ideal of contained sexual identity) led
eighteenth-century Philanthropic pedagogues such as Christian Gotthelf
Salzmann and Christian Karl André to conceive of girls' schools – the
so-called *Philanthropinen* – as replacement families, where charges would
be taught to be perfect wives and mothers. To this end a scholarly
training in Latin and Greek was not even considered.

The sense of a proper *space* for girls and boys, men and women, was
already strikingly evident in the pedagogical use of drama in German
schools of the early modern period. Luther had recommended Latin
school drama for boys not only as language practice but also as a
didactic pointer to the basic tenet of social order: knowing one's place
or space:

For the sake of the schoolboys we should not object to the production of
plays, but approve and allow it; firstly because it gives them practice in the
Latin language, and secondly because drama provides us with artfully contrived and presented examples of characters that instruct us . . . how each and

---

[13] 'en le [= l'homme] livrant à des passions immodérées, [l'Etre suprême] joint à ces passions la
raison pour les gouverner; en livrant la femme à des désirs illimités, il joint à ces désirs la
pudeur pour les contenir'. J. Rousseau, *Emile, ou de l'éducation* (Paris, 1966), p. 468.
[14] Th. von Hippel, 'Über die bürgerliche Verbesserung der Weiber', in his *Sämmtliche Werke*, vol.
VI (Berlin, 1828).

every one of us should behave according to our station in life, as if we were gazing into a mirror.[15]

Ordinances form the Protestant schools of St Elisabeth and St Magdalena in Breslau, which became famous centres for drama and produced some of the most noted playwrights of the period (Gryphius, author of the title quotation, is one example), show performances of Terence and Plautus on the syllabus from 1528. By the first half of the seventeenth century Protestant schools were producing German as well as Latin dramas, while the competing Jesuit academies continued their highly successful productions in Latin. To a modern reader, the plays are likely to appear unconvincing; their characters tend to address one another in flowing periods and in language richly embroidered with emblem and metaphor. But this is an essential part of school drama's *raison d'être*: the plays exemplify and make tangible a classical schooling in rhetoric, taught in the classroom according to the five-point scheme that comprised *inventio* (the conception of the idea), *dispositio* (structure), *elocutio* (style), *memoria* (committing to memory) and *actio/pronunciatio* (delivery).[16] The most obvious function of school drama from the boys' perspective was the rehearsal of *memoria* and *actio*, but the object of rhetorical expertise is *persuadere* – the listener is manipulated, and thus brought to share the view of the author or speaker. In school plays, the whole rhetorical process was divided between the author/pedagogue (usually a teacher or ex-pupil of the school), who provided the conceived idea, the structure and the style, and the student who was in the position of the delivering orator; thus the boys practised prepared eloquence (the pedagogical *exemplum*) in an exercise designed to culminate in *imitatio*. This appropriation of eloquence – of an authorial/authoritative use of language – is a vital part of school drama's didactic effect, and each performance was therefore a linguistically enabling exercise, a pedagogically-directed preparation for the boys' future in the *theatrum mundi* of public life. With this in mind, we need not be surprised that, even in the vernacular, school drama played almost no part in the education of girls. Against the hundreds of such

---

[15] 'Comödien zu spielen soll man um der Knaben in der Schule willen nicht wehren, sondern gestatten und zulassen, erstlich, daß sie sich uben [sic] in der lateinischen Sprache; zum Andern, daß in Comödien fein künstlich erdichtet, abgemalet und fürgestellt werden solche Personen, dadurch die Leute unterrichtet [werden] . . . wie sich ein Iglicher in seinem Stande halten soll im äußerlichen Wandel, wie in einem Spiegel'. M. Luther, *Tischreden* (Weimar, 1912), vol. I, no. 867, pp. 431–2.
[16] See K. Zeller, *Pädagogik und Drama: Untersuchungen zur Schulkomödie Christian Weises* (Tübingen, 1980), pp. 29–30.

plays written for and performed by boys, there is one single surviving example in German for girls, Konrad Porta's *Meidleinschul (School for little maids)* of 1573.[17] This drama functions primarily as propaganda to encourage parents by setting out the advantages – in terms of the acquisition of private or personal morals – of an elementary (non-classical) education for their daughters. A few plays for Dutch schoolgirls were also written, designed to provide instruction in the domestic female roles of housewife, mother, or widow.[18]

The educational difference that is visible in the denial of a linguistic and rhetorical training to women is evidently linked to both their social and their sexual containment. In her chapter in this volume, Jane Stevenson indicates that a classical education is more acceptable in noble and royal women, that is, in women who are already destined for public life. But if eloquence is seen as akin to the wielding of a 'sword' or 'noblest appendage' – that is, as active and masculine – then we need not be surprised that it is considered unnatural or even alarming in the great majority of women, and denied them in the systems of the anxious pedagogues.

In the opinion of Johann Heinrich Campe (1786–1818), a follower of Rousseau, even learning French is too much for the daughters of the German bourgeoisie; he remonstrates with his own daughter (who dared to express a wish to learn) 'that for a young woman *of your class and your station in life*, . . . learning foreign languages is not only useless, but *detrimental*' (Campe's emphasis).[19] The damage, he explains, is caused because the learning process would require time and energy that might better be spent on acquiring the 'natural' female skills of housekeeping and motherhood. Campe's major pedagogical work, *A Father's Advice to his Daughter* (1782), appeared in seven editions to 1808, and is an authoritative paternal directive on the nature of women's educational needs in the light of their destiny in life (*Bestimmung*). This destiny, he instructs his female readers, has been determined by both God and Nature:

---

[17] K. Porta, *Meidleinschul, Ein schön nutzlich [sic] Spiel / darinnen vermeldet / was für nutz aus den Schulen kome / vnd das gleichwohl die Diener und Dienerinnen in denselbigen wenig danck bey Gottlosen groben Leuten verdienen / entlich auch was jnen vnd den jren vber solcher vndanckbarkeit pflege zu begegnen / . . .* (Eisleben, 1573).

[18] See Barth, *Jungfrauenzucht*, pp. 188–9.

[19] 'daß einem jungen Frauenzimmer *deines Standes und deines Berufs* . . . die Erlernung fremder Sprachen nicht nur unnütz, sondern auch *schädlich* ist'. Campe, 'Väterlicher Rath für meine Tochter', in his *Sämmtliche Kinder- und Jugendschriften . . . Neue Gesammtausgabe der letzten Hand* (Braunschweig, 1832), vol. XXXVI, p. 100.

God himself intended . . . that not woman but man should be the head. That
is why the Creator has generally accorded men more muscular strength, . . . and
– usually, I mean – the unmistakeable capacity for greater, further-looking
and wider-reaching intelligence. . . . There is therefore a consensus in Nature
and human society that man should protect and direct woman, and that
woman on the other hand should be his . . . grateful and caring companion
and helpmeet for life.[20]

The differences he identifies lead Campe to oppose all but the most
basic, practical kind of instruction for girls. A classical education (*gelehrte
Geistesbildung*) is entirely undesirable, as it leads to illness, general sickli-
ness, and sloppy housekeeping.[21] The 'natural difference' argument
surfaces again in the writings of the Prussian educational reformer
Wilhelm von Humboldt (1767–1835). Rousseau had summarized the
'natural' interaction of the sexes: 'One must be active and strong, the
other passive and weak: it is necessarily the case that one should feel
desire and be empowered, and it is enough if the other barely resists'.[22]
In his essay *On Sexual Difference and its Influence on Organic Nature*, Humboldt
attests that 'all that is male displays more independent activity, all that
is female more passive receptivity'.[23] The relevance of this to education is immediate: men are to be taught to act and speak and hold
public office, women to accept and be silent in the domestic sphere.
A classical training is not only of no use to them in the light of their
natural *Bestimmung*, it would even invert or subvert it. The crucial
social significance of this is clear when Humboldt ascribes to the established active/passive relation of the sexes the elemental function of
'ordering . . . chaos'.[24] In what is perceived as its most sophisticated
form, classical eloquence, language is therefore denied to women, and
the 'natural' social order is conserved by their lack of the rhetorical
sword.

[20] 'Gott selbst hat gewollt . . . daß nicht das Weib, sondern der Mann das Haupt sein solle.
    Dazu gab der Schöpfer, in der Regel dem Manne, die stärkere Muskelkraft, . . . und – in der
    Regel, meine ich – auch die unverkennbaren Anlagen zu einem größern, weiterblickenden
    und mehr umfassenden Verstande. . . . Es ist also der übereinstimmende Wille der Natur und
    der menschlichen Gesellschaft, daß der Mann des Weibes Beschützer und Oberhaupt, das
    Weib hingegen die . . . dankbare und sorgsame Gefährtinn und Gehülfinn seines Lebens sein
    soll'. Ibid., p. 18.
[21] Ibid., pp. 41–4.
[22] 'L'un doit être actif et fort, l'autre passif et faible: il faut nécessairement que l'un veuille et
    puisse, il suffit que l'autre résiste peu'. Rousseau, *Emile*, p. 466.
[23] 'Alles Männliche zeigt mehr Selbstthätigkeit, alles Weibliche mehr leidende Empfänglichkeit':
    W. von Humboldt, *Über den Geschlechtsunterschied und dessen Einfluß auf die organische Natur*, in
    A. Flitner and K. Giel, eds., *Werke* (Stuttgart, 1960), p. 278.
[24] Ibid., p. 295.

CLASSICAL SCHOOLING: THE PATH TO POWER?

The practice of schooling reflects women's and girls' systematic exclusion in pedagogical theory from the articulate, classically-trained circles of the socially empowered. Prior to the Reformation, the earliest formal schooling in Europe had taken place in ecclesiastical circles, as monasteries educated each new generation of cloistered scholars. Gradually a *schola externa*, for boys who did not intend to become monks, supplemented the *schola interna*. In any case Latin was the essential tool to be acquired, as the first key to an understanding of the divine word manifested in Scripture.[25] It was also the language of communication in the classroom and between scholars, and Latin disputation was a classroom discipline, the art of rhetoric being culled especially from Cicero's *De inventione* and dialectics from Boethius. The acquisition of the heathen *ars eloquentiae* was held to be justified by their use in the service of Christian theological insight.[26]

Some girls, too, found opportunities for education within the institution of the Church. Like the monasteries, convents from around the tenth century began to offer schooling to the visiting daughters of paying families as well as to their own protegées. Predictably, the quality and scope of the teaching depended heavily on the literacy level of the nuns. Despite scholarly disagreement on the details of medieval schooling in the German states, a general consensus seems to have developed that the – few – educated women were not far behind the – few – educated men in this period.[27] While this may be true in practical terms, women were nonetheless consistently excluded from the sphere of real ecclesiastical authority, something which clearly affected their access to and active use of classical scholarship.

In the developing towns of the twelfth and thirteenth centuries, civic schools brought educational opportunities for boys and girls. But an early division between German and Latin schooling is evident; only boys tended to progress beyond the elementary stage in the vernacular to learn Latin, while girls returned home to help their parents and acquire the practical skills of housekeeping and animal husbandry. Alternatively,

---

[25] Knowledge of Greek was rare before the sixteenth century; Latin translations were in general use.
[26] See F. Paulsen, *Das deutsche Bildungswesen in seiner geschichtlichen Entwickelung* [*sic*] (Leipzig, 1906), pp. 10–11.
[27] See e.g. B. Becker-Cantarino, *Der lange Weg zur Mündigkeit: Frauen und Literatur in Deutschland von 1500 bis 1800* (Munich, 1989), pp. 161–2; Hans-Uwe Rump, '"Diu höhe frouwe, so tugentsam und lieb" – Erziehung und Bildung adeliger Frauen im Hochmittelalter', in M. Liedke and J. G. Prinz von Hohenzollern, eds., *Der weite Schulweg der Mädchen* (Bad Heilbrunn, 1990), pp. 98–109; Barth, *Jungfrauenzucht*, pp. 45–6.

they might attend the girls-only 'sewing schools' for instruction in the household arts. The division of the spheres is further evident in the development of small private girls' schools for the provision of elementary literacy; these *Klipp-* or *Winkelschulen* (roughly translatable as 'corner schools') were often run by women, had no civic licence, and stood in contrast to the growing number of municipally-run Latin schools for boys.[28] The first of the new Protestant boys' schools was founded in Magdeburg in 1524. Its Humanist founders aimed to teach (in Latin) reading and writing, the precepts of grammar (for which Terence and Virgil were the usual models), rhetoric and dialectics (using Erasmus's *De duplici copia* as well as Livy, Sallust, Virgil, Horace and Cicero), and prose and verse composition.[29] Some boys might progress to beginners' Greek and Hebrew, but Latin was the essential basis, tool and preparation for further study at one of the new universities, the first of which had been established in Prague in 1348. There were fifteen universities in German-speaking territories by 1506, and they were all (except in a very few exceptional cases) inaccessible to women.

There was, then, no significant change in girls' access to classical education as the Church's monopoly on schooling broke down in the German Protestant states in the early modern period. The real advances pertained to the male half of the population, as influential voices such as Luther's urged parents to help gifted sons to a Latin education to prepare them for jobs in church ministry or secular government. Girls' schooling, meanwhile, continued along its limited path. One Protestant girls' school was run in Wittenberg from 1533 by Elsa Kaunitz, under the aegis of Martin Luther; its curriculum embraced reading, but only optionally writing in German, religious education in the form of catechisms, psalms, hymns and maxims, and needlework. Humanist intellectuals and pedagogues such as Philipp Melanchthon (1497–1560) and Johannes Bugenhagen (1485–1558) advocated Latin schools for boys, but held that girls should not spend more than one or two hours a day at school over a period of one to two years, to learn reading and writing in the vernacular, religion and hymn-singing; their remaining education should be of a practical nature, in the home.[30]

---

[28] Sometimes the (untrained) wives of schoolmasters might take charge of the girls. See Alfred Fickel, 'Mädchenbildung und gesellschaftliche Stellung der Frau im Mittelalter und in der frühen Neuzeit', in *Der weite Schulweg der Mädchen*, p. 120.

[29] See Paulsen, *Geschichte des gelehrten Unterrichts*, p. 182.

[30] See Stock, *Better than Rubies*, pp. 62–3; Ulrich Herrmann, 'Erziehung und Schulunterricht für Mädchen im 18. Jahrhundert', *Wolfenbütteler Studien zur Aufklärung* 3 (1976), pp. 101–27, esp. p. 102.

In the Catholic states female secondary education was just as rare. An exception was the schooling offered by the Ursuline nuns, an active teaching order which by 1687 had even managed to establish itself in the predominantly Protestant town of Breslau (Wroclaw) in Silesia, where an Ursuline girls' school prospered until it was forcibly closed by Bismarck during the *Kulturkampf* of the 1870s. The nuns offered tuition for up to six hours a day, with Latin for girls who could afford to progress beyond the elementary stage.[31] Other female teaching orders, however, adhered to the kind of syllabus also found in Protestant schools: girls learned to read and write in German, Christian precepts, good conduct, and 'female skills' from textile work to dancing. Some civic schools for girls also existed in the Catholic territories, and – as in their Protestant counterparts – the girls were generally excluded from the advanced stage at which their brothers learned Latin and Greek.

An interesting example of early resistance to the idea of educating girls in the classical languages is provided by the case of Mary Ward. Ward, an Englishwoman, founded the Catholic teaching order of the *Englische Fräulein* (English Sisters; *Englisch* also contains a play on the German adjective 'angelic') in 1609. Perhaps because of the powerful example set by Elizabeth I in the previous century, the taboo on classical learning for women was less pronounced in England, and Ward came to Germany expecting to teach girls Latin, modelling her pedagogical plan on the rigorous classical education provided for boys by the Fathers of the Society of Jesus. But her curriculum immediately aroused mistrust and opposition in ecclesiastical circles – especially from the Jesuits. In 1630 a papal bull caused her order to be dismantled and her schools closed, and Ward herself was put in custody. She later did persuade the Pope to allow her to re-open some schools for girls, but their (vernacular) curriculum was placed strictly under the control of the local bishop.[32]

The miserable educational fate even of the daughters of the wealthier classes is well illustrated in the surviving curricula for boys' and girls' schools established by the pedagogue and philanthropist August Herrmann Francke (1663–1727). Francke founded a number of different schools in his home town of Halle towards the end of the seventeenth century. The best known was a school for the advanced education of the sons of the well-to-do: the so-called *Pädagogium*, opened in 1696.

[31] See Stock, *Better than Rubies*, pp. 75–7.
[32] See G. Wiegand, 'Die weibliche Schulorden und die Mädchenbildung', in *Der weite Schulweg der Mädchen*, p. 136.

As we might expect, the essential element in its pupils' studies was
Latin, which accounted for four hours in the daily timetable. Older
boys received all of their instruction in that language as well as progressing to classes in Latin public speaking, and Greek was taught for
up to two hours daily. A few learned Hebrew through Bible reading.
One lesson was taught in German, but with close reference to the boys'
classical training: *teutsche Oratoria* (German oratory), which comprised
the arts of public speaking in the vernacular, letter-writing and poetry.[33]
In 1697, Francke established another school, to provide a more basic
scholarly education for the sons of less elevated families; here they
learned Latin for two hours a day in eight forms or year-groups, Greek
for an hour a day in six forms, optionally Hebrew, and, in conjunction
with Latin, oratory and logic.[34] There was also an orphanage school,
which seems to have been designed not only for orphaned children but
also for single mothers, where boys learnt to read and write in Latin
after they had mastered those skills in German; the girls attended school
for up to four hours per day to acquire basic literacy and to practise
sewing, knitting and spinning. They were encouraged to pray, to keep
quiet, and to stay with their mothers.[35] By 1698 Francke clearly felt the
need to provide secondary education for the daughters of well-to-do
families, and a *Gynecaeum* was founded; even the name betrays that the
girls' sex was of more relevance than their intellect. As well as limiting
access to this school by wealth and class, Francke designed an entirely
different curriculum for his female protegées. They learnt French but
no Latin, Greek or Hebrew, and parental motivation to pay for even
this level of intellectual training seems to have been low: when Francke
died in 1727, the *Gynecaeum* had only eight pupils, and in 1744 it closed
down for good.[36] The Halle parents were fighting shy of an expense they
could at best perceive as unnecessary: intellectual and linguistic training
not only seemed of no use to girls but might even prove detrimental
if it tempted them out of the domestic space assigned them. Even in
the highest-level German girls' schools of the later eighteenth century,
such as the *Ecole des demoiselles* established by Duke Carl Eugen in
Württemberg in 1772, the curriculum was more akin to that of a finishing

[33] See Francke, 'Schriften über Erziehung und Unterricht', in K. Richter, ed., *Pädagogische Bibliothek:
Eine Sammlung der wichtigsten pädagogischen Schriften älterer und neuerer Zeit* (Berlin and Leipzig, 1871),
pp. 271–85.
[34] Ibid, pp. 333–5.   [35] Ibid., pp. 409ff.
[36] See Petschauer, *The Education of Women*, p. 67; Becker-Cantarino, *Der lange Weg*, p. 167.

school than a serious academy, the peak of the young ladies' achievements being Italian conversation and dancing. Similarly, in Dessau, the Antoinette school (founded in 1786) boasted that it would provide girls not with an intellectual training, but with one which would enable them to benefit the household and the community.[37]

Individual German noblewomen did sometimes find a way to a classical education, whether by a father's wish, sharing a brother's tutor, or by their own special efforts. Anna Sophia of Hesse-Darmstadt (1638–1683) acquired a knowledge of the Church Fathers that was reputed to have 'put many a theologian to shame', and Duchess Dorothea Maria of Saxony-Weimar summoned the reforming pedagogue Ratke to her court in 1612 to instruct her and her ladies in Latin.[38] (Her motivation is worth noting, however: it was to provide guinea-pigs for his controversial new teaching methods, which – if successful – she intended to employ in the education of her *sons*.) Juliana Patientia Schultt (1680–1701), who taught for the Pietist pedagogue Francke in Halle, appears to have known Greek, Hebrew, Latin and French;[39] but the special nature of the records that were kept of such women betray that they were the exception, not the rule. The remarkable Dorothea Leporin, who was awarded a doctorate in medicine at Halle in 1754, provides us with a depressing catalogue of men's resistance to female scholarship in her *Thorough Examination of the Reasons Preventing Women from Study* (1742). She begins by describing the pseudo-physiological argument that implicitly evokes the Fall of Eve: that women's moist and cool temperament must render them inconstant and therefore – among other things – unfit for concentrated study. This leads into a discussion of men's reservations regarding mixed-sex classes and of their tendency to dislike bluestockings (although here Leporin swiftly counters: 'Even if a few men are disgusted by learned women, what is that to us? or why should it induce us to shun learning?').[40] She reflects on the factors most regularly cited as proper impediments to female education – the idea that scholarly study is of no use to them, and that with it they are of less use to society – but even Leporin is unable to shake

---

[37] See Petschauer, *The Education of Women*, pp. 180–3; Stock, *Better than Rubies*, p. 120.
[38] See Niekus Morre, *The Maiden's Mirror*, pp. 47–8.   [39] Ibid., p. 51.
[40] 'Gesetzt, es hätten einige Männer einen Abscheu für gelehrten Frauenzimmer, was wird uns solches schaden? oder warum solten wir gehalten seyn, deßwegen die Gelehrsamkeit zu verachten?' Leporin, *Gründliche Untersuchung der Ursachen, die das Weibliche Geschlecht vom Studiren [sic] abhalten, . . . Nebst einer Vorrede ihres Vaters*, ed. by G. Rechenberg (Hildesheim, 1987), p. 108.

off the conviction that women are really destined for the home. She is forced to conclude that they should never let academic work interfere with their domestic duties, using only their leisure hours for study.

From around the middle of the seventeenth century, Sturm's *sapiens atque eloquens pietas* had begun to be augmented in boys' education by the idea of a 'realistic' or practical training. With the end of the Thirty Years War the *Ritterakademien* arose, schools for young noblemen that followed a more secular, courtly curriculum. Latin was still important but so were French, Italian, Spanish, and English, and the timetable expanded to include the so-called *Realien*: sciences, social sciences and physical exercise.[41] More emphasis was placed on the German language, too, a trend that was visible in the growth of the *Sprachgesellschaften*, linguistic and poetical societies which had existed since the early seventeenth century for the advancement of the vernacular. Latin's importance was shifting, but even by the later eighteenth century it had not disappeared; the new 'realistic' function of the classical languages was as transporters of knowledge, authority and experience, as Heyne's praise of Latin (cited previously) suggests.

German female pedagogues at this time betray no similar sense of the importance of classics. Caroline Rudolphi (1754–1811) and Betty Gleim (1781–1827) both practised and published theories on the education of girls, and both were primarily concerned with the need to teach specifically female – especially maternal – skills.[42] Rudolphi's school in Heidelberg concentrated on the girls' moral development and on instilling a sense of duty in them; neither Latin nor Greek featured in her educational programme, nor indeed in Gleim's. The importance of motherhood (particularly for mothers of boys!) is a leitmotif also in male pedagogues' musings on the second sex, especially after Rousseau;[43] the Swiss Johann Heinrich Pestalozzi's *Buch der Mütter* (*Book for Mothers*) first appeared in 1803 and was designed for use in his own girls' schools,[44] and the inimitable voice of Campe joins the chorus:

Truly you are not destined to be mere overgrown children, frivolous dolls, fools or even furies; instead you have been created – and take note of your

[41] See Paulsen, *Geschichte des gelehrten Unterrichts*, p. 379.
[42] Rudolphi's *Gemälde weiblicher Erziehung*, an epistolary account of an ideal upbringing, was first published in 1807 and appeared in four editions to 1857. Gleim's major pedagogical work is her *Erziehung und Unterricht des weiblichen Geschlechts* (Leipzig, 1810).
[43] See Rousseau, *Emile*, p. 475.
[44] Extract from Pestalozzi, *Werke* ed. by G. Cepl-Kaufmann and M. Windfuhr (Munich, 1977), vol. II, pp. 105–9. On Pestalozzi's educational theory and practice for girls see M. Simmel, *Erziehung zum Weibe: Mädchenbildung im 19. Jahrhundert* (Frankfurt a. M., 1980), pp. 67–80.

venerable calling with thankful joy at its great dignity! – to be *wives who gladden their husbands' hearts, mothers who educate,* and *wise stewards of the domestic sphere.*[45]

Campe's conception of a woman's function may not gladden many modern hearts, but it does betray the chink in the armour of the post-Enlightenment patriarchal pedagogue. If all *men* are to be educated from boyhood, then all *women* as potential mothers must be equipped to provide at least the basics of their children's education. As educators, Gleim and Rudolphi exemplified a growing recognition that women's *Bestimmung* might include teaching at an elementary level, as an extension of their childrearing role. From the beginning of the nineteenth century, teaching seminaries for women began to be established, and in 1811 the Prussian minister Stein indicated that women might even teach within the state system in girls' primary schools, where they were employed especially to teach the practical 'female' subjects and religion.[46] Industrialization was under way, and this not only caused a re-assessment of women's economic function and therefore of their educational needs, but also created something of a vacuum in the teaching profession, especially in the lower-status primary area, as men were drawn into commercial and industrial work. But even as women's sphere was permitted to extend beyond the domestic and the education of girls acquired real economic significance, the girls' schools – unlike their counterparts for boys – were not subject to any universal curricular requirements. At the time of German unification under Prussia in 1871 there was no official ordinance for girls' schools in any of the German states. Girls left school at age fifteen or sixteen while boys stayed on until they were eighteen or nineteen; girls could not expect to be taught mathematics and science, and invariably did without Latin and Greek.[47] Women were still systematically denied the access to scholarship and eloquence that men – sometimes even in the poorest circles, as Francke's orphanage demonstrated – might enjoy.

In the male education system, important developments had again been taking place since the early nineteenth century, especially in Prussia. The *Abitur,* or official high school qualification, had been established in 1788. It was examined in Latin, and entitled successful candidates

---

[45] 'Ihr seid wahrlich nicht dazu bestimmt, nur große Kinder, tändelnde Puppen, Närrinnen, oder gar Furien zu sein: ihr seid vielmehr geschaffen – o vernimm deinen ehrwürdigen Beruf mit dankbarer Freude über die große Würde desselben! – um *beglückende Gattinnen, bildende Mütter,* und *weise Vorsteherinnen des innern Hauswesens* zu werden'. Campe, *Väterlicher Rath,* p. 13.

[46] See Paulsen, *Das deutsche Bildungswesen,* p. 147; Stock, *Better than Rubies,* p. 120.

[47] See Stock, *Better than Rubies,* p. 133.

not only to university entry but also to take higher state examinations
and to enter the middle ranks of the civil service. From 1812, preparation for the *Abitur* took place almost exclusively in special classical
schools or *Gymnasien*, which were accorded a status above all other
schools (although from 1878 the so-called *Oberrealschulen*, which taught
a nine-year non-classical curriculum for boys, were also allowed to
prepare students for certain state examinations at technical colleges,
and from 1890 these students were admitted to the universities to gain
teaching qualifications in non-classical disciplines).[48]

Girls, by contrast, not only had no fixed curriculum, but sat no examinations which, it was felt, might encourage unfeminine ambitions in
them.[49] To remedy this state of affairs a meeting of headmasters from
state and private girls' schools was convened in Weimar in 1872, from
which recommendations for a semi-standardized curriculum resulted. It
included French, English, German literature, history, geography, maths,
natural history, physical science, calligraphy, drawing, singing, physical education, and religion;[50] it excluded Latin and Greek, the normal
passport to the *Abitur* and higher education. In case this absence was
not effective enough, the Prussian government in 1879 barred women
explicitly from entering any German university as well as from being
certified as physicians.[51]

Governmental nervousness was probably augmented by the growing
pressure from organized groups of German women for a state-run education for girls that more nearly approximated that of their male peers.
Many of these women were teachers, whose own training now enabled
them to articulate their demands. Louise Otto-Peters (1819–1895), an
intellectual who had demanded full equality for women during the
liberal uprisings of 1848, became president of the General Association
of German Women (*Allgemeine Deutscher Frauenverein* or ADF) when it
was founded in 1865. She did not reiterate her previous revolutionary
demands (a law had been passed in 1851 strictly forbidding women's
involvement in politics), but during the 1870s and 1880s the ADF
proposed expanding the school system to prepare girls for university
entrance to study medicine: a 'caring' profession that was felt to suit the
female constitution (as well as sparing other women the embarrassment
of consulting a male practitioner), but also one that required knowledge

[48] See F. K. Ringer, *Education and Society in Modern Europe* (Bloomington and London, 1979),
pp. 34–9.
[49] See Albisetti, *Schooling German Girls*, pp. 23–4; p. 45.   [50] See Stock, *Better than Rubies*, p. 135.
[51] See Albisetti, *Schooling German Girls*, p. 93.

of Latin at least.[52] A Berlin teacher, Helene Lange, became involved in the ADF and in 1889–90 founded with her female colleagues the General Association of German Women Teachers (*Allgemeiner Deutscher Lehrerinnenverein*). This quickly became the biggest professional association for women in Germany, with 16,000 members by 1900.[53] Other pressure groups included the German Academic Association (*Deutsche Akademische Vereinigung*), later called the Association for Women's Welfare (*Verein Frauenwohl*) led by another teacher, Minna Cauer. Hedwig Kettler's Women's Assocation for Reform (*Frauenverein 'Reform'*) pursued particularly radical aims, demanding for women the same education as for men rather than sticking to the standard 'separate but equal' approach. It was her Association that founded the first ever *Gymnasium* for girls, in Karlsruhe in 1893; the school was officially assimilated the following year by the state of Baden, and thus became the first state-run classical school for girls in Germany.

In Prussia, in the same year, a general curricular ordinance for female secondary schooling was finally imposed, although the specified nine-year course still did not entitle girls to a university place. From 1895, young women could sit the classical *Abitur* examination after five years of supplementary secondary schooling at a female *Gymnasium*: this, however, remained the exception rather than the rule. Until 1896 women could attend university lectures in Prussia only with the special permission of the Minister for Education; after 1896 they might apply directly to the university authorities.[54] They were not allowed to be matriculated for degrees, although in Berlin Helene Lange and her associates were already running privately-funded courses to prepare women for school-leaving examinations (often taken in Switzerland) that would enable them to study abroad.[55]

Even though full matriculation for women was allowed in Baden from 1900 and Bavaria from 1903, Prussia was the last of the German states to accept women students in 1908, the same year that the all-important new ordinance for girls' schools was issued. By this time the nine-year rule (ages 7–16) had given way in most schools to ten years for girls. In the Prussian ordinance of 1908 it was suggested that eleven or even twelve years might be the ideal (as it had long been in the case

[52] See R. J. Evans, *The Feminist Movement in Germany 1894–1933* (London, 1976), pp. 24–7.
[53] See U. Frevert, *Women in German History: From Bourgeois Emancipation to Sexual Liberation* (Oxford, 1989), p. 125.
[54] Ibid., p. 122.
[55] See Stock, *Better than Rubies*, p. 138. The United States had begun admitting women to universities in 1853, France in 1863, and England in 1878.

of boys), and that this should be achieved by appending one to two years in a so-called lyceum to normal secondary schooling. Yet even now the pedagogical aim was not primarily academic or even intellectual, as the text of the ordinance makes clear:

It seems far more important to augment [young girls'] education in the direction of their future tasks as German women, to introduce them to the duties of both the domestic and the broader social sphere, to elements of childrearing and childcare, to home economics, healthcare and the practice of charity as well as to the realms of mercy and neighbourly concern.[56]

Education for girls who wished to attend university had to take place in special institutes of study or *Studienanstalten*. It was in these *Studienanstalten* that girls were finally to receive state-approved instruction, among other things, in Latin or Latin and Greek to the same standard taught in boys' schools. They were prepared for a leaving examination which was not only equivalent in standard to the boys', but also conferred the same rights to university entrance – 'in as far as these are relevant to women'.[57] Even though the *Studienanstalten* were intended to exist only as an optional alternative to and by no means as a replacement for the more usual, 'feminine', educational route, and even though they were designed primarily for the daughters of the upper classes, still they marked a turning-point: for the first time in German history the way to a classical education was officially opened to girls and women.

RECAPITULATION: WOMEN, CLASSICS AND POWER

Luther saw the ancient languages as vehicles of the highest, divine authority in Scripture. In a secular context, the eloquence taught in boys' schools by the example of Greek and Roman authors was intended to prepare them for professions in politics, law or academia, as well as for a position of paternal authority within the home. Until the beginning of this century, girls received no such training. Even an exceptional woman like Dorothea Leporin felt obliged to preface

[56] 'Wichtiger erscheint vielmehr eine Ergänzung [der jungen Mädchen] Bildung in der Richtung der künftigen Lebensaufgaben einer deutschen Frau, ihre Einführung in den Pflichtenkreis des häuslichen wie des weiteren Gemeinschaftslebens, in die Elemente der Kindererziehung und Kinderpflege, in Hauswirtschaft, Gesundheitslehre, Wohlfahrtskunde sowie in die Gebiete der Barmherzigkeit und Nächstenliebe'. See A. Reble, ed., *Zur Geschichte der höheren Schule* (Bad Heilbrunn, 1975), vol. II, pp. 118–19. I am indebted for this reference to Oberstudienrat Kurt Umbach of the Gymnasium Schinkel, Osnabrück.
[57] Ibid., pp. 121–2.

her *Thorough Examination* with an introduction by her father, in which he emphasized her domestic capabilities and her unwillingness to enter the public arena as an author.

Rousseau and his German epigones perpetuated traditional ideas about the ideal locations, private or public, and the related linguistic needs of the sexes. For Campe, women are the 'heart' and men the 'external limbs' of the state; in such metaphors of internal and external organs he unwittingly picks up on earlier ideas of the vagina as inverted phallus, a private or secret place that is emblematic of women's position in society.[58] Women who use their tongues are perceived as phallic women, an inversion of the natural or divine order of things.

At the beginning of this century Paul Julius Möbius, the influential and notorious author of an essay entitled 'On the physiological reasons for women's weak-mindedness', drew on familiar imagery in an outburst of male anxiety regarding female articulacy:

A woman's sword is her tongue, as her physical weakness prevents her from fighting with her fists and her intellectual weakness stops her from using proper argument – so she has to rely on the sheer quantity of her words.[59]

In the history of women's education it is clear that in fact their tongues were to be stilled rather than sharpened like a sword, and that their schooling reflected the norm of their exclusion from public life.

Eloquence is public, eloquence imposes form or order, eloquence is authoritative and masculine. It is therefore unsurprising that male pedagogues excluded women from the classical rhetorical training that was the basis of German education for centuries. Their insistence that women's nature and destiny render them unsuited to language learning, especially of Latin and Greek, is the insistence on a *status quo* that constrains women, subjugating them to paternal and conjugal authority within the home and the state. A classical linguistic training would imply the promotion of women to a status of authority or activity and hence, potentially, to public life and the power sphere. Phyllis Stock has inferred that 'the aim of the educator is to produce an adult who will play a certain desired role in society';[60] for most women of *all* social stations as well as for lower-class men this role has traditionally

---

[58] See J. P. Clark, 'Inside/out: Body Politics Against Large Bodies', *Daphnis* XX (1991), pp. 101–30.

[59] 'Die Zunge ist das Schwert der Weiber, denn ihre körperliche Schwäche hindert sie, mit der Faust zu fechten, ihre geistige Schwäche lässt sie auf Beweise verzichten, also bleibt nur die Fülle der Wörter'. P. J. Möbius, *Ueber den physiologischen Schwachsinn des Weibes* 7th edn. (Halle, 1905), p. 20. Möbius's essay was first published in 1900, and appeared in nine editions to 1907.

[60] Stock, *Better than Rubies*, p. 12.

been one of subordination to authority. The same groups have generally been denied access to a classical, advanced education.

Nonetheless, schooling or applied pedagogy can never be an entirely
effective method of social control; to assume it will be is to underestimate
the liberating potential of literacy, as the Prussian government perhaps
did when training female teachers in the nineteenth century. But the
German example shows how schooling reflects and reproduces the *status
quo* of gender relations, and while it is always worth registering the
achievements of exceptional women and the gradual developments in
women's educational opportunities, observing girls' and women's lack
of access specifically to *classical* learning clearly reveals the differentiating
conceptions of gender and schooling that are at work. The classics have
traditionally been associated with ecclesiastical, intellectual and political power; pedagogical systems have traditionally excluded girls and
women on all counts.

It may finally be worth noting that the formal entry of women into
classical studies in this century has coincided with a decline in the
status of classics, at least as far as university access and public positions
are concerned. We must hope that the new arrivals will still find access
to such swords as may now be necessary to ensure the future of their
discipline.

CHAPTER 4

'What does that argue for us?': the politics of teaching and political education in late eighteenth-century dialogues[1]

Clare Brant

In late eighteenth-century England, dialogues engaged with the literally revolutionary question of who should participate in civic debate. Writers used the idea of taking part in a conversation as a metaphor and a *mise en scène* for taking part in politics, and dialogues as both an implicit and explicit form of challenging old orders and questioning new regimes. Through choosing characters, and aiming at certain readerships, writers tried to control the terrain on which these questions were debated. The two-sided discourse of the simplest dialogues proved useful to writers on both radical and reactionary sides of that political conflict which grew from the 1760s discontent in Britain and acquired additional impetus from upheavals first in America in the 1770s, then in France in the 1780s and 1790s.[2] The discussion which follows shows how, with reference to a selection of dialogues, and suggests how assumptions about classical antecedents could weight the dialogue ideologically.

Both progressive and conservative writers had to engage with the literary history of dialogues when choosing how to use it so as to represent their own times, and the transformative power of education therein. On the one hand, the dialogue's classical antecedents gave it the authority of the ancients, an immensely respectable literary history which seemed to predetermine it towards conservative uses. On the other hand, the assumed relations of this weighty authority were sufficiently stable to

---

[1] I would like to thank Yun Lee Too for constructive editorial comment, and George Myerson for creative discussion about dialogues in general, and the subject of this paper in particular. Place of publication for texts cited is London unless specified otherwise.

[2] To relate the politics of British dialogues in these decades simply to the French Revolution is to mask the significance of home-grown radicalism, and the fact, perfectly understood at the time, that revolutions are no respecters of borders. For an instance of American republicanism influencing British politics, see my discussion of the Bristol election of 1784 in *Eighteenth-Century Letters and British Culture* (forthcoming).

enable rewriting through parody and play. This made the dialogue simultaneously authoritative, and potentially subversive. Different dialogists
exploited the mix more variously, and more adventurously, than one
might suppose. Conservatives, for instance, were as likely to use playful
dialogues as more anarchic spirits, who in turn wrote many openly
didactic dialogues. So, for example, Sir William Jones's *The Principles of
Government, in a Dialogue between a Scholar and a Peasant* (1782) is didactic in
its method of argument, but the catechism is controversial since what
the scholar teaches the peasant is recognition of his rights. Conversely,
in Hannah More's *Village Politics* (1792), a conversation between a black-
smith and a mason involves social equals, one of whom persuades the
other to abandon his dangerous republicanism, in a good-humoured
argument which also amuses middle-class readers with humour at the
expense of both protagonists.

There are dozens of dialogues from the 1780s and 1790s which demonstrate how the form was a prime space in which to discuss whether
it was possible for people to agree to disagree, when contentious issues
involved material forms of power. Most are either anonymous, or by
writers virtually unknown now.[3] The demotic aspects of the genre,
coupled with its long-established pedagogical function, made it addi-
tionally attractive in the late eighteenth century to writers for children
and women writers.[4] The pedagogical methods employed by these
texts include brow-beating, didacticism, gentle persuasion, satire, story-
telling, and role-playing. They construct a range of models of learning,
with a variety of interactions, not always predictable, between ignorance
and information, and between innocence and knowledge. This variety
of models of argument suggests a very flexible understanding during
the Enlightenment of how understanding comes about, even amongst
those who wished to keep certain kinds of knowledge as the preserve of
particular social groups.

Broadly speaking, there are several distinct types of dialogues which
bring together the issues of rights and right answers in this period.

---

[3] For example, John Bowles, *Dialogues on the Rights of Britons, Between a Farmer, a Sailor, and a Manu-
facturer* (1792); Joseph Towers, *A Dialogue between an Associator and a Well-informed Englishman* (1793);
Dialogues between a Reformer and an Antirevolutionist (1794). Conversely, some dialogues are over-
shadowed by their author's fame for other writings: thus William Blake's *An Island in the Moon*,
first printed 1907.

[4] For example, Anna Laetitia Barbauld, Eleanor Fenn, Dorothy Kilner, Mary Leadbeater, Hannah
Neale, Richard Johnson and Priscilla Wakefield, who all wrote dialogues in the 1780s or 1790s.
I discuss the significance of dialogues to women writers further in an essay in Vivien Jones (ed.),
Women and Literature in Britain, 1700–1800 (Cambridge, forthcoming).

There are dialogues for children, which address what they should know and how best they learn; dialogues which take up issues in sexual politics, class politics or international relations, and dialogues which widen – and sometimes constrain – political activism through the use of unschooled protagonists. (There were also dialogues on other subjects, such as religion, which have a comparable typology.) Although some of these dialogues present themselves as being removed from or ostensibly indifferent to politics, the context of revolutions, actual and imagined, connects them to unavoidably politicised discourse. Even the simple narrative scenario of people talking together had political implications, given that meetings and clubs used discussion to disseminate radical ideas. Conservatives also had their own traditions in which clubs functioned as venues for those of like minds to meet and exchange views, in which members could tolerate some dissent. For some educated or aristocratic women, there were opportunities to enjoy rational conversation in mixed, salon-style settings, or via the epistolary conversations of cultured correspondence.[5]

These material contexts of talk fed into a local history of the dialogue. Eighteenth-century dialogues were many and various, but there was a consistent interest in Lucian, and 'dialogues of the dead' were imitated and updated.[6] Typically these feature debates between famous ancients and representative moderns; an underworld location serves to make the discussion contingent on the real world, but at one literary remove from it. In the late eighteenth century, dialogues shifted from playful inquisitions into wrongs to more urgent and solemn enquiries into rights. The change is one of drift rather than leap, and not absolute, but it is epitomised by a revival of interest in Plato's dialogues. If Lucian's dialogues were associated with disruptive comedy, and Cicero's with oratorical smoothness, Plato's dialogues combined a serene *mise en*

---

[5] For example, the Bluestockings, in whose meetings Hannah More intermittently participated. See Sylvia Harcstarck Myers, *The Bluestocking Circle: Women, Friendship and the Life of the Mind in Eighteenth-Century England* (Oxford, 1990). On the 'conversation' as a genre of painting, see David H. Solkin, *Painting for Money: The Visual Arts and the Public Sphere in Eighteenth-Century England* (New Haven and London, 1992), chapters 1 and 2. On letters as talk, see Bruce Redford, *The Converse of the Pen: Acts of Intimacy in the Eighteenth-Century Familiar Letter* (Chicago, 1986) esp. ch.6; Elizabeth Goldsmith (ed.), *Writing the Female Voice: Essays on Epistolary Literature* (Boston, 1988), and Amanda Gilroy and W. M. Verhoeven (eds.), *Prose Studies*, Correspondences: A Special Issue on Letters, Vol. 19, No. 2, August 1996.

[6] Besides translations from the French of Fenelon and Fontanelle, popular collections included Elizabeth Rowe, *Friendship in Death* (1728), and George, Lord Lyttelton, *Dialogues of the Dead* (1760–5). There were new translations of Lucian's dialogues into English by John Carr in 1774–98, and Thomas Franklin in 1780.

scène with unpredictable debate. Translators held up Plato's dialogues
as a model to be admired, though hard to imitate. Plato's principal
achievement, they suggest, was to win arguments by getting opponents
or sceptics to concede defeat. This kind of victory did not require ideological assertion – you have to prove your opponents' errors but not
necessarily your own truths – and hence it suited a certain reactionary agenda, in which the point was to discredit new ideas rather than
demonstrate the virtues of old ones. But Plato was also associated with
an absence of dogmatism – his cleverness was in getting his opponents
to dismantle their own arguments – and with a literary pleasure. Characters were led one way when they thought they were going another;
readers were free to climb in and out of the same traps, or to be ahead
of the game. The winning intellect had to be sharp and precise but not
wounding: there was no place for abuse, and hence rational argument
was synonymous with civilised argument. For those writing across the
edge of Romanticism, this held out contradictory hopes – of calming
inflammatory radical ideas, and of making the radical case more pleasurable and more persuasive.

The translation of Anne Dacier illustrates the complicated attractions
of Platonic dialogues to both radical and reactionary writers. In a prefatory discourse, Dacier praises Plato's handling of the dialogue: like the
unrolling of a picture, truth appears gradually, and so that the mind can
anticipate it even before the representation is completely visible. Plato
is not a wrestler who pins down his adversaries, but a more seductive
figure: 'he softens his Proofs, and makes 'em pleasant, and attracts his
Auditors by the Insinuation of Fables and Examples, which seem to be
contriv'd not so much to convince as to divert 'em.'[7] The image Dacier
foregrounds is that of the accessible, sociable meal, in which conversation, like the food, should be digestible and pleasant: 'The Discourse
at Table ought to be for every one, like the Wine; and such as propose there abstracted and difficult Questions, banish thence this kind
of Community, and renew the Feast of the Fox and the Crane.'[8] Food
imagery suggests ideas which nourish the mind, and do so universally,
but whose presentation goes beyond functionalism in order to delight
the senses and soul. The dialogue then becomes a place in which the
material and abstract meet, which makes it all-embracing, but also
political again, since food was frequently the measure of popular satis-
faction with government. As Hannah More put it in a verse dialogue:

[7] A. Dacier, *The Works of Plato Abridg'd*, 2 vols. (1772, 3rd edn.), I, p. 17.
[8] A. Dacier, *The Works of Plato Abridg'd*, I, p. 17.

'I'm hungry, my lads, but I've little to eat, / So we'll pull down the mills and seize all the meat'.[9]

A less liberal conception of Plato's dialogues was expressed by Thomas Taylor, whose translations were published in the 1790s. He agreed with Dacier that Plato had perfectly united the twin aims of writing as defined in the eighteenth century – to instruct and to entertain; it was Plato's distinction 'to joke seriously, and sport in earnest'.[10] In dialogues, he argued, 'the dialectical energy is triple, either subsisting through opposite arguments, or alone unfolding truth, or alone confuting falsehood.'[11] Where Dacier had been cheerfully insouciant about translation, claiming 'that which is most useful can't be hurt by my Translation', for Taylor, in contrast, dialogues in translation were subject to misreading, not least by those who put philology before philosophy. As he gloomily concluded his summary of the *Cratylus*,

The truth of this account will be evident to every ingenuous mind, from barely reading the dialogue with attention; but is not even suspected by the verbal critic, who as usual dogmatically decides on writings, which he is so far from having studied, that he has not even read them like a rational being; but, totally neglecting the design and sense of the author, has confined himself solely to the pursuit of new words and phrases, different readings, and omissions of accent![12]

Plato's dialogues thus became a trope both for argument and authority in argument. For Dacier, Plato's plain and simple discourse was to be defended as natural, not as some critics claimed, vulgar and trivial. The philosopher 'who is scarce ever to be found out of shops, who talks only of Husbandmen, Smiths, Masons, Carpenters, Shoemakers and Taylors'[13] could be readily taken up as a champion of the people, and the dialogue as a democratic form. The more authoritarian Taylor, however, read into Plato an anticipation of the Romantic sublime. Plato's language had the magnificence of a strong, deep and rapid river, which to a reader in the 1790s might be reminiscent of Alph, the sacred river in Coleridge's *Kubla Khan*, or Wordsworth's spiritually reviving River Wye in *Tintern Abbey*. For Taylor, Plato mingles opposites as perfectly as the balance between Coleridge's domes and caves, and there are more close echoes of Kubla in his praise for Plato as 'marvellous' and 'enchanting'. The sublime however has contradictions:

[9] Hannah More, *The Riot: or, Half a Loaf is Better than no Bread* (1795), ll. 3–4.
[10] Thomas Taylor, *The Cratylus, Phaedo, Parmenides, and Timaeus of Plato* (1793), p. 247.
[11] Taylor, *The Cratylus*, p. 249. [12] Taylor, *The Cratylus*, p. xvi.
[13] Dacier, *The Works of Plato Abridg'd*, I, p. 20.

on the one hand self-evident, in that anyone in its presence is seized
by it, but on the other hand evanescent, in that anyone seized by it
is unable to articulate its full power.[14] For Taylor, this meant Plato's
dialogues were intelligible to 'every ingenuous mind', but his dialectic
was adapted 'to those only whose cogitative power is perfectly pure'.[15]
Plato's universality was thus ironically represented by how accessible
he was to a specific class – and, paradoxically, in terms of a class which
might be labouring or elite, according to an author's ideology.

Ambivalence about whether Plato counted for high or low culture
was not only a matter of the political arguments with which dialogue
in this period was concerned, but the sense of who was using them.
Class difference between protagonists and readership was not restricted
to dialogues – Wordsworth and Coleridge's *Lyrical Ballads* (1798) were
hardly enjoyed by the deprived rural types who featured in them.[16]
Hannah More's *Cheap Repository Tracts* were probably read by readers
of more than one class, although when republished in her *Collected Works*
they were separated out into class-distinct groups, such as *Stories for
Persons of the Middle Ranks*, and *Tales for the Common People*.[17] Whilst dialogues involving juveniles do seem to have had actual pedagogical
use as parents and teachers attempted to make real children imitate
paper paragons, dialogues with labouring protagonists could be given
to labourers (some of whom could read) to disseminate radical ideas,
or to frighten upper orders with representations of the dangerous ideas
with which labourers were entertaining each other. The same texts could
be used to teach literate radicals of any class how to give uneducated
labourers a sense of their rights, and how to divest them of their beliefs
in those rights.

That distributive practices added to the propaganda values of dialogues can be seen from the case of Sir William Jones's *The Principles*

[14] Late eighteenth-century notions of the sublime (not as monolithic as the term 'Romantic
sublime' suggests) took their aesthetic essentials from Edmund Burke, *A Philosophical Inquiry into
the Origin of our Ideas of the Sublime and Beautiful* (1756).
[15] Thomas Taylor, *The Cratylus*, p. xxiii and 127.
[16] See Donna Landry, *The Muses of Resistance: Laboring Class Women's Poetry in Britain, 1739–1796*
(Cambridge, 1990) pp. 22–9.
[17] For further discussion of these complications and More's writings, see Kathryn Sutherland,
'Hannah More's Counter-Revolutionary Feminism' in Kelvin Everest (ed.), *Revolution in Writing:
British Literary Responses to the French Revolution* (Milton Keynes, 1991); Mitzi Myers, 'Hannah More's
Tracts for the Times: Social Fiction and Female Ideology' in Mary Ann Schofield and Cecilia
Macheski (eds.), *Fetter'd or Free? British Women Novelists, 1670–1815* (Athens, Ohio, 1985); Susan
Pederson, 'Hannah More meets Simple Simon: Tracts, Chapbooks and Popular Culture in
Late Eighteenth-Century England', *Journal of British Studies* 25 (1986); Chris Jones, *Radical
Sensibility: Literature and Ideas in the 1790s* (Routledge, 1993).

of Government. The author was designated simply as 'a Member of the Society for Constitutional Information', and the title-page further stressed the text's circulatory aims by declaring that the same society was responsible for printing and distribution *gratis*. This could not protect distributors from prosecution for libel at the behest of government ministers who disagreed that such texts were, as one put it, 'for Public Good'.[18] Sir William Jones's dialogue was notable not just for the stir it caused, or the social disparity of its characters, but for its pedagogical clarity. The scholar is clearly going to know most if not all of the answers, but in keeping with the demotic discourse of dialogue, he needs to learn which questions the peasant can already answer for himself.

The action starts with the peasant reluctant to sign a petition to widen the franchise, preferring to leave to parliament what he and other peasants do not understand. The scholar responds by reassuring him of his reasoning abilities, but stressing that participation in a platonic community of debate is not a matter of abilities, nor even of rights, but of civic obligation: as he tells the peasant, 'You can comprehend more than you imagine; and, as *a free member of a free state*, have higher things to mind than you may conceive.'[19] The peasant, underwhelmed by this, focuses on defining terms: he is free as in out of prison, but unsure what a free state is. The scholar then takes charge of the exchange and asks him a series of questions about the working men's club established in his village, and how its purposes of recreation and mutual protection were established, through a set of rules communally agreed, and upheld, through a mixture of the security of their own collective strength, and the help of agents of ideological apparatuses, alias the village schoolmaster and lawyer. The scholar is in one sense ignorant – he needs to be informed about the workings of the club in order for the dialogue to take the next turn, which is to establish an analogy between this club and the state.[20] '*S*[cholar]. Did it never occur to you, that every state or nation was only a great *club*? *P*[easant]. Nothing ever occurred to me on the subject; for I never thought about it.' The rhetorical affect, so to speak, of this declaration

---

[18] W. Jones, *Principles of Government* (1782), title-page. In a celebrated case in 1784, one distributor of Jones's dialogue was prosecuted for libel.

[19] Jones, *Principles of Government*, p. 1.

[20] This analogy did not go uncontested: one writer passionately argued that clubs were voluntary and not obliged to defend members, whereas being born into a state gave citizens rights and obligations, a quasi-contract not open to choice. See Josiah Tucker, *A Sequel to Sir William Jones's Pamphlet on the Principles of Government, in a Dialogue between a Freeholder in the County of Denbigh, and the Dean of Glocester* [sic] (Glocester [sic], 1784), pp. 3–15.

of blankness is itself blank: the scholar shows neither contempt nor regret for it. But the peasant is not quite a proverbial blank page, in that he is able to absorb new ideas by referring to his own experience. The scholar moves swiftly on to extend the analogy, closely questioning the peasant about the ideal way of electing people to form club rules, or state laws. The critical point of information, that six out of seven men have no vote for the parliament whose laws bind them, is set up as a mildly rhetorical question – 'Can you be ignorant [of this] . . . ?' asks the scholar. The process of asking questions is shown to be crucial within the dialogue as it brings into question a system in which citizens are indeed kept ignorant of their own disenfranchisement.

Asking questions thus unites the educated, who challenge both oppression and the inertia of the oppressed, and the uneducated, who can raise their consciousness by acquiring knowledge, and become politically forceful by demanding answers. The peasant signs the petition with an energy which overcomes poor literacy: 'Give me your pen – I never wrote my name, ill as it may be written, with greater eagerness.'[21] Just in case the peasant forgets the lesson, the scholar makes him practise making analogies: on the basis of how the village club deals with members who won't abide by its rules, how would he react to an autocratic king? The peasant gives the 'right' answer: expulsion, by force if necessary. For this he is rewarded by the present of a musket! The dialogue ends with a classic affirmation of the Socratic process, in which pedagogical success is about realising innate potential. As the peasant parts cheerfully from the scholar, he tells him, 'You have made me wiser and better than I was yesterday; and yet, methinks, I had some knowledge in my own mind of this great subject, and have been a politician all my life without perceiving it.'[22]

Jones's pedagogical project fused politics-out-of-doors with extramural education. Hannah More can be seen as a comparably radical educationalist, establishing a number of charity schools in the Bristol area whose catchment succeeded in reaching people previously thought more or less ineducable. But More's motives were pious rather than political, her aim to produce good Christians rather than good citizens – or rather, to More a good Christian was a model citizen. A restive peasant made unruly through inflammatory ideas showed education gone wrong; instruction should help people to make the most of what is within their grasp, both philosophically and materially. Hence More's

---

[21] Jones, *Principles of Government*, p. 5.   [22] *Ibid.*, p. 6.

emphasis on teaching the poor how to grow and cook vegetables.[23] What Jones deplored as quiescence in an oppressive social order, More promoted as acquiescence in a hierarchy in which social distinction was benignly paternalist, and offset by equality of moral responsibility. The Platonic paradigm of self-amendment was grafted onto a Christian project of self-government; political liberty paled beside liberty of conscience, though this, too, was textual, involving freedom to read the Bible and apply its lessons for oneself.

More's personal energy in setting up her schools under challenging, even dangerous, circumstances[24] had an analogue in her penchant for troping education as athletic. There is a distinct tendency in the eighteenth century for scholars to be associated with mobility; where a Renaissance St Jerome was sedentary in his study, an Enlightenment scholar was more of a rambler, like the classical scholar Elizabeth Carter who strode around the Sussex clifftops in all weathers. An emphasis on the powers of the mind had a particularly positive resonance for women, so obviously disempowered in various ways, and for whom intellectual achievements did demand distinct efforts. The ghostly embodiment latent in tropes of mental vigour and intellectual stamina was not necessarily oppressive, especially since eighteenth-century caricaturists liked to show male scholars as physically decrepit – scrawny, stooped, spindly. This helps explain the robustness of Hannah More's writings, otherwise off-putting to modern readers.

One consequence of the idea of learning as mental aerobics was that paradoxically it generated doubts about whether teachers' efforts were well applied. As Anna Laetitia Barbauld observed, young people often responded to the *ex officio* ideas of teachers:

> it is the sentiments we let drop occasionally, the conversation they overhear when playing unnoticed in a corner of the room, which has an effect on children; and not what is addressed directly to them in the tone of exhortation. If you would know precisely the effect these set discourses have upon your child, be pleased to reflect upon that which a discourse from the pulpit, which you have reason to think merely professional, has upon you.[25]

Dialogues, being less prescriptive than sermons, could engage readers imaginatively. But those which presented two sides of a question, or two

---

[23] Likewise Mary Leadbeater in *Cottage Dialogues among the Irish Peasantry*, 2 vols. (Dublin, 1811–13).

[24] In Nailsea, where More set up one of her schools for the poor, glass-workers gave their houses names like 'Botany Bay' and 'Little Hell'. See Jeremy and Margaret Collingwood, *Hannah More* (Oxford, 1990), p. 85.

[25] Anna Laetitia Barbauld, *Works* 2 vols. (1825), II, p. 312.

opposed views, could split the pedagogical subject. One commentator worried that readers might take the 'wrong' side when reading Plato's dialogues: 'superficial minds are ready to grasp at any shadow of authority that may seem to justify their quibbling'. But Plato, he claimed, represented two sides of an argument not to perplex truth, or from carelessness; 'if the whole matter in question is not always fully determined, yet it is always put in a fairer way of being determined afterward.'[26] In this respect, dialogues offered a diffusion of pedagogical authority rather than a surrender of authorial authority. But the Platonic method encouraged students to become their own teachers, at least in terms of a negative pedagogy of recognising their own errors. Plato's dialogues were thus 'a kind of *mirror-writing*. In them you may discern the errors of your own mind, and when it is liable to wander from the truth.'[27] If dialogues taught a way to teach oneself, ironically, Plato could make all other teachers redundant.

This pitted reason against authority, and Barbauld, for one, puzzled over possible complications, finally resolving them on the grounds that it could be reasonable to accept authority as a better reason for believing something than your own rational inquiries. It was, for instance, not unreasonable to accept a mathematical truth on the authority of Sir Isaac Newton. This leaves teachers free to enjoy the fantasy of having pedagogic authority, and ironically restored to Plato that authority subtracted from him by the Socratic method. But Barbauld also felt that teaching, whether by reason or authority, intrinsically generated resistance. The child struggled to escape from a net of truth:

The calm repose of his mind is broken, the placid lake is become turbid, and reflects distorted and broken images of things; but be not you alarmed at the new workings of his thoughts, – it is the angel of reason which descends and troubles the waters.[28]

So the difficulties one might have with dialogues could happily (for a teacher) be attributed to student difficulty, not teacher failure. This makes dialogues arguably the ultimate teaching fantasy: for all their mirror-writing and troubled waters, they propose a scenario in which something is learnt which extends the scenario of learning beyond the frame of the dialogue, though without surrendering pedagogic authority. On the one hand, the student is doing the work; on the other, the teacher is necessary. The student can be the teacher (which pleases

---

[26] Ebenezer Macfaite, *Remarks on the Life and Writings of Plato* (Edinburgh, 1760), pp. 84–5.
[27] Macfaite, *Remarks on the Life and Writings of Plato*, p. 85.   [28] Barbauld, *Works*, II, pp. 334–5.

students), but the teacher still produces the student (which pleases teachers). Signs of distress can be laid at the door of angels of reason (which pleases teachers); the entertainment value of dialogues makes students less restive than formal genres like sermons or catechisms (which pleases students and teachers).

Given these pedagogical politics, it is no wonder that dialogues were taken up by eighteenth-century writers of both radical and conservative persuasions. What they pursued was the pedagogic fantasy at the heart of the Platonic dialogue, whose scenario ends with something under-stood, the teacher's authority intact (because asserted so subtly) and the student's reasoning powers advanced. This magic formula explains dialogues' recurrent appeal: education was naturalised. There was no force involved (the only violence being the struggles of students), which increased its appeal to sophisticates, in contrast to unprogressive types who preferred the ferula, cane or whip. And the dialogic fantasy of never being at a loss for either an answer or a question makes regular con-verts. As one eighteenth-century writer put it, Cicero was so delighted with Socrates' way of establishing truth, that he subsequently chose to write dialogues: '*here*, says he, *every doubt may be proposed and answered.*'[29] This fantasy offsets what might otherwise be the genre's liabilities – that knowledge is laboriously disseminated; there are too many inter-ruptions; it is all too drawn out, too slow. For all the historically-specific inflections of this fantasy, it also has a core of continuity, which can roughly be described as a post-Enlightenment situation in which ideas (new-fangled or old-fashioned) are tested against reason, defined or inferred to be 'common sense'. The democratic nature of the dialogue then comes into its own, as different participants test out what they can agree in common.

At this point one should consider what advantages dialogues offered writers outside parliamentary politics who wanted to argue for certain forms of government, and to integrate those arguments with recog-nisably educational discourses. Some dialogues, like catechisms, give authority to the questioner, whose dominance is expressed structurally through the power or the right to ask questions. Those with answers may, ironically, be more vulnerable: testing may show their knowledge to be imperfect or ill-founded. Other dialogues identify the educator as the person with the answers, and make the questioner one thirsty for knowledge who can be satisfied by certain answers. Some dialogues,

---

[29] Robert Hodgson, *Arcana, or the Principles of the Late Petitioners to Parliament* (Cambridge, 1774), p. 104.

especially those with more than two protagonists, make education a process of exchange where learning is mutual but contested, where one voice may prove decisive but where every voice may carry weight, and where the product of learning may be as open-ended as the process. Like interrogators in spy fiction, those who ask questions may do so in order to secure information about what their adversaries know; in this sense, although they know something, they present themselves as learners in order to serve a strategic end and to underscore the value of certain knowledges in ideological struggle. In dialogues, as in spy fiction, the scene of learning may involve resistance, threats and surprises.

Usually, one of the narrative pre-conditions of dialogues is that they should not foreground transference between the characters' life-world and the readers' life-world, unlike some forms of epistolary debate, in which letterwriters or their personae see further circulation of a text as a sign of its persuasiveness. Both letters and dialogues make criss-cross connections between oral and print culture. Dialogues mimic speech in written conventions, but aim to generate debates about themselves; they are usually meant to be read, but may be read aloud. There are two pedagogical situations in a dialogue: a narrative one, in which characters may or may not learn something, and a metanarrative one, in which a reader may or may not learn something. A reader's conclusion may converge with or diverge from what characters conclude, and the most influential arguments may not be the concluding ones anyway. All these potential instabilities make dialogue writers alert to the frustrations of teaching as well as its successes. They also contribute to an anxiety about reading, which is exacerbated by the inflammatory powers of radical texts in the late eighteenth century.

Ideological bonds forged through a naturalised rhetorical process of discussion can be seen in Hannah More's *Village Politics*. Conversation restores social harmony, as Jack disabuses Tom of foolish notions. Jack is initially relaxed. His interjections are built around possibilities which may or may not be discountable: 'and suppose the French were as much in the right as I know them to be in the wrong; what does that argue for *us*?' Producing no evidence for his knowledge, he shifts the burden of proving relevance onto Tom. Jack is sometimes emphatic: 'No, Tom, no', and refuses to accept the terms of revolutionary discourse, garbled by Tom into 'hard words' like '*organization* and *function*, and *civism*'. These he denounces as 'nonsense, gibberish, downright hocus-pocus'.[30] When Tom accuses the rich of lolling about in their coaches and living off

---

[30] More, *Works*, p. 62.

the fat of the land, Jack responds with a fable from his daughter's schoolbook, in which the limbs rebel against a belly until, starved of nourishment, they are forced back to work. This fable, from Aesop by way of Shakespeare's *Coriolanus*, puts labourers on a level with schoolchildren even as it offers nominal equality for all adults within the body politic.[31] Occasionally peremptory, as if with a fractious child – 'Do be quiet' – Jack prefers to disguise paternalism in persuasion, until he has worn down Tom's defences. Tom begins to crack: 'I begin to think we are better off as we are . . . I begin to think I'm not so very unhappy as I had got to fancy.'[32] A range of pedagogic skills are displayed by Jack – refutation, counter-analogy, leading questions, discursive switches, counter-definition, parody, irony and so on. This makes discussions fraternal even when a character opposes revolutionary fraternity.

At critical moments, however, Jack relies on a colloquial force which locates authority in homespun experience. Telling Tom grim tales of how in France there is no longer respect for Sunday, respect for property or respect for life, Tom asks 'And dost thou think our Rights of Man will lead to all this wickedness? *Jack.* As sure as eggs is eggs.'[33] This circular rhetoric, echoing the mental protein of Platonic symposia, is part of the discourse of British empiricism triumphing over fancy (often foreign) theory – reminiscent of Samuel Johnson refuting Berkeley's metaphysics by kicking a stone in his way.[34]

For the conservative's ideas of French Revolutionists in the 1790s, one could plausibly substitute the conservative's ideas of certain poststructural theorists in the 1990s. The reassuringly material analogy tries to control the radical's sign substitutions,[35] ironically making interference with meaning a sign of social disorder. Anti-revolutionary lexicographers in France and Christian moralists in Britain faced the same problem, of how to deny the language of their opponents, without silencing them. 'A logomachy breaks out over a Revolution which is itself qualified as a "logomachy" by its protagonists.'[36] Jack cannot silence Tom, because Tom must disown his views if the dialogue is to foreground its power to teach readers.

[31] The politics of More's use of this fable is further discussed in my *Eighteenth-Century Letters and British Culture*.
[32] More, *Works*, p. 62.   [33] Ibid.
[34] As reported by Boswell in R. W. Chapman (ed.) *Life of Johnson* (Oxford, 1953 repr. 1985), p. 333; 6 August 1763.
[35] Contrast Gertrude Stein's famous dictum, 'A rose is a rose is a rose is a rose.'
[36] Philippe Roger, 'The French Revolution as "logomachy"', in John Renwick (ed.), *Language and Rhetoric of the Revolution* (Edinburgh, 1990), p. 10.

This shift from things to words, but also words to things, is a perpetual
current whose toing and froing charges Reality and Language by turns. This
common conviction animates counter-revolutionary lampoons and Jacobin
decrees alike; both emanate from an epistemology of representation whose
'natural' result is a shared belief in the dangerous powers of language. Some
may be aristocrats, others democrats, but *all* are semiocrats.[37]

Tom signals his conversion to his teacher's view by singing a snatch of
a nourishing patriotic song, 'The Roast Beef of Old England'; popular
culture takes over from populist politics as the common ground best
for the common man.[38]

Singing turns party politics into partying, temporarily less problematic as a form of political education than reading. Tom's 'mistakes'
have come from reading the wrong texts. Foreign ideas generate literal
xenophobia when they can be attributed to that old enemy of British
kings, people and philosophers, the French. Here conservative writers
like More got into a tangle. On the one hand, the poor were to be
encouraged to read the Bible, but they had to be discouraged from
reading the works of Tom Paine. Somebody had to read Paine, though,
in order to prove exactly how it was wicked nonsense. Middle-class
protagonists in dialogues admitted they had read Paine's works, but at
the behest of others: 'During my late confinement I read them at the
request of a friend', as a fictional farmer put it, neatly merging his own
illness with a lack of (bodily) freedom feared as the consequence of
Paine's agenda.[39] Reading leads to the danger of teaching oneself the
wrong things, though British writers of all persuasions were careful to
uphold the freedom of the press as a desirable, if sometimes problematic liberty. Even More's conservative Jack restrains Tom from making
a bonfire of his book at the end of *Village Politics*. Dialogues redirect
ignorant characters whilst being careful not to impinge on the freedom
of readers to read dialogues.

The solidarity between radicals established by common reading for
the common man could also be broken up by allusions to upper-class
texts which confuted populist beliefs. Tom is not interested in securing
treasure in heaven by reading his Bible as Jack does; he wants a share of
treasure in this world, as Paine tells him the French have. Jack responds:

[37] Roger, 'The French Revolution as "logomachy"', p. 10.
[38] It is tempting to note here how the composer Vangelis's 'Theme for the Common Man' was
used by the Social Democrat party, and how Conservative education ministers in the 1990s
have stressed hymn-singing in school assemblies – both instances of how music is part of political education. Songs are prescripted, which means people temporarily in unison.
[39] John Bowles, *Dialogues on the Rights of Britons*, p. 8.

'Tis all a lie, Tom. Sir John's butler says his master gets letters which *say* 'tis all a lie. 'Tis all murder, and nakedness, and hunger, many poor soldiers fights without victuals and march without clothes. These are your *democrats*! Tom.[40]

Manuscript correspondence here overrides print culture, with More's dialogue able to mediate its lessons to the masses.

Tom can be persuaded out of his views both because his arguments are bad, and because Jack's arguments are better. But this can weaken rather than strengthen the pedagogic power of dialogues, as it changes questioning into quietism. Dialogues also had to separate out questions of rights for working men from the related causes of women's rights, slave emancipation, and the rights of children. They also had to dis-associate modern radicalism from the successful removal of an earlier British king in the 'Glorious Revolution' of 1688, universally agreed to be the foundation of British liberty, and whose centenary in 1788 led writers to look back to British Levellers as well as across to French Jacobins.[41] Dialogues suspend the pedagogic power of examples from history in favour of a less overtly didactic discourse, the supposedly informal chat. The 'we' divided by class envy and radical politics is reunited into a new 'us' by the shared narrative of conversation. Edu-cation takes place when people meet in discussion, displacing the com-munity of those who read the same books.

Given the recent rapid expansion of higher education, the dialogue's fantasy of including those previously thought uneducable would appeal to governments who want to broaden the educational franchise – and do so on the cheap, since symposia appear to require no resources other than teachers possessed of reasoning powers common to all. The revolutionary-minded could appropriate the free-marketeers' rationale of transferable skills to justify handing out muskets. The issue of plum-meting academic standards miraculously vanishes, since dialogues meas-ure success either by supposedly self-evident standards of reason, or by internal rhetorical standards of persuasion, though no doubt auditors would find a way to quantify numbers of labourers persuaded to be content with their lot, or to award institutional funding on the basis of student evaluation of the painlessness of persuasion. On the other hand, the anarchic potential of the dialogue, its articulation of doubt, its expression of the way that an argument can have many sides,

---

[40] More, *Works*, p. 61.
[41] For example, *A Dialogue on the Revolution* (1788), pro-radical; *Principles of Order and Happiness* (1792), anti-radical. Fourteenth-century rabble-rousing was also invoked: see *A Dialogue between Wat Tyler, Mischievous Tom, and an English Farmer* (1793).

and how a resolution dependent on mirror-writing is also dependent
on reversals and doubleness – all these features make the dialogue a
powerful fantasy for teachers who resist fantasies both of their power
as instructors, and of their powerlessness in the shrinking public service
of malign governments.

CHAPTER 5

Women and classical education in the early modern period

Jane Stevenson

INTRODUCTION

The relevance of classical education to women was very much a subject of debate in the sixteenth and seventeenth centuries.[1] There is an enormous literature concerned with the proper extent of female learning, much of it in the form of lists, or catalogues, of learned women (to be discussed later in this chapter). Clearly, many were against it: equally clearly, many educators, both male and female, spoke in favour of educating girls, and a good few actually did so. My chapter will attempt to focus on both the debate itself, and its social and cultural consequences.

What complicates this subject is the enormous mass of evidence more or less indirectly *about* educated women, compared with the small quantity of actual surviving works *by* women. This means that, even today, discussions of women's opportunities and achievements tend to consist of the bandying about of secondary authorities. The same few names, linked by phrases such as 'is said by contemporaries to . . .' appear all too often. Male defenders of women's education have in effect intruded themselves as spokesmen for early modern women rather than allowing them to speak for themselves, a situation not without its parallels among more recent male feminists. Consequently, my focus in this paper is specifically on women who write in Latin and Greek: on writers, because we have no means of assessing the actual level of knowledge of a woman merely *described* as prodigiously learned, and particularly on poets, because the ability to compose metrical poetry is

---

[1] See for instance C. Jordan, 'Feminism and the Humanists: the Case of Sir Thomas Elyot's *Defence of Good Women,*' *Renaissance Quarterly* 36.2 (1983), 181–201, and G. Kaufman, 'Juan Luis Vives on the Education of Women,' *Signs* 3.4 (1978), 891–96. There is an interesting polemic by Marie Burghope, written in 1699, against men's attitudes to women's education (M. Ezell, *The Patriarch's Wife: Literary Evidence and the History of the Family* (Chapel Hill and London, 1987), 125–6).

the nearest possible thing to an unequivocal indication that the writer
in question had received an education comparable to that of a man.

In assessing women's actual writing, it may be helpful to reflect that
the resonance of the word 'author' was until recently entirely male.[2]
An author is a begetter, and also an authority: thus Frances Burney, in
the eighteenth century, apostrophises her father as 'Sole Author of my
Being' as if she imagines that she was born, like Minerva, from Charles
Burney's head.[3] This has made it difficult, both for contemporaries and
for subsequent writers, to think clearly about women's writing, particularly that of women educated 'like men', since the idea of 'authorship'
seems to exclude women. Actually, though it obviously did so in the
minds of some men (and women), others found ways of accommodat-
ing the idea of the woman writer. There is, moreover, more surviving
writing by women in Latin and Greek than is sometimes thought, and
I shall, in this chapter, attempt to distinguish between actual and alleged
achievement. Most of this chapter will be devoted to a survey of the
social context, extent, and purpose(s) of women's formal education
in the classics (particularly Latin), but it will also consider the case for
and against: the restrictions governing women, the nature, level and
bases of prejudice against female authorship, but also men's support
for women's education, and women's support for one another.

EVIDENCE FOR LEARNED WOMEN

The level of public interest in the educability of women is suggested
by the extremely large number of highly similar works written in the
fifteenth, sixteenth and seventeenth centuries which list learned and/
or remarkable women, beginning either with Sappho, Corinna, Nossis
and so forth, or with Minerva and the Muses (such catalogues often
show a pretty indifference to the distinction between myth and history),
and continuing with the writer's contemporaries.[4] This suggests that
European intellectuals were increasingly concerned about educated
women and the problem they represent. Woods and Fürstenwald, for
example, list twenty Northern European catalogues of learned women

---

[2] Classical Greek writers combined a belief in the male as sole parent with the metaphoric understanding of authorship as fathering (e.g. Plato, *Phaedrus*, 275d–276a). But even now, the resonance
of authorship is specifically male. For example, the contract I signed for the production of this
chapter asserts my 'right of *paternity* (the right always to be identified as the author of the essay)'.
[3] R. Lonsdale, *Eighteenth Century Women Poets: an Oxford Anthology* (Oxford and New York, 1990) p. 356.
[4] See G. McLeod, *Virtue and Venom. Catalogs of Women from Antiquity to the Renaissance* (Ann Arbor,
1991).

and dissertations on women's education from before 1800,[5] and many more, including examples from Italy and Spain, are listed in Bond's edition of William Bercher's 1559 treatise, *The Nobility of Women*, which is itself an example of the genre.[6] The authors of these works pillage those of their predecessors with enthusiasm, and have a tendency to bandy names rather than examples of the work of the women themselves, but they represent a rising tide of evidence for the educability and intellectual capacity of women.

The importance of these catalogues is twofold. First, they were an academic industry in themselves; a witness to the early modern concern for comprehensive list-making and sorting. From the beginning of the sixteenth century, most authors of any kind of general literary survey seem to have considered it *de rigueur* to include a chapter on women. Bernardino Scardeone, for example, author of *On the Antiquity of the City of Padua and Distinguished Paduan Citizens* printed in Basel in 1560, includes a chapter entitled *Distinguished Paduan Women*. This survey includes one Julia Bigolina, who 'wrote both in rhythm (i.e., poetry) and in composed speeches'.[7] Secondly, by their very nature, these catalogues put women's writing into a continuum; they equip the woman scholars of their own immediate social context with a past stretching back into the remotest mists of antiquity, which must surely have implications for women's authorial self-confidence.

Such surveys are, of course, virtually useless to any quibbling modern scholar who wants to know what any particular Tenth Muse, Fourth Grace or Second Sappho actually *wrote*. An index of their unsatisfactoriness for the purposes of modern scholarship is Count von Baldhoven's edition in 1606 of the remarkable Latin poetry of Elizabeth Jane Weston (1582–1612), a woman who relied significantly on patronage secured by her own writing. It concludes with a *catalogue of learned maidens and women* (sig. F.3–F.8), which places her in the context of other women poets, starting with Minerva and Corinna, and ending with learned women contemporaries, who include 'the virgin Helena Maria Wackeriana à Wackenfels, [who] died in Prague' (sig. F.8). The daughter of the Count von Wackenfels died at the age of nine. She was a child brilliant and remarkable enough to attract an epigram on her death from Johannes

[5] J. M. Woods and M. Fürstenwald, *Schriftstellerinnen, Künstlerinnen und gelehrte Frauen des deutschen Barock*, 2 vols. (Stuttgart, 1984) I, pp. xii–xxiv.
[6] R. W. Bond, ed., *The Nobility of Women, By William Bercher, 1559*, 2 vols. (London, 1904).
[7] B. Scardeone, *De Antiquitate Urbis Patavii et claris civibus Patavini libri tres* (Basel, 1560), p. 368. I know of no surviving trace of this woman's oeuvre.

Kepler,[8] but her contribution to literature was nil. Von Baldhoven, like many other enthusiasts for learned maids, makes no distinction between the genuine achievement of Weston, and the mere potential of this unfortunate child. Thus, it is only when the writer's work actually survives that it is possible to assess the real meaning of such undiscriminating praise. These catalogues show that learned women existed, and were known to exist, throughout Europe in the sixteenth and seventeenth centuries. But their existence also bespeaks a certain uneasiness, or lack of confidence, in women and their male defenders. The sheer number of these catalogues might either suggest that the point had to be made over and over again, and that it was never possible simply to accept that girls were educable and get on with it; or alternatively, that male scholars were engaged in creating a sort of canon: a controllably small number of exceptional women.[9]

The education of women is often demonstrably affected by events completely outside their control. As far as the English court élite were concerned (which would include, of course, most though not all of the Englishwomen of immediate concern to this study), the accession of the markedly misogynist and patriarchal James VI/I meant a marked diminution of women's opportunities to take part in public life.[10] Almost all poets at this period were dependent on patronage, and James VI disliked, and disapproved of, women in general, and particularly of learned ones: 'even a Man who was vain and foolish, was made more so by Learning, and as for Women, who he said were all naturally addicted to Vanity, where it did one good, it did harm to twenty'.[11] For example, Aemilia Lanyer, an English woman poet of the court milieu, seems to have experienced difficulties under the new régime.[12] Elizabeth Jane

[8] J. Kepler, *Gesammelte Werke*, W. von Dyck and Max Caspar eds., 38 vols. (Munich, 1937), IV, p. 96.

[9] There is a possible analogy in the way that the gay male community used to resort to an apologetic litany of 'Plato, Michelangelo, Shakespeare, Wilde (etc.)' to validate their collective identity, but now seldom seems to consider this necessary.

[10] See J. Goldberg, *James VI and the Politics of Literature* (Baltimore, 1983).

[11] According to the eighteenth-century memoir of Frances Erskine, based on the family records of the Earls of Mar, James forbade his daughter Elizabeth to study Latin and Greek. Counter-claims that Elizabeth did in fact learn to write and speak Latin might either suggest that he changed his mind when it looked as if the poor health of his sons might bring her to the throne, or that she learned Latin in adult life because her situation as Queen, then ex-queen, of Bohemia demanded it. [Frances Erskine], *Memoirs relating to the Queen of Bohemia by One of her Ladies* (n.p.: privately printed, 17–?), p. 109, quoted in B. K. Lewalski, *Writing Women in Jacobean England* (Cambridge, MA and London, 1993), p. 341, n. 14.

[12] 'It is evident from [her later] poems that Lanyer does not enjoy in the court circle of King James the associations and the favours she attracted in Elizabeth's court.' B. K. Lewalski 'Of God and Good Women: The Poems of Aemilia Lanyer,' in M. P. Hannay, ed., *Silent but for the*

Weston sent a fulsome Latin ode from Prague to congratulate James on his accession (dropping some none too subtle hints about patronage as she did so): no direct reply seems to have been forthcoming; and she was furious to discover that the court had been left under the impression that they had been ghost-written for her.[13] James's response to a learned young woman poet who presented herself in person (almost certainly Bathsua Rainolds) was positively hostile:

when a learned maid was presented to King James for an English rarity, because she could speake and rite pure Latine, Greeke and Hebrew, the King ask'd, – 'But can shee spin?'[14]

The later Stuarts, similarly, did not foster women's education in Latin, let alone Greek: of course, as the seventeenth century progressed, Latin became less and less important as a diplomatic language even for men.

In the seventeenth century, hostility to women's authorship also continued to be a factor in potential poets' self-perceptions, and consequent self-censorship. Lucy Hutchinson (1620–after 1675), the wife of an important Puritan general during the English Civil War, was tutored in Latin at the express desire of her father (Sir Allen Apsley, Lieutenant of the Tower of London), and became a good enough Latinist to translate Lucretius. But she presents her translation with hesitation, commenting 'I did attempt things out of my own Sphere', and seems genuinely to have felt that it was inappropriate for her as a woman to use Latin, even to translate it.[15]

Her attitude is explicable in the light of the general attitude to the education of English girls in this period, exemplified by the family of the earls of Huntingdon. George (the eighth earl) was sent to Foubert's Academy and Wadham College, Oxford, where he read New Testament Greek, and Latin and English verse. His sister was only given

---

Word: Tudor Women as Patrons, Translators and Writers of Religious Works (Kent, OH, 1985) 203–24, p. 206. For an extended discussion of the importance of patronage to poets of both sexes in the Renaissance, see M. Brennan, *Literary Patronage in the English Renaissance: the Pembroke Family* (London, 1988), pp. 1–18.

[13] E. J. Weston, *Parthenicon Elisabethae Ioannae Westoniae, virginis nobilissimae, poetriae florentissimae, linguarum plurimarum peritissimae,* ed. G. Martin à Baldhoven (Prague, [1606]), iii sig. A7–8; L. Schleiner, *Tudor and Stuart Women Writers* (Bloomington and Indianapolis, 1994), p. 265.

[14] W. J. Thoms, *Anecdotes and Traditions, Illustrative of Early English History and Literature, Derived from MS Sources* (London, 1839), p. 125, from London, BL Add. MS 3890 (1633), f. 129. It is worth noting here that Bathsua Rainolds, daughter of Henry Rainolds, is the same woman who is better known by her husband's name as Bathsua Makin (F. Teague, 'The Identity of Bathsua Makin', *Biography* 16.1 (1993), pp. 1–17).

[15] G. Greer, S. Hastings, J. Medoff, M. Sansone, eds., *Kissing the Rod: An Anthology of Seventeenth-Century Women's Verse* (London, 1988), p. 216.

lessons in dancing and music: she was intelligent and ambitious, and later became a patron of Mary Astell.[16] But it is precisely at this time that several learned Englishwomen, notably Mary Astell, Bathsua Makin (née Rainolds), and Dorothy Drury (née Moore), began to write in support of women's education: a new development of the seventeenth century since pro-woman Renaissance educationalists had all been men.[17]

Another new aspect of this generation of learned women is the self-conscious way they correspond and carefully foster a sense of community. Anna Maria van Schurman (1607–1678) provides a very clear-cut example.[18] In the 1630s, she wrote a treatise on the education of women which was published in 1641[19] and translated into English as *The Learned Maid or, Whether a Maid may be a Scholar* in 1659, à propos of which she corresponded with Bathsua Makin in Greek, and with Dorothy Drury in Hebrew. A third notable polemicist for the intellectual rights of women with whom she corresponded was Marie de Gournay (1565–1645), about whom she wrote a poem.[20] For van Schurman, who corresponded with de Gournay in the latter's extreme old age, she was a link with the brilliant world of the Pléiade and the Parisian Academies, which had (as she knew) contained a number of women scholars, such as Marguerite de Valois, Anna Pallantia and Camille de Morel.[21] Van Schurman also wrote in French to Madame Contel, Anne de Rohan (author of poetry in French), and Mademoiselle de Moulin,[22] and was friendly with Elizabeth of Bohemia.[23] Her considerable output of occasional verse also includes a Latin panegyric poem in support of

[16] R. Perry, *The Celebrated Mary Astell: an Early English Feminist* (Chicago and London, 1986), p. 104.
[17] It is not a development confined to England: Lucretia Marinella in 1600 and Marie de Gournay in 1622 also published defences of women's abilities and educability (*Le nobiltà e excellenze delle Donne e i diffetti e mancamenti de gli huomini* (Venice), and *L'égalité des hommes et des femmes* (Paris), respectively).
[18] L. Miller, 'Anna Maria van Schurman's Appeal for the Education of Women,' in A. Dalzell, C. Fantazzi, R. J. Schoect, eds., *Acta Conventus Neo-Latini Torontonensis: Proceedings of the Seventh International Congress of Neo-Latin Studies, Toronto, 8 August to 13 August 1988* (Binghamton, NY, 1991), pp. 491–98.
[19] R. M. van Schurman, *Nobiliss. Virginis Annae Mariae a Schurman Dissertatio De Ingenii Muliebris ad Doctrinam, & meliores Litteras aptitudine* (Leiden, 1641), pp. 162–4.
[20] Marie was a prodigious autodidact, who contrived to teach herself Latin, Greek and English, and came to the notice of Montaigne, who proclaimed her his 'fille d'alliance'. She was author of a number of poems and translations, and also of *L'egalité des hommes et des femmes* (see note 17) which prompted van Schurman's tribute in *De Ingenii Muliebris*, p. 303.
[21] F. Yates, *The French Academies of the Sixteenth Century* (London and New York, 1947), pp. 32–4.
[22] R. M. van Schurman, *Nobiliss. Virginis Annae Mariae a Schurman Opuscula Hebraea, Graeca, Latina, Gallica: prosaica et metrica* (Leiden, 1648), pp. 149–76.
[23] K. M. Wilson and F. J. Warnke, *Women Writers of the Seventeenth Century* (Athens, GA, and London, 1989), pp. 171–74.

a young Danish noblewoman, Birgitte Thott (1610–1662), who translated the works of Seneca into Danish.[24] Thus, van Schurman was in contact with educated women interested in the education of their own sex in the Low Countries, France, England, and Scandinavia, and, importantly, was aware through Marie de Gournay that hers was *not* a generation of pioneers.[25]

If we look at women outside court circles in early modern England, the picture seems to confirm Margaret Spufford's thesis that, in some families, a 'tradition of literacy' existed independent of economic factors.[26] In the case of women Latinists, we are dealing with the very special case of fathers who saw fit to educate their daughters like their sons. Bathsua Makin is an obvious case in point: she proudly records both her father's status as a schoolmaster and his interest in language on her title-page. It is reasonable to assume that she was educated by him at home. Similarly, at the end of the century, one Anne Baynard (1674–97) developed a specialist interest in Protestant theology, and disputed with Socinians[27] in 'severe satyrs written in the Latin tongue'.[28] She was the daughter of Edward Baynard, a physician and surgeon practising in the City of London,[29] but a bibliophile by inclination: the catalogue of his books sold after his death in 1721 lists some 300 works in Greek, Latin, French, and Italian.[30] He may be presumed to have supported and encouraged his daughter's education. Anne Baynard's funeral sermon, by John Prude, was published at the request of her circle of (female) friends and relatives. This points to the existence of circles of scholarly and thoughtful countrywomen; a reminder that the fashions and values of metropolitan education did not necessarily represent those of the country as a whole. There was already a history of

[24] M. Alenius, 'Learned Scandinavian Women in the Seventeenth and Eighteenth Centuries', in A. Dalzell et al., eds., *Acta Conventus Neo-Latini Torontonensis*, pp. 177–88, p. 181. Thott's book is called *Lucii Annæi Senecæ . . . Skrifter, som om Sæderne oc et skickeligt Lefnit handler* (Sorøe, 1658).

[25] Thott illustrates the thesis that learned women tend to run in families: she was almost certainly related to one of the most distinguished Danish women of letters, Sophie Brahe.

[26] M. Spufford, *Contrasting Communities: English Villagers in the Sixteenth and Seventeenth Centuries* (Cambridge, 1974), pp. 203–4.

[27] Proto-Unitarians, who doubted the doctrine of the Trinity.

[28] J. Prude, *A Sermon at the Funeral of the Learned and Ingenious Mrs Ann Baynard . . . preached at the Parish Church of Barnes in the County of Surrey the 16 June 1697* (London, 1697).

[29] One of the last English women poets writing in Latin (before, doubtless, a number of twentieth-century university poets, products of a wholly different intellectual culture) is the well-known bluestocking Elizabeth Carter, translator of Epictetus and friend of Dr Johnson, who could turn a competent Latin epigram: see M. Pennington, *Memoirs of the Life of Mrs Elizabeth Carter* (London, 1807), p. 26.

[30] D. Gardiner, *English Girlhood at School: A Study of Women's Education through Twelve Centuries* (London, 1929), p. 383.

Latinate women of comparable background. In the sixteenth-century, there were Elizabeth Lucar, daughter of a citizen of London, and Rachel Jevon, daughter of a Royalist Anglican clergyman deprived of his living during the Civil War, and author of two long, complex poems on the Restoration of Charles II, one in English, one in Latin.[31] Lucy Hutchinson has been mentioned as an example of the self-limiting woman who felt that it was inappropriate for her to write in Latin: it is therefore worth observing the existence of Rachel Jevon, a product of the same generation and of similar status, who seems to have felt no such thing.

Both the community-building of educated women, and the enabling of well-disposed men, are well illustrated in a letter from Jeanne Otho (b. *c.* 1545) to Camille de Morel (b. 1547). Both women became published Latin poets: Jeanne late in life,[32] while de Morel began early, and published an unknown number of poems scattered through the works of contemporaries.[33] Camille and her sisters Lucrèce and Diane were tutored by one of the foremost humanists of the age, Charles Utenhove (1536–1600),[34] who himself had been a pupil at Otho's father's school of ancient languages in Ghent (opened in 1545), Utenhove's native city.[35] The positive interest which Utenhove took in the children of his old master is shown by a poem he wrote to Jean de Morel, father of Camille, published in his *Xenia, To the same* [Jean de Morel], *to recommend J. Otho, child of the writer's teacher Johann Otho*. With Utenhove and her brother Johann as links, it is hardly surprising that Jeanne Otho got to hear of Camille de Morel.[36] Jeanne finally wrote to Camille in 1556, shortly after Utenhove had visited her and her father, probably at the same time as Utenhove was writing to Jean de Morel about Johann.

[31] Elizabeth Lucar, discussed in G. Ballard, *Memoirs of Several Ladies of Great Britain Who Have Been Celebrated for Their Writings or Skill in the Learned Languages, Arts and Sciences* (Oxford, privately printed, 1752) pp. 36–7. R. Jevon, *Carmen θριαμβευτικον regiae maiestatis Caroli II principum et Christianorum optimi in exoptatissimum eius restaurationem* (London, 1660).

[32] J. [Jeanne] Otho, *Carminum diversorum libri duo* (Strasbourg, 1616) and *Poemata sive lusus extemporanei* (Antwerp, 1617).

[33] Camille was on very friendly terms with Ronsard, Boissard, and other poets associated with the Pléiade and the French Academy. See R. L. Hawkins, 'A Letter from One Maiden of the Renaissance to Another', *Modern Language Notes* 22.8 (1907), pp. 243–45, p. 244.

[34] W. Janssen, *Charles Utenhove: sa vie et sa oeuvre* (Maastricht, 1939).

[35] On the witness of Charles Utenhove, *Xenia* (Basel, 1560), and of the letter quoted below, see also N. C. Kist, 'Johanna Otho en Karel Utenhove, eene bijdrage tot de hervormings-geschiedenis von Gend', *Kerkhistorisch Archief* (Amsterdam) 2 (1859), pp. 419–26.

[36] Utenhove's close friend Paul Melissus Schede (another enthusiast for learned women) was also a friend of Elizabeth Jane Weston's (*Parthenicon* III, sig. A12): this offers one possible route for Weston to have heard of the Morel sisters, which, as we see from her poem quoted later, she clearly had.

This was three years after he had ceased to tutor Camille and her sisters, and apparently before Jeanne Otho's marriage to Willem Mayart.

When Sir Charles Utenhove came to us from England (a man among those my father once instructed in letters for whom he feels a unique affection), he gave me your poem. When I read it, I cannot describe how pleased I was. For in this country, I have heard of no maiden particularly skilled in humane letters; for which reason, it is appropriate that I should congratulate you equally on your good fortune, wit and education, since you do not blush to conjoin Latin and Greek letters with maidenly conduct within such a re- nowned family, and you do not deem the mysteries of Phoebus and the nine Muses unworthy of your studies. For me, indeed, if I am to admit the truth, no pleasure can come my way which is so great that, through concern for it, I would be able to give second place to Latin and Greek letters. It is by them that I measure not only my enjoyment, but indeed my happiness. If only I were able to spurn domestic cares (something which, in us, most people regard as a crime/which most of us [women] think a crime) for their sake! I would not at all mind dedicating myself to the Muses alone. Forgive my audacity, illustrious virgin, in daring to burden your most erudite ears with this unsophisticated letter. Sir Charles Utenhove asked my father that I should send you some piece of writing, albeit in prose, and slide myself into your acquaintance through the medium of letters; so if this is an error, your kind- ness will attribute it entirely to Sir Charles Utenhove. Farewell, most learned Camilla, and deign to inscribe me in the list of your servants. I have a brother in Paris. I wish that, through your recommendation, he could live in your pious family or somewhere else, rather than looking after himself. Again, farewell. From Duisberg [in the duchy of Cleves], the day before the calends of October [30 September].[37]

The letter is interesting for its reference to tension between domestic responsibility and the life of a scholar, especially since Otho is unmar- ried: housewifery is often advanced as a reason why learned girls should not marry, but clearly, continuing to live with one's father was no pro- tection from household chores. It is also interesting for the way in which an intellectually ambitious girl hearing of another promptly seeks to make a connection, though in tones of becoming modesty. Camille's public career started very young: with her father and Utenhove's back- ing, she was publishing in her early teens, while Jeanne, though she was later to play a public part in the intellectual life of Antwerp, the city in which she settled,[38] was not at the time of this letter a published author. The manuscript in which this letter is preserved, München,

[37] München, Bayerische Staatsbibliothek, Collectio Camerariana 33, clm. 1084, ff. 250–54 (poem) and 279–80 (letter) (1556).
[38] F. Sweertius, *Athenae Belgicae, sive Nomenclator infer. Germaniae scriptorum* (Antwerp, 1628), pp. 468–9.

Bayerische Staatsbibliothek clm. 1084, also includes a poem of Jeanne Otho's to Camille de Morel (ff. 250–54), which suggests that this is more than simply a letter of recommendation for brother Johann backing-up Utenhove's poem to Camille's father.

Another salient part of the context of women's learning in the early modern period is the importance of a few men (other than fathers) sympathetic to women's learning, who act as mediators: such men as von Baldhoven, Melissus, and Utenhove.[39] Nothing necessarily prevented women engaging in international scholarly *amicitia* through the medium of letters. For example, when the Silesian nobleman Count von Baldhoven was travelling in the Low Countries in 1603, he recommended the name of his brilliant young protégée, Elizabeth Jane Weston, to some of the most distinguished humanist scholars in the Low Countries. She reports the results to him as follows:

> Meanwhile, I give you eternal thanks for the letters of such great men, written to me, and procured through your patronage. I have replied in two letters to those most celebrated duumvirs of the republic of letters, Master Scaliger and Master Dousa. From Heinsius, whom you commend to me so much, I have seen nothing as yet.[40]

Justus Scaliger and Janus Dousa, philologists, jurists, poets, and leading lights of the Northern Renaissance, sent well-turned letters: Dousa was in fact still more generous, sending two graceful poems, and several more to von Baldhoven himself; the jurist Daniel Heinsius had not sent anything at the time of writing, though he did later.[41] In this exchange, von Baldhoven seems to be acting like any conscientious patron of any protégé: gender is not directly an issue. Similarly, Charles Utenhove seems to have sought to open channels between his erstwhile pupil Camille de Morel and Queen Elizabeth I, an obvious possible source of patronage for her in the future. In neither case is the able young

---

[39] See, for example, Kist, 'Johanna Otho'; F. Leys, 'Deux documents sur l'amitié entre Jacques Yetzweirt et Jeanne Otho', *Latomus* 48 (1989), pp. 424–34; P. de Nolhac, *Un poète rhénan ami de la Pléiade: Paul Melissus*, (Paris: Bibliothèque littéraire de la Renaissance, n.s. 11, 1923); J. E. Phillips, 'Elizabeth I as a Latin Poet: an Epigram on Paul Melissus', *Renaissance News* 16.4 (1963), pp. 289–98.

[40] *Parthenicon* II, sig. C9: Prague, 8 March, 1603.

[41] There is an undated poem from him in *Parthenicon* II, sig. E. 10. A similar rebuff by silence from Guarino traumatised Isotta Nogarola (c. 1416–1446) (see A. Grafton and L. Jardine, *From Humanism to the Humanities: Education and the Liberal Arts in Fifteenth- and Sixteenth-Century Europe* (London, 1986), p. 38): Weston appears quite unconcerned. Perhaps we should take this as a reminder that it is not necessarily helpful to read one humanist culture in terms of another: it must be becoming very clear that Western and Central Europe in the late sixteenth and seventeenth centuries were very different from Italy in the fifteenth, not least in the constraints governing women scholars.

woman in question being treated like a monster or a prodigy, though obviously her gender gives her a certain rarity value which is in some sense a selling-point. It must be remembered that too many would-be literati were always chasing too few patrons.

WOMEN'S EDUCATION IN CONTEXT

Much writing from, and about, the early modern period gives the strongest of impressions that women were excluded from the academy.[42] Walter Ong, for example, goes so far as to suggest that Latin learning was *specifically* patriarchal, in that by the end of the middle ages, it had become a male *rite de passage* involving

isolation from the family, the achievement of identity in a totally male group (the school), the learning of a body of relatively abstract tribal lore inaccessible to those outside the group . . .[43]

More recently, Robert Adams Day picked up on this anthropological approach to the teaching and learning of the classics in the early modern period and extended it, suggesting that not merely did classical learning function as part of the glue that held male society together; it deliberately, rather than inadvertently, excluded women:[44]

If clean[45] literature is bounded by the lines laid down in antiquity and if clean literary practitioners are men of position, by definition trained in the classics, clean women cannot of course practice literature for the simple reason that they never did, except for the two ancient Greek monsters, Sappho and Corinna.

These works, and others like them, suggest that there is simply no point in looking for classically educated women. They did not exist; and if they did, they were so anomalous as to be 'monsters'. This *a priori* position effectively obscures the realities of the relationship between women and the academy in the sixteenth and seventeenth centuries: in fact, it represents *one* position taken by contemporary male scholars, and one, at that, which was the subject of vigorous debate.

Day and Ong are also incorrect in assuming that there were no women writers in the classical languages. In fact, there are many women

[42] L. Jardine, '"O decus Italiae virgo", or the Myth of the Learned Lady in the Renaissance', *Historical Journal* 28 (1985), pp. 799–819, for example, demonstrates the force of opposition.
[43] W. J. Ong, SJ, 'Latin Language Study as a Renaissance Puberty Rite', *Studies in Philology* 56 (1967), pp. 103–24, see also Ong, *The Presence of the Word* (New Haven, 1959) p. 251.
[44] R. A. Day, 'Muses in the Mud: the *Female Wits* Anthropologically Considered', *Women's Studies* 7 (1980), pp. 61–74, p. 68.
[45] He uses the word in the anthropological sense developed by M. Douglas, *Purity and Danger: An Analysis of the Concepts of Pollution and Taboo* (London, 1966).

practitioners of literature beyond Sappho and Corinna; and many of them were known, at least by name, in the early modern period. It is modern scholarship, rather than early modern, which has caused the woman scholars of the sixteenth and seventeenth centuries to vanish. My discussion in this chapter is focused on Latin, the more widely used of the two classical languages, but I will just note here that the tradition of Greek writing by women continues after the sixth century BC through the whole history of Greek literature.[46] Similarly, several classical Latin women poets are known to have existed, including one (Sulpicia) whose work survives to this day.[47] It is possible to construct a *continuous* tradition of women's poetry in Latin from antiquity to the eighteenth century. This was far better known to contemporaries than it is now, principally through the lists and catalogues discussed above.

Let us, for example, notice two poems, one from the late sixteenth, one from the early seventeenth century, both of which make reference to the tradition of women's poetry in Latin and Greek. The first is by Elizabeth Jane Weston, writing in Prague in the 1590s to Erich Lymburch, a councillor at the court of Rudolf II in Prague:

> I should not be said to be able to conquer Praxilla, Sappho
> and learned Corinna with my songs.
> I do not seek to be set in front of you, learned Fulvia;
> since my tiny genius flows from a dried-up fountain.
> O, if only my Muse were comparable with the skilful Morellae,
> a praise which was worthy of me would arise from my Muses.
> Supposing you think that I savour of the holy-uttering bards
> in my wit, my manners, my art, my poetry,
> with you as my judge, I would be criticised;
> but with you as my tutor, even my only one, O Erich,
> I would learn to despise the menaces of envy.[48]

In addition to demonstrating that she knew of three ancient Greek poetesses, Praxilla, Corinna and Sappho, the poem also shows that she was aware of several contemporary women poets writing in Latin; the recently deceased Italian, Olympia Fulvia Morata (1526–1551), and

---

[46] It includes such writers as Nossis, and in the Roman period, Theophila (Martial II.69) and Julia Balbilla; Byzantine Greek writers, who include the fourth-century empress Eudocia, the ninth-century hymnodist Kassia, and the medieval epic poet Anna Comnena; fifteenth-century Italians such as Alessandra Scala, and the seventeenth-century Englishwoman Bathsua Makin, though there is less of a connected history to be drawn for the use of Greek (at least in Western Europe) than there is for Latin. See J. McIntosh Snyder, *The Woman and the Lyre: Women Writers in Classical Greece and Rome* (Bristol, 1989).

[47] J. Stevenson, 'Rereading Sulpicia' (forthcoming).   [48] *Parthenicon* I, sig. C.3.

the three learned daughters of Jean de Morel in Paris, whom we have already met, Camille, Lucrèce and Diane.[49]

The second poem is in honour of the Dutch polymath Anna Maria van Schurman, by her friend and admirer Jan Smet.[50]

> To the most noble Belgian Anna, shown forth as an incomparable virgin, these others are shown, and you may read their very own Latin epigrams in the works of Grudius and Posthius.

Anna ⎰ Suys, a nun,   in Nicholas Grudius
⎱ van Pallandt ⎱
⎱ Utenhove   ⎰ in Iohann Posthius
⎱ MARIA à SCHURMAN

> The spacious antiquity of the world remembers three Annas;[51]
> Ten lustra (fifty years) of the present age have brought three.
> Now, our little Northern kingdom vaunts with praise for another,
> And Belgia sings of three Annas in our own time.
> Whoever wishes, may praise the ages and times past;
> Our own times give me their own Annas.
> It is right to add three to the Muses, and there will not nine be as before;
> But twelve, in the company that makes up the Muses' chorus.
> What Annas will envious Spain set against ours?
> Whom will Italy, or learned France give that are similar?
> Or any nation lying anywhere under the sun which is famous
> For glory, for scholarship or for genius?
> If, however any country were to count equal ones [Annas], there comes a fourth
> Who must be held the equal of them all, and must be placed before all others:
> She who doubles the name of Anna [*Anna* Schurm-*anna*], from the stock of Schurman,
> Anna, the eternal ornament of all Annas and of her sex:
> This will be the Anna for me. Nor will you, our Anna Perenna, find
> An equal for your tongue, and hand, and mind.[52]

---

[49] S. F. Will, 'Camille de Morel: a Prodigy of the Renaissance', *PMLA* 51 (1936), pp. 83–119.

[50] Who for some obscure reason signs it in English form as I. Smith. The text is in van Schurman, *Opuscula*, p. 342.

[51] By the three Annas of antiquity he probably means the Old Testament Anna, or Hannah, mother of the prophet Samuel, the New Testament Anna, the prophetess mentioned in Luke 2.36–38, and the Carthaginian Anna, sister of Dido, in the fourth book of the *Aeneid*.

[52] Anna Perenna is a minor Roman goddess associated with the turning of the years: Smet suggests that Anna van Schurmann's unsurpassed learning gives her semi-divine status. Ovid made an identification between the Carthaginian Anna, sister of Dido, alluded to in the first line, and the Roman goddess Anna Perenna (*Fasti* III, 545). This is a further indication of how consciously witty, clever and allusive this epigram is.

Smet thus proclaims his friend Anna van Schurman's unique quality, but
in the context of her being the fourth learned Anna to grace the Low
Countries. Evidence for the abilities of the first three is not dependent on
Smet's assertion alone. As he declares, a verse exchange between Anna
Suys and Nicholas Grudius is preserved in the latter's *Epigrammata*,[53] while
some verses of Charles Utenhove's two talented nieces, Anna Pallantia
(b. *c.* 1560) and Anna Utenhovia (dates unknown), are printed in Johannes
Posthius' *Parerga*.[54] Thus, in both Weston's poem and Smet's, the literary achievements of learned women are mapped against those of their
near-contemporaries: their achievement, therefore, is necessarily seen as
outstanding rather than freakish. These women, *pace* Day, are not represented as 'monsters'. We may note that when the new university of Utrecht
was founded in 1636, its rector, Gisbert Voetius, asked van Schurman
to write the customary Latin ode for the inaugural ceremony: a very
public honour.[55] Voetius also arranged for her to attend lectures there
(though unseen by the male students, which implies a special arrangement rather than the establishment of a precedent for co-education).

Moreover, though Smet's rhetoric implies the answer 'no', the question, 'Quas Latium, aut similes Gallia docta dabit?' is readily answered
positively. Learned women can be found, neither singly nor in battalions,
but in small groups, not only in Italy and France, but also in England
and Spain and Portugal, in the sixteenth century.[56] Italy produced such

[53] Ranutius Gherus [Jan Gruter], *Delitiae Poetarum Belgicorum, huius superiorisque aevi illustrius*, 3 vols.
(Frankfurt, 1614) II, p. 586. She is also noticed in M. Balen, *Descriptio urbis Dordracenae (Beschrijvinge
der Stad Dordrecht)* (Dordrecht, 1677), p. 203, in a section on 'Geleerde Mannen en Jonk-vrouwen
van Dordrecht' (learned women are listed beside men: there was another contemporary
woman student of Latin (and Greek) in Dordrecht, Margarita Godewyk).
[54] J. Posthius, *Iohannis Posthii Germershemii parergorum poeticorum pars prima et pars altera* (Heidelberg, 1595)
139, 204, 339–40. Some further distichs by both young women are also printed in J. Monavius,
Symbolum Iacobi Monavi . . . variis variorum auctorum carminibus (Görlitz, 1595), pp. 221–3, unknown
to Smet.
[55] *Inclytae et antiquae urbi Trajectinae nova academia nuperrime donatae gratulatur*: she also wrote a Dutch
version, separately printed (*Sermoen van de Nutticheydt der Academien ende Schoelen mitsgaders der
Wetenschappen ende Consten die in de selve gheleert werden . . . door Gisbertus Voetius* (Utrecht, 1636)).
She makes a pointed comment in this address about the exclusion of women from the student
body. A very similar situation is found in Padua in 1487, when Cassandra Fedele, Maiden of
Venice, was invited to give the gratulatory oration for Bertucio Lambero, who was receiving
the honours of the liberal arts: 'there is not a little irony in the fact that Cassandra was invited
to address a body of scholars among whom she was not allowed to study' (M. L. King and
A. Rabil, *Her Immaculate Hand: Selected Works By and About the Woman Humanists of the Quattrocento*
(Binghamton, NY, 1983), p. 69).
[56] Smet is of course writing in the seventeenth century (when, indeed, Italy, France and Spain
would show a smaller tally of women writing in Latin); but since his three Low Countries
Annas other than Anna Maria van Schurman are all products of the late sixteenth century, it
is fair to compare the picture across sixteenth- rather than seventeenth-century Europe.

women writers in the ancient languages as Olympia Morata, Cassandra Fedele, Angela and Isotta Nogarola,[57] and Laurentia Strozzi;[58] France had a number of women associated with the court or the 'Pléiade', including the Morel sisters, Louise Sarrasin, and Marie de Gournay;[59] in England, there were women such as the Cooke sisters, most of the female relatives of Henry VIII, Bathsua Makin, and Rachel Jevon;[60] Spain and Portugal had Beatriz Galindo ('La Latina'), Joanna Contrera, and Luisa Sigea, among many others.[61] The presence of women in educated humanist groups is an international phenomenon of the sixteenth century.

The story of women and education has always tended to concentrate on the relatively familiar and well-surveyed territories of England and Italy. But one of the most significant things about humanism was its ability to overleap political and linguistic boundaries, facilitated by the adoption of common languages (Latin, Greek, later French). While the Romance-speaking countries of Europe increasingly tended to agree in leaving Latin to men in the seventeenth century, a surprising number of learned women (some of them prodigiously so) continued to appear in Germany, the Low Countries, and Scandinavia. The principal reasons for this difference between Northern Europe and the rest are probably religious, and to some extent political. By the early seventeenth century, Italy and Spain were in the grip of the counter-reformation, a movement prejudicial to both learning and women, while the French language had acquired a commanding position not merely in France itself, but also in England and central Europe; and the status of *all* national vernaculars had noticeably risen. The extreme North was relatively aloof from these developments, and thus continued to have more of a place for women Latinists. Calvinist and Lutheran circles in Germany, the Low Countries and Scandinavia positively encouraged textual scholarship, while Protestantism defended (up to a point)

[57] See M. L. King, 'Thwarted Ambitions: Six Learned Women of the Italian Renaissance', *Soundings* 59 (1976), pp. 276–304, and 'The Religious Retreat of Isotta Nogarola', *Signs* 3 (1978), pp. 807–22; King and Rabil, *Her Immaculate Hand*.

[58] G. Pierattini, 'Suor Lorenza Strozzi, poetessa domenicana (1514–1591)', *Memorie domenicane* 59 (1942), pp. 113–15, 142–45, 177–83; 60 (1943), pp. 19–25.

[59] See Will, 'Camille de Morel'; L. Feugère, *Les femmes poètes au xviᵉ siècle*, (Paris, 1860); M. H. Ilsley, *A Daughter of the Renaissance: Marie le Jars de Gournay: Her Life and Works* (The Hague, 1963); L. Clark Keating, *Studies on the Literary Salon in France, 1550–1615* (Cambridge, MA, 1941); W. Gibson, *Women in Seventeenth-Century France* (Basingstoke, 1989).

[60] Gardiner, *English Girlhood*; Ezell, *The Patriarch's Wife* and *Writing Women's Literary History* (Baltimore, 1993); Schleiner, *Tudor and Stuart Women Writers*.

[61] D. G. Molleda, 'La cultura femenina en la epoca de Isabel la Catolica', *Revista de Archivos, Bibliotecas y Museos* 61 (1955), pp. 137–95; T. Oettel, 'Una cathedrática en el siglo xvi, Lucía de Medrano', *Boletín de la Real Academia de la Historia* (1935), p. 310.

women's right to form independent judgements. Protestant interest in accurate Bible-texts led to the cultivation not only of Latin, but of Greek and Hebrew. A number of the scholars involved were blessed with clever daughters, and educated them in these tongues.

Early modern women Latinists in Germany, the Low Countries and Scandinavia fall almost entirely into three familiar categories. They are either the daughters of university professors, or they are royal, or they are noblewomen from families with a strong commitment to culture. Although by the seventeenth century, Italian women of the élite culture wrote in Italian, many of the Fürstinnen, Herzoginnen and Prinzessen of Northern Europe were highly educated, and the knowledge of Latin was quite widespread among them. There were some spectacularly well-educated German noblewomen at this time, for example, Catherine Albertus (fl. c. 1600) and the princess Ernesta Augusta Anhalt-Bernburg (1636–1659), both of whom read Hebrew, Greek and Latin. It is therefore not surprising to find that much of the women's Latin poetry of this period is court poetry. Elizabeth Koolaart (née Hoofman), still writing in Hesse in the early eighteenth century, seems to stand at the end of this tradition of educated women writing very public verse.[62] Similarly, there is a goodly number of professors' daughters, of whom the most distinguished was the already-mentioned Anna Maria van Schurman, the most outstanding woman scholar of early modern Holland. She was known far beyond the Low Countries, especially after the publication in English of *The Learned Maid* (1659). She learned Latin, Greek, Hebrew, Syriac, Coptic, and Chaldaic, and acquired a very public position as a woman scholar, exchanging letters and poems with a wide variety of correspondents, male and female, including Salmasius and Descartes. Her circle in Holland included other learned women, notably the Roemers sisters, Anna and Maria (nicknamed Tesselschade).[63] Other late-sixteenth- and seventeenth-century Northern

[62] Woods and Fürstenwald, *Schriftstellerinnen*, p. 1. Other early modern German princesses who wrote surviving Latin poetry include Catharina Ursula, Landgräfin von Hessen-Kassel (1593–1615), and Sybille Ursula, Herzogin von Holstein-Glücksburg (1629–1671) (ibid., pp. 51 and 53). On Koolaart, see J. Hoeufft, *Parnasus Latino-Belgicus, sive plerique e poetis belgis latinis, epigrammate atque adnotatione illustrati* (Amsterdam and Breda, 1819), p. 201.
[63] For an account of various aspects of van Schurman's life, work and significance, see now M. de Baar, M. Löwensteyn, M. Monteiro, A. A. Sneller, eds., L. Richards, tr., *Choosing the Better Part: Anna Maria van Schurman (1607–1678)* (Dordrecht, Boston and London, 1996). For the general standard of women's education in the Low Countries, see M. A. Nauwelarts, 'Opvoeding van meisjes in de 16ᵉ eeuw', *Spiegel Historiael* 10 (1975), 130–37.

European woman scholars of similar background include Elizabeth Rings of Frankfurt, Euphrosine Aue of Colberg, and Hélène Sybille Moller of Altdorf.[64]

Scandinavia produced few women writing original poetry in Latin, but a goodly number of women scholars and bibliophiles. An interesting list by a seventeenth-century Dane of the learned women of his country reveals a rich and fascinating culture.[65] Many of the cultivated Danishwomen he mentions read Latin, and some of them are on record as having translated works from Latin, but all the works by women that he mentions are in Danish. Birgitte Thott, though she translated Seneca's works, wrote no Latin poetry of her own. Like Lucy Hutchinson, she perhaps did not consider it appropriate. Queen Christina of Sweden was, as is well known, deeply cultivated, and a great collector both of manuscripts and of scholars. She has considerable importance to the history of culture as a patron and bibliophile, and in this respect, she had a female counterpart in Denmark, the noblewoman Catherine Brahe, who belonged to one of the most important intellectual families in Renaissance Denmark, and who built up a stupendous library in her house at Hredholm (frequently mentioned by Schecht).

If the poem attributed to her is actually her own work, the most distinguished woman Latin poet in early modern Scandinavia was another female member of the Brahe clan, Sophie Brahe (c. 1556–1643), sister of the famous astronomer Tycho. During her twelve-year engagement to her future second husband, a penurious astrologer, a long, verse letter in Latin, *Urania Titani*, celebrating her love for the absent Erik, was published by Tycho Brahe at Uraniborg. The work is either by Sophie, or by Tycho writing in her name.[66] Other Scandinavian women Latin poets, whose authorship is unambiguous, include Cille Gad (1675–1711)[67] and Sophie Brenner (1659–1730).[68]

---

[64] G. C. Lehms, *Teutschlands galante Poetinnen* (Frankfurt am Main, 1715), pp. 169–71, Woods and Fürstenwald, *Schriftstellerinnen*, pp. 3 and 71.

[65] M. Schecht, 'Schediasma, exhilbens specimen de eruditis mulieribus Daniae', *Nova Literaria Maris Balthici et Septentrionis* (Lübeck, 1700), pp. 209–219.

[66] The text is *Urania Titani: Urania til Titan*, in *Resenii Inscriptiones Hafniensis* (privately printed, Uraniborg, 1594). On the authorship question, see J. L. E. Dreyer, *Tycho Brahe: A Picture of Scientific Life and Work in the Sixteenth Century* (Edinburgh, 1890) 202n.

[67] M. S. Jensen, ed., *A History of Nordic Neo-Latin Literature* (Odense, 1995), p. 77. There is a poem of Gad's in Th. Jacobæus, *Dissertatio de oculis insectorum*, Copenhagen, University Library, Oslo, 1708.

[68] S. Brenner, *Poetiska dikter* (Stockholm, 1713 and 1732). K. M. Wilson, *Encyclopedia of Continental Women Writers*, 2 vols. (Chicago and London 1991) I, p. 171.

THE PURPOSES OF WOMEN'S EDUCATION

In order to understand the position of learned women, it may be as well to begin by asking what women might be educated *for*. The uses of Latin in the Renaissance were various: Latin was the language of the clerisy, of the universities (Europe's universities started to be founded in the twelfth and thirteenth centuries: by the Renaissance, Bologna, Paris, Oxford, Salerno and some others were well established); and also of lawyers, diplomats, scientists, and doctors – people whose professional lives made it necessary, or at least useful, to maintain a community of culture which crossed the boundaries imposed by national languages.[69] It is often assumed that women would have none of these uses for Latin. Jardine, for example, has seen an absence of productive purpose in women's writing, stating that women were not involved in retrieving the residue of antiquity (a central preoccupation of humanist scholarship).[70]

This was perhaps not universally the case. The detailed and technical letter of Franciscus Modius to Joanna Pallantia on the text of the letters of the younger Pliny suggests that she, at least, was actively a part of the international world of textual scholarship.[71] Margarita Velsen, wife of Conrad Peutinger, not only shared very fully in her husband's antiquarian pursuits, but even wrote an antiquarian study of her own, on the statues, representations and inscriptions of Augustus found at Vienna.[72] Both women were certainly unusual; but their correspondents, again, do not represent them as freaks of nature. Similarly, a very few women were independent members of the clerisy, and became university professors or scientists, though only in very exceptional circumstances, and almost invariably in succession to their fathers' positions.[73]

---

[69] Note that P. Burke, *The Art of Conversation* (Cambridge, 1993), pp. 34–65, suggests the continued use of Latin as a means of communication down to the nineteenth century in many contexts *beyond* those of the academy: his argument is not addressed to the issue of gender, but is clearly relevant to it.

[70] Jardine, 'O decus Italiae', pp. 812–17.

[71] F. Modius, *Francisci Modii Brug. Novantique lectiones, tributae in Epistolas centum et quod excurrit* (Frankfurt, 1584), pp. 49–54.

[72] München, Bayerische Staatsbibliothek, clm. 4018 (1511).

[73] The latter, a very interesting group, include Constanza Calenda, who became a lecturer at Naples in the fourteenth century, Dorotea Bocchi at Bologna in the fifteenth, and Francisca Lebrija at Alcalà in the sixteenth: all succeeded their fathers. It is necessary to observe, lest this seem bizarrely anachronistic, that in the sixteenth century, a professor was generally an individual licensed to lecture at home: he (or she) did not necessarily appear in a lecture-hall before crowds of students, nor was he (or she) necessarily burdened with all the additional business of a twentieth-century professor.

An important question in addressing the status of learned women, and the relevance of learning to more than the occasional talented freak, is whether learning in a woman is perceived as compatible with marriage. In Renaissance Italy, as is well known, aspiration to authorship was generally (though not invariably) understood to preclude the possibility of marriage. A female scholar was expected to be a virgin. Her position was understood by male contemporaries as that of a Sibyl or a Muse rather than a co-worker. This is clearly illustrated by the biographies of the sisters Isotta and Ginevra Nogarola. Isotta Nogarola remained in the world, but as a spinster, a situation which caused her a great deal of difficulty. She seems to have found the ambiguities of her position, and the ambivalence with which she was treated, increasingly hard to deal with, and retreated into depressed isolation.[74] Ginevra, on the other hand, married, and stopped writing. Her loss of virginity is perceived by some contemporaries, notably by Damiano Borgo, who says as much in a letter to Isotta, as a contamination which prevents her from continuing to write.[75] But this quite well-known feature of Italian humanism has perhaps occupied too much space in the overall picture of educated women's lives in Renaissance Europe. Even in Italy, the issue of virginity is not always raised: such women as Battista Malatesta or Isabella d'Este married without losing their status as scholars (their far more important roles as patrons represented a powerful incentive for humanist men to avoid invoking the paradigm of virginity which they applied to the daughters of the professional classes). We may also note the existence of Clara Lanzavegia, wife of Iacobo Lanzavegia, and author of verses to Mario Philelphus,[76] and the marriages of Laura Cereta, Cassandra Fedele, and the scholarly prodigy, Olympia Morata.[77]

Outside Italy, the devaluation of perpetual virginity as a sanctified state in Protestant society and the value placed on marriage may have helped women who wished to combine scholarship with a relatively conventional life-pattern (some, such as Anna Maria van Schurman and Camille de Morel, did not so wish; in both cases, their continued celibacy was not for want of proposals). Paul Melissus Schede (correspondent of a number of learned women, including Queen Elizabeth

[71] King, 'The religious retreat'.

[75] L. Jardine, 'Isotta Nogarola: Women humanists – education for what?', *History of Education* 12 (1983), pp. 231–44, p. 236 (see also King and Rabil, *Her Immaculate Hand*, pp. 11–13).

[76] E. Abel, ed., *Isotae Nogarolae Veronensis Opera quae supersunt omnia*, 2 vols. (Vienna, 1886), II, pp. 361–4.

[77] King and Rabil, *Her Immaculate Hand*, pp. 22–23.

and Camille de Morel) was married to Aemilia Jordan, daughter of a councillor in the Palatinate, who wrote Latin and French poetry.[78] His friend the doctor and poet Johann Posthius was married to Rosina Brosamerus, who has left at least one poem.[79] Similarly, the fact that the mother of the published Latin poet Camille de Morel, Antoinette de Loynes, was also a published poet (in French) is an indication that French humanists, also, did not believe education was an impediment to women's marriage. We might also note in passing that Balthasar Venatori's panegyric on Jan Gruter mentions that his mother, Catharina Tishem, read Latin, Greek, French, Italian, and English, though she wrote nothing: such accomplishment is presented by Venatori as unusual rather than prodigious.[80] Other respected women Latin poets of the educated bourgeoisie (rather than the high aristocracy) who married include Elizabeth Jane Weston (Leon), Olympia Morata (Grundler), Luisa Sigea (de Cuevas), Anna Pallantia (Rulant), Jeanne Otho (Mayart), Bathsua Rainolds (Makin), and Elizabeth Hoofman (Koolart).

The learned and well-connected Sir John Harington may have spoken for many, and certainly speaks for what most modern scholars would a priori assume to be an early modern male reaction,[81] in writing his epigram, 'A refusall of a learned wife'.[82]

> You wished me to a wife rich fair and yung,
> Which hath y[e] Latine French and Spanish toung.
> I thanke you Sir, but I will haue none such
> For why, I thinke one toung to bee to much.
> But loue you not y[e] learned? – As my life
> The learned scoller, not y[e] learned wife.

[78] P. Melissus Schede, *Schediasmata* (Paris, 1586), pp. 631–2, 672.
[79] Posthius, *Parerga*, pp. 296–7.
[80] L. Forster, *Janus Gruter's English Years* (Leiden, 1967), pp. 88–89.
[81] Harington's sentiments may be paralleled by those of a slightly younger contemporary, John Owen, in his *Epigrammatum Ioannis Owen Oxoniensis Cambro-Britanni libri tres ad Henricum Principem Cambriae* (London, 1622), II, no. 104:

> Mulier quale animal?
> Sensu intacta caret virgo, cum nupta maritum
> sensit, habit sensum, sed ratione caret.

(What kind of creature is a woman? An intact virgin is lacking in sensibility; but when she is married and experiences a husband, she has sensibility, but loses reason): here is a direct statement that in Owen's view, sexual and intellectual fulfilment for women were completely incompatible.
[82] Oxford, Bodleian Library MS eng. poet. e. 14, f. 87. Punctuation is mine. Also printed in J. Harington, *Orlando Furioso in English Heroical Verse, with his Epigrams*, 3rd edn (London, 1634) IV, no. 7, in a variant form: the most significant variant is in the last line: 'A learned *Mistris*, not a learned wife'.

However, we cannot simply let him speak for all sixteenth-century male humanists, or even assume that this was the only thing Harington himself had to say on the subject. He was personally friendly with the learned and virtuous Cooke sisters (indeed, he quotes one of Catherine's poems in the notes to his translation of *Orlando Furioso*), all four of whom were classically educated to the extent of Latin and Greek verse composition by their father, Sir Antony Cooke. Far from finding that their learning condemned them to spinsterhood, the four girls became the wives of some of the most politically significant men in Elizabethan England.[83] We must ask ourselves, in fact, whether Sir Antony educated his daughters precisely *in order* to make such brilliant matches – his own career, let it be noted, was distinctly in eclipse by the time they reached adulthood.[84] While the average man, even the average nobleman, might not have cared for an educated wife, the element of Elizabethan society which was internationalist and progressive seems to have seen the matter rather differently.

But a more significant influence on the appropriation of humanist education on the male model for women is that it was considered appropriate for potential rulers of either sex. The number of princesses thus educated almost certainly exceeds the number of professors' wives and daughters referred to in preceding paragraphs. The use of Latin, including the composition of Latin verse, was necessary training for a ruler. Queen Isabella of Spain, who found herself ruling as a widow, had painfully to acquire a mastery of the discourse of rule (which meant not merely Latin, but the ability to understand and manipulate classical allusions) as a grown woman.[85] In consequence, she made sure that her daughters, who included Catherine of Aragon, were well educated. In turn, Catherine took great pains over the education of her daughter (Mary Tudor), as we may see from a letter she wrote her:[86]

And for your writing in Lattine I am glad that ye shall change frome me to Maister Federston, for that shall doo you moche good, to lerne by him to

---

[83] Respectively, Mildred married William Cecil, Lord Burghley, Anne married Sir Nicholas Bacon, Lord Keeper of the Great Seal, Elizabeth married first Sir Thomas Hoby then Lord Russell, Katherine married the diplomat Sir Henry Killigrew. Their children included Robert Cecil and Sir Francis Bacon.

[84] See M. E. Lamb, 'The Cooke Sisters: Attitudes towards Learned Women', in Hannay, ed., *Silent but for the Word*, pp. 107–25; Schleiner, *Tudor and Stuart Women Writers*; J. Stevenson, 'The Cooke Sisters' (forthcoming).

[85] G. Mattingly, *Catherine of Aragon* (London, 1942), pp. 16–18.

[86] H. Ellis, ed., *Original Letters Illustrative of English History*, 3 vols. (London, 1824) II, pp. 19–20, from London, British Library Cotton Vespasian F. xiii, f. 72.

write right. But yet some tymes I wold be glad when ye doo write to Maister
Federston of your own enditing when he hath rede it that I may se it. For it
shalbe a grete comfort to me to see You kepe your Latten and fayer writing
and all.

Other princesses of Mary's generation were similarly educated for
rule.[87] As an indication of this, we have brief Latin epigrams by Queen
Elizabeth, by Mary, Queen of Scots and by Lady Jane Grey.[88] Poetry
was not the business of these women's lives, but it was one of the ways
that they indicated their fitness for their real work of ruling.

It is also sometimes the case that daughters of the aristocracy whose
fathers had ambitions of inserting them into the royal family had them
educated in Latin. Certainly, the Latin education of three of the daughters of Edward Seymour, Duke of Somerset, who was Lord Protector,
and brother of Queen Jane Seymour, may be understood as directly
political. Seymour was accused of plotting to marry off Jane (1541–
61), the youngest of the three, to the sickly young prince, Edward VI
(whose early death brought Mary Tudor and then Elizabeth I to the
throne) in order to graft his own dynasty onto that of the Tudors. The
Seymour sisters had Thomas Norton as one of their tutors for three
years,[89] and the French littérateur, Nicholas Denisot, as another: Denisot
arrived in England rather suddenly, fleeing troubles of his own, and it
seems very much as if the Duke pounced on him as a useful adjunct to
his master-plan.[90] Similarly, the granddaughters of Thomas Howard,
the third Duke of Norfolk, another highly ambitious nobleman, are
believed (on rather less direct evidence) to have received education in
Latin together with their brother.[91] Norfolk was certainly suspected of

[87] Mattingly, *Catherine*, pp. 140–2. The level of power and responsibility actually exercised by
Catherine of Aragon is stressed by Jordan, 'Feminism and the Humanists', pp. 198–201.
[88] Some evidence for the Latinity of all three is collected in G. Ballard, *Memoirs of Several Ladies
of Great Britain Who Have Been Celebrated for their Writings or Skill in the Learned Languages, Arts and
Sciences* (Oxford, 1752).
[89] C. H. Cooper and T. Cooper, *Athenae Cantabrigienses* (Cambridge 1858–1913, 3 vols.), I, p. 485.
[90] C. Jugé, *Nicolas Denisot du Mans (1515–1559): Essai sur la vie et ses oeuvres* (Le Mans and Paris, 1907),
pp. 45–58. Denisot was later the editor of the sisters' distichs for Marguerite of Navarre.
[91] William Bercher says of the Howard girls, 'off this ffamelye be thre Systers [Jane, Catherine
and Margaret] whearof one lady Iane haward[,] who is of such marvelous towardnes in
learnenge as ffewe men may compare wth her. bothe greke and lattyne is vulgare vnto her. her
composycon in versis so notable, that all the world dothe acknowledge her a worthye daughter
of a most worthy ffather' (Bord, ed., *The Nobility of Women*, I, p. 154). R. M. Warnicke, *Women of
the English Renaissance and Reformation*, (Westport, CO, and London, 1983), p. 101, points out that
the eminent Dutch scholar, Hadrianus Junius, became tutor to the Howard children in 1544:
Jane, the oldest (b. 1537) is likely to have benefited most.

seeking a marriage between his son and Mary Tudor, then Princess of Wales, in 1530/31, and may also have had designs on the young Edward for one of his granddaughters.[92] The classical education of Lady Jane Grey and her sister Katherine, and that of Arbella Stuart (who had a somewhat tenuous claim on the throne as a great-great-granddaughter of Henry VII), also points in the same direction.

In consequence, the Latinity of royal women and the high aristocracy created a potential window of opportunity for other women. Much of the patronage available to humanist scholars was bound up with the education of noble children, and some humanist scholars may have intentionally educated their daughters for a future as tutors. Certainly, a number of daughters of educated bourgeoisie and professors became teachers in their turn. Among other possible examples, the multilingual Luisa Sigea became tutor to the Infanta Maria of the royal court of Portugal, the young Olympia Morata took service with Renée d'Este, Duchess of Ferrara, who invited her to court as a companion to her daughter Anne, and in the next century, Bathsua Makin became the tutor of Charles I's daughter Elizabeth. Some careful parents may have seen competent female teachers as extremely desirable: the dangers of a princess reading with a male tutor are exemplified by the story of Paolo and Francesca, told in Dante's *Inferno*.[93]

The life of Bathsua Makin shows that education might be of some use to women in seventeenth-century England who needed, or wanted, to earn their livings, just as it had been in Renaissance Italy. Her first public manifestation is as the sixteen-year old author of *Musa Virginea* (a slim volume of poems in Latin, Greek, Italian, and French, with a few lines of Hebrew for good measure), which is quite manifestly aimed at attracting royal patronage, in which she failed for reasons outlined earlier.[94] However, she was more successful under Charles I, less overtly misogynistic than his father had been. Remarkably learned (she read Latin, Greek and Hebrew, French, Italian and Spanish), she was later chosen by Charles I as tutor to his daughter, the Princess Elizabeth (born 1635). In old age, she opened a school for gentlewomen at Tottenham High Cross in 1673, which promised her pupils a remarkably sophisticated curriculum:

---

[92] Warnicke, *Women*, pp. 38–9.   [93] *Inferno* v, 73–142.

[94] Interestingly, the contents of *Musa Virginea* (1616) suggest that she was setting her cap not only at James, but at Anne of Denmark: the queen's capacity for independent literary patronage is remarked on by L. L. Peck, *Court Patronage and Corruption in Early Stuart England* (London, 1993), pp. 68–72.

Gentlewomen of eight or nine years old that can read well may be instructed
in a year or two (according to their Parts) in the Latin and French Tongues;
by such plain and short Rules accommodated to the Grammar of the English
Tongue, that they may easily keep what they have learned . . . Those that
think one Language enough for a Woman, may forbear the Languages, and
learn onely Experimental Philosophy . . . the Rate certain shal be 20*l.* per
annum.[95]

But despite the best efforts of Bathsua Makin and others, daughters of
the educated classes in seventeenth-century England were not normally educated as their brothers were. Aphra Behn, the playwright, for
instance, probably a gentleman's daughter, and able to read and translate French, was defensive about her lack of acquaintance with Latin
and Greek.[96] John Norris, a philosopher sympathetic to women's learning, sent a long letter to his friend Elizabeth Thomas, with a sort of
curriculum, in which he says: 'for some of them [the authors listed]
there will be a Necessity of a Language or two, Latin is more difficult,
and French will now answer all, which therefore I would have you learn
out of Hand. It is the most commanding, and therefore most useful
Language at present'.[97]

Thus, seventeenth-century Englishwomen were advised to learn
French rather than Latin, if they learned anything at all. Men, also,
though Latin continued to function for them as a social marker (a
function it did *not* have for women), found that in practice, once they
had reached adulthood, 'French would now answer all'. Since, I would
suggest, much of women's education in Latin was for practical ends,
the declining value of Latin in society at large resulted in fewer women
taking an interest in either Latin or Greek. It is a significant indication
of changing trends that the most important French woman classicist
of the seventeenth century, Anne Dacier, confined her work entirely to
translation.

Another kind of life which might lead to a woman learning, or
even teaching, Latin is that of a religious, since some convents did
(though increasing numbers did not) educate girls in Latin. The tradition
of Latin learning for nuns seems to have lingered longest in the Low
Countries. The Flemish Augustinian convent of St Ursula in Louvain
harboured a number of English Latinists in the sixteenth century who

[95] Gardiner, *English Girlhood*, p. 224. See also pp. 230–1 on the sophistication of Makin's educational principles.

[96] In 'An epistle to the Reader', printed in J. Goulianos, ed., *By a Woman Writt: Literature from Six
Centuries by and about Women* (London, 1974), p. 99.

[97] Perry, *The Celebrated Mary Astell*, pp. 484–5, n. 60.

have left translations and some prose letters,[98] and the learned nun of Dordrecht mentioned earlier, Anna Suys (fl. c. 1600), was able to write Latin verse.[99] In Italy, Spain and France, however, Latin learning appears to be less and less important in convents. Laurenzia Strozzi (1514–91), an outstandingly learned Dominican nun who became a highly competent Latin poet, did so in rather exceptional circumstances. She was brought up in the Dominican convent of San Niccolò in Prato, and at thirteen decided to remain there and make her profession as a nun. Her education cannot be taken as characteristic of Italian convent life. A special tutor (presumably paid for by her wealthy and highly-educated family, who included a number of noted scholars) was sent to teach her Latin and Greek.[100]

One rather under-researched group who might have a particularly pressing reason to educate their daughters is that of recusant Catholics in Protestant countries.[101] Since Catholics were debarred from the Northern European universities (except in the liberal Netherlands), Catholics under Protestant rule had great difficulties in educating their children. Thus, they tended to educate daughters alongside sons, since these daughters would thereby be enabled to preside in turn over at least the early stages of their own children's education. There is some interesting evidence of this in the case of Anna Alcox, an English Catholic child who wrote two long and surprisingly competent poems (in English) at the age of six: plainly, Anna was receiving a great deal of instruction, and not only in the mysteries of her faith.[102] In the Catholic countries, the polarising of religious positions under the stress of Reformation left most convents sadly reduced in the opportunities they offered women: nuns increasingly spent their time in embroidery and confectionery.[103] Early modern Mexico appears to have been something of an exception, though Latin was abandoned in favour of the

---

[98] Warnicke, *Women*, pp. 134–5.   [99] See above, n. 53.

[100] Wilson, *Encyclopedia* II, pp. 1199; Pierattini, 'Suor Lorenza'.

[101] The importance of recusant Englishwomen in holding together the English Catholic families is emphasised by Sr. J. D. Hanlon, 'These be but women', in C. H. Carter, ed., *From the Renaissance to the Counter-Reformation: Essays in Honour of Garrett Mattingly* (London, 1966), pp. 371–397.

[102] Oxford, Bodleian Library, MS Eng. Poet. B.5, pp. 50–51. The only identified author in this rich collection of recusant poetry:

> 'This Anna above exprest, as you shall understand
> Is a little mayd of six yeares old who writ it with her hand.'

[103] Though see A. Hatherly, ed., *A Preciosa de Sóror Maria do Céu: Edição actualizado do Códice 3773 da Biblioteca Nacional prededida dum estudo Histórico*, (Lisbon, 1990) for the very substantial vernacular oeuvre of a Portuguese nun, Sóror Maria do Céu, and an account of the context of women's writing in Spanish and Portuguese convents in the sixteenth and seventeenth centuries.

vernacular.[104] The Protestant countries did not evolve any sort of institution comparable to the convent, though, as is well known, the English feminist Mary Astell argued that they should.[105]

As with all other generations of learned women, the chance of a classical education for young women in the seventeenth century was a matter of luck and sympathetic parents. This can be illustrated by an important Dutch humanist, Constantijn Huygens, who wrote warmly to, and in support of, various learned women, notably Anna Maria van Schurman, and the brilliant Roemers sisters, Anna and Tesselschade. Huygens was deeply concerned with education, and supervised that of his sons with meticulous care. He wrote the boys many poems, mostly in Latin, emphasising the importance of study. There is only one poem to his daughter, which is in simple Dutch, and about pies. While it suggests warmth, affection and a happy family life, it makes it absolutely clear that she is in a different category from her brothers. Interestingly, it was the sad history of Anna van Schurman which made him decide not to teach his daughter languages. He seems to have concluded from van Schurman's ultimate descent into heresy and subsequent social ostracism that educating women simply caused them to go mad.[106] He may have had a point, though not the one he thought he was making: Calvinism, even as interpreted in socially liberal Holland, laid great stress on patriarchal male authority, while the Labadists, the rather Quaker-like sect which van Schurman joined in late life, allowed her to preach and teach in a wholly independent manner. The attraction of this for a woman of intelligence and spirit is obvious.

The conclusion to such an essay as this, which covers two centuries or more and the whole of Europe, necessarily has a flavour of 'on the one hand . . . while on the other'. Nonetheless, some conclusions can usefully be drawn. First, women scholars were more involved in the humanist enterprise of the late fifteenth and sixteenth centuries than is often believed to be the case. Second, the forces ranged against the education of early modern women are various, but not monolithic. Social consensus as to whether women of a particular social class and milieu needed a classical education or not depended on the overall status of Latin: the declining number of women Latinists in the seventeenth

---

[104] See, for example, O. Paz, *Sor Juana: her Life and her World* (London, 1988) on Sor Juana Inés de la Cruz (1648–1695), a brilliant Spanish poet and playwright.

[105] Perry, *The Celebrated Mary Astell*.

[106] See M. de Baar, 'Now as for the faint rumours of fame attached to my name . . .', in de Baar et al., *Choosing the Better Part*, pp. 87–102.

century has to do with the triumph of the vernaculars as well as with the changing position of women as such. The fact that fewer women received advanced education in Latin and/or Greek from the end of the sixteenth century relates at least in part to the prodigiously enhanced possibilities offered by the great rise in status of Italian, French, English, and Spanish, and the consequent decline in the social usefulness of Latin. This is not so true in Northern Europe (i.e. the German-speaking regions and Scandinavia), where the absence of a language/dialect with the status of Tuscan Italian, Parisian French, London English, or Castilian Spanish left Latin more diplomatically and socially useful in the seventeenth and even the eighteenth century than was the case elsewhere.

Education-for-rule aside, a classical education did not have, for women, the function of marking social divisions which it did have for men. Throughout the early modern period, a male of the rank of 'gentleman' or above would normally be Latinate, but his wife or daughter might be anything from a Mildred Cooke to functionally illiterate, without this having any effect on her status. Therefore, women's education was not directly a function of class, but rather, even within the élite, dependent on the educational theories, social context, and aspirations of her immediate family, particularly those of her father.

Men's attitudes to the education of their own and other peoples' daughters cover an enormously wide range. One man might envisage his daughter's education in terms of pudding-making and the knitting of socks; another, of the same social class, generation, and milieu, might be looking about for a Greek tutor for his. The power of the daughters themselves to influence this is obviously limited; though at least one of the women discussed here, Marie de Gournay, acquired her education in the teeth of total parental indifference. We might also note that both Anna Maria van Schurman and Luisa Sigea established their right to benefit from lessons initially intended for their brothers by sheer force of will: while institutionally powerless, daughters were not inevitably passive victims of parental intentions.

CHAPTER 6

Pilgrimage to Parnassus: local intellectual traditions, humanist education and the cultural geography of sixteenth-century England

Warren Boutcher

INTRODUCTION

The Renaissance – so scholars have said for centuries – witnessed the rise of a new scholarship and a new education. Professional humanists and young aristocrats alike bathed themselves, for five to ten years, in ancient prose and verse, before they entered on active careers in State, Church or School. Reading – informed reading of classical texts – became the preferred preparation for leadership. So much is well known.[1]

So much is well known, but we have not begun to appreciate how local, how personalised, and how applied the traditions and the uses of humanistic literacies were in early modern Europe. From the new political history of the Victorian scholar, James Anthony Froude, to the new social history of Lawrence Stone in the 1960s, the notion that sixteenth-century England experienced an educational revolution has been given a special place in accounts of political and social change in the post-Reformation period.[2] Insofar as textual and cultural studies have engaged with these histories, they have most usually done so via the literary analysis of printed and documentary sources in relation to 'political thought' and 'political culture', now established fields in early

This paper was completed during a period of leave in 1995/1996 granted under the Research Leave Scheme by the Humanities Research Board of the British Academy. I am very grateful to the Board for its support.
[1] A. Grafton, 'Quotations on Demand: The Rise and Fall of the Renaissance Soundbite', *Times Literary Supplement* January 31 (1996), p. 10. This quotation is also an acknowledgement that the pioneering work in the field to which this chapter is intended to be a contribution was undertaken by Anthony Grafton and Lisa Jardine in the 1980s. See in particular A. Grafton and L. Jardine, *From Humanism to the Humanities: Education and the Liberal Arts in Fifteenth- and Sixteenth-Century Europe* (London, 1986).
[2] J. A. Froude, *History of England from the Fall of Wolsey to the Death of Elizabeth*, fourth edition, 12 vols. (London, 1867–70), vol. I, pp. 47–50; L. Stone, 'The Educational Revolution in England, 1560–1640', *Past and Present* 28 (1964), 41–80.

modern studies.[3] Whether explicitly stated or not, one of the premisses of such work is that the educational revolution helped produce at the cultural level the integrated national consciousness that the state was seeking to impose at the political and administrative level.

Thus Frank Whigham, summarising the picture that emerges from the work done since 1950 by J. H. Hexter, Mark H. Curtis, Lawrence Stone, Kenneth Charlton, Joan Simon, Hugh Kearney and James McConica, writes as follows:

> So the ruling classes of the English Renaissance came to share a political and intellectual and stylistic self-concept, rather than the limited military one of the armed knight. . . . The combative chivalric ideology of moralized force was altered by new cooperative pressures of nationally centralized life; problems of power once solved by force were now submitted to a rule of words, of laws and principles that often seemed to the old order to be effete fraud and trickery. . . . English adoption of these ideas aroused a presumption of national destiny in the young man at the university.[4]

Relying implicitly on assumptions such as these, the study of political thought and culture usually involves a contextualised approach to the language and ideological arguments of a (usually printed) source conducted against the background of the court or the state and its battles with factions, subversives, rebels, and provincials. The poetic products of the English literary renaissance, together with translations, and rhetoric or courtesy manuals, are enlisted in this way for the study of the relationship between literature and the growth of court-centered cultural nationalism, or, in the early seventeenth century, between literature and oppositional or republican cultural nationalism – the 'country' ideology, blamed famously by Thomas Hobbes on the classical curriculum at Oxbridge.[5]

For British social historians anxious to reintegrate the history of local and regional communities with the history of national society, the consensus drawn out by Whigham about the effects of education provides a convenient axis of cultural differentiation for the plotting of

---

[3] For instances of both the strengths and the limitations of the former kind of work see *The Varieties of British Political Thought, 1500–1800*, eds. J. G. A. Pocock, G. J. Schochet and L. G. Schwoerer (Cambridge, 1993). For the latter kind of work see K. Sharpe, *Criticism and Complement: the Politics of Literature in the England of Charles I* (Cambridge, 1987); *Politics of Discourse: The Literature and History of Seventeenth Century England*, eds. K. Sharpe and S. N. Zwicker (Berkeley, 1987); A. Hadfield, *Literature, Politics and National Identity: Reformation to Renaissance* (Cambridge, 1994).

[4] F. Whigham, *Ambition and Privilege: the Social Tropes of Elizabethan Courtesy Theory* (Berkeley, 1984), pp. 13, 191–2.

[5] See Sharpe, *Criticism* and Hadfield, *Literature*.

change in the history of society. For Keith Wrightson and David Levine it is important to be able to state that men of yeoman status and above, through increased access to educational provision at grammar schools, private schools, universities and inns of court, enjoyed greater participation in the 'political and cultural life of the nation' at the expense of 'local loyalties and identities'. For it is the corollary to their argument that at the village level itself 'elements of local cultural homogeneity' were broken down in the early modern period, and a more marked differentiation became observable 'in terms of attitudes, education, and manners'.[6]

Pursuing a different argument, Mervyn James sets up a related contrast. On the one hand, the new humanist education disseminates a 'style of thinking' within which 'generalized propositions could be stated, and a discourse sustained which could claim universal validity', 'creating the systemized literary culture of school and university'. On the other hand, a more thoroughly local style of education still bound by the 'lineage culture' persists in households in the northern and border regions. In these households, the approach was 'personal and particularized', the 'validity of the modes of acceptable behaviour' was taken for granted within the 'restricted world to which alone they had relevance: that of the specific household community and its related clientele'. The thinking of this society 'was less philosophical and discursive than mythological, expressed in terms of exemplary myth and tale'.[7]

The argument of this chapter will be that as a matter of pedagogical and cultural practice, sixteenth-century English humanism retained elements of 'local' and 'household' education, that it too was personal and particularised, and expressed in terms of exemplary myth and tale. The social-structural and statistical study of the social composition of those going into higher education in the sixteenth and seventeenth centuries has combined with certain 1950s and 1960s anthropological assumptions about the universal developmental effects of literacy, and idealistic approaches to the history of technical rhetoric, to leave us with too Whiggish a framework for the reconstruction of the culture of educational and intellectual life in early modern England. An alternative strain in anthropology tells us, for example, that a particular form

---

[6] K. Wrightson and D. Levine, *Poverty and Piety in an English Village: Terling, 1525–1700*, second edition (Oxford, 1995), pp. 2, 14–15.
[7] M. James, *Society, Politics and Culture: Studies in Early Modern England* (Cambridge, 1986), pp. 270–1, 273.

of literacy cannot be detached from the social context in which it is transmitted and learned, that it should not be imagined as a kind of neutral technology autonomously productive of ' "empathy", "abstract context-free thought", "rationality", "critical thought" ', of 'the distinction of myth from history, the elaboration of bureaucracy, the shift from "little communities" to complex cultures'.[8]

Brian Street gives the example of a form of 'maktab' literacy particular to a village on the border between North East Iran and Afghanistan. In an atmosphere of economic expansion generated by oil money, local middlemen and traders would pick up this form of literacy in local religious schools ('maktabs') but then adapt it to the requirements of their new commercial positions. Street offers this as an example of the non-autonomous, the 'ideological' nature of literacy practice:

It was rooted in village institutions, and in the social relations of 'tajers' [middlemen] with other villagers and with city dealers on which their commercial success depended. The construction of this particular literate form was neither an individual matter nor was it a product of specific formal training. Although it emerged from 'maktab' literacy, for instance, it was not a product of 'maktab' pedagogy, which was directed towards a different cluster of meanings and usage. It was a development at the level of ideology, a social construction of reality embedded in collective practice in specific social situations.[9]

The terms of this anthropological analysis can and should be turned upon the history of the relationship between religious pedagogy and elite European Latin literacy in the late medieval and early modern periods. Until 1500 or so, the dynamic of even the elite young's education in literacy was exclusively religious, while Latin literacy was offered in localities by a European institution, the Roman Catholic Church, and oriented towards the pan-European professions and philosophies of theology, civil and canon law, and medicine. As clerks and middlemen between the nobility and the people the notaries of the Italian city republics had begun the secularisation of this tradition by adding in the teaching of classical literature and expertise in rare books and manuscripts.[10] The new, northern humanist, mass-produced print pedagogies of first Desiderius Erasmus then Petrus Ramus continued the

---

[8] B. V. Street, *Literacy in Theory and Practice* (Cambridge, 1984), pp. 1–2, 5.

[9] Street, *Literacy*, pp. 11–12.

[10] M. T. Clanchy, *From Memory to Written Record: England 1066–1307*, second edition (Oxford, 1993), pp. 13–14.

progressive secularisation of this church tradition, already turning an education in Latin towards a different 'cluster of meanings and usage' derived from the particularities of academic politics in international centres of learning such as Louvain and Paris, but adaptable to the requirements of the new ruling classes across Europe.[11]

Still more varied clusters of meaning and usage come into play, however, when we narrow in on the case of England, and even on 'border' localities in England, and throw in the question of the relationship between Latin and the vernacular.[12] For we should not allow the undeniable fact that the humanist pedagogies of Desiderius Erasmus and Petrus Ramus infiltrated the structure and practice of arts education in English grammar schools, universities and inns of court between 1520 and 1580 to be sufficient explanation of the culturally embedded nature of such humanistic literacy practices as resulted. They too were adaptations rooted in particular sets of social relations between local and more central institutions, between local middlemen and city politicians and traders, they too were neither an individual matter, nor a product of specific formal training, and they too gave rise to 'a social construction of reality embedded in collective practice in specific social situations' – new, elite versions of English cultural nationhood.[13] There may even be a case for saying that Tudor humanistic literacy as represented in the much studied vernacular pedagogical and rhetorical manuals is likewise predominantly an ideology linking borders, university and city, or subjugating borders to city, if we stretch the term 'border' to include any self-consciously 'local' place in the 'countries' outside the 'civilised' lowland core around London.

At the higher level, the chief institutional symptoms of educational revolution in the Tudor college were the appearance of the undergraduate or 'gentleman' commoner and the evolution of the office of the college tutor. In arts teaching, the tutor offered personally directed readings in antique and contemporary humanistic culture: such personally directed readings in textbooks and the works of canonical authors with a view to subsequent compilation and composition are at the core of arts pedagogy at all levels from early grammar to advanced study in this period. The curriculum as a whole offered a blend of dialectic, moral philosophy, history and rhetoric which could accommodate,

[11] Grafton and Jardine, *From Humanism to the Humanities, passim.*
[12] For a definition of border localities in Tudor England see note 82 below.
[13] Street, *Literacy*, p. 12.

if required, serious study in the quadrivium, or in 'science' (itself a blend of arithmetic, astronomy, geometry and geography).[14] From the point of view of the arts undergraduate, the revival of interest in Aristotelianism in Renaissance Oxford was but 'an element in a wider humanistic culture where the art of rhetoric with its ancillary disciplines of logic, history and modern languages prepared the university graduate for travel, government and statecraft as well as for the general discourse of cultivated society'.[15] A smattering of civil law and a course in the common law at the inns of court would complete the all-round education.

The overall service of varied and occasional teaching that resulted from this educational transformation helped the Tudor gentry 'supply their households with educated servants, and to provide their kin and other dependents with a secure and familial environment in which they would become acceptable members of polite society'.[16] In a letter of advice to his son, the provincial gentleman and magistrate, Sir Richard Grosvenor, made it clear that the mediation of his very local Cheshire concerns by national perspectives on religion and culture could be traced to the influence of his tutors at the Queen's College, Oxford: '"Tutores . . . are the fathers off spiritts, as haveing more influence over the resemblance off soules then carnall fathers over bodies"'.[17]

With, then, issues in cultural geography (as it might be called) in mind, the following investigation will approach Tudor humanism diachronically as a matter of increasingly local and eclectic intellectual traditions, and synchronically as a matter of personalised and heavily applied tutorial and reading contexts. In the process an attempt will be made to suggest a fresh perspective on one of the categories of literature – grammar and rhetoric manuals – which underpin the study of political thought and culture in the early modern period.

[14] In *The History of the University of Oxford*, Volume III, *The Collegiate University*, ed. J. McConica (Oxford, 1986) see J. McConica, 'The Rise of the Undergraduate College' pp. 1–68 (65–6); J. M. Fletcher, 'The Faculty of Arts', pp. 157–99 (168); J. Barton, 'The Faculty of Law' and 'Appendix: The King's Readers', pp. 257–93 (279–80); J. McConica, 'Elizabethan Oxford: The Collegiate Society', pp. 645–732 (693–6, 704, 716–22).

[15] McConica, 'Elizabethan Oxford', p. 721.

[16] J. McConica, 'Scholars and Commoners in Renaissance Oxford' in *The University in Society*, ed. L. Stone, 2 vols. (Princeton, 1974), vol. I, pp. 151–81 (181). See also, in *ibid.*, L. Stone, 'The Size and Composition of the Oxford Student Body 1580–1909', pp. 3–110 (24–6).

[17] Grosvenor's remark is quoted from Grosvenor MSS., item 45, Memoranda book p. 41 (held at Eaton Hall, Cheshire) in R. Cust and P. G. Lake, 'Sir Richard Grosvenor and the Rhetoric of Magistracy', *Bulletin of the Institute of Historical Research* 54 (1981), 40–53 (41).

LOCAL INTELLECTUAL TRADITIONS

In the third act of Shakespeare's *King Henry VIII* (1610–11), the king discovers that the great Cardinal who informs him he is committed to 'th'good of your most sacred person, and / The profit of the state' has been corruptly accumulating wealth in order – as Wolsey himself puts it – 'to gain the popedom / And fee my friends in Rome'. The writ sued against the Cardinal by his enemies is a *praemunire* – for those who illegally assert papal jurisdiction in England.[18] Two scenes later, adapting a passage from Holinshed's *Chronicles*, Shakespeare invents an exchange between the dowager Queen Katherine and Griffith, her gentleman usher, who has informed her of Wolsey's death and repentance. In dying, Wolsey had sought charity at an abbey in Leicester, but Queen Katherine begs leave 'to speak him / And yet with charity' (ironically?) as an ill example to the clergy, 'one that by suggestion / Tied all the kingdom'. Griffiths, however, undertakes to speak his good:

> *Griffiths:*   This cardinal,
> Though from an humble stock, undoubtedly
> Was fashion'd to much honour. From his cradle
> He was a scholar, and a ripe and good one,
> Exceeding wise, fair-spoken and persuading:
> Lofty and sour to them that lov'd him not,
> But to those men that sought him, sweet as summer.
> And though he were unsatisfied in getting
> (Which was a sin) yet in bestowing, madam,
> He was most princely: ever witness for him
> Those twins of learning that he rais'd in you,
> Ipswich and Oxford; one of which fell with him,
> Unwilling to outlive the good that did it,
> The other (though unfinish'd) yet so famous,
> So excellent in art, and still so rising,
> That Christendom shall ever speak his virtue.[19]

Two scenes previously we have seen Wolsey showing sweetness to men that seek him. In his valedictory speech, anticipating a time when he will be forgotten, he asks his secretarial protégé Thomas Cromwell, the son of a clothmaker, to 'say I taught thee . . . a way . . . to rise in, / A sure and safe one, though thy master miss'd it', exhorting him furthermore to 'Let all the ends thou aim'st at be thy country's,/ Thy

---

[18] William Shakespeare, *King Henry VIII*, ed. J. Margeson (Cambridge, 1990), III. 2. 173–4, 212–13, 340. I am putting to one side here as irrelevant the still vexed question of the extent of Fletcher's or another's co-authorship of the play.

[19] *Ibid.*, IV. 2. 32–3, 35–6, 43–4, 48–63.

God's and truth's'.[20] The qualified rehabilitation of Wolsey's reputation, continued by Griffiths, is part of the preparation for the Christian
georgic of Cranmer's prophecy of prosperity and peace under Elizabeth
I and James I that is to follow in act five. Said by early writers to have
been a butcher's son, Wolsey is described earlier in the play by his
enemy Buckingham as '[t]his Ipswich fellow', a 'butcher's cur' equipped
with a 'beggar's book' which '[o]utworths a noble's blood'.[21]

Faced with the task of showing Wolsey in a charitable light, and of
demonstrating his allegiance to his country rather than his friends in
Rome, Griffiths emphasises Wolsey's local roots and the specific way
in which he has sought to honour them. He claims that Wolsey has
tried to make a continuing reality of the pastoral story of his own rise
through 'natural' scholarship in humane learning from humble stock
to honour, by turning that story into a permanent social and intellectual tradition twinning his own local point of origin, Ipswich, with the
University of Oxford. The financial means, of course, is the tradition
of charitable endowments which, as we shall see, pre-dates and is trans-
muted by the Reformation, and which in this case briefly gave rise to
the Cardinal's College, Ipswich and Cardinal College, Oxford – later
Christ Church.[22]

The important point is that in the play, which needs to redeem
Wolsey for dramatic reasons, the chief evidence of Wolsey's commitment
to country and commonwealth rather than to international Roman
Catholicism, is his foundation of a local intellectual tradition redolent,
anachronistically, of secular Elizabethan and Jacobean benefactions.
In practice, both of Wolsey's foundations were failures and his suppression of monasteries in Suffolk caused much local antagonism; he
built up no personal property or contact with the county gentry in
the area; his family was only known amongst Ipswich's borough elite
and the source of his power lay in the political spaces between Oxford
and the court. So much is implied, in fact, in the opening acts of the
play itself, where the confrontation between Wolsey and Buckingham

---

[20] *Ibid.*, III. 2. 431–48; p. 203.
[21] *Ibid.*, I. I. 120, 122–3, 138. For Cranmer's prophecy see v. 4. 14–75.
[22] The college at Ipswich was a college of secular canons with a school attached, founded in 1528
   by the appropriation of local churches and the suppression of local monasteries – acts approved
   both by Pope Clement and Henry VIII. It was dissolved upon the fall of Wolsey in 1530. See
   The Victoria History of the Counties of England: Suffolk, ed. W. Page, 6 vols. (London, 1907–), vol. 2,
   pp. 142–4. The building of Cardinal College, Oxford began in 1525 but after Wolsey's fall it
   barely survived until re-founded as Christ Church in 1546 (McConica, 'Rise of the Undergraduate College', pp. 29–33).

is structured by the former's status as a self-made man of the court lacking in any local, landed substance.[23]

More typical of Tudor reform of the social and institutional arrangements linking the universities to the country than this route between East Anglia (in the event tied more firmly to Cambridge) and Oxford were the ties which linked Cambridge and the northern counties. Of the six Oxford and Cambridge colleges founded between 1496 and 1525, only Cardinal College was not the work of northcountrymen. John Fisher presided over the pre-Reformation Catholic reform of Cambridge, bringing Erasmus to Queens', founding two large colleges (St John's and Christ's), and turning the university into an international centre of learning. When he arrived, however, as a mercer's son from Beverley, Yorkshire, some time around 1483, his tutor at Michaelhouse was his fellow townsman William Melton. Forty years later, caught up in international theological controversy and defending the Real Presence in a work printed at Cologne, his stated model for strict attention to a (biblical) text was his fellow countryman and *praeceptor*'s admonition in a university tutorial to attend to all the details in a Euclidean geometrical diagram.[24]

Here, in this pre-Reformation context, an affectionate friendship and scholarly relationship is invoked as a bit of local colour for the pious fabric of Roman Catholic Latin Christendom (compare Griffiths' 'That Christendom shall ever speak his virtue'), and it was in such a cultural context that charitable endowments were offered by wealthy prelates in the fifteenth century and earlier.[25] With the Reformation, however, the interest of the landed and mercantile classes in the universities reached a new pitch, and with that interest came a new era in the foundation of local intellectual traditions linking particular localities with particular colleges. Endowed with land in specific places, colleges were drawn into the local and county communities of the landed gentry, and vice-versa. Likewise, grammar schools were founded with closed exhibitions to specific colleges attached, and the colleges would become

[23] D. MacCulloch, *Suffolk and the Tudors: Politics and Religion in an English County 1500–1600* (Oxford, 1986), pp. 151, 227–8. Norfolk says of Wolsey to Buckingham that 'being not propped by ancestry, whose grace / Chalks successors their way, not called upon / For high feats done to th'crown, neither allied / To eminent assistants, but spider-like / Out of his self-drawing web – O! gives us note, / The force of his own merit makes his way, / A gift that heaven gives for him, which buys / A place next to the king' (I. I. 59–66).
[24] D. R. Leader, *A History of the University of Cambridge*, Volume 1, *The University to 1546* (Cambridge, 1988), pp. 264–7, incl. n.8.
[25] V. Morgan, 'Cambridge University and "The Country" 1560–1640' in *University in Society*, ed. Stone, vol. I, pp. 183–245 (197).

involved in the selection of both schoolmasters and scholars. This new breed of benefactor thought more concretely of his or her 'native community' than grand Catholic prelates like Fisher and Wolsey, or international Latin pedagogues like Erasmus, and around these formal institutional links between colleges and local communities accumulated other 'customary patterns of patronage and connection'. Even the choice of a tutor for a young member of the county elite was often based on common local origins – fellows at Gonville and Caius tended for statutory reasons to be Norfolk or Suffolk men, and they tended as tutors to attract East Anglian clients.[26]

Nevertheless, no hard and fast distinction can be made between Catholic 'medieval' and Protestant 'renaissance' endowments as elements in educational reformation. Nor must the sense in which colleges could be extensions of the founders' households and careers – even in the sixteenth century – be neglected.[27] The statutory arrangements of Corpus Christi, the Oxford foundation of the bishop of Winchester, Lincolnshire-born Richard Fox, were designed to give it a very specific geographical constituency derived from the origins and careers both of the founder and of another great benefactor, Hugh Oldham, the Lancashire-born bishop of Exeter (kin of Oldham's steward, William Frost, were also preferred). In practice these arrangements weighed equally with another factor: counties and dioceses in which the college held lands and collected rents. Although Lincolnshire and Lancashire were represented, 'the general result was a society made up of men chiefly from the home counties, west country and south, with a significant concentration of strength also from the west midlands', especially in the case of the commoners whose counties of origin can be identified.[28] Even allowing for the fact that these statutory and institutional arrangements were flexible in practice, this begins to suggest that not just courtly images of the 'country', but specific cultural relationships to land, locality, household, and even lineage and kin, the factors which partly structured routes into higher education and the selection of tutors, cannot be dissociated from the social conditions in which humanistic literacy was acquired, and thus from the mentalities thereby formed.

The case of Corpus Christi – undoubtedly a 'renaissance' college – and its geographical constituency in the south-east also suggest a different

---

[26] *Ibid.*, pp. 190, 192–4, 197, 205, 206, 211–13. The quotations are from p. 197 and p. 205 respectively.

[27] McConica, 'Scholars and Commoners', pp. 177–9.

[28] McConica, 'The Collegiate Society', pp. 670–1.

slant on the traditional sources for the study of Tudor pedagogy. For as far as the ideology of Tudor humanism evident in vernacular ped-agogies and arts of rhetoric is concerned, the core of educational reform in the mid-Tudor period was the proliferation of institutional and customary ties between particular schools and towns in the northern counties, the north-west, Wales and the Welsh borders, and particular Oxford and Cambridge colleges, most notably Trinity (Cambridge) and the early Elizabethan seminary of establishment Protestant human-ism, St John's College (Cambridge). These areas relied more heavily on certain key 'feeder' schools and the endowment of specific, local intellectual traditions than the more 'civilised' south-eastern counties such as Norfolk or Kent, and the institutionalisation of such ties began to accentuate a sense of individual student county identities from within the traditional medieval division of northerners and southerners.[29] The local end of this can be seen at work in documentation pertaining to the relationship between St John's College, Cambridge, and Pock-lington School in Yorkshire, originally founded by Dr John Dowman (a Pocklington man) along with five scholarships (funded by lands in Yorkshire and Derbyshire) linking the school to the College. St John's had the power to prefer candidates for the headmastership, and the extant correspondence between the two institutions shows very clearly how grievances about the running of the school and the diversion of the 'Schollershipps belonginge our Schoole . . . to straungers' contribute strongly to the formation of political consciousness in this particular 'country' ('The Contry that do depend upon this fundacon [Pocklington School] is great, and therefor your care had not nede but be so also').[30] This is just one of many examples of the college's connections with schools in outlying regions: St John's also had the power to prefer candidates for the head- and under-masterships at Shrewsbury's gram-mar school, and would normally take the opportunity to advance one of its own graduates from the area. The regional bias at St John's was so strong, in fact, that the original foundation statutes ordaining that 'at least' half of the twenty-eight 'foundress's fellows' should come from the nine northern counties were amended to a stipulation of 'at most' half, probably on orders from the court.[31]

[29] Morgan, 'Cambridge University', pp. 193–4, 198–9, 209.
[30] R. F. Scott, *Notes from the Records of St John's College, Cambridge* (privately printed, 1889–99), extract from the *Eagle* [the St John's College Magazine], vol. 19, no. 111, December 1896, pp. 1–2, 7, 9, 17.
[31] Morgan, 'Cambridge University', pp. 194, 201–2.

Once at Cambridge, northern and north-western grammar school boys were more likely to pick up court connections or to benefit from the greater and more frequent and more intimate permeability of the university to the societies of the more proximate or 'Home' counties – avid for educated servants of various kinds (tutors, chaplains, secretaries, stewards, and advisers) – than they were to return immediately north. For their principal acquisition was 'an eligibility for employment in [or – we might add – marriage into] more hospitable southern counties', and this probably led to an internal brain-drain that exacerbated regional differentiations.[32]

The contemporary cultural model for the hospitable southern county was, by the time the scholar William Lambard published his pioneering *Perambulation*, undoubtedly Kent. In Shakespeare's representation (*c*.1589–92) of the rebellion mounted against London by Jack Cade and his Kentish companions, the rebels capture the Chancellor Lord Say and blame him for the corruption caused by the bringing in of grammar schools, books and printing, literacy and the justices of the peace. Seeking to save his skin Say invokes the local intellectual tradition which has taken scholars and courtiers from the universities and the court *to* Kent:

> *Say*: Kent, in the *Commentaries* Caesar writ,
> Is termed the civil'st place of all this isle:
> Sweet is the country because full of riches,
> The people liberal, valiant, active, wealthy. . . .[33]

This is the civilised Kent of Lambard, who likewise records Caesar's comments on its inhabitants' 'humanitie and gentlenesse', placed in a contemporary context by Lambard's later observations that this civility is more recently due to the transplantation of '*Courtiers, Lawyers, & Marchants*' and with them 'good letters and, . . . the knowledge of the lawes', from London.[34] From Say's elite, educated perspective, Kent is '*bona terra, mala gens* [a good land, bad people]', a place which needs to be repopulated with more deserving inhabitants.[35] But this civilised,

---

[32] Morgan, 'Cambridge University', pp. 194, 209–210; V. Morgan, 'Country, Court and Cambridge University, 1558–1640: a Study in the Evolution of a Political Culture' (Ph.D. thesis, University of East Anglia, 1983), p. 132.

[33] William Shakespeare, *The Second Part of King Henry VI*, ed. M. Hattaway (Cambridge, 1991), IV. 7. 49–52.

[34] W. Lambard, *A perambulation of Kent: conteining the description, hystorie, and customes of that shyre* (London, 1576), sigs. A4[r], B1[v].

[35] Shakespeare, *Second Part of King Henry VI*, IV. 7. 46. I am grateful to Niall Livingstone for this point.

internally colonised Kent on behalf of whose 'countrymen' Say claims to have 'parleyed unto foreign kings', this Kent of the new men of Tudor administration, masters of the media of law and letters, is not recognised by Cade and the rebels, who duly behead him (IV. 8. 66, 98).

Of course, between the local intellectual traditions taking scholars typically (in the *ideology* of Tudor humanism) from northern, north-western, Welsh border and western counties *to* university, and *from* university to households in the hospitable southern counties, most typic-ally Kent, lay the opportunities of scholarly service with courtiers and state officials. For emphasis on the regional link should not obscure the other and perhaps better known if not better explored of the uni-versities' connections, that with the court. In terms of the traditions and institutional arrangements that lined up local men for particular places, the court was often not so much a connection as an interference, seeking to prefer its own candidates on arguments from merit. Royal privilege clashed with local liberties in the structuring of educational and intellectual careers, as the court and state sought more intensively to supervise and control the universities.[36]

Indeed, the whole development described above can still obviously be seen from another perspective as conducive to state formation. It is relatively well known how from the 1530s and 1540s, and with greater urgency from the 1560s, the court and government increasingly called on the universities for services of various kinds to the state, from opinions on the royal divorce to scholarly secretaries to the broader provision of a graduate laity ready to go back into the shires as ministers and magistrates. The rise of humanism in most northern 'arts' universities can be characterised as the emergence of an alliance between the state and the lecturers; it being the latter, now paid by local secular author-ities, who undertook a reform of the medieval curriculum in line with the state's requirements. Although, compared with Cambridge, there was no serious attempt at statutory change of the curriculum in Oxford, both universities began to answer, in informal collegiate contexts, the demand for a humanistic training which had arisen particularly amongst the 'active, dynamic and richer classes of the late sixteenth century'.[37] Recent work surrounding documents such as the letter allegedly written

---

[36] Morgan, 'Cambridge University', pp. 221–2, 225; Morgan, 'Country, Court and Cambridge University', chs. 1 (re the politics of the election of the Duke of Buckingham as chancellor during the mid-1620s), 4 (re the 'Cambridge connection'), 8 (re outside intervention in elections to scholarships and headships, and in the allocation of leases).

[37] Fletcher, 'Faculty of Arts', pp. 157, 172–3, 179–80, 185, 188, 199. The quotation is from p. 199.

by the second Earl of Essex to Fulke Greville (dated to *c*.1599–1600) has offered fascinating detail of the way in which court figures treated the universities as a recruiting ground for scholarly advisers and servants. Essex apparently writes to Greville offering him advice on how he should set about '"going to Cambridge . . . to get a Scholar to your liking, to live with you and some 2, or 3 others to remain in the University, and gather [research] for you"'.[38] An earlier document (*c*.1589–90) shows that Greville had already done this at least once: Lionel Sharpe of King's College had acted as an intermediary and sought to recruit John Coke of Trinity College at a stipend of £30 a year if he committed his work in the arts to Greville alone.[39]

Nevertheless, it is still legitimate to stress the weight of 'local' cultural baggage which scholars continued to carry with them as a direct result of their university experience and the ongoing likelihood that they might return to points of local origin to participate in regional society (as the university-educated scholar and court facilitator Gabriel Harvey eventually did for half of his adult life).[40] One of the most important things they learned at college was, indeed, 'to identify "the country" with the social world of their own regional societies'.[41]

Such, at any rate, is the conclusion that follows from the model of the educational revolution proposed in the pioneering work of Victor Morgan, upon which I have principally been drawing here. The important innovation in this model is that it is not founded on a Whiggish nineteenth-century version of the relationship between regional or

---

[38] P. E. J. Hammer, 'The Earl of Essex, Fulke Greville, and the Employment of Scholars', *Studies in Philology* 91 (1994), 167–80 (p. 174). See also L. Jardine and A. Grafton, '"Studied for Action": How Gabriel Harvey Read his Livy', *PP* 129 (1990), 30–78; W. H. Sherman, *John Dee: The Politics of Reading and Writing in the English Renaissance* (Amherst, 1995).

[39] Hammer, 'Earl of Essex', pp. 178, 180.

[40] V. F. Stern, *Gabriel Harvey: His Life, Marginalia and Library* (Oxford, 1979), pp. 130–4.

[41] Morgan, 'Cambridge University', p. 243. Morgan summarises as follows (pp. 219–20): 'Of what loyalties was a boy conscious as a student at early 17th century Cambridge? Surely one loyalty was that to his home "country", as he pored over books reserved for boys from that country, perhaps used and marked in his days as a student by the schoolmaster who had started him on his academic career; working in a study built out of the benefactions of a man from his own country, sharing a chamber with a boy from the same town or region, overseen by a tutor who was a member of the college by right of the same regional dispensation, whose acquaintance or companionship he could expect to enjoy in his subsequent careers; surrounded by other boys from other parts of the kingdom, attending the college under analogous regulations; his sojourn there financed by the fruits of those fields he had known as a child, would know again as a man, perhaps tilled by his father and brothers or tenanted by his patron. Herein lay the roots of that strong bond of sentiment attaching him to his country; sentiments originating in the realities of a physical place and reinforced in the college by the ever present mnemonics of his dependence.'

local consciousness, a grammar school and university education in classical literacy, and service to the imperial state; namely, that such education prepares for the latter by *alienating* the student from the former. Instead, Morgan's model takes account of the evidence that in the sixteenth century the normal experience of the young gentleman just out of university did not exclusively involve aspiration to participate in centralised state bureaucracy or the 'national' court media, but retained a strong orientation towards 'regional' life and administration (whether secular or ecclesiastical). His school and university experience, furthermore, did not necessarily alienate him from such life, and may actually have strengthened his 'cultural regionalism' *as a fundamental aspect of* his commitment to the 'country' as a whole; his 'culture', indeed, may precisely have been participation in social and communication networks *linking* country, university and court, not transcendence of localities in which – because of his education – he could *only* live an alienated existence. For Cambridge 'acted as an exchange for the social, political, theological, and cultural "information explosion" of the late 16th and early 17th century'. Alienation from regions and gravitation towards the court doubtless occurred, but not as an automatic product of the educational experience.[42]

TUDOR RHETORIC: NORTH BY NORTH-WEST

We can test these observations briefly against the details of one obscure scholar's career and two well known but very different works of Tudor pedagogical literature. Christopher Watson was born in the parish of St Oswald's, Durham, in 1545/46, and according to the earliest extant Treasurer's book (*c.*1560–61) was one of the first pupils to proceed (1558–59) as a Queen's scholar of grammar, 'poor and destititute of friends', through (what is now called) Durham School after it was re-founded by Henry VIII. The full details of the local intellectual tradition – perhaps

---

[42] On networks and occasions linking university and country societies see Morgan, 'Cambridge University', pp. 225–234 (229). Lawrence Stone, in 'Educational Revolution' (76), was perhaps still working with rather Whiggish assumptions in this respect, though there is no doubt that his characterisation gels with the disillusionment evident, say, in the end-of-century University entertainments known as the 'Parnassus' plays: 'Having finished at the university, the young gentlemen were obliged to return home to their muddy shires, marry a barely literate girl, and find what intellectual stimulus they could in the dull grind of a seat on the bench at quarter and petty sessions, together, if they were lucky, with a few weeks' excitement every few years at one of the rare sessions of Parliament.' For the culture of regionalism, see V. Morgan, 'The Cartographic Image of "The Country" in Early Modern England', *Transactions of the Royal Historical Society* 5th series 29 (1979), 129–54 (131).

very recent – or local patronage which took him to St John's College, Cambridge are not yet clear, but he matriculated there in 1562, while the school's connection with the college was formalised by an endowment of George Baker in the next century. At university he certainly picked up connections amidst the Norfolk gentry and he certainly became a minister in the south-east of England; if the standard biographical authorities are correct, he was ordained deacon and became a rector in East Anglia.[43] The interesting point is that Watson left one testimony to the training in humane learning he received at St John's, and one to the development of his ministerial and scholarly interest in the antiquities of Durham and Northumbria: it is the link between them that interests us here.

Before he proceeded to M. A. in 1569, Watson had published (1568) an English translation of the first book of Polybius's *Hystories*, dedicated to 'the right worshipful Thomas Gaudy Esquier' from 'my chamber in your house at Gaudy Hall' in Redenhall, Norfolk, where Watson perhaps spent time in vacations on the invitation of a gentleman keen to have Cambridge scholars in the house.[44] By 1573–74 he was making collections of authorities on the history of Durham and Northumbria which are preserved in the Cotton MSS in the British Library.[45] Given his origins, his background at one of the oldest bishop's schools in the country, and his profession, these collections make sense. But is the 'local' sense they make to be completely dissociated from the humanistic work on Polybius, which Mervyn James might want to see as evidence of Watson's transcendence of local roots, of his access to a universal cultural system via humanistic pedagogy?[46] Unusually, Watson, in an epistle 'To the Questioners', tells his readers exactly how he became interested in publishing the translation. In his study at St John's College, his eyes had strayed from Aristotelean philosophy to Edward Hall's *Union of the Two Noble Houses of York and Lancaster* and been caught – due to his training in rhetoric – by a vernacular oration delivered

[43] *Dictionary of National Biography; The Parish Registers of St Oswald's, Durham, containing the Baptisms, Marriages, and Burials, from 1538 to 1751*, ed. A. W. Headlam (Durham, 1891), p. 5; P. R. O. (Prerogative Court of Canterbury 49 Arundell) Prob. 11/62 fol. 393ᵛ; C. H. Cooper and T. Cooper, *Athenae Cantabrigienses: Volume I, 1500–1585* (Cambridge and London, 1858), p. 434; *The Victoria History of the Counties of England: Durham*, ed. W. Page, 3 vols (London, 1905–28), vol. 1, pp. 374–6; *Durham School Register*, ed. T. H. Burbridge, third edition (Cambridge, 1940), pp. 125, 691.

[44] Polybius, *The hystories . . . of the warres betwixt the Romanes & Carthaginenses*, tr. C. Watson (London, 1568), sig. A4ʳ

[45] British Library Cotton MS Vitellius C. IX. fols 63ᵛ–128ʳ.

[46] James, *Society, Politics and Culture*, pp. 270–1, 273.

before Henry V (actually made up by Hall) by Ralph Neville, Earl of
Westmorland, at the time high warden of the West Marches in the
northern border territories. In the oration, the Earl uses memorable
examples from Polybius. Further detail is not needed to make the point
that is relevant here. Watson's eyes are attracted to the rhetoric of this
particular oration because of the long history of the Neville family in
the social and political affairs of the Scottish Border marches and the
Durham region. It is very probable, indeed, that the contemporary
Nevilles were partly instrumental at some point in the arrangements
that took Watson south to Cambridge: he vows to translate the text into
English 'under the protection & governance of ye most worthy sequele
& hautie successours of ye incomparable Earle, trusting so much to
their bountiful benevolence & accustomed gentlenes, which naturally
is planted in ye stock, so they would gratefully accept my good wil
towards them'. At the very least, this makes it clear that this arts student
read not only with a rhetorical but also with a regional eye.[47]

The best known and most influential vernacular work of Tudor
pedagogical literature was written by a Yorkshireman and a fellow of
St John's College, Cambridge, but is not very flattering about northern
schools and is difficult to square with the case of Christopher Watson,
even though it was written between 1562 and 1568, the precise period
during which the Durham scholar took his B. A. and M. A. Roger
Ascham was born at Kirby Wiske in the North Riding of Yorkshire in
1515 or 1516, but left no trace of any interest in Yorkshire antiquities.
Whether he received any local education is not clear, but his route to
university was via the cultivated Suffolk household of Sir Humphrey
Wingfield of Brantham, a lawyer and royal commissioner who employed
a tutor to teach Latin and some Greek to the promising young men
brought up in learning under his aegis. Another pupil of Wingfield's,
John Christopherson, also went on to St John's, suggesting that this
'was the normal pattern with Sir Humphrey's brighter pupils'.[48]

In *The Scholemaster* (published posthumously in 1570), Ascham tells the
reader how as a 'new Bacheler of arte' at St John's (1534), he chanced
amongst his companions 'to speake against the Pope'. The master of
the college, the benign Papist Nicholas Metcalfe, nevertheless 'privilie
procured' Ascham his fellowship, and Ascham goes on to record how
Metcalfe's goodness,

---

[47] Polybius, *Hystories*, sigs. N4^v–N7^r (N6^r).
[48] L. V. Ryan, *Roger Ascham* (Stanford and London, 1963), pp. 7, 11–12; MacCulloch, *Suffolk*,
pp. 146–7.

flowed aboundantlie over all that Colledge, and brake out also to norishe good wittes in every part of that universitie: whereby, at his departing thence, he left soch a companie of fellowes and scholers in *S. Johnes* Colledge, as can scarse be found now in som whole universitie: which, either for divinitie, on the one side or other, or for Civill service to their Prince and contrie, have bene, and are yet to this day, notable ornaments to this whole Realme: Yea *S. Johnes* did then so florish, as Trinitie college, that Princely house now, at the first erection, was but *Colonia deducta* out of *S. Jhones* [*sic*], not onelie for their Master, fellowes, and scholers, but also, which is more, for their whole, both order of learning, and discipline of maners: yet to this day, it never tooke Master but such as was bred up before in *S. Johnes*: doing the dewtie of a good *Colonia* to her *Metropolis*, as the auncient Cities in Greice and some yet in Italie, at this day, are accustomed to do.[49]

When Ascham talks here of service to 'contrie' and just beforehand of the college fellowship he won as 'the whole *foundation* of the poore learning I have' (my italics), an 'order' and a 'discipline' proper to this one institution, he means something more specific than may at first appear: a local intellectual tradition which in this case has privily prevailed over international confessional solidarities that might have blocked Ascham's appointment. Metcalfe himself was from Aysgarth in Richmondshire, one of the heartland college counties north of the Trent favoured both by the foundress and by subsequent benefactors, while Ascham was from the most favoured county of all, Yorkshire. Ascham observes earlier in the same passage that Metcalfe increased the annual expenditure of the college from two hundred to a thousand marks a year, by a wise encouragement of benefactors. Almost all of these were 'Northenmen: who being liberallie rewarded in the service of their Prince, bestowed it as liberallie for the good of their Contrie'. Metcalfe may have been 'parciall to Northrenmen' as a result, but Ascham is sure 'Northrenmen were parciall, in doing more good, and geving more landes to the forderance of learning, than any other con-trie men in those dayes did'.[50] The 'foundation', then, of Ascham's fellowship and of his learning, is a four-way transaction between north-countrymen, their 'countries' (Yorkshire, Richmondshire), the college,

---

[49] R. Ascham, *The scholemaster, or plaine and perfite way of teachyng children, to understand, write, and speake, the Latin tong, but specially purposed for the private brynging up of youth in ientlemen and noble mens houses, and commodious also for all such, as have forgot the Latin tonge, and would, by themselves, without a scholemaster, in short tyme, and with small paines, recover a sufficient habilitie, to understand, write, and speake Latin* (London, 1570), sigs. Q2ᵛ–3ʳ. I give the full title as it makes Ascham's priorities and intentions very clear. All 'i's, 'u's and 'v's have been transcribed according to modern spelling conventions.

[50] Ascham, *Scholemaster*, (1570), sig. Q2ʳ⁻ᵛ.

and the Prince: 'order of learning, and discipline of maners' qualifies
them for 'Civill service', the rewards for which are realised as northern
'lands' for the college. The livings from these lands are realised in turn
by Metcalfe as private exhibitions for the maintenance of young men –
particularly northern men such as Ascham – 'geven to new learning'.[51]

The book tells us what this 'new learning' as applied to the early,
pre-university preparation of young men in Latin should be. In doing
so it consistently invokes two entirely different settings within which the
boy can be taught Latin, representing two different approaches to the
'breeching' of the boy, two different kinds of textbook, and two ways
of using particular paradigms of good Latin.[52] One is the 'common
order in common scholes, for making of latines', in which the pupil is
made to translate brief English phrases as Latin speech. Masters might
make up these phrases (*'vulgaria'*, 'vulgars', or 'Englishes') themselves,
and the boy might be beaten naked and unbreeched if in the judgement of the master the Latin translation is not well made: 'the scholer,
is commonlie beat for the making, when the master were . . . many
times, . . . as ignorant as the childe, what to saie properlie and fitlie to
the matter'. This process is no better even when printed textbooks
of *vulgaria* are involved: Ascham names the 'beggarlie gatheringes' of
William Horman and Robert Whittinton, textbooks not current at
the time of writing but redolent of Ascham's own schooldays.[53] At the
beginning of the second book, Ascham gives a more specific location
to this barbaric process:

I remember, whan I was yong, in the North, they went to the Grammer schole,
litle children: they came from thence great lubbers: always learning, and litle

<hr/>

[51] *Dictionary of National Biography*; Morgan, 'Cambridge University', p. 201; Roger Ascham, *The Scholemaster*, ed. J. E. B. Mayor (London, 1863), pp. 250–1; Ascham, *Scholemaster*, (1570), sig. Q2ᵛ.
[52] From this point I am indebted to the discussion in A. Stewart, *Close Readers: Humanism and Sodomy in Early Modern England* (Princeton, 1997), ch. 3. I am grateful to Dr Stewart for allowing me to see a copy of the unpublished manuscript of his work. It is the first thorough account of the vexed sexual and power politics of the new sixteenth-century forms of intimacy between humanist pedagogues / secretaries and their pupils / patrons, and includes analysis of the way in which within the terms of male pedagogical culture the schoolmaster's beatings unmanned the newly breeched young boy.
[53] Ascham, *Scholemaster*, sigs. C1ʳ, N2ᵛ; W. E. Miller, 'Double Translation in English Human-istic Education', *Studies in the Renaissance* 10 (1963), 163–74 (165–6). A manuscript set of *vulgaria* (British Library, MS Royal 12. B. xx, fols. 35–49) intended for use at Magdalen College School sometime between its foundation in 1478–80 and about 1549 is typical in that it is clearly composed by a schoolmaster from the College itself and features the everyday life and work of the school '"here at Oxford"': teaching materials, in other words, local to a particular institution. See N. Orme, 'An Early-Tudor Oxford Schoolbook', *Renaissance Quarterly* 34 (1981), 11–39 (13).

profiting: learning without booke, every thing, understandyng with in the booke, litle or nothing: Their whole knowledge, by learning without the booke, was tied onely to their tong & lips, and never ascended up to the braine & head, and therfore was sone spitte out of the mouth againe: They were, as men, alwayes goyng, but ever out of the way: and why?[54]

With this thoroughly vulgar process in northern schools is contrasted Ascham's own method: double translation. The setting for this is very clearly suggested. For Ascham's 'Præface to the Reader' sets the scene as a December day in 1563, when Queen Elizabeth was at Windsor Castle, and when the core of the early Elizabethan political establishment found themselves in the Principal Secretary William Cecil's chamber. The historical and conversational setting sketched in this preface, combined with the contemporary allusions sprinkled throughout the treatise, indicate that Ascham's work should be considered as a Tudor English version of Cicero's dialogue, *De oratore* and the *Cortegiano* of Baldessare Castiglione. For Ascham's anecdotal and historical commentary amounts to a socio-political and academic pedigree of English reformed humanism equivalent to Cicero's identification of Roman political culture with the tradition of the Scipionic circle, and Castiglione's of the successful courtier with particular figures in Urbino's court culture.[55]

More particularly, for our purposes, the setting is nearby Eton, for the conversation with which the preface deals starts from the news Secretary Cecil has had that morning about scholars running away from that grammar school 'for feare of beating'. One participant in the conversation, Walter Haddon, is in passing held up as a famous scholarly product of the school, but Ascham seizes the occasion to mount his argument that 'yong children were soner allured by love, than driven by beating'.[56]

At the beginning of the treatise proper, Ascham reveals that the key to his alternative, less painful route to the 'making of latines' is the substitution of *vulgaria* – teaching materials local to a particular institution

[54] Ascham, *Scholemaster*, sig. K3^v.

[55] *Ibid.*, sigs. B1^r, E3^v–4^r (Lady Jane Grey), G2^r (Francis I of France), G2^v (Sir Roger Cholmley), G4^v–H1^v (Sir Thomas Hoby, King Edward, Duke of Suffolk, Lord Henry Maltravers, Sir John Cheke, John Redman, Queen Elizabeth), H3^r (Sir Richard Sackville), H3^v (Thomas Watson, Bishop of Lincoln, educated at St John's College), K4^r–L1^r (Sir Anthony Denny, John Whitney, Queen Elizabeth), L3^r (Queen Elizabeth), N3^v (Walter Haddon, Sir Francis Bryan – for his 'lustie' style), O1^v (Bishop Stephen Gardiner, for having a 'quicke head, and a readie tong'), P4^r, Q4^v–R2^r, R4^r (Cheke and Watson), S1^r ('the noble Lord Th. Earle of Surrey' – Henry Howard).

[56] Ascham, *Scholemaster*, sigs. B1^v–2^r.

– by a standard textbook edition of Cicero's letters: 'let the master read unto hym the Epistles of *Cicero*, gathered togither and chosen out by *Sturmius*, for the capacitie of children'. Ascham must have known that exactly this edition was placed on the new curriculum drawn up for Eton school shortly before the Windsor conversation, *c.*1560. In the use of this textbook, all speaking of Latin is deferred, though not because spoken Latin is by its nature more corrupt. Indeed, the ideal setting for learning is 'a house, or . . . Schole, where the latin tonge were properlie and perfitlie spoken', such as the house of the Gracchi: the problem for Ascham is that in the sixteenth century no such house or school exists.[57]

The text-bound method which is to compensate for the lack of such houses works as follows: the master first helps the child construe and parse a passage from Sturm's edition of Cicero's letters; the child then translates the passage into English on his own in a paper book; the master then takes from him the textbook; after an hour, the child translates his own English back into Latin in another paper book; then the master lays the textbook, Ciceronian 'original' alongside the child's effort, and without chiding, gently shows him where Cicero would have used a different word, or syntactical arrangement.[58] In this way the associated dangers of corrupt colloquial Latinity and physical beating are avoided by reference back to authoritative textual paradigms of Latin style: 'examples of good authors' and Ascham's own printed guidance on how gently to use them supplant the 'naked rewles of *Grammarians*' and the speech and violence of the live, vulgar northern schoolmaster: 'learning without the booke . . . tied . . . to . . . tong and lip' is replaced by learning within the book tied to two exemplary and complementary texts, Sturm's edition of Cicero and Ascham's *Scholemaster*.[59]

This method is, of course, itself the formalisation in print of a local teaching tradition: a letter of William Cecil's indicates that it was his own and Ascham's Cambridge tutor, Sir John Cheke, who used the practice in the late 1530s. Rooted in, and authorised by particular

---

[57] Ascham, *Scholemaster*, sigs. C1ᵛ–2ᵛ. For Sturmius and the curriculum at Eton see T. W. Baldwin, *William Shakspere's Small Latine & Lesse Greeke*, 2 vols. (Urbana, 1944), vol. I, pp. 353, 355, 375; vol. II, pp. 255–6, 263–4. In practice in grammar schools, Cicero's *Epistles* were rarely used as the *sole* basis for early exercises in translation. J. E. B. Mayor records an edition of this schoolboy selection published in Strasbourg in 1539 (Ascham, *Scholemaster*, ed. Mayor, p. 208). The British Library has a copy of an edition published at Paris in 1554: *M. T. Ciceronis Epistolarum libri tres a Ioanne Sturmio puerili educationi confecti*. Further editions were issued well into the seventeenth century, indicating that it became a standard grammar school textbook.
[58] Ascham, *Scholemaster*, sig. C1ᵛ; Baldwin, *Shakspere's Small Latine*, vol. I, pp. 264–9.
[59] Ascham, *Scholemaster*, sig. N2ᵛ.

tutorial friendships of exemplary moral, social and political significance, it spawned others: Ascham describes how he had 'a profe hereof, tried by good experience, by a deare frende of myne, whan I came first from Cambridge, to serve the Queenes Majestie, than Ladie *Elizabeth*'. The dear friend is a 'yong ientleman, . . . my bedfeloe', John Whitney, who is able within just seven months to reproduce Ciceronian Latin by this method, but who tragically dies. His loss is grieved by the Queen, and lamented by Ascham in a vernacular elegy to Whitney's moral and religious purity inserted in the text of *The Scholemaster*.[60] In the third of the satirical 'Parnassus' plays performed at St John's (*c*.1601–2), it is the piety, physical intimacy and social expectancy attached to tutorial relationships of this kind which makes the encounter between a tutor, Academico, and his ex-pupil and gentleman-commoner at St John's, Amoretto, so wickedly funny for the latter. Describing to his page how he has fobbed off Academico's hopes of a living with his father in the country, Amoretto mocks his ex-tutor thus:

Sirrha, this prædicable, this saucy groome, because when I was in *Cambridge*, and lay in a Trundlebed under my Tutor, I was content in discreet humilitie to give him some [meane] place at my Table . . . he thought himselfe therefore eternally possest of my love, and came hither to take acquaintance of me, and thought his old familiaritie did continue, and would beare him out in a matter of weight.[61]

The orbit, though, of Ascham's 'familiaritie' does not extend out into the country, or if it does, only to the home counties mansions of rich courtiers like Sir Humphrey Wingfield and Sir Anthony Denny, whose Cheshunt residence was the scene of Whitney's tuition. Here, we should notice that what Frank Whigham, summarising the secondary literature on the educational revolution, called the 'new cooperative pressures of nationally centralized life' will also serve as a description of the carefully constructed ideological effect of *The Scholemaster*.[62] Civilised life is pressurised within a bubble that takes in, geographically and topographically, Cambridge and London and courtly locations nearby, namely Windsor and Cheshunt; institutionally, prestigious southern

---

[60] Baldwin, *Shakespere's Small Latine*, vol. I, pp. 266–7; Ascham, *Scholemaster*, sigs. K4ʳ–L1ʳ.

[61] *The Three Parnassus Plays (1598–1601)*, ed. J. B. Leishman (London, 1949), 'The Second Part of the Return from Parnassus', II. 6. 943–53. The editor glosses 'trundlebed' as a 'trucklebed', a 'small bed shifted about upon wheels', and encloses within square brackets words which appear in the extant manuscript versions of the play but not in the 1606 quarto edition, upon which he bases his text.

[62] Whigham, *Ambition and Privilege*, p. 13.

grammar schools like Eton and Westminster and by extension St Paul's and Winchester, as well as St John's College, Cambridge; intellectually, the group of Cambridge orators who, like Cicero and his correspondents, 'lived all in one time, . . . like in authority' – John Redman, John Cheke, Thomas Smith, Walter Haddon, and Thomas Watson;[63] socially and politically, the Privy Council, the Queen, and those 'serving hir in verie good place'[64] – William Cecil, Sir William Petre, Sir John Mason, Nicholas Wotton, Richard Sackville and Walter Mildmay; religiously, establishment Protestant conformism tolerant of reformed Catholic piety (Metcalfe's); pedagogically, the Cambridge tutor and his aristocratic or royal pupil (the treatise was written for the education of Robert Sackville, grandson of Richard Sackville and son of Thomas Sackville, who became Lord Buckhurst and Earl of Dorset);[65] linguistically, Ciceronian Latin style learned primarily as a textual medium by use of printed editions of Sturm's Cicero and Ascham's *Scholemaster*.

This 'pressure' makes it clear that Ascham's reformed pedagogy is not, ultimately, the ideology of a local intellectual tradition linking northern communities with St John's. It is, rather, the ideology of the 'Cambridge connection' that for a short period seized the centre of national political life. Based in common schoolboy and university experience of Latin-learning (and, to a lesser extent, Greek-learning) with particular tutors at particular places near London, or in the common desire to transcend in gentle fashion the brutality and vulgarity alleged to be characteristic of local teaching traditions, this connection linked prestigious southern grammar schools and aristocratic households with university and court, and, across a bridge from the 1540s to the 1560s, shaped the early Elizabethan regime in government and church.[66] This connection undoubtedly became the period's central ideological model for the 'cluster of meanings and usage' gathered around elite humanistic literacy, but, again, we should not let it obscure the varieties in practice of the local contexts and places in which such literacy was transmitted and used.

---

[63] Ascham, *Scholemaster*, sigs. S3ʳ, Q1ᵛ–4ʳ.   [64] *Ibid.*, sig. B1ʳ.   [65] *Ibid.*, sig. B2ʳ.

[66] On the early Elizabethan council see W. MacCaffrey, *The Shaping of the Elizabethan Regime*, first published 1968 (reprinted: London 1969), pp. 34–5, 128–9. For an important development of MacCaffrey's notion of the new Elizabethan 'establishment' ('a loose grouping of friends') by means of a discussion of the importance of the Cambridge background (including mention of Ascham's *Scholemaster*) see W. S. Hudson, *The Cambridge Connection and the Elizabethan Settlement of 1559* (Durham, NC, 1980), pp. 29–42 and *passim*. See also M. Dewar, *Sir Thomas Smith: A Tudor Intellectual in Office* (London, 1964), and for the lower political profile and very different experiences during Mary's reign of Ascham (as compared with Cheke and Smith) see the introduction to Roger Ascham, *Letters*, tr. M. Hatch and A. Vos, ed. A. Vos (New York, 1989).

Take, for example, the evidence of John Hoskyns' manuscript treatise, 'Directions for Speech and Style', of which four copies are extant (one incomplete), none of them holographs.[67] The fact that two of these have survived in the Harley family's famous collection of manuscripts as acquired by the British Library is one piece of evidence for identifying the student of rhetoric for whom they were written as Robert Harley, '"son and heir-apparent of Thomas Harley of Brampton Castell, Herefordshire"'. As a new student at the Middle Temple, Harley was 'bound' with Hoskyns (who as a Herefordshire man had himself been bound with older students upon his entrance in 1593), on 24 October, 1599. Since the treatise is dateable to the latter half of 1599, and since it is written as a favour to the father of a young man come up from the country, Harley seems the only plausible candidate.[68]

Though the treatise may indeed have been written specifically for Harley, its broader context is very clearly an informal humanistic teaching tradition which extends at the Middle Temple the local intellectual tradition that has brought Hoskyns himself from Herefordshire via Winchester College and New College, Oxford to the inns of court. This secular tradition of landed gentlemen from the southern Welsh borders grows in Hoskyns' case out of a particular aspect of the medieval ecclesiastical patronage of William of Wykeham, who, building principally upon the example of the existing relationship between the King's Hall, Cambridge and the chapel royal, twinned his new foundations of Winchester grammar school (1382) and New College (1379), providing for a salaried tutorial system whereby senior scholars acted as *informatores* to the then still relatively new category of undergraduate juniors during their first three years. Endowments such as these were

---

[67] My interest in Hoskyns' treatise was revived by David Colclough's excellent unpublished paper, '"I meane to kill your Speaker": Manuscript Miscellanies and the Politics of Free Speech in Jacobean England'. I am very grateful to Dr Colclough for providing me with a copy of his paper. The manuscripts of the 'Directions' are British Library, Harleian MSS 4604 and 850 (incomplete), Additional MS 15230; Bodleian Library MS. Ash. Mus. d. 1. See L. B. Osborn, *The Life, Letters, and Writings of John Hoskyns, 1566–1638* (New Haven and London, 1937), pp. 112–113; J. Hoskyns, *Directions for Speech and Style*, ed. H. H. Hudson (Princeton, 1935), pp. xxxviii–lv; B. W. Whitlock, *John Hoskyns, Serjeant-at-Law* (Washington, 1982), pp. 164–5. Hudson's text is a partially modernised edition of Harleian MS. 4604 and is the one used here. Osborn also uses the Harleian MS, but neither editor knew of the Additional MS, which Whitlock states to be more complete and more accurate, but which remains unpublished. For the reader's convenience I have preferred to quote from a printed edition, and I have used the spelling 'Hoskyns' (Hudson uses 'Hoskins').

[68] Whitlock, *Hoskyns*, pp. 90, 101 (quoting from the *Middle Temple Records*, ed. C. H. Hopwood, 4 vols., London, 1904–5, vol. I). Osborn, Hudson and Whitlock all support the identification of the unnamed student with Robert Harley.

to insure that the foundation upon which higher education in the arts and sciences had to be built was a strong grasp of grammar.[69]

Born to a farming family in Monkton in Herefordshire, Hoskyns may have spent a year at Westminster School before entering Winchester College as a scholar in 1579 (he may have been there earlier as a commoner), by virtue not of his being a Founder's Kin, which was one possibility under Wykeham's statutes, but of his being a native of a parish in which one of the twinned colleges held property. Winchester had extensive holdings in Herefordshire, one of which, Titley Manor, two miles south of the Welsh border and about five miles from other Hoskyns family properties, John Hoskyns leased from the College on 11 January, 1600.[70]

Having followed through from New College to Middle Temple, building a brilliant reputation in the process, Hoskyns had by the late 1590s supplemented his local substance with new county and important court connections. In August 1598 he was able to mobilise three powerful court patrons – Thomas Egerton, the Lord Keeper; Thomas Howard, Lord High Admiral; William Knollys, Privy Councillor – in an attempt (unsuccessful) to speed his younger brother John on the path from Winchester to New College. Meanwhile, as an increasingly senior student at the Temple, he was beginning to assume responsibility for younger gentlemen students.[71] He tells the addressee of the 'Directions' that, 'bound to your father's love and yours', he will make 'somewhat more of you than one of my young masters of the Temple'.[72] The first 'young master' for whom Hoskyns was bound in 1595 was Kentish in origin, suggesting he was already known (via Henry Wotton and his future Kentish wife, Benedicta Bourne) and respected by families in Kent. But the locality whence students most frequently sought his guidance was Herefordshire. In particular, from 1597 he began to share his knowledge, and in one or two cases very probably his chambers, with a series of young masters from that county: on 4 November 1597 he was bound with Mr Henry Kyrle of Much Marcle, on 16 November

[69] McConica, 'Rise of the Undergraduate College', pp. 2–3; A. B. Cobban, 'Colleges and Halls, 1380 1500' in *The History of the University of Oxford*, Volume II, *Late Middle Ages*, ed. J. I. Catto and T. A. R. Evans (Oxford, 1993), pp. 581–633 (581–98).

[70] Whitlock, *Hoskyns*, pp. 5, 16, 28–9, 127. For the statutes see Cobban, 'Colleges and Halls', p. 584: after founder's kin preference was given to scholars from Winchester,

'first to candidates from the places and parishes where Winchester College had spiritual or temporal holdings; then to scholars from Winchester diocese; then to those from named counties in the southern half of England; and finally those from the remaining parts of the country.'

[71] Whitlock, *Hoskyns*, pp. 124–30.   [72] Hoskyns, *Directions*, ed. Hudson, p. 3.

with William Vaughan from Winforton, on 15 January 1598 with John Vaughan of Clerewood, on 10 May with Richard Phillips of Rushmor (Carmarthenshire), and finally, on 29 October with Robert Harley of Brampton Castle. Beyond Robert Harley, then, the treatise could equally well be addressed to a generic young master from an important family in Herefordshire looking for some humanistic and legal polish before going back into county society.[73]

In his prefatory epistle, Hoskyns invokes in broad terms the classical and technical tradition of writers on oratory and rhetoric, supplemented by their northern humanist interpreters, upon which he has drawn: 'Aristotle, Hermogenes, Quintilian, Demosthenes, Cicero, and some later, as Sturmius and Talaeus [Omer Talon, associate of Ramus]'.[74] One of Hoskyns' editors has demonstrated the extent to which, and the sense in which he did variously draw on and refer his student to contemporary editions of works by these writers.[75] When treating of the means to remove ambiguities by '*distinctio*', Hoskyns refers the student not only in general to Castiglione's *Courtier* and to the second book of Cicero's *De oratore*, but in particular to paradigms marked by printed marginal notes in particular editions of works by Quintilian and Erasmus. It is interesting for the purposes of the comparison being made here, furthermore, that Hoskyns notes apropos of the figure 'contentio' (the use of balanced antitheses) that 'Ascham told Sturmius that he taught the Queen of England [this figure], and that she excels in practice of it' (referring to a printed Latin epistle of Ascham's published in 1551).[76] The principal aim here, though, is not to re-assign Hoskyns' collected observations to their places in a homogeneous and technical tradition of rhetorical thought common to the intellectual community throughout northern Europe, but to retrieve (from circumstances without and clues within the text) Hoskyns' local teaching methods, his socially and intellectually specific modes of mediation of that tradition. Ultimately, most sixteenth century grammatical and rhetorical manuals are not reflections of independent thought about the schemes of classical pedagogy, but reflections of and upon teaching practices.

The first thing to emphasise is that although Hoskyns' 'Directions' do refer to the Latin rhetorical textbook tradition, they are twinned most explicitly with a specific copy of the 1590 edition of Philip Sidney's *Arcadia* (now referred to always as the *Countess of Pembroke's Arcadia*), in which

[73] Whitlock, *Hoskyns*, pp. 97–8.   [74] Hoskyns, *Directions*, ed. Hudson, p. 3.
[75] *Ibid.*, pp. xxii–xxvii.   [76] *Ibid.*, pp. 43, 37, 86–7.

Hoskyns himself has in manuscript marked up for attention particular paradigms of various kinds. Where there are metaphors worthy of note he has put the letter '(M:)' in the margin and the student is invited to compare all the places in the book thus marked. Instead of reading Theophrastus' *Ethical Characters* ('*Theophrasti Imagines*') and Aristotle's *Rhetoric* in order to learn the techniques for rhetorical representation of psychological and moral qualities, the student can follow Hoskyns' directions to the passages in Sidney where the fruits of 'our learned knight['s]' reading in those two authors are apparent in his own practice of imagining 'the thing present in his own brain'. In particular, the student will find '&c' alongside passages illustrative of 'policy' at work in particular 'actions of persons'; 'des:' alongside 'evident and lively descriptions'; ':dc:' alongside passages 'where the person is aptly fitted with speech and action'.[77]

If thought of in this way as Sidney's vivid vernacular re-imagining of classical paradigms, the *Arcadia* becomes, then, a respectable textbook for teaching a rhetorical vernacular, not Latin style. To such paradigms as he has marked in the 1590 copy, Hoskyns adds a large number of rhetorical paradigms of his own invention – the equivalent to the more localised grammatical exercises, or *vulgaria* Ascham had sought to displace – either from previous set-piece compositions, or from topical matters of political or legal debate, or from the 'conversation' he might actually be having with his student (a standard pedagogical tactic). Some of those in the second category relate to diplomatic issues which Ascham might have expected his aristocratic or royal pupil to be able to deal with in Latin as a result of his/her training in classical orators such as Cicero and Demosthenes. So Hoskyns' pupil learns how to compare Sir Francis Drake and Vascus Gama as explorers and colonialists on the classical model of a Plutarchean comparison between Themistocles and Coriolanus, to justify an aggressive foreign policy on the model of the actions of early heroes of the Roman empire, and to compare as 'things different' the King of Spain's assisting the Irish ('a people untrue in their treatises, uncivil in their manners') with the Queen of England's aiding the Netherlands ('a nation peacable in their lives, free by their

---

[77] *Ibid.*, pp. 8–9, 41–2 and Osborn, *John Hoskyns*, pp. 122, 156. In the case of the marginal marks to which Hoskyns refers his student, I have preferred Osborn's transcriptions from the manuscript, which are more accurate than Hudson's (especially '&c', which Hudson emends to 'pc'). Hoskyns has seen Sidney's manuscript translation of Aristotle's *Rhetoric* in the hands of another Winchester and New College man, Henry Wotton (Hoskyns, *Directions*, ed. Hudson, p. 41).

privileges').[78] Discussions of other paradigms in this category, as you would expect at the inns of court, smack more of the law-courts than anything you would find in Ascham: one paradigm argues the point as to whether the marriages of heads of houses and colleges are as lawful as the marriages of 'Doctors of the Arches or Clerks of the Chancery'; 'sententiae' in general are judged 'better for the bench than the bar'. At the end of the incomplete Harleian MS of the 'Directions' are found rhetorical exercises in plea-making based on a fictional case between a husband and a wife borrowed from a contemporary printed manual – *The Orator* (London, 1596), by Alexander van den Busche. This suggests pragmatic contexts of use continuous with some of Hoskyns' own paradigms.[79]

Thus, even though Ascham is writing about earlier stages in a student's humanistic education, we can still say that by comparison Hoskyns' treatment is pragmatised, secularised and, obviously, vernacularised: the nitty-gritty of live, contemporary arguments in law and politics is more evident; there is no attempt to associate elegant style with religious and moral probity (only with the avoidance of 'discredit'); the key textbook is not a humanistic edition of Cicero's epistles in Latin, but a vernacular romance.[80] Nevertheless there are structural continuities which provide opportunities for assimilation of Ascham and Hoskyns to the 'same' northern humanist, pedagogical tradition. In both cases an informal and intimate teaching relationship between tutor and pupil is mediated by a pair of texts (a book of paradigms edited or produced by an exemplary modern humanist with directions how to use them) that provide a briefer route to elegant style than formal curricula in schools and universities, while the ultimate reference is to an established textbook tradition in Latin (and, comparatively, Greek) rhetoric and oratory. Both courses, furthermore, have their foundations in the teaching of epistolary skills. One should be wary, also, of too clean a distinction between the apparently more personalised, manuscript context of Hoskyns' instruction and the print-based pedagogy of Ascham: while it may be true that Hoskyns' *Arcadia* was a single, treasured artefact now apparently lost, it is also true that his 'Directions' were known in the universities and circulated in manuscript, finding their way in part into print in Ben Jonson's *Timber* (published in Jonson's *Works* in

---

[78] *Ibid.*, pp. 17–21 (19–20).   [79] Hoskyns, *Directions*, ed. Hudson, pp. 20–1, 40, 106–7.
[80] On avoiding 'discredit' see *ibid.*, p. 2.

1641, at London), and in Thomas Blount's *Academie of Eloquence* (London, 1654). Hoskyns' readings in the arts were a known and sought-after commodity, even amongst 'Masters of the Universities'.[81]

Panning back from the textual detail to questions of social and cultural provenance may help re-localise both Ascham's and Hoskyns' pedagogies. It is striking that both ultimately appear to derive from local intellectual traditions which trace a trajectory from locations in Diarmaid MacCulloch's 'second tier' of territories adhering to the Tudor English state: those not directly under the Crown's jurisdiction, not self-consciously a part of lowland, 'civilised' England, but part of a 'second tier'.[82] This includes both Yorkshire and the southern Welsh borders, and it would take in as well the localities from which other grammatical and rhetorical 'arts' of this period emerge: Thomas Wilson's Lincolnshire ('my Countrey'), Richard Mulcaster's northern border territories, Abraham Fraunce's northern Welsh borders.[83]

---

[81] Unacknowledged borrowings first pointed out by L. B. Osborn in the *Times Literary Supplement* for May 1 (1930). In composing a paradigm of 'paralipsis' (a figure of amplification), Hoskyns imagines himself telling his student (ed. Hudson, p. 31):

'I value not my pains in collecting these observations, I will forget that I denied the earnest entreaties of many kinds of gent[lemen] that sued unto me for such helps, I am loth to tell you they are notes of whom your Masters of the Universities have thought the author as great a reader and a greater observer thereof than themselves'.

[82] D. MacCulloch, 'The Consolidation of Tudor England, 1485–1603' in *The Oxford Illustrated History of Tudor and Stuart Britain*, ed. J. Morrill (Oxford, 1996), pp. 35–52 (pp. 35–6):

'The heartland was the south-east, centred since the twelfth century on government institutions at Westminster beside London. Medieval England was more centralised than any other large European state, but only in this area of prosperous lowland farming country – the Thames valley, the south coast from Kent to Dorset, East Anglia, and the Midlands – did Westminster's writ fully run. . . . Beyond this was a more miscellaneous area – the second tier – Devon and Cornwall, along the Welsh border to Cheshire, Lancashire, the Peak District, the Yorkshire Ridings, and Lincolnshire. The hills tended to fill the horizon more menacingly above lowland prosperity, and the crown's authority was often expressed in indirect form, through jurisdictions like the Duchies of Cornwall and Lancaster, the Earldom of Chester, or the scattered territories of the Duchy of York. . . . From these areas, fewer citizens and burgesses than in the heartland were summoned as city and borough representatives to Parliament; Cheshire returned no MPs at all until 1545. The real outliers – the third tier – were still further out, to the south, north, and west: Calais and the Channel Islands; the borders with Scotland; Wales; Ireland.'

[83] Wilson went via Eton to King's College, Cambridge, and was appointed tutor to the sons of the Duchess of Suffolk. For his roots in Lincolnshire, see T. Wilson, *Arte of Rhetorique*, ed. T. J. Derrick (New York, 1982), pp. x, xiii–xvi, xx–xxi, xxvi–xxvii, 7, 45–6, 285–6, 327–8, 417. Richard Mulcaster, author of two pedagogical manuals (*Positions* and *The first part of the Elementarie*, 1581 and 1582 respectively, both at London), was of an old border family, and went via Eton to King's College, Cambridge, before transferring to Christ Church, Oxford. See Richard Mulcaster, *Positions*, ed. R. H. Quick (London, 1888), pp. 299–300. Abraham Fraunce (author of *The Arcadian rhetorike* and *The lawiers logike*, both of 1588, both at London) was born at Shrewsbury, sometime in 1558–60, and was a pupil at the school Philip Sidney attended from 1564 to 1568, Shrewsbury School, by the time that all boys were re-inscribed after the promulgation of new

Consumers of these arts who had followed such a trajectory in turn became patrons of the local intellectual traditions within which they flourished. The structure of Sir Thomas Egerton, Baron Ellesmere's educational and political patronage linked his native country – the northern lowland region of the Welsh marches – and his later acquisitions of land nearer London in Buckingham and Hertfordshire with the London metropolitan scene via specific Oxbridge colleges and inns of court: Brasenose (which had eighteen out of twenty-one fellows from his own area when Egerton matriculated there in 1556) and Jesus in Oxford, St John's in Cambridge, and Lincoln's Inn in London. Part of the educational package that brought him 'into the mainstream of English life on the Midland plain' stretching out below the estates of the landed gentry in the northern borderlands of England and Wales was skill in Ramistic analysis and the new logic, which he began to apply to the interpretation of statutes and the drafting of legal arguments in the period 1575–85, and which he supported directly and indirectly as a patron thereafter.[84]

The suggestion, then, is that there is at this time an English tradition of both Latin and vernacular 'arts' of rhetoric and logic specific to the cultural trajectory between second tier and lowland core territories and spaces, a tradition that is a response to the task of teaching the trivium in a 'reformed' manner to non-specialists from outlying provinces following (often extra-curricular) courses in general humanistic culture. These non-specialists are beneficiaries of the local intellectual traditions taking increasing numbers of grammar school boys from specific 'countries' to universities and inns of court. The tradition's cultural and ideological centre of gravity in the sixteenth century is St John's College, Cambridge, and it attracts not only members of the 'new' Cambridge colleges, but 'new men' arriving with scholarships

statutes on January 11, 1571/2. When Shrewsbury School was established in 1561, Thomas Ashton, a contemporary of Cheke and Ascham, was recruited as its first headmaster. Ashton had been at St John's College, Cambridge, from the 1520s to the 1540s, and thus brought the 'Cambridge connection' to Shrewsbury. Fraunce matriculated as a pensioner with Sidney's financial help at St John's College, Cambridge on May 26, 1576, and became a fellow there in 1580/81. See Abraham Fraunce, *Victoria, A Latin Comedy*, ed. G. C. Moore Smith, 'Materialien zur Kunde des älteren Englischen Dramas Band XIV' (Louvain, 1906), pp. xiv–xvi, xviii–xix; B. Coulton, 'The Establishment of Protestantism in a Provincial Town: A Study of Shrewsbury in the Sixteenth Century', *Sixteenth Century Journal* 27 (1996), 307–35 (312, 314–15, 317–18).

[84] L. A. Knafla, 'The "Country" Chancellor: The Patronage of Sir Thomas Egerton, Baron Ellesmere' in French R. Fogle and Louis A. Knafla, *Patronage in Late Renaissance England: Papers Read at a Clark Library Seminar, 14 May 1977* (Los Angeles, 1983), pp. 33–115 (34, 42–3, 48, 50–1, 53–8, 67–8, 74–80). Knafla's perspective is compatible with Morgan's in most respects and is another major source for the approach taken to educational patronage in this chapter.

and exhibitions at the older Oxbridge colleges. It may be that by 1579, the figure of the northern or north-western grammar school boy who comes south to Cambridge and on the advice of his new friends takes employment in lowland counties (such as Kent) has become a literary paradigm: this is the story, at any rate, at the heart of Edmund Spenser's *The shepheardes calender* (1579), in which the shepherd Hobbinol (Gabriel Harvey – at Pembroke Hall, Cambridge with Spenser) gives the poet just such advice. The political issue behind Spenserian pastoral may be as much the specific question of court appropriation and manipulation of local intellectual tradition as the general question of political and religious reform.[85]

The hypothesis of an English rhetorical tradition specific to the sixteenth-century influx of arts students from second tier territories finds remarkable confirmation in a passage from the opening of the first of the St John's College 'Parnassus' plays, mentioned earlier. 'The Pilgrimage to Parnassus' (1598–9) starts with two prospective college arts undergraduates (Philomusus and Studioso) taking advice from Consoliodorus about the route up to 'greene Parnassus hill' and the return thence with 'refined tounge' to the valleys. Earlier, we heard Ascham refer to an 'order of learning, and discipline of maners' specific to St John's and exported to Trinity College in the same university, Cambridge. The foundation of this 'order' in the first two years of the arts degree was logic or dialectic, and the homegrown textbook which introduced fifteen year-old students at St John's and other colleges across the university to reformed Aristotelian dialectic (learned alongside and sometimes in tension with the rhetoricised dialectic of Agricola, then Ramus) was produced by two fellows of St John's. John Seton, admitted as a Fisher scholar in 1529 (presumably from Yorkshire), first printed his *Dialectica* in 1545, but it did not assume its definitive form until Peter Carter, one of the many St John's students from Lancashire who came down on Hugh Ashton's foundation (admitted 1554), first added his annotations in the edition of 1572 after having returned to Preston as a schoolmaster.[86] It is first year college students' encounter with this textbook that is allegorised in the following speech of Studioso:

[85] The reference here is to the annotations on the June eclogue in Spenser's work.
[86] *Dialectica Joannis Setoni Cantabrigiensis, annotationibus Petri Carteri, vt clarissimis, ita breuissimis explicata* (London, 1572). On Seton's and Carter's manual and its place in the Cambridge B. A. see L. Jardine, *Francis Bacon: Discovery and the Art of Discourse* (Cambridge, 1974), pp. 9–10, 35–8, 66–7; W. S. Howell, *Logic and Rhetoric in England, 1500–1700* (Princeton, 1956), pp. 49–56. Bishop Fisher's private foundation stipulated that his two scholars were to be chosen 'out of the county of York' while two of Hugh Ashton's scholars were to be chosen in the first instance from natives

The firste lande that wee muste travell in (as that oulde Hermite toulde me) is Logique. I have gotten Iacke Setons mappe to directe us through this cuntrie. This Iland is, according to his discription, muche like Wales, full of craggie mountaines and thornie vallies. There are two robbers in this cuntrie caled Genus and Species, that take captive everie true mans Invention that come by them; Pacius in his returne from Parnassus hadd beene robt by these twoo forresters, but for one Carterus, a lustie clubman, much like the Pinder of Wakfield, that defended him.[87]

Earlier I described how between the local intellectual traditions taking scholars typically (in the *ideology* of Tudor humanism) from northern, north-western, Welsh border and western counties *to* university, and *from* university to households in the hospitable southern counties, most typically Kent, lay the opportunities of scholarly service with courtiers and state officials. There is no space here to demonstrate how the allegorisation and satirisation of precisely such a cultural, political and geographical trajectory is the basis for the *Parnassus* plays as a whole: Philomusus and Studioso retire at the end of 'The Second Part of the Return from Parnassus' to 'the downes of Kent'.[88] What we can see in this passage, however, is that the rough 'cuntrie' whence the students escape with the help of Seton's 'mappe' and Carter's club is allegoric-ally associated both with Wales and, via the famous impounder of stray cattle for Wakefield (the Pinder) who held out against Robin Hood and company, Yorkshire. If we add Ralph Lever, Abraham Fraunce and Everard Digby to Seton and Carter, we begin to see just how Johnian and how north by north-west the orientation of the sixteenth-century discussion of English logic-teaching really is.[89]

There is still plenty of scope within this common cultural orienta-tion, however, for different kinds of 'pilgrimage' to and 'return' from

of Lancashire, or, in default, from natives of the diocese of Chester, another one from natives of the county (or, in default, diocese) of York, and another one from natives of the bishopric (or, in default, diocese) of Durham. See *Dictionary of National Biography*, 'Carter, Peter (1530?–1590)', 'Ashton, Hugh (d.1522)'; Thomas Baker, *History of the College of St John the Evangelist, Cambridge*, ed. J. E. B. Mayor, 2 vols. (Cambridge, 1869), vol. 1, pp. 94–5, 100, 282, 286, 352–3.

[87] *Parnassus Plays*, ed. Leishman, 'The Pilgrimage to Parnassus', I. 1. 17, 102, 130–9. 'Pacius' is a highly topical allusion to a logic manual by Vicenzan Julius Pacius just published (1597) in Cambridge. See also Howell, *Logic*, pp. 242–5.

[88] *Parnassus Plays*, ed. Leishman, 'The Second Part of the Return from Parnassus', v. 3. 2153.

[89] Ralph Lever's brother Thomas became Master of St John's. They were natives of Lancashire, and Ralph probably wrote his *Arte of reason* (London, 1573) while a fellow at St John's in 1549–51. See the *Dictionary of National Biography* and Howell, *Logic*, pp. 57–8. Digby came from Rutlandshire and after his *Theoria Analytica* (London, 1579) became involved as an anti-Ramist in a polemic about logical method with William Temple of King's College, Cambridge. See Baker, *History of the College of St John the Evangelist*, vol. 1, p. 289, and Jardine, *Francis Bacon*, pp. 59–64.

Parnassus, and this is where we can begin to differentiate between
Ascham and Hoskyns once again. As stated previously, the foundation of Ascham's learning was a four-way transaction between north-
countrymen, their 'countries' (Yorkshire, Richmondshire), the college
and the Prince, but there is little sense in *The Scholemaster* of any 'return'
to or for a Yorkshire imagined as a concrete regional community. The
work is premissed on the stark contrast between vulgar brutalities in
northern schools and the civilised practices employed by Ascham in
court service with his aristocratic and royal pupils. Despite his religious
politics, Ascham's career and intellectual expectations as a Latinist and
provider of pedagogical services are structured by the forms of patronage of Latinity associated on the one hand with ecclesiastical magnates
like Thomas Wolsey, John Fisher and Nicholas Metcalfe, patronage
designed primarily to produce great diplomats and persuasive theologians for ecclesiastical and court chancelleries, and on the other hand
with royalty, desirous of a Latinity appropriate to the royal court. When,
in 1540–2, long after taking his M. A., an impecunious and ill Ascham
finds himself stuck back in Yorkshire, he relies for a paid route back to
Cambridge on the composition of a Latin epistle to impress the conservative, anti-Erasmian archbishop of York, Edward Lee.[90]

Ascham, then, is answering and profiting from a demand from the
centre; as such, the idea that the educational revolution produced a
nationally centralised life via a universal and systematised literary culture
captures the case of his secularisation of late medieval ecclesiastical
Latinity as the ideology of the 'Cambridge connection' quite well, but
it does not begin to cover the consequences of the diffusion in demand
for an arts education, nor the developing complexities of the educational culture linking countries, universities and court in this period.
For within this 'centralisation' the clusters of meanings and usage around
elite humanistic literacy rapidly diversified as the demand for localised
and applied services of teaching, preaching and reading in both Latin
and the vernaculars spread widely amongst the yeomanry, gentry and
aristocracy, as they employed tutors, chaplains, secretaries, and advisers
for their households.

At first sight, the foundations of John Hoskyns' learning seem remarkably similar to Ascham's. In the course of collecting paradigms
of the form of rhetorical amplification he calls 'progressio', Hoskyns
introduces and then offers to his student an example of a piece of

---

[90] Ryan, *Ascham*, p. 33.

rhetoric directly redolent of Griffiths' praise of Cardinal Wolsey and of Ascham's praise of the northern benefactors of St John's:

Or to give that bishop his right that built two absolute colleges at his own charges and endowed them with lands, look downwards:

> How rare it is in these days for a prelate not to grant long leases, diminish the revenues of his see; how laudable it is but to repair the ruins of his own decayed palaces and churches; how magnificent a thing it is thought for a nobleman to build an hospital, how royal for two or three princes to erect one college: and can there be such unthankfulness as to bear but one ordinary remembrance of him that enriched his bishopric, built two of the most famous nurseries of learning in the land, was liberal to all wants in his life, and left worthy bequests to all degrees at his death?[91]

Hoskyns, as his students would have known, is here praising the founder of Winchester and New Colleges, Bishop William of Wykeham, and alluding to the local intellectual tradition that brought him eventually to the inns of court. He grafts on to this the newer secular trends in charitable endowments symbolised by the mention of noblemen building hospitals and princes founding new colleges such as Trinity. In this case, however, we must conclude from the difference in the nature of the demand for tutorial services placed upon Hoskyns, that the rhetoric of local intellectual tradition is less perfunctory than in the case either of Griffiths or Ascham.

For where in the case of *The Scholemaster* there is no 'return' to or for a Yorkshire imagined as a concrete regional community, we must remember that Hoskyns writes his treatise at a moment when he is informally tutoring a whole string of young masters from the landed yeomanry and gentry of Herefordshire, while at the same time beginning to accumulate more land in the vicinity. Some of the paradigms he composes reflect the pressure of these circumstances. As an example of 'paralipsis . . . when you say you let pass that which notwithstanding you touch at full' (i.e. when you discuss fully something you say you are not going to discuss at all), Hoskyns composes a speech in which he touches at full the expectations and jealousies which surround the student's educational progress back in his 'country': 'I urge not to you the hope of your friends . . . I lay not before you the necessity of the place you are to furnish . . . I omit the envious concurrencies and some prepared comparisons in your country etc. . . .'. This is continuous

---

[91] Hoskyns, *Directions*, ed. Hudson, p. 27. The editor has distinguished Hoskyns' introductory comment from the paradigm itself by indenting the latter. In the manuscript no such layout is used – see Osborn, *John Hoskyns*, p. 141.

with the story told by the last paradigm of any substantial length in the treatise, and one of the longest found throughout: a rhetorical deliberation using 'occupatio' of the social and political strategies open to a worthy local gentleman and judge facing a 'factious country': 'Are you judge amongst your neighbors and inferiors, be precisely just and equal. Are you assistant to your friend, be advisedly but throughly partial. You would be accounted liberal: testify seldom, but publicly and worthily'.[92]

CONCLUSION

Both Ascham's and Hoskyns' texts are products of the greatly increased sixteenth-century demand for the provision of localised and applied services of arts teaching and reading to the yeomanry, gentry and aristocracy. The differences between them can be approached diachronically and synchronically.

Diachronically, the distance between Ascham's and Hoskyns' treatises is the range in the full career of a humanist education between early, pre-university preparation in the ethos and style of pure Latin, and late, post-university training in applied, vernacular reasoning; between, also, courtly and civic contexts for the exercise of humanistic skills. Ascham's, furthermore, is an officially endorsed and protected pedagogical manual that goes through five editions between 1570 and 1589; the 'tradition' it standardises is an exclusive escape route from local teaching practices via a private aristocratic academy in Suffolk.[93] Hoskyns' notes, though quite widely used and circulated, do not assume the same 'manual' status and relate to a particular local intellectual tradition linking Hereford-shire and the Court and courts at London, a tradition which produces a specific demand on the part of the Herefordshire 'country' for reliable tutorial services in the capital. To a certain extent, the distance in question is also, then, that between an official pedagogical standard and the varieties of local teaching traditions and local teaching materials (like the *vulgaria*) to be found at work in practice. The extent to which this can, in turn, be assimilated to the political distance between official and unofficial knowledge is hard to discern from the nature of the 'Directions' alone. It is interesting, however, that by the 1610s, both the

---

[92] Hoskyns, *Directions*, ed. Hudson, pp. 49–50.
[93] Stewart, *Close Readers*, p. 115, cites the well-known entry in the Stationer's Register for 6 March, 1581, which makes permission to print Mulcaster's *Positions* conditional upon its not containing anything 'preiudiciall or hurtfull to the booke of maister ASKHAM'.

figure of Hoskyns and the texts of his works were key elements in what David Colclough has characterised as networks of unofficial knowledge indulging habits of informal and oppositional political analysis via the collection and circulation of manuscript materials and news between London, the universities and 'countries' such as Shropshire. One such politically satirical manuscript miscellany, a key source for Hoskyns' poems, dates from *c.*1630–40 and appears to have been written by a Wykehamist at Oxford.[94]

There is, however, also a distance to be measured synchronically. By the end of the 1590s, the father of a student like Robert Harley is less likely to be taking advice such as Ascham's on the available methods for cultivating the young in a pure Latin environment. Although the ideal scene for early education remains gently recreational and thus still 'pure', not practical, the smart money is now paid out for lessons which place an early emphasis on vernacular learning (not only in English, but most frequently in French), and on the process of making moral, political and historical judgements. Thus early education is more likely by the 1590s to have been conceived as a preparation for the new, eclectic, pragmatic, Latin-and-vernacular style of humanist philosophy in demand by that period. The transitional figure is Michel de Montaigne, who offers a pedagogical conception of this kind, while also recalling the details of his father's imperfectly realised attempt to provide his son with pure, spoken Latin as a first language.[95]

Though the exemplars, paradigms and mentalities of a secularised version of late medieval ecclesiastical Latinity of course persist, between Ascham and Hoskyns the lay foundations of humanist learning go deeper into the localities. One result of this is that the cultural geography and topography of 'civilised' England begins to emerge more distinctly as the laity of the outlying and border territories make pilgrimage to Parnassus with their textbook and tutorial guides and return into the valleys with their refined tongues. We should not assume, however, that during the sixteenth century an aristocratic ethos of court Latinity was replaced by a commonwealth ethos of local intellectual tradition which automatically spread power to the localities. Let us not

---

[94] Bodleian MS Malone 19. My information here is derived from Colclough, 'Manuscript Miscellanies'.

[95] Indicative of this shift is a treatise such as James Cleland, ΗΡΩ-ΠΑΙΔΕΙΑ, *or, the institution of a young nobleman* (Oxford, 1607), especially sigs. K3ᵛ, L2ʳ. See also W. Boutcher, 'Vernacular Humanism in the Sixteenth Century' in *The Cambridge Companion to Renaissance Humanism*, ed. J. Kraye (Cambridge, 1996), pp. 189–202; Michel de Montaigne, *Œuvres complètes*, eds. A. Thibaudet and M. Rat (Paris, 1962), pp. 152, 172–3.

forget the complaint of the Pocklington worthies that their scholarships had been usurped by strangers.

Let us recall, also, the fate of the Suffolk scholars in Robert Greene's play of the late sixteenth century, *The honorable historie of Frier Bacon, and Frier Bongay*. This pseudo-historical comedy of royal and aristocratic marriage includes sharp satire on the consumer demand excited at court by the promise of the services available from proponents of the new learning in sixteenth-century England. Prince Edward and his followers go to Oxford to find a scholar to help them in their designs on Margaret, the fair maid of Fressingfield in Suffolk.[96] The Prince offers Friar Bacon – a scholar resident in Brasenose College in Oxford – '[l]iving and lands to strength thy colledge state' if Bacon will conjure the maid for him.[97] In fact, Bacon's services are desperately needed all round. The Doctors of Oxford need him to defeat the 'science' of the terrifying German scholar who accompanies King Henry's royal visitors as they progress to the university for evidence of its learning.[98] Bacon has intelligence of all, and can conjure a vision of what is happening in private places anywhere in the southeast with his magic glass.[99] But although he promises to wall the coast of Kent and Sussex against invaders with brass, he cannot teach his own poor scholar Miles a pure Latin, and resorts to beating him in frustration.[100]

Meanwhile, two local Suffolk gentlemen begin to vie aggressively for the affections of the most precious of the county's local assets, Margaret, affections which have already been secretly won by the fair-spoken courtier Lacy, the Earl of Lincoln.[101] It is at this point that two humble young Suffolk scholars of the kind imagined in Griffiths' speech in *King Henry VIII* (discussed earlier) arrive at Bacon's cell in Brasenose. They declare themselves 'colledge mates', that is, '*Suffolke* men and neighbouring friends' whose fathers possess adjoining lands in two neighbouring villages of the county ('in *Crackfield* mine doth dwell, / And his in *Laxfield*'). The experience of being college mates at Oxford has clearly – as we heard Victor Morgan describe earlier – strengthened their identification with their 'country' because they ask if Bacon will focus his 'glasse prospective' on their fathers down in Suffolk.[102] What Bacon's learning helps them to see, however, is their fathers in the

---

[96] Robert Greene, *Plays and Poems*, ed. J. C. Collins, 2 vols. (Oxford, 1905), vol. II, 'Frier Bacon and Frier Bongay', I. I. 94–7. I am very grateful to my colleague Dr Lorna Hutson for drawing my attention to this play.
[97] *Ibid.*, II. 3. 588.   [98] *Ibid.*, II. 4. 818–22.   [99] *Ibid.*, I. 2. 286–330.
[100] *Ibid.*, I. 2. 229–37; II. 2. 523–35.   [101] *Ibid.*, III. 3 passim.   [102] *Ibid.*, IV. 3. 1764–73.

act of viciously duelling for the hand of Margaret. The tragedy, the only tragedy in the play, is that the two scholars in Bacon's study react to this vision by stabbing each other to death. What is, in truth, less a tragic than a tragi-comic moment is quickly forgotten, however, in the courtly pageant of royal and aristocratic marriage which concludes the play, as Margaret marries the Earl, and Prince Edward marries Princess Elinor of Castile.[103]

Here, then, local intellectual tradition finds itself thoroughly defeated and corrupted by forms of new learning enthralled in the service of court interests. What we see, though, is not the emergence of a distinction between a local and a national culture founded statically on a new self-concept (as Frank Whigham put it earlier), or a universal style of thinking. We see the very local dynamics of this 'national' culture comically – if satirically – endorsed. We see the dynamics of the powerful interests employing the services of the new men of learning tutoring in the colleges to link together interested parties from the sphere of international imperial politics, the English court, Oxford University and the rich county of Suffolk, and to spin those dynamics as a matter of national destiny.

[103] *Ibid.*, IV. 3. 1781–816; V. 3 *passim*.

CHAPTER 7

'Not so much praise as precept': Erasmus, panegyric, and the Renaissance art of teaching princes[1]

David Rundle

Erasmus was well acquainted with the arrogance of power; indeed, he could be accused of having abetted the powerful's illusions of grandeur. For example, in outlining his preferred *Education of the Christian Prince*, he freely declares that a country owes everything to its good prince. However, on Erasmus' calculation, this national debt of gratitude should be accounted to someone else's credit: for making the good prince what he is, the country is indebted to his educator.[2] This is not just a Northern bout of Italian *prepotenza*; rather, it reflects the realisation or belief that, to use their power properly, rulers are dependent on the teaching of the learned. This realisation is what could be dubbed the pride of pedagogy. Erasmus was certainly not alone among Renaissance scholars in being blessed with the self-confidence that such a belief instils: those who devoted their lives to contemplation of the *studia humanitatis* often claimed that the education they promoted had a political importance.[3] If they themselves could not combine, as it were, poetry and power, they could at least teach others how to negotiate the active life.

Teaching in the Renaissance was not only dignified, it was also lucrative. 'Humanists' might be definable as those members of scholarly coteries who formed the *soi-disant* intellectual avant-garde of fifteenth-century Italy and sixteenth-century Europe; but the term originates in

---

[1] I would like to thank Dr George Garnett and Dr James McConica, as well as the vigilant editors, for their detailed and helpful comments on an earlier draft of this paper. In this chapter, all translations of passages of Latin are my own; the original is quoted in the footnotes unless there is an accessible twentieth-century edition, in which case the bibliographical reference alone is given.

[2] O. Herder (ed.), *Opera omnia Erasmi*, IV/I [hereafter ASD IV/I] (Amsterdam, 1974) ll. 47–8.

[3] For a little-known statement of this common belief, see Lapo da Castiglionchio's unedited *Comparatio studiorum et rei militaris*, in (for example) Oxford: Bodleian, MS. Auct. F.5.26, esp. pp. 128–9.

umanista – a paid teacher of a defined curriculum of subjects.[4] At the same time, the humanists could claim to be no ordinary schoolmasters. For, following their classical role-models, they could boast a better quality of pupil as well as of education. For example, of Guarino's *studio*, founded at Ferrara in the 1440s with funds from the ruling dynasty, it could be claimed: 'as is said of Isocrates, countless princes came out of his school, as many as out of the Trojan horse.'[5] The prospect of humanist education was the preparation of future leaders for action, although the reality may have been more mundane. Guarino's lessons may well have been dominated by heavy grammatical analysis of classical texts – but we would underestimate his skill if we imagined that he had not mastered the pedagogical trick of holding his pupils' attention by occasionally turning away from his text and adding more general, more political observations.[6] However this may be, the humanists were anyway not just teachers during school-hours: they were pedagogues for life. They found opportunities to teach outside the classroom. This chapter is concerned with one such form of pedagogy: the prose panegyric addressed to secular princes.

The panegyric might seem an unlikely method of teaching; as the classical textbooks of rhetoric demonstrate, panegyric is not a forensic, nor a deliberative but an epideictic oration.[7] It is Erasmus' own claim that the panegyric could be not so much praise as precept, and this discussion will centre on his contribution to the genre. In 1504, Philip the Handsome, Duke of Burgundy, returned to the Low Countries after a two-year excursion to Spain, where he had married the Catholic Monarchs' daughter, Juana (whose extreme or excessive mourning on her husband's death two years later earned her instead of sympathy the sobriquet 'the Mad'). Erasmus was called upon to celebrate his

---

[4] For a recent restatement of his narrow definition of 'humanist', see P. O. Kristeller, 'Humanism' in C. B. Schmitt and Q. Skinner (eds.), *The Cambridge History of Renaissance Philosophy* (Cambridge, 1988) pp. 113–137.

[5] Ludovico Carbone in his funeral oration to Guarino (paraphrasing Cicero, *De oratore*, II.94), edited in E. Garin (ed.), *Prosatori Latini del Quattrocento* (Milan, 1952) pp. 382–417 at p. 392.

[6] *Pace* A. Grafton and L. Jardine, *From Humanism to the Humanities* (London, 1986) ch. 1; see, for example, Pietro del Monte's comments on his time in Guarino's school in Poggio Bracciolini, *Opera omnia* (ed. R. Fubini) IV (Turin, 1969) pp. 615–639.

[7] Quintilian, *Institutio Oratoria*, II.x.11; III.viii.7. On the theory of praise in both antiquity and the Renaissance, see O. B. Hardison, *The Enduring Monument: a Study of the Idea of Praise in Renaissance Literary Theory and Practice* (Chapel Hill, 1962) ch. 2. The prose panegyric to princes is naturally only one small part of the Renaissance epideictic tradition; for other elements, see J. W. O'Malley, *Praise and Blame in Renaissance Rome* (Durham, NC, 1979) and J. M. McManamon, *Funeral Oratory and the Cultural Ideals of Italian Humanism* (Chapel Hill and London, 1989).

Duke's return in an oration to be delivered at the attendant festivities – the commission resulted in his *Panegyricus*.[8] At the same time, Erasmus produced a justification for the genre which reveals how he – and other humanists – appropriated the classical tradition. We need first, however, to outline the difficulties humanists faced in employing the panegyric.

Europe before the fifteenth century was acquainted with examples of panegyrical writing.[9] Claudian's addresses to Honorius were well known, as were Optatianus' clever acrostics, but these were all in poetical form. There was another tradition, that of the religious panegyric of saints.[10] However, the prose panegyrics to secular princes were, in one sense, a Renaissance rediscovery: to be precise, they were reborn in the summer of 1433. Their midwife was Giovanni Aurispa, who is perhaps best remembered for his felicitous plundering of Byzantine libraries.[11] In the early 1430s, he enjoyed less exotic climes: he was attending the Council of Basel when he decided to go on pilgrimage to Cologne, a journey in which the humanist combined Christian devotion with archival archaeology. Tracing the path of the Rhine up through Germany, he stopped at Mainz and there, in the cathedral library, unearthed, among other things, a codex containing what became known as the *panegyrici veteres*: twelve panegyrics to Roman emperors, mainly from the late third and early fourth centuries, but headed by an oration to Trajan written by Pliny the Younger in AD 100.[12] Aurispa transcribed the speeches and, on his return to Basel, publicised his discovery.[13] Copies of the *panegyrici veteres* soon circulated both in Italy and further afield: for example, six or so years after their discovery, the English prince Humphrey, Duke of Gloucester, received an elegant manuscript

[8] The text is edited in ASD IV/1, pp. 1–93. An English translation has appeared in the *Complete Works of Erasmus*, 27 (Toronto, 1986) pp. 1–79. The work is discussed by V. de Caprariis, 'Il panegyricus di Erasmo a Filippo di Borgogna', *Rivista storica italiana*, 65 (1953) pp. 199–221; J. D. Tracy, *The Politics of Erasmus* (Toronto, 1978) pp. 17–22.
[9] E. R. Curtius, *European Literature and the Latin Middle Ages* (Princeton, 1953) pp. 154–166.
[10] See O'Malley, *Praise and Blame*.
[11] For Aurispa's biography, see *Dizionario Biografico degli Italiani*, vol. 4 (Rome, 1962), *sub nomine*.
[12] *XII Panegyrici latini*, most recently edited by R. A. B. Mynors (Oxford, 1964); English translation of all but Pliny's now available in C. Nixon and B. Rogers (eds.), *In Praise of Late Roman Emperors* (Oxford, 1994), while Pliny's is available in the second volume of B. Radice's Loeb edition, *Letters and Panegyricus* (Cambridge, MA, 1969).
[13] Aurispa himself relates his discovery in R. Sabbadini (ed.), *Carteggio di Giovanni Aurispa* (Rome, 1931) pp. 81–3; see also Sabbadini's note in *Studi italiani di filologia classica*, 11 (1903) pp. 263–6. For the future Nicholas V's involvement in editing the speeches, see A. Manfredi, 'Un' *Editio* umanistica dei *Panegyrici Latini Minores*: il codice Vaticano Lat. 1775 e il suo correttore', in L. Belloni, G. Milanese and A. Porro (eds.), *Studia classica Iohanni Tarditi oblata* (Milan, 1995), vol. II, pp. 1313–25.

of these fashionable texts, and his copy was itself copied soon after its arrival.[14]

The Duke of Gloucester was supplied with his codex by the Milanese scholar, Pier Candido Decembrio, who committed to paper his own response to the *panegyrici veteres*. In a short letter, Decembrio expresses extravagant praise for Pliny's text – 'there is nothing more perfect, more beautiful, more embellished' – and concludes with a telling variation on the conventional complaints about the modern world: 'would that our age had either such praisers or princes fully worthy of such praise.'[15] Few Renaissance princes may have taken up the challenge to be like Trajan but, as we shall see, there soon appeared panegyrists eager to imitate Pliny. For the moment, however, what is notable is that Decembrio's comments concentrate on Pliny's work. This was not unprecedented: Aurispa himself had stressed that the Mainz manuscript included 'a Panegyric of Pliny to Trajan; I have never read anything more elegant than this.'[16] From the very start, then, the *panegyrici veteres* attracted unequal attention. Together the panegyrics might have constituted a rediscovered genre, but this paled into insignificance beside the fact of the first author's identity; the other eleven speeches were merely supporting cast, often relegated to back-stage. The pull of the 'big name' is reflected in those surviving manuscripts which include Pliny's and omit the other speeches. Yet, this is not to suggest that the first *Panegyricus* achieved much of a solo-career: only a few manuscripts exist in which the Pliny stands alone, and certainly it was never printed alone in the late fifteenth and early sixteenth centuries.[17] The *Panegyricus*

---

[14] Humphrey's codex survives as Paris: Bibliothèque Nationale, MS. lat. 7805, on which see A. C. de la Mare's description in *Bodleian Library Record*, xiii (1988–91) pp. 115–8; Pier Candido Decembrio's characteristic pointing hand appears at fol. 95ʳ. Oxford: Balliol College, MS.315, fol. 69–148 is, as Mynors suggested [*XII Panegyrici latini*, p. vi], a copy of this ms., excluding the third and fourth panegyrics; it was owned by William Gray, bishop of Ely (1454–1478). On Decembrio, see below.

[15] The letter, noted by R. Sabbadini (*Le Scoperte dei Codici Latini*, ii (reprint) (Florence, 1967) p. 243), is printed by V. Zaccaria, 'Pier Candido Decembrio, Michele Pizolpasso e Ugolino Pisani', *Atti dell'Istituto Veneto di Scienze, Lettere ed Arti*, 133, (1974–5) pp. 187–212 at p. 203. I have compared the copy printed there with that in Seville: Biblioteca Colombina, MS. 7/4/20, fol. 2, on which manuscript see my 'A Renaissance Bishop and his books: Pietro del Monte, bishop of Brescia (d. 1457)', *PBSR* (forthcoming). On Decembrio generally, see *Dizionario Biografico degli Italiani*, vol. 33 (Rome, 1987) *sub nomine*.

[16] Sabbadini (ed.), *Carteggio di Aurispa*, p. 82. It was also Pliny's panegyric, rather than all twelve speeches, that, probably at Decembrio's suggestion, Humphrey of Gloucester requested: A. Sammut, *Unfredo Duca di Gloucester e gli umanisti italiani* (Padua, 1980) pp. 37, 189.

[17] For manuscripts comprised solely of the Pliny, see for example London: British Library, MSS. Add. 12008 & Royal 15.B.v. London: British Library, MS. Arundel 154, meanwhile, includes the popular translation of the Ps-Phalaris letters and Pliny's epistles as well as his *Panegyricus*.

may have been separated from its original companions but it simultaneously found new textual partners.

Pliny's speech failed to build an independent circulation, in part, for the same reason that it became semi-detached from the other panegyrics. When the *Panegyricus* was rediscovered, the younger Pliny was already well-known not only for the (spurious) *de viris illustribus* but also for his (imperfectly disseminated) letters; to these epistles the *Panegyricus* made a fitting supplement, especially as it was mentioned in a couple of them.[18] So, for example, in 1508 Aldus Manutius published an edition of Pliny's works which boasted a fuller collection of his letters than previously available; the *Panegyricus* is also included, primarily, the preface says, for reasons of comprehensiveness – 'I thought it most appropriate to publish it at the same time in a single volume.'[19] However, Aldus goes on to add a second reason: the work is so elegant, so learned, that its author appears to surpass himself, and everyone (but especially great men) should read it. Indeed, Aldus is bold enough to suggest that the *Panegyricus* is even greater than Xenophon's *Cyropaedia*:

> [Cyrus] was portrayed with not historical accuracy but the model of just government in mind . . . Trajan, on the other hand, was the same sort of man in reality as our reading tells us he was. So, just as Scipio not without reason rarely let Xenophon's work out of his hands because there was nothing in it which could be neglected for the duty of careful and ordered government, similarly we should not let this *Panegyricus* of our Pliny out of our hands since, through the example of the best man, the most powerful Emperor, the most just prince, we can make ourselves his like.[20]

Over seventy years after its second birth, the *Panegyricus* still attracts effusive praise; yet, this may not be a wholly positive sign. The very fact that those scholars who were closely involved in its circulation

---

For incunabula, see Hain 13116–18; in these as in the early sixteenth century printings (e.g. Beroaldo's edition (Venice: Albertinus Vercellensis, 1501)) the speech is paired with some version of the letters as well, often, as the *de viris illustribus*.

[18] Decembrio, in the letter mentioned above (Footnote 15), alludes to one of these epistolary references.

[19] *C. Plinii Secundi . . . epistolarum libri decem . . .* (Venice: Aldus Manutius, 1508) fol. iv: convenientissimum existimavi in uno volumine simul edere. On the ten-book tradition of the letters, see L. Reynolds (ed.), *Texts and Transmission* (Oxford, 1983) pp. 317–320.

[20] Aldus, fol. iv': qui quidem ipso Cyro Xenophontis maior quod illo non ad historiae fidem scriptus sed ad effigiem iusti imperii . . . hic autem re vera talis fuit qualem fuisse legimus. Quare, ut Africanus ille Xenophontis libros non sine caussa de manibus ponere non solebat quia nullum esset praetermissum in his officium diligentis & moderati imperii sic nos hunc Secundi nostri Panegyricum de manibus ponere non debemus ut optimi viri fortissimi Imperatoris, iustissimi Principis exemplo tales et ipsi efficiamur. This passage relies for its references to Xenophon and Scipio on Cicero, *Epistolae ad Quintum fratrem*, i.i.23.

– from Aurispa to Aldus – felt it necessary to protest so much about its elegance might suggest that this was not an irrefutable claim. Moreover, the central conceit of Aldus' phrases might hint at the limits to the *Panegyricus*' popularity. The editor is flattering Pliny's speech by comparison with an established classic and claiming that this work should have similar canonical status – by implication, it does not have that yet.[21] Modern commentators have been quick to note the stylistic shortcomings of Pliny's *Panegyricus*; perhaps Renaissance readers (despite their protestations) were not insensible to these longueurs.[22] Perhaps the early claims for the work can be credited with having as much veracity as most dust-jàcket recommendations.

If stylistic flaws in part account for the *Panegyricus*' mixed fortunes, another reason was surely the chosen genre. For, in post-classical Europe, panegyric had long had a bad name. Early Christian writers, from Augustine on, had reacted against the perceived excesses of pagan panegyrics to Roman emperors; this response was succinctly summarised in the early seventh century by Isidore of Seville:

Panegyricum est licentiosum et lasciviosum genus dicendi in laudibus regum, in cuius compositione homines multis mendaciis adulantur. Quod malum a Graecis exortum est, quorum levitas instructa dicendi facultate et copia incredibili multas mendaciorum nebulas suscitavit.[23]

This was a definition with a long history ahead of it. The tactful might prefer to equate panegyric with praise but the less charitable adjudged it adulation. Flattery was a vice which should be avoided, as John of Salisbury (for example) pointed out at length in his enduringly popular *Policraticus*.[24] Moreover, the humanists found in Plutarch's *How to Tell a Flatterer from a Friend* a new text to teach the same lesson. This work was not only adapted in the 1430s by Guarino for his princely patron, Leonello d'Este; it was also translated seventy years later by the main protagonist of our story, Erasmus. The history of what might be called the Isidorean tradition, condemning panegyric as flattering lies, could be continued beyond the 1500s. English dictionary definitions of the late sixteenth and early seventeenth centuries have a familiar ring to them:

---

[21] On the popularity of the *Cyropaedia*, see Y. L. Too's chapter in this volume; D. Marsh, 'Xenophon' in V. Brown (ed.), *Catalogus translationum et commentariorum*, VII (Washington, 1992) pp. 75–196, esp. pp. 81, 83–5, 116–38.

[22] B. Radice, 'Pliny and the *Panegyricus*', *Greece & Rome*, 15 (1968) pp. 166–172 at pp. 169–70.

[23] St Isidore, *Libri Etymologiarum*, VI.8.7.

[24] Johannes Salisbriensis, *Policraticus*, III.14 (ed. C. C. I. Webb (Oxford, 1909) vol. I, pp. 221–32). On humanist interest in this work, see A. Linder, 'The knowledge of John of Salisbury in the late middle ages', *Studi medievali*, 3rd ser., 18 (1977) pp. 881–932, esp. pp. 906–7 and 912–13.

Panegyricum. A licentious and lascivious kinde of speaking or oration in the praise and commendation of Kings, wherein men do ioyne many lyes with flatterie.[25]

The dictionary-compiler felt no need to provide an original definition; all that was necessary was to anglicise Isidore's words.

So, panegyrics had, as it were, an unflattering reputation. It was, moreover, one which lasted through that period we call 'the Renaissance'. The rediscovery of Pliny's rhetoric did not persuade many to reject completely the 'medieval' criticisms of the genre. There were a few – like the seventeenth century translator, Sir Robert Stapylton – who believed that what others called sycophancy was actually a demonstration of due respect. In the turbulent England of 1644, writing in Oxford, the surrogate royal capital, Stapylton produced the first English rendition of Pliny's *Panegyricus* and dedicated it to Charles, Prince of Wales. The translator's agenda was patently not purely scholarly; as he explained in his preface:

in the present eruption of *Licentious pamphlets*, I conceive it seasonable to publish a modest worke and necessary to intitle it to inviolable protection. Humbly therefore I consecrate to your highnesse *Pliny's* Panegyricke, which hath lived many ages with constant approbation . . . and . . . may have the honour to out-live all those abortives of the Presse.[26]

This, though, was the lesser tradition. More frequently, Renaissance authors accepted that panegyric and veracity were rarely bedfellows. Two influential examples of this come from Florence in the decades immediately preceding Aurispa's discovery. In his last years, Coluccio Salutati (1331–1406), chancellor of Florence and pedagogue to the first generation of humanists, admitted that poetic panegyrics were deceitful but thought they could still have a positive function:

[25] Thomas Thomas, *Dictionarium Linguae Latinae et Anglicanae* (1587), quoted by J. D. Garrison in his *Dryden and the Tradition of Panegyric* (Berkeley, 1975), pp. 6–7; as Garrison shows, this definition was followed by Blount in 1656. An alternative, fuller translation of the Isidore would be: 'Panegyric is an unguarded and wanton form of speaking in praise of kings, in the composition of which men flatter with many lies. This evil began with the Greeks, whose shallow eloquence [*levitas*] with their educated skill in speaking and their amazing abundant style aroused many clouds of lies.'

[26] *Pliny's Panegyricke: a speech in senate* (Oxford: s.n., 1644) sig.A2ʳ⁻ᵛ. The English were late in producing a vernacular version of the speech: for example, in the fifteenth century, there were versions in both Castilian and Portuguese, on which see J. Lawrance, 'Humanism in the Iberian Peninsula' in A. Goodman and A. Mackay (eds.), *The Impact of Humanism on Western Europe* (London, 1990) p. 235, as well as a *volgare* version by Aurelio Brandolini (*Iter Italicum*, 7 vols. (Leiden, 1963–97) III, pp. 309, 310), while in the early sixteenth century a German translation was produced for Frederick the Wise, Elector of Saxony (*Iter*, III, p. 393).

If praise has been devised untruthfully [*de falsis*], as is the case whenever it is dressed up in panegyrics, it warns its subject that he has not been praised as much as told what he should do; it spurs on those who are praised into trying to become like the people they see themselves being praised as, even in error.[27]

Salutati's most illustrious pupil, Leonardo Bruni (1369–1444), provided a rather different defence of panegyric. Bruni, an immigrant to Florence from hilltop Arezzo, had in the first years of the fifteenth century demonstrated his loyalty to his adoptive city by writing a *Praise of the Florentine city*.[28] Thirty years later, belatedly justifying that work's exaggerated claims, Bruni produced what is surely the first humanist definition of the panegyric. He pointed out that his *Praise* was based on good classical precedents, being imitative of Aristides' panegyric of Athens. He went on to explain that 'what the Greeks call panegyric is not designed to be refined rhetoric but to be pleasing to the people. In this genre, every opportunity for praise is seized and raised to the heights in words.' For Bruni, panegyric contrasts with history: 'history certainly must follow the truth, but praise raises many things above the truth.'[29] Neither Bruni nor Salutati imagine that panegyrics are truthful; they merely claim that their lies are meant to do good or give pleasure.

Salutati and Bruni were working with separate traditions; one was acquainted only with Latin verse panegyrics, the other was consciously imitating Greek praises of cities. Later writers, with knowledge of the Latin prose panegyrics to individuals, had an even less positive attitude. Ermolao Barbaro, for example, in a 1486 speech to Maximilian, King of the Romans, which was later published in the Froben edition of ancient and modern panegyrics, includes a disclaimer:

I have in mind no panegyric, most famous king, I am not stretching the meaning of words, I amplify nothing, I gloss over nothing; instead I race through point by point and touch the bare heights of your deeds.[30]

[27] C. Salutati, *De Laboribus Herculis*, ed. B. L. Ullman (Zurich, 1951) p. 68.

[28] The *Laudatio Florentinae urbis* is published in H. Baron, *From Petrarch to Bruni* (Chicago, 1968) pp. 232–63.

[29] L. Bruni, *Epistolarum libri VIII*, ed. L. Mehus (Florence, 1741) ep. VIII.4 [II, pp. 111–2]: id Graeci panegyricum vocant nec ad subtilitatem dicendi sed ad plausum multitudinis accomodari, omnisque laudandi occasio arripienda est in eo genere ac verbis extollenda . . . Aliud est historia, aliud laudatio. Historia quidem veritatem sequi debet, laudatio vero multa supra veritatem extollit.

[30] E. Barbaro, *Epistolae, orationes et carmina*, ed. V. Branca (Florence, 1943) II, p. 113. The Froben edition of *panegyrici quotquot* was published at Basel in 1520; it includes the *panegyrici veteres*, Eumenius' *oratio per scholis Cliviensibus instaurandis* and four speeches contemporary with the period of publication: apart from Barbaro's, there is Erasmus' *Panegyricus*, Panulfo Collenucio's panegyric to the Emperor Maximilian (1494) and Georg Sauroman's *de laudibus Maximiliani Augusti Carolo & Ferdinando* (1519).

Likewise, twenty years later, Erasmus was concerned how he would be
perceived when his *Panegyricus* was published. Indeed, in an important
letter to Jean Desmarais, he claimed that he had actually been accused
of writing flattery; he took the opportunity to reject the charge and
retort that he was the victim of its antithesis – calumny.[31] Unfortunately, the only evidence we have of his *Panegyricus* being attacked on
these grounds comes from Erasmus himself – writing to John Colet, he
complained that he wrote the work reluctantly because the style of
panegyric was too close to adulation for comfort.[32] It may well be that
there were other detractors but we might equally be allowed to be
sceptical about this; claiming that he had been slandered was a useful
fiction for Erasmus. In the first place, it allowed him to publicise his
own aesthetic of the panegyric, a rationale to which we will return in
a moment. It also pre-empted criticism which was highly likely – so
probable indeed that it might seem inevitable. From Pliny's panegyric
onwards, it was conventional to claim that all earlier speeches, unlike
your own, were mendacious flattery.[33] This topos may, in fact, help
explain the resilience of the Isidorean tradition. The genre required that
panegyrists, like their critics, dismissed this type of text as usually full of
adulation – each orator differed only in claiming that their own work
was the exception to the rule. In effect, the rhetoric of a panegyric provides its own criticism.

For whatever reasons, then, the art of the panegyric was often
despised but it was also practised, with the critic and the practitioner
often the same person. For example, Filippo Beroaldo the Elder – an
early editor of Pliny's *Panegyricus* – pronounced in his tract *On the Best
State* that panegyrics of the living are a pure mockery; this treatise,
however, was printed in editions of Beroaldo's *opuscula* which also included his own *Panegyric to the illustrious prince Ludovico Sforza* – who, at
the time of writing, was very much alive.[34] Such inconsistency might
only be natural; after all, financial necessity impelled a humanist to act
the panegyrist. Humanists' sellable commodity was their eloquence;
for a scholar like Beroaldo, employed as a royal secretary, part of the

[31] P. S. Allen, *Opus Epistolarum Des. Erasmi Roterodami*, 12 vols. (Oxford, 1906–58) (hereafter Allen)
ep. 180. Note Erasmus' self-image here as Apelles, ll. 7–12.
[32] Allen, ep. 181, ll. 54–8.
[33] Pliny, *Panegyricus*, 3.4; ASD IV/1 ll. 40–41. See also Filippo Beroaldo the Elder, *Varia . . . opuscula*
(Basel: sn, 1517) fol. xxᵛ.
[34] In *Varia Philippi Beroaldi opuscula*, the *panegyricus* is at fol. xviiᵛ–xxᵛ, *de optimo statu* at fol. cxxiiiᵛ–
cxxxiiiᵛ, with the reference to panegyrics at fol. cxxxi. On Beroaldo's edition of Pliny's *Panegyricus*,
see above n. 17; for his life, see *Dizionario Biografico degli Italiani*, 9 (Rome, 1967) *sub nomine*.

job-description was to provide orations on demand, while others, like Erasmus, were hired for the special occasion. Whether receiving or seeking patronage, all were required to concoct speeches of eloquent praise. Yet, this involved them in practising a form of flattery which was at best risible, at worst reprehensible; how could this accord with grand humanist claims to educate society to the good? For some, perhaps, the inconsistency in their works actually served a purpose, with their true opinions confined to a few of their texts. Erasmus, on the other hand, was concerned not to appear so changeable. This brings us to his defence of panegyric.

Erasmus published his *Panegyricus* late in 1504.[35] Two years later, however, the oration's subject, Philip the Handsome, died with woeful bad timing, considering he had just negotiated for himself and his wife the crown of Castile. His death was also unfortunate as it undoubtedly reduced the immediate significance of Erasmus' work, undermining its optimistic predictions about Philip's future. Yet, by the mid-1510s, the humanist had found another context in which to circulate his speech. In 1516, Philip's eldest son, Charles, surpassed his late father by becoming king of both Castile and Aragon. Erasmus took this opportunity to dedicate to him both his own translation of Isocrates' popular treatise of advice to the Cyprian king, *To Nicocles*, and his own Isocratean mirror-for-princes, *Education of the Christian Prince*. In publishing these, he also reprinted as their companion piece his earlier *Panegyricus*.[36] The intention of this volume is clear: a prince is supposed to learn from this book. In his educational programme, Erasmus' *Panegyricus* was a core text. It was in such terms that Erasmus had justified his speech when he first claimed it had been attacked: it was not flattery but advice or, as he put it, not so much praise as precept.[37]

---

[35] On the work's print history, see ASD IV/1, pp. 17–21.

[36] Erasmus did not intend this textbook for the future Charles V alone; he also presented a copy to Henry VIII – see C. H. Clough, 'A presentation volume for Henry VIII. The Charlecote Park Copy of Erasmus' *Education of the Christian Prince*', *Journal of the Warburg and Courtauld Institutes*, 44 (1981) pp. 199–202.

[37] Allen, ep. 179, ll. 41–42. Apart from this letter and Allen ep. 180, which defend the *Panegyricus*, Erasmus adumbrates his aesthetic of the panegyric in an earlier work. This is a letter addressed to Adolphus of Heere which is dated 1498 but was first published, significantly, in Erasmus's 1503 *Lucubratiunculae* (Antwerp) [I have worked from the 1509 reprinting of this]. Only parts of this *epistola exhortatoria ad capessendam virtutem* are edited as Allen ep. 93; for our purposes the *praefatiuscula* is relevant for its discussion of panegyric. Allen omits the last two sentences of this, so after Allen ep. 93, ll. 1–16 add:

Nihil igitur erat aliud ista laudatio quam delicatum monendi blandumque exprobrandi genus ac plane pharmacum necessarium quidem illud sed amarum eoque melle praelitum. Id quod olim regum barbatorum violentiae dabatur non tam turpiter (ut ego opinor) quam prudenter . . .

In 1504, Erasmus did not simply claim that his *Panegyricus* had a pedagogical purpose; he also provided for it an educational pedigree. In his letter to Jean Desmarais, he stridently declared that those who believed panegyrics are plain sycophancy do not know what they are talking about:

Those who think that panegyrics are nothing other than pieces of flattery seem to have no idea by what thinking and to what end this genre of writing was devised by the most sagacious men. For, surely, in this rulers were confronted with a vision of virtue so that dishonourable princes might be corrected, the honourable may benefit, the uncouth be educated, the erring warned, the negligent aroused and finally the reproached blush at themselves. Or is it really to be believed that as great a philospher as Callisthenes, who sang Alexander's praises, or Lysias and Isocrates, or Pliny and countless others besides, when they threw their efforts into this genre, had any other end in view than to encourage to virtue under the pretext of praise?[38]

This, as we shall see, is a curious team of classical authors, but the last of them, at least, is familiar. Erasmus' statement of the panegyric's purpose actually echoes Pliny's own text, but the latter's didactic aim is rather different from that of his humanist followers.[39] Pliny explained his intention in a well-known letter. He hoped:

first, to commend our emperor's virtues to himself with honest praise and also, to advise future princes in advance (not, as it were, through a teacher, but rather with an example) what route they could best take to shining with the same glory. For, to lay down what sort of prince one should be might be a worthy but surely a heavy – and nearly arrogant – task; on the other hand, to praise the best prince and by so doing to show his successors, as if in a mirror, what light they should follow, that, indeed, contains no presumption and some utility.[40]

This was a section of Pliny's epistle that the early editors of the *panegyrici veteres* were fond of quoting: they claimed that their publication of the speeches meant that latterday princes too could learn not from a teacher but from an example.[41] The editors are producing manuals, as it were, to teach yourself leadership; if their claims – or Pliny's – were true,

---

[38] Allen, ep. 180, ll. 39–48.
[39] Pliny, *Panegyricus*, 4.1; this is directly quoted at Allen, ep. 93, ll. 15–16.
[40] Pliny, *Epistolae*, III.18.2–3, see also III.18.7.
[41] See for example the preface of Puteolano in L. Hain, *Repertorium Bibliographicum* 4 vols. (Milan, 1948) no. 13119, reprinted in *C. Plinii Secundi de viris illustribus* [and *Panegyricus*] (Bologna: Benedictus Hectoris, 1502); Giovanni Maria Cataneo's preface to his commentary on the *Panegyricus* in *C.Plinii Caecilii Secundi epistolarum libri novem* . . . (Venice: Johannes & Bernardinus Vercellenses, 1510) fol. 177 – see also his commentary on the appropriate letter at fol. 62.

the schoolmaster would be made redundant. Kingship, it appears, is a skill which needs to be learnt but not within a classroom: this is pedagogy without a pedagogue. Yet, Pliny's statement also suggests that his panegyric is not even, in the first instance, didactic: the speech is not persuading Trajan to virtue, it is merely describing his virtues. At the point of writing, this panegyric is educational only in potential; it does not begin to teach until its subject is dead and others have to learn to rule virtuously. What is descriptive of Trajan is exhortatory to his successors.

The suggestion – which is happily accepted by Renaissance readers like Aldus – is nothing less than that Trajan was an ideal prince made real.[42] Such extreme optimism was alien to Erasmus. According to him, 'nobody remains unaware' that panegyrics reflect not their subjects' merits but their authors' own ingenuity.[43] The logic of this position is less than complimentary to the subjects of the humanist panegyrics. By emphasising the advisory aspect of the genre, Erasmus is implicitly suggesting that modern princes are no Trajans.[44] Unlike Pliny's emperor, these rulers need teachers in some form or other. In this respect, Erasmus' agenda differs from that of the author he was emulating – humanist panegyric actually increases the didactic element of the genre. Ironically, of course, Erasmus claimed Pliny as one of the classical precedents for this present pedagogical use – but did he really believe this reflected the Roman consul's true intent? In other words, did he imagine that Pliny, in good Erasmian fashion, was disingenuous when he spoke fulsome praise to his prince?[45] Or is the enlisting of Pliny to the humanist educational cause itself disingenuous? There is no certain answer to this quandary but there is one piece of suggestive evidence in the letter to Desmarais. As I have mentioned, Pliny is the last name in the list of classical panegyrists. Of the other three, the most intriguing inclusion is the first named: Callisthenes.

This companion of Alexander the Great has such a varied reputation that he might seem to constitute a split personality.[46] Erasmus was being somewhat generous when he described him as 'so great a philosopher'; his credentials consisted of his being the nephew of Aristotle,

[42] Aldus recognised this in the preface to his edition; see above p. 152.
[43] ASD IV/1, *Institutio*, ll. 1335–7.   [44] Cf. Allen ep. 180, l. 159.
[45] For a modern statement of this possibility, see S. Bartsch, *Actors in the Audience: Theatricality and Double-Speak from Nero to Hadrian* (Cambridge, MA, and London) ch. 5.
[46] On Callisthenes in general, see *OCD*, 2nd ed. (Oxford, 1970) *sub nomine*; D. M. Lewis, J. Boardman, S. Hornblower, M. Ostwald (eds.), *Cambridge Ancient History* 6 (Cambridge, 1994: 2nd ed.), pp. 10–11, 626–7, 810, 872–3.

who supposedly warned him (as Erasmus notes in a later work) to say only pleasurable things to his master – advice that Callisthenes ignored at the cost of his life: he was executed for his supposed part in a conspiracy against the Emperor.[47] Yet, earlier in his life he arguably took his uncle's dictum too much to heart: he is also remembered – and this is what Erasmus is explicitly referring to in this list – as the first encomiastic historian of Alexander, who claimed, for example, that the emperor was the son of Zeus.[48] There is nothing to mark Callisthenes out as an author of panegyrics, in either the formal or the didactic sense. So, Callisthenes might provide an object-lesson in how flattery is the only safe policy when addressing monarchs, but he surely does not fit his billing as one of the 'most sagacious men' who invented the didactic genre of the panegyric.[49] Even more strikingly than Pliny, he does not match the description Erasmus provides of him. Now, to refer apparently in error to one classical forefather might be regarded as a mistake, but to mention two in this manner looks like carefulness. In other words, it is possible that Erasmus adopted these figures fully aware of the irony involved. Indeed, this would seem likely if we imagine Erasmus' letters as an exercise in creative writing, in which fictions form 'purposive narratives.'[50] Erasmus might not have been the only or the first humanist so consciously to construct his correspondence, but he is perhaps the most artful. And in this process, I would suggest, the (ab)use of classical references played its part. In effect, the intellectual pedigree of the panegyric in the letter to Desmarais is an example of how Erasmus' use of classical authors is more ingenious than ingenuous.

---

[47] Erasmus quotes this anecdote in his *Lingua*, ASD IV/IA p. 62; around the same time, Castiglione alludes to it, *Il libro del cortegiano* (Milan, 1972) p. 327. The story appears to originate from Valerius Maximus, but there is perhaps an echo of it in Plutarch's *Vita Alexandri*, c. lii. Plutarch also terms Callisthenes a philosopher; Cicero in *De oratore*, II.58 calls him a philosopher turned historian. For another reference to Callisthenes in Erasmus' works, see footnote 49 below.

[48] Plutarch, *Vita Alexandri*, c. xxxiii. From Casaubon's time, Callisthenes has been known as the (spurious) author of an Alexander novel on which much of the medieval Alexander legend is based; see G. Cary, *The medieval Alexander* (Cambridge, 1956) ch. 2; D. J. A. Ross, *Alexander Historiatus* (Frankfurt, 1988 [2nd ed.]) pt. 1. Erasmus was no admirer of the Alexander romances, which he believed were unsuitable reading for rulers: *Institutio Christiani Principis*, ASD IV/1, ll. 420–6.

[49] In 1513, in the letter to Henry VIII prefacing his translation of Plutarch's *quo pacto possis adulatorem ab amico dignoscere*, Erasmus mentions Callisthenes as the one companion Alexander relied on not for flattery but for sincere advice. However, I would suggest that this letter is another fine example of Erasmus' irony: he supplies a list ostensibly of *liberi amici* to monarchs, but the examples taken together demonstrate how difficult it is honestly to advise a prince. The translation is edited in ASD IV/2 pp. 117–162; the preface to Henry is also in Allen, ep. 272.

[50] L. Jardine, *Erasmus: Man of Letters* (Princeton, 1993); see also Jill Kraye's comments in her review of this book, *The Library*, 6th ser., 17 (1995) pp. 77–80.

The list might claim to provide a credible and creditable historical pedigree for Erasmus' style of panegyric, but its relevance is by no means so straightforward. It does not attempt truthfully to describe what Callisthenes and Pliny wrote; instead, it prescribes how such praise should be read. In effect, Erasmus is succinctly implying that what might appear straightforward sycophancy should be treated more suspiciously. After all, as Erasmus points out both explicitly and more subtly with his reference to Callisthenes, the context of their composition did not allow plain speaking: to dress up philosophical precepts in praise was only prudent.[51] At the same time, Erasmus is directing modern authors to write panegyrics which accord with how they have just learnt to read ancient ones. This, though, is not to suggest that Erasmus' aesthetic for the panegyric depends merely on a revised reception of ancient *laudes*; it is not completely without classical precedent. In the first place, Pliny's *Panegyricus* clearly has some didactic purpose, even though it is not identical to Erasmus'. Moreover, between Callisthenes and Pliny, Lysias and Isocrates appear in Erasmus' short list. Lysias is significant perhaps not so much in his own right as for his supposed influence on the other Attic orator mentioned.[52] For, Isocrates is, I would suggest, essential to Erasmus' definition of panegyric, although his influence (as we may have come to expect) is less than straightforward. Isocrates' oeuvre includes a *Panegyricus*, the first surviving speech with this title, but this was hardly a popular work in the fifteenth or early sixteenth centuries. Unlike his Cyprian orations, it was rarely translated and, though the Greek text was printed in 1493, it was in an edition that could not be called a publishing sensation of the late *quattrocento* (copies of the first impression remained unsold in 1535).[53]

[51] Allen, ep. 180, ll. 48–51; see also the extract from the letter to Adolphus of Heere, above n. 37. This attitude naturally calls into question the honesty of Pliny's claim that freedom of speech existed in Trajan's empire; see *Panegyricus*, 3.4 and *Epistolae* III.18.7.

[52] Lysias wrote an *Olympiacus* which constituted a panegyric in the sense of being spoken at a public festival; but this survives only in fragments. However, the pseudo-Plutarchan *Lives of the Ten Orators* asserts that Isocrates' *Panegyricus* was indebted to works of Gorgias and Lysias [837F, see also 836D]. Another possible reason for referring to both orators was that both their panegyrics urged internal Greek unity and war against the barbarians – an agenda which dovetails with Erasmus' concern for peace within Christendom and crusade against the Ottomans [e.g. ASD IV/I ll. 122–127]. This potential parallel certainly seemed to be on G. M. Cataneo's mind when he translated Isocrates' *Panegyricus* five years later (Rome: Iacobus Mazochius, 1509) – see his preface at sig.ai[v].

[53] I have used *Iter Italicum* to trace the history of latinised versions of Isocrates' orations – only two copies of the *Panegyricus* appear: *Iter*, I, p. 169 and III, p. 520. The 1493 edition was printed by Chalcondyles at Milan (Hain 9312) – see N. G. Wilson, *From Byzantium to Italy* (London, 1992) p. 96. An edition by Erasmus' favourite printer, Aldus, appeared in 1513.

So, it is by no means certain that Erasmus would have known this work in 1504. If he did, he would have found that the speech – ostensibly advising war against the barbarians but mainly providing a praise of Athens – hardly fitted his specific description of a panegyric. On the other hand, he could have found a classical pedigree for his emphasis on the speeches' educational power by turning to Isocrates' didactic Cyprian orations – most notably, *Nicocles* and *To Nicocles*, which Erasmus later translated.[54] So, the significance of Isocrates may be less that he wrote a panegyric than that he provided examples of pedagogical rhetoric. As Erasmus defines it, then, the humanist panegyric derives not just from its Roman namesake but also from the ancient tradition of hortatory literature. It is usually argued that his *Panegyricus* combines elements of panegyric and *speculum principis*.[55] I would suggest, however, that this is too limited an analysis: what Erasmus is doing in his letters and in the speech itself is nothing less than redefining the panegyric. In his hands, it has become a means of serving up lessons to a prince by making them palatable with praise.

Given this painstaking construction of a justification for his *Panegyricus*, Erasmus' text itself might (at first sight) seem something of a disappointment. Certainly, we can see the humanist's aesthetic in action, endowing even the highest praise with a monitory aspect. At points, he sounds like a latterday Callisthenes, referring to princes as godlike figures; yet, for Erasmus, such claims give a ruler not freedom but duties.[56] He sees no conflict between extravagant praise and a belief in limited kingship. For example, he introduces the doctrine that the prince's word is law, but only so that he can explicitly stigmatise it as a maxim worthy of Nero; Erasmus' Philip does not think of himself as above the laws.[57] Such statements, along with diatribes against tyranny or the iniquities of war, are quintessential 'Erasmus.'[58] However, not only

---

[54] Garrison, *Dryden and the Tradition*, pp. 21–2 suggests Erasmus' debt to *To Nicocles* on the 'external evidence' of the 1516 volume (on which, see above p. 157). The chronology, of course, is problematic. In contrast, I would argue that the relevance of the Cyprian orations can be posited from internal evidence. At the same time, this would allow the possibility that, *pace* J. D. Tracy [*Politics*, p. 17], Erasmus' attitude to his *Panegyricus* did not vary greatly over time: his outlook when it was written, I would suggest, was fairly consistent with his perception of it in 1516.

[55] O. Herder in ASD IV/1 pp. 6–14, followed by J. D. Tracy, *Politics*, pp. 17–21.

[56] ASD IV/1 ll. 1047–1048: there seems to be an echo here, appropriately, of Seneca, *De Clementia*, I.2. See also Beroaldo's comments on the god-like nature of good kings in *De optimo statu* in *Varia . . . opuscula*, fol. cxxv.

[57] ASD IV/1, ll. 1164–2002. On 'constitutionalism' in the *Panegyricus*, see Tracy, *Politics* p. 19.

[58] On tyranny, see for example ll. 304–5; on pacifism, see below pp. 166–7.

are such precepts familiar from other works in his oeuvre, many of them can also be found in other – earlier – panegyrics. Indeed, I would contend that, while Erasmus is the most explicit in his pedagogical rationale, his justification would have surprised few of his fellow humanists. Erasmus merely provided a novel explanation for the didactic element which occurred in many contemporary panegyrics. So, for instance, the emphasis on reminding the prince of the duties rulership puts upon him is also to be found in Panulfo Collenucio's 1494 panegyric to the Emperor Maximilian:

it is indisputable that kingship is in no way an idle task; instead it is troublesome, full not of rest and relaxation for the soul but of cares and labours.[59]

Again – and unsurprisingly – Erasmus is certainly not alone in urging his prince to patronise literature. As Beroaldo tells Lodovico 'il Moro':

You are the glory and the guardian of the learned . . . and indeed the best princes can do nothing better than to support the educated and to encourage the learned, by whose writings they are made immortal . . .[60]

Humanists, then, did not need to wait for Erasmus' 1504 letters to learn to endow their panegyrics with didactic elements. In fact, as was briefly mentioned above, something of this sort of justification goes back to Salutati – in other words, to before the rediscovery of the prose panegyrics.[61] What is unusual about Erasmus' work, in the first place, is merely the sophistication with which he explains the genre's purpose. At the same time the subtle – even covert – method with which he used classical references to express this aesthetic foreshadows an even more striking feature of his *Panegyricus*: I wish in the final pages to argue that what makes this work particularly remarkable is the insertion of a critical element. Erasmus, as it were, does not just teach his royal pupil, he also berates him. On one level, this is perhaps intrinsic to Erasmus' aesthetic of panegyric. As I have already suggested, the humanist agenda assumes that the prince needs teaching but that this can not be done in an open manner: the panegyric is pedagogy's means of overcoming censorship. This in itself warns us not to take the

[59] *Panegyrici quotquot*, p. 511: principatum constat nequaquam segnem rem esse sed laboriosum non ocio & animi remissione sed curis & laboribus abundantem . . . ; cf. ASD IV/1, ll. 2002–2004.

[60] Beroaldo, *Varia . . . opuscula*, fol. xix^v: tu decus et praesidium es eruditorum . . . et profecto nihil melius agere possunt optimi principes quam sublevare doctos, fovere eruditos, quorum scriptis immortales efficiuntur; cf. ASD IV/1, ll. 2169–2170; see also Barbaro's stress on learning in his panegyric, *Epistolae*, p. 114.

[61] See above, pp. 154–5.

praise at face-value. However, not content with the inherent irony of the redefined genre, Erasmus also secretes subversive elements in both the work's structure and its prose style.

In the first place, Erasmus adopts and adapts to critical ends the basic structure of Pliny's *Panegyricus*. One central device Pliny employed to heighten his praise of Trajan was to suggest the novelty of good government – his reign is contrasted with the preceding tyranny of Domitian. Erasmus is faithful enough to his classical prototype to reproduce this diachronic structure, even though he can not describe either achievements as great or iniquities as egregious as those related by Pliny. The changes, however, are not only a matter of degree; the very purpose of the structure is transformed by Erasmus' decision to contain the temporal division within a much smaller timespan. Past sorrow and present joy are no longer divided between different reigns: Philip's rule serves for both sides of the dichotomy. The Burgundians' delight is occasioned by their prince's return from Spain; their sorrow was caused by his departure in the first place. Explicitly, this dichotomy reflects Erasmus' fellow subjects' constant devotion to their prince, but its implications for the image of Philip are not totally uncritical. For example, at a couple of points, Burgundy's reaction to Philip's departure is subtly paralleled with Dido's grief at being abandoned by Aeneas.[62] At least, though, Aeneas had an excuse for displaying male perfidy – his heaven-sent destiny was to found a new city. In contrast, Philip's birthright is to be Burgundy's own ruler; indeed, the early section of the oration centres on a long apostrophe by the *patria* to Philip, chiding him as if she were his mother for his extended absence.[63] For Erasmus, good kingship depends on the prince's presence; he compares a country without its king to the world without a sun:

Take the sun from the world and straight away all the radiant face of nature will become barren and unkempt. Remove the prince from the mother-country and immediately whatever before flourished and grew, of necessity will be frosted and wither away.[64]

If Philip is the sun-king, it is his duty to shine upon his country; by his absence on his foreign travels, he has been guilty of dereliction of that duty. Erasmus' *Panegyricus* revolves around not a comparison of two

---

[62] ASD IV/1, ll. 181, 214–5. Note also the repeated quotations from Terence's *The Brothers* in this section: ll. 179–80, 208, 382.

[63] ASD IV/1, ll. 292–335. For a less critical reading of this element, see Garrison, *Dryden and the Tradition*, pp. 50–1.

[64] ASD IV/1, ll. 107–109.

rulers but a contrast between one prince's past and present actions. Effectively, Philip is made to act not only as Trajan but also as Domitian.

It is not only through what might be called parodying Pliny's structure that Erasmus endows his work with a critical element; this is also a key feature of the *Panegyricus'* style. I will confine myself here to four examples, the first two of which concern Erasmus' turn of phrase. The very first sentence of the speech opens in a fashion so idiomatic it defies felicitous translation: *Velis nolis boni consulas oportet saedulitatem atque adeo licentiam nostram . . .* [Like it or not, it is your duty to take in good part our assiduousness and even freedom].[65] This collection of phrases has an imperious tone – Philip is bound by necessity to listen; he is subjected to the speech. The strikingly arrogant tone was not lost on the early readers; the printed marginalia in the editions of the *Panegyricus* from 1516 excuse Erasmus' licence by commenting: 'this style is used not without reason as it clears the prince of any suspicion of seeking flattery [*affectatae laudationis*].' Yet, the studied use of language is not confined to these first words. For example, Erasmus enjoys employing the verb *blandiri* which the modern English translation translates as 'to tempt' or 'to be pleasing'; it could, though, have a more critical meaning – 'to flatter'. So, Burgundy was worried during Philip's absence in Spain – *verebatur ne qua pars orbis magis blandiretur oculis tuis* [she feared lest some other part of the world might be more pleasing to your eyes].[66] On my submission, the ambiguity in such lines is not accidental: Erasmus is a careful selector of his words, allowing the intelligent reader to savour the resonances of his choice.

Perhaps more important than his turn of phrase, however, is another technique that we have already met when discussing the 1504 letters: the employment of classical examples to subversive or ironic effect. In the *Panegyricus* itself, there is used, for example, a rhetorical tool which could be called illusory hyperbole.[67] At one point, Philip is said to surpass a series of classical rulers:

you excel Cecrops in nobility, Polycrates in happiness, Croesus in riches, Xerxes in resources, Caesar in victories, Pompey in triumphs . . .[68]

[65] ASD IV/1, l. 7. The first phrase, *velis nolis*, is used at the opening of one of the *panegyrici veteres* [VII.I.I], perhaps significantly in addressing Maximian who had returned to political affairs from retirement. The phrase *boni consulas* is employed on three occasions in the *panegyrici* but, if Erasmus had any specific use of it in mind, it may well have been Seneca, *De beneficiis*, I.viii.I.

[66] ASD IV/1, ll. 200–1 (contrast *Complete Works of Erasmus*, 27, p. 32); see also ll. 125–6, 295. Erasmus has a similar penchant for the term *simulo*.

[67] Quintilian, *Institutio Oratoria*, VIII.vi.54–7, 67–76.   [68] ASD IV/1, ll. 367–9.

This piling-up of favourable comparisons with ancient figures appears impressive – but it is no more than appearance. Cecrops' nobility consisted in his autochthonous birth, Polycrates' happiness culminated in his crucifixion, neither Croesus' riches nor Xerxes' forces prevented their defeats, and both Caesar and Pompey were assassinated. The six figures, then, divide into three pairs. The first comprises characters who have a dubious claim to the stated attribute; the second, rulers who, despite a wealth of resources, failed; the third, generals of the late Roman Republic whose military credentials sit uneasily with the pacifist message of the *Panegyricus*. What appears grandiloquent praise is, on closer inspection, quite underwhelming.

It is not just through references to classical characters that Erasmus adds irony to his praise; he also employs allusion to ancient literature in a subversive fashion. For example, at one point, he compares Philip's travels to Hercules' labours:

No-one would so excessively [*tam superstitiose*] favour antiquity that they thought Hercules' labours – which were I do not know how spectacular but certainly disastrous – comparable with your most fortunate journey. Indeed, if all of your expedition bears a very close resemblance to the most attractive triumph, what else, I ask you, do Hercules' wanderings look like than some sort of brigandage [*latrocinii speciem*]? He fought monsters with gladiatorial recklessness, while monsters surrendered to your majesty. He killed one or two thieves and brought peace to (I would guess) just a few fields, you acted as the conciliator of the greatest empires. On whatever region your highness shone, you brought, by some destiny, not only peace, but also incomparable happiness. But let Hercules be. For it is a show of effrontery to compare you with that man, with whom Alexander the Great did not allow himself to be contrasted, however briefly.[69]

Any alert contemporary reader was unlikely to miss the allusion here to Augustine's well-known anecdote of the pirate and Alexander the Great: the pirate, captured and berated by the emperor for his lawless activities, responded that Alexander's deeds seem to him merely piracy on a much greater scale.[70] Erasmus sets up clear sign-posts to this allusion: if the verbal resonance in *latrocinii speciem* passed the reader by, the explicit reference to Alexander could hardly fail to direct their attention to the anecdote. Recognising the reference, the reader would remember that Augustine originally employed the story as support for his rhetorical question: 'take away justice and what are kingdoms

---

[69] ASD IV/I, ll. 682–693.   [70] Augustine, *De civitate dei*, IV.4.

but large-scale brigandage?' Erasmus' passage, therefore, gains greater depth. It becomes (as so often in the *Panegyricus*) uncomplimentary to Alexander, but it also includes a subtle warning to Philip: it is not (as it may seem) the magnitude of the achievements that make them praise-worthy, but their nature. If Philip's actions did not tend towards peace and justice, he too would be no better than a brigand.

These are only a few examples of the ironic praise which repeatedly occurs in the *Panegyricus*; to pinpoint all such instances would certainly take more space than is available here and probably would demand a page-by-page commentary. However, on the basis of the sample that I have given, I would argue that, far from being a set of 'effusive com-pliments . . . elaborated *ad nauseam*', Erasmus' *Panegyricus* is (to para-phrase the author's own claim) not so much praise as both precept and subtle criticism.[71] If the work accordingly gains greater depth than it is usually credited with having, it equally provides extra testimony for the recent claim that Erasmus 'asked a great deal from at least the best of his early readers.'[72] What is more, though, some of those early readers were certainly capable of responding fully to the text. For, Erasmus was not unique in his nuanced use of classical *exempla*. There may have been few who were able or willing to use their learning to subvert their praise but there is at least one parallel case of which I am aware: it concerns Erasmus' English friend Thomas More.[73] His *Carmen gratu-latorium* on Henry VIII's accession in 1509 is usually assumed to be unmitigated, if uncharacteristic, rejoicing. However, a closer reading reveals that this poem, like Erasmus' *Panegyricus*, is essentially ambival-ent; it, too, by its phrasing and its use of classical anecdotes, subverts its praise. On the other hand, this ambiguity was perhaps already lost to intelligent readers by the early seventeenth century, when More's *Carmen* was praised by Henry Peacham and imitated by Ben Jonson without any sign that they had appreciated its subtly subversive nature.[74] In the face of such evidence, it would seem that what might be called the Erasmian moment was shortlived.

[71] B. Radice in the preface to the *Complete Works of Erasmus*, 27, p. 4.

[72] Jardine, *Erasmus*, p. 26.

[73] For the following sentences, see my article, 'A New Golden Age?: More, Skelton and the Accession Verses of 1509', *Renaissance Studies*, 9 (1995) pp. 58–76, esp. pp. 67–74. The More poem is available in C. H. Miller, L. Bradner, C. A. Lynch, R. P. Oliver (eds.), *Complete Works of St* [sic] *Thomas More*, III/ii (New Haven, CT, 1984).

[74] On Jonson's reading of More's poem and its influence on his own 'Panegyre', see R. C. Evans, *Habits of Mind: Evidence and Effect of Jonson's Reading* (Lewisburg, 1996) ch. 6. I would like to thank Prof. Blair Worden for bringing this work to my attention.

This brief survey has necessarily left many questions unasked, let alone answered. There is, however, one issue which should be raised: how successful could the project of the panegyric as precept be? In other words, could this form of pedagogy actually teach the powerful? I wish, by way of conclusion, to point out a couple of structural difficulties in the use of panegyrics as teaching instruments.

Pliny, describing how his panegyric had developed, explained that after he had delivered it in the Senate, he reworked and lengthened its text. Noting this passage in his copy of Pliny's letters, Guillaume Budé remarked: 'the spoken panegyric is one thing, the written another.'[75] Such revision of a work is the wont of scholars torn between deadlines and perfectionism: it seems that Erasmus' *Panegyricus* also underwent refinement in its passage from oration to printed text.[76] Inevitably, we are hostages to the written word: we are not at liberty to know what might have been the spoken version. Plutarch, in an anecdote that Erasmus was fond of quoting, tells how Demetrius of Phalerum advised his prince, Ptolemy I, to read books on the office of king since he would find there the advice his friends would not dare to tell him.[77] If this was really so, perhaps the spoken panegyric was less didactic than the printed version. Perhaps, surrounded by the court's magnificence and the prince's bodyguard, the orator's intent to take the occasion as a class dissipated even more swiftly than the words he recited.

This potential inconsistency would be no difficulty if we could assume that the prince paid as much attention to the written as to the spoken word. As it is, such hopes should probably be treated with scepticism – after all, as Aeneas Sylvius Piccolomini commented, only a fool thinks that kings read books.[78] But even if one were to imagine a prince who was an avid reader, there is another structural difficulty. For, in the end, the force of a panegyric depends less on what is written or said than on what is understood or read. It is, effectively, up to the prince whether he takes it as adulation or admonition. Erasmus recognised this in his *Education of the Christian prince*:

---

[75] Pliny, *Epistolae*, III.18.1; Budé's copy is in the Bodleian, Auct.L .4.3, on which see E. T. Merrill, 'On a Bodleian copy of Pliny's letters', *Classical Philology*, 2 (1907) pp. 129–156. This marginal comment occurs at fol. 46: *aliter dictus et aliter scriptus panegyricus*.

[76] Tracy, *Politics*, pp. 20–21; see Allen, ep. 179, ll. 24–32; ep. 180, ll. 149–53, 402.

[77] *Panegyricus*, ASD IV/1, ll. 82–86; *Institutio Christiani principis*, ASD IV/1, ll. 413–414. The source is Plutarch, *Moralia* 189D. Cf. Isocrates, *To Nicocles*, 2–4.

[78] Quoted by A. Black, *Monarchy and Community* (Cambridge, 1970) p. 114. For an example of a humanist patron who was less than attentive to his library's contents, see my comments on Humphrey, Duke of Gloucester in 'On the Difference Between Virtue and Weiss' in D. Dunn (ed.), *Courts, Counties and the Capital* (Stroud, 1996) pp. 181–203 at pp. 194–198.

Therefore the young prince should be forewarned that he should mentally [*sibi*] turn those titles which he is forced to hear, to his own advantage. He hears 'father of the fatherland'; let him think that there was never any title attributed to princes which squares more closely with 'good prince' than 'father of the fatherland'. Accordingly, he should act so that he might appear worthy of this title. If he thinks thus it will be advice, if not, on the contrary, it will be adulation [*Ita si cogitat admonitio fuerit, sin secus adulatio*].[79]

For a panegyric to have didactic force, the prince must realise that, despite the lack of classroom walls, he is a pupil; not only that, but he must be willing to learn. There needs to be an inclination to appreciate the praise as precept. Yet, if this inclination already existed, there would surely be little need to dress the lessons up as flattery. Panegyric, then, is directed to those who are least likely to read it as advice: it is an attempt to teach problem pupils – an attempt which is perhaps both laudable and idealistic. Faced with probable unresponsiveness, some teachers turned to the last resort of the arrogant pedagogue: they moved from praising to blaming their princely 'students'.

[79] ASD IV/I, ll. 381–5.

CHAPTER 8

Teachers, pupils and imperial power in eleventh-century Byzantium

Panagiotis A. Agapitos

To Aris Spanos
Χάρις χάριν γάρ ἐστιν ἡ τίκτουσ' ἀεί.

The negative image of Byzantium drawn by historians of the Enlighten-ment and Romanticism is well known.[1] In an attempt to correct this image Byzantinists have repeatedly pointed to the continuous cultivation of ancient learning during the Christian Greek Middle Ages.[2] Yet the Byzantines themselves were partly responsible for both negative and positive images, which are to a substantial degree misrepresentations,[3] in that, within their highly conservative society, they very often pre-sented their thoughts in a manner seemingly unaltered since Hellenistic antiquity.[4] Pedagogy is just such a case: viewed superficially, nothing changed from late antique grammarians to the end of the Byzantine Empire in the mid-fifteenth century. However, during specific periods of Byzantine history a series of ideological clashes lead to important changes in education and in the perception of pedagogy. These clashes were primarily and most importantly conducted between philosophy and theology in order to define the meaning and function of ancient learning within a Christian society.

The present paper will focus on one period in Byzantium's millenium-long history, the eleventh century, when it appeared as if involvement

---

[1] The works of Edward Gibbon (1737–1794) and Jakob Philipp Fallmerayer (1790–1861) have been seminal in this respect. On the development of this image, see P. A. Agapitos, 'Byzantine Literature and Greek Philologists in the Nineteenth Century', *ClMed* 43 (1992) 231–60, in par-ticular pp. 233–9 with further bibliography.

[2] See, for example, the influential study by J. M. Hussey, *Church and Learning in the Byzantine Empire 867–1185* (London, 1937).

[3] See A. P. Kazhdan and S. Franklin, *Studies on Byzantine Literature of the Eleventh and Twelfth Cen-turies* (Cambridge and Paris, 1984), pp. 1–22 (the chapter is entitled 'Approaches to the history of Byzantine civilization: from Krause to Beck and Mango').

[4] See the bitter remarks by C. Mango, *Byzantine Literature as a Distorting Mirror* (Oxford, 1975), reprinted in his *Byzantium and Its Image* (London, 1984).

with ancient learning would lead to a new approach to knowledge. The eleventh century was a period of change in Byzantium's history,[5] and its peculiar mixture of politics, religion and pedagogy characterises a state which at that point obsessively promoted its claim to ecumenical power and culture.[6] During it, a problem formulated in Late Antiquity was the starting point of a clash between a group of innovative scholars, their pupils and the conservative state. I will examine this late antique problem briefly and move to the eleventh-century developments, which culminated in a partly successful attempt at reconciliation.

I

On 17 June 362 AD Emperor Flavius Claudius Iulianus, better known as Julian the Apostate, issued the following decree:

School teachers and professors must be distinguished first for their character and then for their eloquence. Since I cannot be present myself in each city, I order that whoever wishes to teach should not take up this task hastily and thoughtlessly. The candidate should be judged worthy by his own city's council and should receive the necessary permit with the agreement of the outstanding among the councillors. This permit must be submitted to me for inspection, so that through my ratification the prestige of those who are about to teach in the cities of the empire will be raised.[7]

The seemingly harmless decree was in reality highly insidious. It served the ruler's intention to exercise control over every teacher in the imperial dominion, and this meant the exclusion of the 'Galilaeans', as Julian contemptuously used to call Christians, from traditional education. The emperor revealed his hidden purpose in a letter which details his thought on 'correct education':

I think that correct education is not the rich harmony of words and style but the healthy judgement of a mind displaying prudence and pronouncing proper opinions on what is good and bad, beautiful and ugly. The person then who believes in certain things but instructs his pupils otherwise, is as far removed from education as from being an honest man. . . . I consider it unacceptable

---

[5] P. Lemerle, *Cinq études sur le XIe siècle byzantin* (Paris, 1977) and A. P. Kazhdan and A. W. Epstein, *Change in Byzantine Culture in the Eleventh and Twelfth Centuries*. The Transformation of the Classical Heritage 7 (Berkeley, Los Angeles and London, 1985).

[6] H. Ahrweiler, *L'idéologie politique de l'Empire byzantin* (Paris, 1975), pp. 60–74.

[7] *Cod. Theod.* xiii 3.5.10–15 (= *Cod. Iustin.* x 53.7). For the Latin text with commentary and translation see J. Bidez, *L'Empereur Julien: Oeuvres complètes. Tome I, 2e partie: Lettres et fragments* (Paris, 1972, 3rd ed.), p. 72 and B. K. Weis, *Julian: Briefe* (Munich, 1973), pp. 321–2. Except where otherwise indicated, all translations are my own.

that those who interpret the writings of the ancients should at the same time dishonour the gods whom these writers honoured. However, I do not say that, because I personally judge this practice unacceptable, they should be forbidden from conversing with youths. Consequently, I give to future teachers the choice either not to teach those things which they do not consider serious or to teach first by their conduct. . . . And if they think that they have erred in respect to the venerable gods, let them go to the churches of the Galilaeans and expound there Matthew and Luke.[8]

Julian stated the problem bluntly: Christian teachers – and most teachers in the fourth century were Christians[9] – overlooked the disjunction between their faith and the current pedagogical practice which pre-scribed Greek education as the only basis of 'correct education'. For Julian, Greek education, which was an essential part of Hellenism, could not be separated from Hellenic religion; so there was in his case a complete identification of education and religious belief. Accordingly, the exclusion of Christians from this education would result in their gradual exclusion from the State and ultimately in their social extinc-tion.[10] Julian's ruling that Christians should only teach the Gospels was an ingenious stroke. Christian intellectuals had been almost exclusively brought up within Greek education;[11] they recognized very well that teaching based solely on the 'vernacular' Gospel texts would mean a decline in the command of the Greek language and a concomitant spiritual impoverishment.[12]

The reaction of the Christian circles to Julian's decree was of the utmost importance for the course of education in Byzantium. In par-ticular, the two Cappadocian Fathers Gregory of Nazianzus (329–391) and Basil of Caesarea (ca. 330–379) were leading figures in establishing

---

[8] Jul. 422a-b, 423a, 423d (Bidez 1.2, pp. 73.2–8, 74.13–18, 75.8–11).

[9] On education in Late Antiquity, see H.-I. Marrou, *Histoire de l'éducation dans l'antiquité* (Paris, 1956, 7th ed.), pp. 431–89; R. A. Kaster, *Guardians of Language: the Grammarian and Society in Late Antiquity* (Berkeley, Los Angeles and London, 1988); P. Athanassiadi, 'From Polis to Theoupolis: School Syllabuses and Teaching Methods in Late Antiquity', in Θυμίαμα στὴ μνήμη τῆς Λασκαρίνας Μπούρα, vol. 1 (Athens, 1994), pp. 9–14.

[10] The harshness of the decree was criticised even by the historian Ammianus Marcellinus, Julian's admirer and contemporary: 'The law forbidding professors of rhetoric and grammar to teach if they adhered to the Christian faith, was inhuman and should be covered by eternal silence' (*Rer. gest.* 22.10.7).

[11] On the issue, see J. Bidez, *La vie de l'Empereur Julien* (Paris, 1930), pp. 261–72, and the diverg-ing interpretations of G. W. Bowersock, *Julian the Apostate* (London, 1978), pp. 83–5 and P. Athanassiadi-Fowden, *Julian and Hellenism. An Intellectual Biography* (London, 1992, 2nd ed.), pp. 1–12.

[12] On the religious and intellectual relation between pagans and Christians during the first centur-ies of the Christian era, see, for example, P. Brown, *The Making of Late Antiquity* (Cambridge, MA, 1978) and P. Chuvin, *The Chronicle of the Last Pagans*, tr. B. A. Archer (Cambridge, MA, 1990).

the principles concerning the acceptable use of Greek, *qua* pagan, literature.[13] Apart from the numerous comments found in his theological homilies and his poems, Gregory developed his thoughts more systematically in the first of his two invectives against Julian.[14] For Gregory the problem was a question of the correct definition of the word 'Hellenism'. In response to the controversial decree, he writes:

First of all he (sc. Julian) transferred the meaning of the word to matters of faith, as if Greek discourse belonged to religion and not to language; thus he chased us, not unlike thieves of foreign property, from education and – according to his judgement – from every Greek craft; this he did since he thought that, because the two terms were homonymous,[15] education was his domain.[16]

And he continues, addressing the Apostate directly:

Whence did this thought come to you, superficial and greedy man, to deprive Christians of education? . . . To what Hellenism does education belong, how is this Hellenism called and how is it defined? . . . If Hellenism belongs to religion, show us where and by what priests was this Hellenism sanctioned, as it happened with sacrifices, namely of what kind these are and to what deities they are offered. . . . If Hellenism belongs to language, and you, considering it your patrimony, exile us from it, then I simply cannot understand your argument. Because certain people who hellenise as to language, hellenise also as to religion, this does not mean that education belongs to religion and that consequently we should be banished from it. . . . Let me ask you, philhellene and philologist you, at what are you aiming? To exclude us completely from the Greek language, that is from the common and everyday words used by the crowd, or just from the elegant and elevated discourse which only cultivated men may attain?[17]

Gregory is attempting to make two points here: first, Greek religion and Greek education, a common good, are not identical; second, education

---

[13] On the appropriation and use of Hellenic literature by Christian authors see the sympathetic presentation by W. Jaeger, *Early Christianity and Greek Paideia* (Cambridge, MA, 1961) and the somewhat polemical approach by P. Athanassiadi-Fowden, 'The Idea of Hellenism', *Philosophia* 7 (1977) 323–56; on the same issue from the pagan perspective see now G. W. Bowersock, *Hellenism in Late Antiquity* (Cambridge, 1990), pp. 1–13. For a more general overview, see G. A. Kennedy, *Greek Rhetoric under Christian Emperors* (Princeton, 1983), pp. 180–264 and 'Christianity and Criticism', in G. A. Kennedy (ed.), *The Cambridge History of Literary Criticism. Volume I: Classical Criticism* (Cambridge, 1989), pp. 330–46.

[14] New critical edition by J. Bernardi, *Grégoire de Nazianze. Discours 4–5: Contre Julien.* Sources Chrétiennes 309 (Paris, 1983); see also the recent commentary by A. Kurmann, *Gregor von Nazianz: Oratio 4 gegen Julian. Ein Kommentar.* Schweizer Beiträge zur Altertumswissenschaft 19 (Basel, 1988).

[15] The word 'Hellenism', Gregory implies, is used to describe both pagan Greek religion and Greek education.

[16] *Orat.* iv 5.1–6 (Bernardi, p. 92).

[17] *Orat.* iv 101.1–2, 103.4–5, 103.10–12, 104.1–8, 105.1–5 (Bernardi, pp. 248, 252–4, 254–6, 256).

should be connected to language, which has nothing to do with faith. To these two arguments Basil of Caesarea added his own thoughts in his famous essay *To Youths on How to Profit from Greek Literature*.[18] Basil, addressing his nephews, writes:

We are led to future life by the Holy Scriptures through mysterious teaching. However, until your age allows you to grasp the depths of this teaching, it is good to exercise your soul with other books which are not wholly different from the Holy Scriptures but which resemble them like shades or mirrors. ... The dyers first prepare with various methods the material which they are about to dye and then they apply colour, red or any other. So it is with us; if we wish to preserve our opinion of virtue unfaded, we must prepare ourselves with ancient wisdom and then comprehend the holy and mysterious teaching: our eyes must first get used to seeing the brilliance of the sun when it is reflected on the water and then look at the real light. If indeed there exists an affinity between these two sources of wisdom, then their knowledge is clearly profitable. If not, still it is useful to place them side by side, because what is in fact better will become immediately apparent through their differences.[19]

Here we find the third reason for the appropriation of Greek education by the Christians: it is the usefulness of 'outer' (*qua* pagan) writings for the understanding of 'inner' (*qua* Christian) truth. Ancient literature was subordinated to the Holy Scriptures and formed a first preparatory step to Christian *paideia*. To the problem posed by Julian in the middle of the fourth century, the two Church Fathers proposed a solution along the three lines of argument mentioned above: separation of Greek education and Greek religion, identification of language and education, gradation of outer and inner education as to their usefulness. At that moment the problem seemed to have been overcome.[20]

II

The *Imperium Romanum* of Late Antiquity gradually transformed itself, but particularly so in the seventh and eighth centuries, into the medieval state which is conventionally called the Byzantine Empire.[21] It was a

---

[18] Critical edition by F. Boulenger, *Saint Basil: Aux jeunes gens sur la manière de tirer profit des lettres helléniques* (Paris, 1935); see also N. G. Wilson, *Saint Basil on the Value of Greek Literature* (London, 1975).

[19] *Ad adolesc.* 2.26–31, 2.39–3.4 (Boulenger, *Saint Basil*, pp. 43–4).

[20] On the fortunes of pagan education up to the sixth century, see P. Lemerle, *Byzantine Humanism: the First Phase. Notes and Remarks on Education and Culture in Byzantium from its Origins to the Tenth Century*, trs. H. Lindsay and A. Moffatt. Byzantina Australiensia 3 (Canberra, 1986), pp. 43–79.

[21] On the historical context of this change, see J. F. Haldon, *Byzantium in the Seventh Century. The Transformation of a Culture* (Cambridge, 1990) and W. Treadgold, *The Byzantine Revival 780–842* (Stanford, 1988).

major change marked by the reduction of state territory, the general redisposition of civil and military administration, the reformation of legislation, the final formation of the cosmological substratum of orthodox faith, the spread of the Greek language in civil administration, and – what concerns us here – the reorganization of education. The system of education, as it took shape especially in the tenth century,[22] was dominated by three figures: the *grammatistes* who directed a small school for the first phase of children's education, the *maistor* who was responsible for the second cycle of studies, and finally the 'patron'. The last was usually a civil or ecclesiastical high functionary who supported financially the maistor and his school and secured for him a certain social prestige. The patron *par excellence* was obviously the emperor who, besides supporting particular teachers in Constantinople, chose the outstanding professors in the various disciplines to teach at the imperial university.[23] The crucial role of this institution is lucidly described by an anonymous tenth-century historian in his discussion of the reforming measures of Emperor Konstantinos VII Porphyrogennetos (913–959) around 950:[24]

The knowledge of good and praiseworthy things, as well as of the philological arts and of the sciences, had been neglected and left to waste in our state – I do not know exactly how and why. What then did that most learned monarch think of? He knew that practice and theory bring us closer to God, and that practice is better suited to political affairs, theory to intellectual matters; thus he supported the one through the other, taking care that the practical aspects were cultivated through rhetoric and the theoretical through philosophy and the mathematical sciences. And he chose the best professors: to the *protospatharios* Konstantinos,[25] who until then was his personal secretary, he gave the chair of philosophy; to the metropolitan of Nicaea Alexandros, the chair of rhetoric; to the patrician Nikephoros, who was the son-in-law of the city prefect Theophilos Erotikos, he gave the chair of geometry; and to the chief secretary Georgios, the chair of astronomy. The emperor showed particular interest and care for

---

[22] On the system of education in the ninth and tenth centuries, see Lemerle, *Byz. Humanism*, pp. 205–353. The term 'system of education' is to be understood here very loosely, since there existed nothing even remotely similar in stability, breadth and organization to modern pedagogical systems and institutions.

[23] P. Speck, *Die kaiserliche Universität von Konstantinopel*. Byzantinisches Archiv 14 (Munich, 1974). Again, the term 'university' has to be taken broadly.

[24] On this important monarch and his times, see A. Toynbee, *Constantine Porphyrogenitus and His World* (London, 1973); A. Markopoulos (ed.), *Constantine VII Porphyrogenitus and his Age. Second International Byzantine Conference (Delphi, July 1987)* (Athens, 1989); I. Ševčenko, 'Re-reading Constantine Porphyrogenitus', in J. Shepard and S. Franklin (eds.), *Byzantine Diplomacy*. Society for the Promotion of Byzantine Studies 1 (London, 1992), pp. 167–95.

[25] *Protospatharios* ('first sword-bearer') was during the 9th and 10th centuries the highest honorary title bestowed on state officials who stood in the emperor's personal service.

the students, whom he invited almost every day to dine with him, supported with donatives and with whom he conversed in a most friendly manner. A short time elapsed and, with the emperor's help and prudence, these important arts and sciences were restored; thus choosing among the students, he appointed them judges, officials and bishops. In this way, he adorned the empire of the Romans and enriched it with wisdom.[26]

The final stage in education was obviously an affair of the state. The teachers came from the highest ranks of civil and ecclesiastical administration; the students in their turn were groomed to take over key positions. In this context education aimed at the preservation of the status quo. The anonymous historian stresses the clearly utilitarian essence of knowledge and its programmatic role in the formation of the governing élite. This was not a system which furthered research but which collected, selected and ultimately codified knowledge for its easier manipulation and control.[27] The presence of the ruler legitimated this control and elevated it to a pedagogical dogma of prime political importance.

At the turn of the eleventh century the empire was governed by Basileios II Boulgaroktonos (976–1025), one of Byzantium's outstanding military rulers.[28] Basileios was never particularly interested in education; he neglected the institution of the imperial university and tried to control the government's bureaucratic élite. The intellectual climate in Basileios' day is commented upon by an eleventh-century historian in the following manner:

(Basileios) payed no attention to learned men, but rather despised these people profoundly – I mean scholars. I am therefore surprised by the fact that, although the emperor showed no interest whatsoever in the progress of letters, it is exactly during his time that philosophy and rhetoric blossomed; I can find but one answer which might best explain this paradox: in those days men did not devote themselves to letters for profit but cultivated learning on their own, whereas most scholars do not follow this path in matters of education, since they consider money as the prime reason for occupying themselves with learning; it is with such a goal in mind that they devote themselves to studying and if their goal is not immediately fulfilled, they give up their task.[29]

---

[26] *Theoph. Cont.* VI.14 (ed. I. Bekker (Bonn, 1838), p. 446.1–22).
[27] On this issue, see now P. Odorico, 'La cultura della Συλλογή', *BZ* 83 (1990) 1–21.
[28] For good overviews of his age, see G. Ostrogorski, *A History of the Byzantine State*, tr. J. M. Hussey (Oxford, 1968, 2nd ed.), pp. 298–315 and A. Christophilopoulou, Βυζαντινὴ Ἱστορία. *B.2: 867–1081* (Athens, 1988), pp. 150–82.
[29] Psel. *Chron.* 1.29.11–24 (S. Impellizzeri (ed.) *Michele Psello: Imperatori di Bisanzio. Cronografia* (Milan, 1984), vol. 1, p. 42; for a complete English translation of the *Chronographia*, see Michael Psellus, *Fourteen Byzantine Rulers*, tr. by E. R. A. Sewter (Harmondsworth, 1966)).

The emperor's attitude is manifestly criticized. The more important point, however, is the author's observation that at the beginning of the eleventh century a group of learned men, having been excluded from the state, 'cultivated learning on their own' which must mean that they pursued scholarly research as such. The historian who makes this highly critical and perceptive remark is Michael Psellos (ca. 1018–ca. 1079), a towering figure of letters in his time and one of the most important intellectuals of Byzantium.[30]

Most prominent among the scholars who cultivated learning on their own was Ioannes Mauropous (ca. 1000-ca. 1085), Psellos' beloved teacher and close friend.[31] At a very young age, Mauropous already directed a small school run in his house. There, enclosed in his own space, he studied ancient authors, historians and philosophers in particular,[32] and there he taught those who made the effort to find him. Psellos, in a laudatory oration he wrote for Ioannes many years later,[33] described the attitude of his teacher in those days:

He did not stand out like a statue displaying his external form, but he was only visible to those who truly wished to see. . . . Because of this attitude a real struggle was necessary to track down this man and to find him. I also had to search for him, almost as if digging; I knew what fountains he hid inside himself and I wished to drink from the spring of his wisdom. From a very young age I found myself close to this magnificent man, literally parched by the thirst for education; drawing deeply from his strong river, I indeed acquired the correct foundations for every branch of learning.[34]

Mauropous had as a fellow-student Konstantinos Leichoudes (ca. 1000–1063), who became a prominent lawyer; moreover, he had, besides

[30] On his life and works, see E. Kriaras, 'Psellos, Michael', *RE Suppl.* 11 (1968) 1124–82; J. N. Ljubarskij, *Michail Psell. Ličnost i tvorčestvo: K istorii vizantijskogo predgumanisma* (Moscow, 1978); R. Volk, *Der medizinische Inhalt der Schriften des Michael Psellos*. Miscellanea Byzantina Monacensia 32 (Munich, 1992), pp. 1–48.

[31] On Mauropous' life, see A. Karpozilos, Συμβολὴ στὴ μελέτη τοῦ βίου καὶ τοῦ ἔργου τοῦ Ἰωάννη Μαυρόποδος. Δωδώνη. Παράρτημα 18 (Ioannina, 1982), pp. 23–50. Recent suggestions for a revision of basic dates in Mauropous' life by A. Kazhdan, 'Some Problems in the Biography of John Mauropous', *JÖB* 43 (1993) 87–111 have been refuted by A. Karpozilos, 'The Biography of Ioannes Mauropous Again', *Hellenika* 44 (1994) 51–60.

[32] Maur. *Epigr.* 47 (J. Bollig and P. de Lagarde, *Iohannis Euchaitorum metropolitae quae in Codice Vaticano Graeco 676 supersunt*. Abhandlungen der hist. -philol. Classe der kgl. Gesellschaft der Wissenschaften zu Göttingen 28 (Göttingen, 1882), pp. 24–6); see Karpozilos, *Symbole*, pp. 26–8.

[33] The oration was delivered in 1075 (see Karpozilos, *Symbole*, pp. 46–7). New critical edition by G. T. Dennis, *Michaelis Pselli orationes panegyricae* (Stuttgart and Leipzig, 1994), pp. 143–74 (older edition by K. N. Sathas, Μεσαιωνικὴ Βιβλιοθήκη vol. 5 (Paris, 1876), pp. 142–67); Italian translation with introduction and notes by R. Anastasi, *Michele Psello: Encomio per Giovanni, piissimo metropolita di Euchaita e protosincello* (Padua, 1968).

[34] Psel. *Enc. Maur.* 150.194–196, 200–207 Dennis (Sathas, *MB* 5, pp. 147–8).

Psellos, another outstanding pupil, Ioannes Xiphilinos (ca. 1010–1075); they all became close friends.[35] When Leichoudes was summoned by the new Emperor Konstantinos IX Monomachos (1042–1055), he took the two younger men with him; within a short time the three of them became the monarch's chief advisers.[36] Leichoudes became *mesazon*, a kind of unofficial prime minister, to the emperor;[37] Psellos was honoured with the title of 'consul of philosophers', teaching philosophy in his private school, while as *nomophylax* ('guardian of the law') Xiphilinos engaged himself with the reformation of legal education on the highest level.[38] It should be pointed out that the decree issued in 1047 for the establishment of a law school was written at the emperor's request by Mauropous himself.[39] Moreover, both Leichoudes and Xiphilinos became patriarchs of Constantinople (1059–1063 and 1064–1075 respectively), while after 1056 and for approximately the next twenty years, Psellos was a close collaborator of all governments, attaining the summit of his power during the reign of his pupil Michael VII Doukas (1071–1078).[40]

[35] The chronological frame and the relation of the four men to each other presented here differs in certain points from the two most recent treatments: Volk, *Der medizinische*, p. 360 considers Mauropous, Leichoudes and Xiphilinos as co-students, while A. Sideras, *Die byzantinischen Grabreden: Prosopographie, Datierung, Überlieferung. 142 Epitaphien und Monodien aus dem byzantinischen Jahrtausend.* Wiener Byzantinistische Studien 19 (Vienna, 1994), p. 136 thinks of Leichoudes as a pupil of Mauropous. However, the sources (for which see notes 37 and 38 below) do not allow such conclusions.

[36] On the various offices held by the three men, see G. Weiß, *Oströmische Beamte im Spiegel der Schriften des Michael Psellos.* Miscellanea Byzantina Monacensia 16 (Munich, 1973), pp. 78–89; on their role in education see Lemerle, *Cinq études*, pp. 193–248. For a historical survey of the eleventh century see M. Angold, *The Byzantine Empire 1025–1204. A Political History* (London, 1984), pp. 1–113; for a survey of ecclesiastical history during this period, see H.-G. Beck, *Geschichte der orthodoxen Kirche im byzantinischen Reich. Die Kirche in ihrer Geschichte* I, D1 (Göttingen, 1980), pp. 142–7.

[37] On Leichoudes, see Psellos' praise in *Chron.* vi.178 (Impellizzeri, *Cronografia* II, p. 126) and the funeral oration in memory of his old friend (K. N. Sathas, Μεσαιωνικὴ Βιβλιοθήκη, vol. 4 (Paris, 1874), pp. 388–421; Italian translation with introduction and notes by U. Criscuolo, *Michele Psello: Orazione in memoria di Constantino Lichude.* Letteratura e civiltà bizantina 1 (Messina, 1983)); on the oration see moreover Volk, *Der medizinische*, pp. 359–62 and Sideras, *Die byzantinischen Grabreden*, pp. 136–8.

[38] Psellos composed also for him a lengthy funeral oration (Sathas, *MB* 4, pp. 421–62), for which see Volk, *Der medizinische*, pp. 374–81 and Sideras, *Die byzantinischen Grabreden*, pp. 145–7. On legal education at the time see the studies by W. Wolska-Conus, 'Les écoles de Psellos et de Xiphilin sous Constantin IX Monomaque', *TM* 6 (1976) 223–43 and 'L'école de droit et l'enseignement du droit à Byzance au XIe siècle: Xiphilin et Psellos', *TM* 7 (1979) 1–107.

[39] The text of the decree in Bollig and de Lagarde, *Iohannis Euchaitorum metropolitae*, pp. 195–202 (see Karpozilos, *Symbole*, pp. 145–7).

[40] It is no coincidence that in the one and only surviving depiction of Psellos, he is represented together with his imperial pupil (S. Pelekanides and P. Christou, Οἱ θησαυροὶ τοῦ Ἁγίου Ὄρους. Σειρὰ Α´: Εἰκονογραφημένα χειρόγραφα, vol. 3 (Athens, 1979), p. 157 and pl. 255). In the manuscript (Athos, Pantokrator Mon. 234, f. 254r) the picture precedes a theological text written specifically for the young ruler. On the miniature, see I. Spatharakis, *The Portrait in Byzantine Illuminated Manuscripts* (Leiden, 1976), p. 232 and Volk, *Der medizinische*, pp. 6–7.

For a relatively long period, Mauropous' friends, aptly referred to as 'the government of philosophers',[41] dominated political and intellectual life in the eleventh century. The feeling of belonging to a privileged group was instilled in his pupils by Mauropous himself. For example, when Psellos assumed the teaching of philosophy at the imperial court, Mauropous sent him a letter of congratulation. He first praises the knowledge and the character of Psellos' pupils, who are worthy of their teacher, and then gives him specific advice concerning a teacher's duties. The sense of a spiritual community is inculcated. Mauropous, addressing Psellos with his lay name Konstantinos, writes:

I was recently surrounded by the sacred chorus of divine philosophy, my wise friend and true leader of philosophers. With them I conversed no less in a friendly than in an intellectual way, and in the end we separated admiring one another. What they admired in me I do not know (I myself am not conscious of anything praiseworthy in me) but there was a lot for me to admire in them: noble nature, intelligence, sagacity, decency, love of learning, erudition, desire and enthusiasm to attend to literary topics (because this is what you call their all-consuming ardour) and above all their common understanding and aspiration for what is good or perfect. What could be better than the promotion and election of my wise Konstantinos to the honours of wisdom and his reception of a teaching chair? ... And to you, my dear and honoured friend, I offer everything that I have and contribute it to your support ... Take this task in hand with great determination and adhere to this undertaking with diligence and courage, under the good guidance of God, who shall bring it to an auspicious end.[42]

This sense of a spiritual community among teachers and pupils, as it is expressed in their surviving correspondence,[43] is something new for medieval Byzantium. Moreover, it clearly distinguishes these eleventh-century scholars, whose families came from the middle strata of Constantinopolitan society (Psellos, Leichoudes) or from the provinces (Mauropous, Xiphilinos), from the tenth-century officials who belonged to the capital's bureaucratic aristocracy. To a certain extent it was this spiritual community, which stood in contrast to the older social

---

[41] Lemerle, *Cinq études*, p. 193.
[42] Maur. *Epist.* 23 (translation quoted from A. Karpozilos, *The Letters of Ioannes Mauropous Metropolitan of Euchaita. Greek Text, Translation and Commentary.* Corpus Fontium Historiae Byzantinae 34 (Thessaloniki, 1990), pp. 98–100).
[43] On Mauropous' correspondence, see Karpozilos, *Symbole*, pp. 107–32 and *id.*, *The Letters*, pp. 199–256 (prosopographical commentary); for the notion of intellectual friendship in Psellos' letters, see F. Tinnefeld, 'Freundschaft in den Briefen des Michael Psellos: Theorie und Wirklichkeit', *JÖB* 22 (1973) 151–68.

élite,[44] that gave a new direction to the cultivation of letters, since it allowed scholars, at least initially, to operate as a group outside the strict control of the state.

The method of teaching first in Mauropous' school, then in those of Xiphilinos and Psellos, took a new form. Teaching was not restricted to the simple transmission of codified knowledge but included a more interpretive approach to the texts of ancient Greek and patristic literature.[45] Psellos' comment on the teaching methods of the maistor Niketas, his old fellow-student in Mauropous' school, is indicative:

With what care did he teach poetry and how well did he know to analyse his poems! What other proof is needed for this claim of mine than the number of his pupils who have become a paradigm of the hermeneutic art for all youths? Because Niketas knew that the Greeks were difficult and obscure authors, hiding the truth under the external cover of eloquent discourse, he raised the veil and presented the hidden meaning. . . . His knowledge of Homer, Archilochus, Pindar and the other poets was vast; thus, he did not – like most teachers today – stop at the letter of the texts, content with the analysis of metre and of the apparent meaning, but, penetrating with his thought into the depths of the text, he advanced towards the mysterious beauty of the various works.[46]

Psellos himself taught in the same manner, as many of his surviving philosophical and theological lectures reveal.[47] Often in his writings, he pointed to the importance of teaching, and especially of teaching as a result of scholarly research. Moreover, he insisted on the interaction of

---

[44] The surviving letters of tenth-century scholars and officials reveal a very different, socially defined, perspective in the codes of communication; see A. Markopoulos, 'Οἱ διανοούμενοι καὶ τὸ περιβάλλον τοῦ Κωνσταντίνου Πορφυρογέννητου', in A. Markopoulos (ed.), *Constantine VII Porphyrogenitus and his Age. Second International Byzantine Conference (Delphi, July 1987)* (Athens, 1989), pp. 155–64.

[45] For an overview of the education system and the various intellectual changes in the eleventh century, see Angold, *The Byzantine Empire 1025–1204*, pp. 76–91 and Kazhdan and Epstein, *Change in Byzantine Culture*, pp. 120–58; see also N. G. Wilson, *Scholars of Byzantium* (London, 1983), pp. 148–79, whose analysis, however, is not always based on a proper appreciation of the historical context (see P. Speck, *Klio* 68 (1986) 615–25 and K. Alpers, *CP* 83 (1988) 342–60).

[46] Psel. *Fun. Orat. Nik.* (Sathas, *MB* 5, p. 92); the passage is also translated by Wilson, *Scholars*, p. 149. For a new edition with Italian translation see A. M. Guglielmino, 'Un maestro di grammatica a Bisanzio nell' XI secolo e l' epitafio per Niceta di Michele Psello', *SicGymn* 27 (1974) 421–63, the above passage on pp. 454.161–71 and 456.184–8; on the oration, see also Volk, *Der medizinische*, pp. 373–4 and Sideras, *Die byzantinischen Grabreden*, pp. 141–5.

[47] See the various texts in the three recent volumes of Psellos' works: P. Gautier, *Michaelis Pselli theologica*. Vol. I (Leipzig, 1989); J. M. Duffy, *Michaelis Pselli philosophica minora. Vol. I: Opuscula logica, physica, allegorica, alia* (Stuttgart and Leipzig, 1992); D. J. O'Meara, *Michaelis Pselli philosophica minora. Vol. II: Opuscula psychologica, theologica, daemonologica* (Leipzig, 1989). As an indicative example, especially for its pedagogical perspective, one might mention the 95th theological lecture (Gautier, *Michaelis Pselli theologica*, I, pp. 368–73), where Psellos discusses a passage from an oration of Gregory Nazianzenus (*Orat.* xxxviii 12 = *Patrologia Graeca*, vol. 36, col. 324C).

the various disciplines with each other in order to achieve a better understanding of the spiritual and material world.[48] Psellos firmly believed in free scholarly curiosity – an essential prerequisite for scientific knowledge – as opposed to a technocratic and utilitarian gnoseology.[49] At the same time, he emphatically stressed the importance of ancient Greek philosophical writings, which he considered the basis of a correct syllogistic process, especially within the framework of teaching.[50]

Yet this academic attitude entailed obvious dangers because it could be interpreted as an aberration in the direction of a heretical, potentially paganistic, cosmology which would overturn the social status quo and the dogmas of the Church, even more so if this attitude was combined – and in the case of Psellos it was combined – with reformatory attempts in education and pedagogy. These dangers became a reality when in the autumn of 1054 Emperor Konstantinos Monomachos, suffering from a debilitating disease, succumbed to the pressure of the then most powerful Patriarch Michael Keroularios (1043–1058).[51] The 'government of philosophers' was removed from court and Psellos was forced to submit a public admission of orthodox faith;[52] he voluntarily donned the monastic habit and went in exile to a monastery on Mt Olympus of Bithynia.[53] However, after Monomachos' death a few months later in the spring of 1055, Psellos returned to Constantinople. When his old fellow-student Ioannes Xiphilinos reprimanded him for going beyond accepted boundaries in engaging with Plato even now that he was a monk,[54] Psellos replied with a passionate defence of academic freedom:

---

[48] Most important in this respect is his extensive autobiographical excursus in the *Chron.* VI.35–44 (Impellizzeri, *Cronografia* I, pp. 282–90). See also his remarks in his lecture *On the Genealogy of Christ from Adam* (*Theol.* no. 114 = Gautier, *Michaelis Pselli theologica*, I, pp. 445–7).

[49] See, for example, his *Funeral Oration on his Mother* 27a–28d (U. Criscuolo, *Michele Psello: Autobiografia. Encomio per la madre* (Naples, 1989), pp. 144.1685–148.1801), where phrases and words about delight and curiosity in research abound (θέλγει γάρ με, οὐκ ἐᾷ με ἡσυχάζειν, ἀναγκάζει με πολυπραγμονεῖν, ἄγαμαι, πολυπραγμοσύνη, θέλγητρα).

[50] *Fun. Orat. on his Mother* 30a (Criscuolo, pp. 150.1865–151.1874). On Psellos' philosophical and theological opinions, see B. Tatakis, *La philosophie byzantine* (Paris, 1959, 2nd ed.), pp. 161–210; see also the references below in note 88.

[51] On whom see F. Tinnefeld, 'Michael I. Kerullarios, Patriarch von Konstantinopel (1043–1058): kritische Überlegungen zu einer Biographie', *JÖB* 39 (1989) 95–127.

[52] A. Garzya, 'On Michael Psellus' Admission of Faith', *EEBΣ* 35 (1966–7) 41–6 (repr. in his *Storia e interpretazione di testi bizantini* (London, 1974) no. 6), and J. Gouillard, 'La religion des philosophes', *TM* 6 (1976) 305–24 (repr. in his *La vie religieuse à Byzance* (London, 1981) no. 3).

[53] These events are described in the *Chron.* VI.191–9 (Impellizzeri, *Cronografia* II, pp. 138–48). For the role of Keroularios in this affair, see A. Michel, 'Schisma und Kaiserhof im Jahre 1054: Michael Psellos', in *1054–1954: L' Église et les Églises*, vol. I (Chevetogne, 1954), pp. 351–440.

[54] On the sometimes tense relation between the two men, see U. Criscuolo, 'Sui rapporti tra Michele Psello e Giovanni Xifilino', *Atti Accad. Pontaniana* N.S. 24 (1975) 1–8.

Plato is mine, most holy and wise lord, Plato is mine? Oh earth and sun, to use a phrase from the tragic stage! If you accuse me that I once dealt in depth with his dialogues and admired the quality of his interpretive and syllogistic power, why then do you not also accuse the great Fathers who refuted the arguments of so many heretics with the exactitude of their syllogisms? . . . I indeed fell in love with Plato and Chrysippus – could it have been otherwise? –, but in depth and beyond their smooth surface. Some of their teachings I immediately passed over, while other ones which would support my own analyses, I accepted after I harmonised them with the Holy Scriptures, as at any rate it had been done by Gregory and Basil, the two grand luminaries of the Church.[55]

Without expressly stating it, Xiphilinos had brought to the surface the problem of the relation between faith and teaching, which Julian had formulated, only this time from the Christian perspective.[56] Psellos' main line of defence was that his teaching of and research on ancient philosophy fully agreed with the practice of Gregory and Basil. In this way he inverted Xiphilinos' criticism and placed himself on the side of the Church Fathers whose generally accepted authority offered him the protective cover for the vindication of his academic freedom. The reference to the two Cappadocians is not a mere excuse for external consumption. Psellos had in his lectures systematically analysed the theology of Gregory,[57] whom, moreover, as we shall see, he deeply admired as a stylist; to a far lesser degree he had also discussed the works of Basil.[58]

As Psellos' position of proximity to the new Emperor Isaakios I Komnenos (1057–1059) increased, the scholar politician did not hesitate to criticize Patriarch Keroularios himself. In the autumn of 1058, Psellos wrote to him a letter where he clarified his position concerning knowledge and juxtaposed it to the authoritarian, but at the same time populist, theology of the patriarch. Psellos writes:

[55] Psel. *Epist. Xiph.* 1a, 4a (U. Criscuolo, *Michele Psello: Epistola a Giovanni Xifilino*. Byzantina et Neo-hellenica Neapolitana 14 (Naples, 1990, 2nd ed.), pp. 49.1–8, 52.102–8).

[56] The problem of faith and teaching in connection with the attempts of State and Church to exercise control over 'dissidents' has been dealt with by R. Browning, 'Enlightenment and Repression in Byzantium in the Eleventh and Twelfth Centuries', *PP* 69 (1975) 3–23 (reprinted in his *Studies on Byzantine History, Literature and Education* (London, 1977), no. 15) and J. Gouillard, 'Quatres procès de mystiques à Byzance (vers 960–1143): Inspiration et autorité', *REB* 36 (1978) 5–81.

[57] This is indicated by the lectures nos. 2–4, 16, 19, 40, 43–58, 86–87 in Gautier's edition, *Michaelis Pselli theologica*, (as above n. 47). In most of these lectures various theological issues are connected to problems of Platonic and Neoplatonic philosophy and are interpreted accordingly. On the whole subject, see now E. V. Maltese, 'Michele Psello commentatore di Gregorio di Nazianzo: note per una lettura dei Theologica', in Σύνδεσμος. *Studi in honore di Rosario Anastasi*, vol. 2 (Catania, 1994), pp. 289–309.

[58] *Theol.* no. 6 (Gautier, *Michaelis Pselli theologica*, 1, pp. 22–27), where Psellos discusses Basil's opinions on the material world in connection with Platonic philosophy and the Peripatetics (see also *Theol.* nos. 79 and 109).

I admit that I am human, a living nature which alters and changes, a logical soul which needs a body, a strange mixture of unfitting parts. Sometimes, whenever I am able, I strive towards that higher nature in order to unite with it in whatever way I can, casting off the heavy burden of my own nature; again sometimes . . . – but I do not intend to blaspheme! You, however, alone amongst all the rest of us, are unalterable and unmovable, a nature different from ours, which moves and stands by its own will. . . .

I gathered knowledge gradually and by myself; we are almost of the same age! I often conversed with books, and searching for their doctrines, I discovered some of them myself through pure research and based on acknowleged principles; again, other doctrines I received as a student from those who knew the science of teaching. From then on I strengthened my knowledge of philosophy and I cleansed my discourse through the art of rhetoric; I collected the subject-matter of geometry, being the first one to teach this science to my pupils; I analysed the mathematical proportions in music and I corrected numerous points in the theory concerning the movement of the heavenly sphere. Moreover, I clarified the hermeneutic approach to Christian literature, I taught the central dogmas of theology, I expounded at length the allegorical interpretation of the Old Testament, and in general – may the arrow of envy not strike me! – I dealt systematically with all disciplines.

You, however, obtained wisdom and theology from other principles which I do not know nor did I ever learn, except if you mean 'the tablets of Zeus'.[59] You never engaged yourself with philosophy or solid geometry, you never conversed with books, you never read any Greek or other author. You call yourself self-science and self-wisdom; it seems that you have not been made from heart and liver, as the specialists have diagnosed for the human nature, but only from mind, something like the Absolute Idea. Do you see now how many mountains, how many seas, how many lands separate us? Neither can you imitate me, but neither can nor will I try to imitate you.

Mark also the following: your descent is from both sides glorious. Your grandfather and great-grandfather are still renowned and talked about by everyone; it is with this glory above anything else that you adorn your patriarchal robe. But I – and together with me old Phocion,[60] so as not to mention the Prophets – do not possess such a glorious race, or if I do, I keep silent about it. I do not wish to be known because of some lifeless and decaying arrogance but because of my youthful and vigorous scientific discourse.[61]

---

[59] See, for example, Lucian *De merc. cond.* 12 (M. D. Macleod, *Luciani opera*, vol. 2 (Oxford, 1974), p. 219.22).

[60] The Athenian general Phocion (402/1–318 BC), pupil of Plato. Psellos here obviously refers to a comment by Plutarch in the *Life of Phocion* about the general's low social origin (*Phocion* 4.1 = Ziegler 11.1, p. 3.29–31).

[61] Psel. *Epist. Cerul.* 2a–3a (U. Criscuolo, *Michele Psello: Epistola a Giovanni Cerulario.* Byzantina et Neo-hellenica Neapolitana 15 (Naples, 1990, 2nd ed.), pp. 22.32–23.40, 23.47–24.80). Psellos went one step further and wrote towards the end of 1058 the lengthy accusation against Keroularios when the latter, having fallen from power, was to be tried by the Holy Synod (G. T. Dennis, *Michaelis Pselli orationes forenses et acta* (Stuttgart and Leipzig, 1994), pp. 1–103); the

It is obvious that we are faced with a declaration of intellectual preferences that is essentially secular: priority is given to man as a living entity which thinks and develops; knowledge is defined as a process of learning, research and teaching, things independent of social context and of possible political expediencies.[62] Of course, Psellos was a man of politics and he knew well how to hover between his own beliefs and the prevailing opinions of Byzantine society. Except for the brief clash with Keroularios, he never found himself in a complete ideological opposition to the social status quo. His powerful personality nonetheless did exercise a profound influence on his pupils, especially those who had a natural inclination towards philosophical inquiry.

Such a pupil was Ioannes Italos, the best known among his students. Italos was born in Southern Italy and went to Constantinople around 1049. He quickly learned Greek, and even more quickly mathematics and philosophy under Psellos.[63] Yet in contrast to his teacher, Italos never became interested in rhetoric. Furthermore, although it seems that he consciously refused to subordinate his discourse to the compulsory eloquence of Greek intellectuals, his thought was so clear and his argumentation so convincing, that even Psellos, who gave extreme importance to cultivated speech, accepted him as an exceptional thinker:

His art is powerful but the elegance of his style non-existent. Thus, for the inattentive listener his discourse is distasteful – it merely consists of syllogistic theses –, yet for the attentive conversant it is neither careless nor burdensome. He does not instil graces in the soul, but he forces others to think and to pay attention to what he is saying. He does not convince by his grandiloquence and rhetoric (after all he does not know how to ensnare by means of a graceful discourse), he does not entice with his style nor does he attract with sweetness, but he conquers and subdues his listener with the content of his arguments.[64]

oration was never delivered because Keroularios died in January of 1059. Psellos composed four years later an equally lengthy funeral oration (Sathas, *MB* 4, pp. 303–87), for which see Sideras, *Die byzantinischen Grabreden*, pp. 133–5. On Psellos and Keroularios, see the somewhat disappointing study by Ja. N. Ljubarskij, 'The fall of an intellectual: the intellectual and moral atmosphere in eleventh-century Byzantium', in S. Vryonis (ed.), *Byzantine Studies: Essays on the Slavic World and the Eleventh Century* (New Rochelle and New York, 1992), pp. 175–82.

[62] See the studies by U. Criscuolo, Tardoantico e umanesimo bizantino: Michele Psello', *Koinonia* 5 (1981) 7–23 and 'Πολιτικὸς ἀνήρ. Contributo al pensiero politico di Michele Psello', *Atti della Società Nazionale di Scienze, Lettere e Belle Arti di Napoli* 93 (1982) 95–130.

[63] A bare outline of Italos' life is drawn by Anna Komnene (1083-ca. 1150), daughter of Emperor Alexios I Komnenos (1081–1118), in her *Alexiad* v.8–9 (B. Leib, *Anne Comnène: Alexiade. Tome II: Livres V–X* (Paris, 1943), pp. 32–40; see also *The Alexiad of Anna Comnena*, tr. E. R. A. Sewter (Harmondsworth, 1969), pp. 173–80); in general, see P. E. Stephanou, *Jean Italos philosophe et humaniste* (Rome, 1949).

[64] Psel. *Enc. Ital.* 4 (A. R. Littlewood, *Michaelis Pselli oratoria minora* (Leipzig, 1985) pp. 71.67–72.75).

The passage comes from a short essay of Psellos in praise of Italos, where the teacher recognises with clarity the astuteness of his pupil. Psellos, however, also recognised another trait of Italos' character, the almost violent passion which got hold of him when he involved himself in philosophical debates while searching for the path to knowledge.[65] Often enough did Ioannes clash with his co-students in Psellos' school.[66] This trait of his does not seem, however, to have diminished his popularity; on the contrary, when he directed his own school in the capital, he had many loyal pupils.[67] When Psellos resigned from the office of consul of philosophers around 1074, possibly for reasons of health,[68] the Emperor Michael Doukas appointed Italos as his successor to the coveted position. Moreover, the government used Italos because of his origin as an ambassador to the Normans in Sicily for a series of delicate diplomatic contacts.

Italos had reached the peak of success. In his lectures he analysed Platonic philosophy in an interpretive manner, while he applied logic to the understanding of the highest theological problems, like, for example, the mystery of Divine Hypostasis or the Incarnation of Christ.[69] His hermeneutic method, where pagan philosophy and Christian theology achieved proximity, provoked objections.[70] Doubts were raised as to

---

[65] In the essay *To Ioannes the Italian when he forced him to interpret science more quickly (Orat. min.* 18 = Littlewood, *Michaelis Pselli oratoria*, pp. 65–9); see also the negative portrait of Italos in the *Alexiad* v.8.7 (Leib II, p. 36.12–24). The quarrelsome aspect of Italos' character is also stressed by the anonymous author of the satiric dialogue *Timarion*, when he depicts Italos getting into a fight in Hades with the Cynic philosopher Diogenes (*Tim.* 44 = R. Romano, *Pseudo-Luciano: Timarione*. Byzantina et Neo-hellenica Neapolitana 2 (Naples, 1974), pp. 88.1093–89.1122, and M. D. Macleod, *Luciani opera*, vol. 4, (Oxford, 1987), pp. 467.16–468.14; see also B. Baldwin, *Timarion. Transl. with an Introduction and Commentary* (Detroit, 1984), pp. 73–4).

[66] See Psellos' essay *To two of his pupils on having exchanged pamphlets against each other (Orat. min.* 20 = Littlewood, *Michaelis Pselli oratoria*, pp. 73–6).

[67] Anna Komnene (*Alexiad* v.9.1–2 = Leib II, p. 37.11–29) underlines the enthusiastic presence of young people in Italos' lectures and mentions by name some of his pupils who came from the highest strata of society, like, for example, Ioannes Solomon, of whom we find a grotesque portrait in *Tim.* 43 (Romano, *Pseudo-Luciano*, p. 88.1085–92; Macleod, *Luciani opera* IV, p. 467.8–15). For the brilliant identification of Solomon with the ἀνδράριον ἡμιάνδριον of the *Timarion*, see D. R. Reinsch, 'Zur Identität einer Gestalt im Timarion', *BZ* 86–7 (1993–4) 383–5.

[68] On the gradual withdrawal of Psellos from public affairs, see Volk, *Der medizinische*, pp. 36–44.

[69] Very few of Italos' works have survived and those that have are not particularly revealing as to his hermeneutic approach (see, for example, P. Joannou, *Johannes Italos. Questiones quodlibetales* (Ettal, 1956)). For a brief presentation of his views see Kazhdan and Epstein, *Change in Byzantine Culture*, pp. 158–66 and Angold, *The Byzantine Empire 1025–1204*, pp. 115–8.

[70] We know his opinions primarily from the highly biased acts of the 1082 synod (J. Gouillard, 'Le procès officiel de Jean l'Italien: Les actes et leurs sous-entendus', *TM* 9 (1985) 133–74) and the synodical condemnation chapters (J. Gouillard, 'Le synodicon de l'Orthodoxie', *TM* 2 (1967) 1–316 and in particular pp. 57–61).

his orthodoxy.[71] Nonetheless, during the reigns of Michael Doukas and of his successor Nikephoros III Botaneiates (1078–1081), Italos' position remained unshaken.

However, when in April of 1081 the young Alexios Komnenos (1057–1118), member of a distinguished military family from Asia Minor,[72] ascended the throne through a *coup d' état*, the situation changed radically. The emperor, in order to meet pressing external military threats, had a large part of the Church's movable property confiscated; it was a clear case of state authoritarianism. In an attempt to appear as protector of the Church, while at the same time strengthening his own position, Alexios proceeded to remove officials and intellectuals of the previous regime. The members of the once 'government of philosophers' had died. As the next in line, Italos was asked to defend his theological teaching, but Patriarch Eustratios Garidas (1081–1084) was positively disposed towards him. During a public debate in February 1082 the patriarch tried to dissuade Italos on a personal level from adhering to his theophilosophical beliefs, and of course failed.[73] One month later, on the Sunday of the Feast of Orthodoxy,[74] the displeased emperor called together at the palace a private council consisting of church and state officials. The choice of the Feast of Orthodoxy was unquestionably a political act. On that day, which had been established since the ninth century to commemorate the restoration of the cult of images, the Synodikon of Orthodoxy condemning all heresies and affirming the orthodox creed was read aloud in all the churches of the empire: it was the day when State and Church celebrated their triumph over their religious adversaries. At the council Italos was accused on the basis of fabricated evidence by an informant;[75] Italos was forced to publicly renounce his works and anathematise his doctrines.[76] The emperor personally composed the text of the judicial decision and had it sent to the patriarch for final ratification.[77] During the final session of the Holy

---

[71] On an inofficial investigation conducted in 1076/7 under Patriarch Kosmas (1075–1081), see Gouillard, 'Le synodicon', pp. 188–9; a set of 10 chapters against hellenising philosophers was composed at that point but was not specifically directed at Italos.

[72] On the Komnenoi, see now the exhaustive study by K. Barzos, Ἡ γενεαλογία τῶν Κομνηνῶν. Βυζαντινὰ Κείμενα καὶ Μελέται 20.1–2 (Thessaloniki, 1984), on Alexios in particular, vol. 1, pp. 87–113 (no. 15). For a re-evalutaion of Alexios and his reign, see M. Mullett and D. Smythe (eds), *Alexios I Komnenos. I: Papers*. Belfast Byzantine Texts and Translations 4.1 (Belfast, 1996).

[73] Guillard, 'Le procès', pp. 143.128–145.151.

[74] The date was 13 March 1082; Gouillard, 'Le procès', p. 159.426–30.

[75] Gouillard, 'Le procès', pp. 145.152–157.409.

[76] The scene is depicted with an obvious bias against Italos in the *Alexiad* v.9.5–7 (Leib II, pp. 39.6–40.22).

[77] Gouillard, 'Le procès', p. 157.394–409.

Synod on April 11 Italos' anathema was confirmed; five of his pupils were examined and, having admitted their error, were lightly punished.[78] Moreover, it was decided to incorporate into the Synodikon of Orthodoxy twelve chapters condemning Italos' teachings; two of them touch specifically the question of Hellenic beliefs in education:

> Those who profess to be pious, but who in fact impudently or rather impiously introduce into the orthodox and catholic Church the impious beliefs of the Hellenes concerning human souls, heaven, earth and other creations, let them be anathematised!
>
> Those who offer courses on Hellenic subjects[79] and do not teach these subjects solely for the sake of education, but who follow the vain opinions of the Hellenes and believe in them as being true, and thus, considering them to be correct, induce others – either secretly or even publicly – to follow them and instruct them without second thoughts, let them be anathematised![80]

Just as Emperor Alexios had, in the name of the state's welfare, exercised his power of authority to gain economic control over the Church, so now he had succeeded in repressing any innovative intellectual movement which could potentially endanger the stability of his recently established and still insecure regime. Seen in the light of Byzantine history of the tenth and eleventh centuries, the trial of Ioannes Italos was an unheard of interference of the State in the affairs of education.[81]

III

At this point we must interrupt the chronological sequence of our narration in order to move backwards to the middle of the eleventh century. During that time a sense among the faithful was taking shape that the two Cappadocian Fathers Basil of Caesarea and Gregory of Nazianzus together with the Antiochene John Chrysostom formed a 'triad', conventionally known as the Three Hierarchs. Representations

---

[78] Gouillard, 'Le procès', pp. 157.410–161.470. For an analysis of the imperial and patriarchal decrees concerning the trial, see F. Dölger, *Regesten der Kaiserurkunden des Oströmischen Reiches. 2. Teil: Regesten von 1025–1204* (Munich and Berlin, 1925) pp. 26–7 (nos. 1078–9), and V. Grumel and J. Darrouzès, *Les regestes des actes du Patriarcat de Constantinople. Fasc. II et III: Les regestes de 715 à 1206* (Paris, 1989, 2nd ed.) pp. 400–3 (nos. 923–7).

[79] 'Courses on Hellenic subjects' freely renders the original ἑλληνικὰ μαθήματα ('Hellenic lessons'); the phrase must refer to ancient philosophy as taught by the school of Psellos, since the acts of the synod specifically mention Iamblichus and Proclus (Gouillard, 'Le procès', p. 147.199–203), Psellos' favourite neoplatonic philosophers.

[80] Gouillard, 'Le synodicon', pp. 57.190–3, 59.214–8.

[81] On the affair, see Gouillard, 'Le synodicon', pp. 188–202; L. Clucas, *The Trial of John Italos and the Crisis of Intellectual Values in Byzantium in the Eleventh Century*. Miscellanea Byzantina Monacensia 26 (Munich, 1981); Gouillard, 'Le procès', pp. 161–9, who revises some of Clucas' conclusions.

in illuminated manuscripts, mosaics and portable icons testify to the interest of Church and artists in grouping together these three out-standing theologians of the fourth century.[82] We also know that there was a growing interest in the literary merits of the works of the three Church Fathers.[83] During the reign of Emperor Michael Doukas this interest led to a philological dispute about who of the three hierarchs was the best rhetorician.[84] It is probably in connection with this dis-pute that Psellos wrote two essays on the topic. In the first essay he deals exclusively with his beloved Gregory, where he analyses in detail Nazianzenus' style and learning, comparing him with the orators of antiquity, Isocrates in particular.[85] His second and shorter essay is entitled 'The Literary Character of Gregory the Theologian, of Basil the Great, of Chrysostom, and of Gregory of Nyssa'.[86] Here Psellos briefly outlines the literary qualities of the 'triad' with the inclusion of their contemporary Gregory of Nyssa (Basil's older brother), but con-centrates on Gregory of Nazianzus' works and shows a clear prefer-ence for them.

By the time Alexios Komnenos ascended the throne this dispute had taken on serious dimensions. The scholars in the capital had divided themselves into three 'parties', each of them supporting their own hierarch. The problem cannot have been only a philological one. It must be remembered that Plato and Aristotle represented at that time two different philosophical approaches to knowledge.[87] Similarly, each of the three hierarchs stood for a different theological approach to the knowledge of God and the Scriptures: Gregory of Nazianzus as the more

---

[82] N. Drandakes, *Εἰκονογραφία τῶν Τριῶν Ἱεραρχῶν* (Ioannina, 1969), pp. 5–34. See also Mauropous' epigram 86 on an icon depicting the three Hierarchs, which he gave as a present to an archbishop (Bollig and de Lagarde, *Iohannis Euchaitorum metropolitae*, pp. 41–2).

[83] Note, for example, the mostly literary commentary of Niketas of Herakleia (ca. 1040–ca. 1120) on sixteen orations of Gregory (R. Constantinescu, *Nicetae Heracleensis commentariorum XVI orationum Gregorii Nazianzeni fragmenta* (Bucharest 1977).

[84] This dispute is described in the hagiographical synaxar for January 30, of which two versions survive. The longest and oldest version dates from the end of the 13th century but is still unedited (cf. G. Przychocki, *Eos* 16 (1910) 133); the shorter version, from the 14th century, has been edited in the *Patrologia Graeca*, vol. 29, col. 390–3.

[85] Edited by A. Mayer, 'Psellos' Rede über den rhetorischen Charakter des Gregorios von Nazianz', *BZ* 20 (1911) 27–100 (text on pp. 48–60), and P. Levy, *Michaelis Pselli de Gregorii Theologi charactere iudicium* (Leipzig, 1912); see also Wilson, *Scholars*, pp. 166–72.

[86] See J. F. Boissonade, *Michaelis Pselli de operatione daemonum* (Nuremburg, 1838), pp. 124–31 (= *Patrologia Graeca*, vol. 122, col. 901–8).

[87] On the image of Plato and Aristotle in Byzantium of the eleventh and twelfth centuries, see I. N. Pontikos, *Anonymi Miscellanea Philosophica. A Miscellany in the Tradition of Michael Psellos (Codex Baroccianus Graecus 131). Critical Edition and Introduction.* Corpus Philosophorum Medii Aevi. Philosophi Byzantini 6 (Athens, Paris and Brussels, 1992), pp. xli–lxxxiv.

flexible and most philosophical, Basil of Caesarea as the more austere and most exegetical, John Chrysostom as the more rhetorical and most openly polemical against pagan learning. The three of them also had different social images: Gregory was seen as the solitary poet theologian, Basil as the bishop politician and John as the defender of the lower classes. These schematic views of the 'triad' meant that their partisans supported opinions, which in the partisans' eyes corresponded to those of their particular hierarch. It is indicative that the innovative scholars around Psellos preferred Plato and Gregory,[88] while the theologians of the establishment, like Michael of Ephesos (early 12th century), chose Aristotle and Basil.[89] In this sense, we might possibly discern behind the philological dispute of these 'parties' over the literary merits of the three Church Fathers conflicting attitudes concerning matters of theology and education. It was therefore surely not accidental that the dispute reached its peak as Emperor Alexios intensified his efforts to control the free course of learning by having Italos condemned.

At that critical moment, in the summer of 1082, Psellos' old teacher Ioannes Mauropous, approximately eighty years of age, made a last appearance on the stage of history.[90] Mauropous lived withdrawn at the Monastery of St John the Forerunner at Petra in Constantinople, having resigned in 1075 from the bishopric at Euchaita.[91] He appealed to Patriarch Eustratios and proposed to the Holy Synod to establish a joint feast for the three hierarchs, not to celebrate the memory of the 'splendid triad' – the appropriate individual feast-days did, in fact, exist –, but to commemorate their collective contribution to education and the cultivation of eloquence.[92] Mauropous suggested that this day should be the thirtieth of January so as to form the crowning conclusion

[88] See above pp. 180–1, as well as L. Benakis, 'Michael Psellos' Kritik an Aristoteles und seine eigene Lehre zur "Physis" und "Materie-Form"-Problematik', *BZ* 56 (1963) 213–27, and Ch. Zervos, *Un philosophe néoplatonicien du XIe siècle: Michel Psellos. Sa vie, son œuvre, ses luttes philosophiques, son influence* (New York, 1973, 2nd ed.).

[89] A. Preus, *Aristotle and Michael of Ephesus. On the Movement and Progression of Animals* (New York, 1981); in general, see G. Podskalsky, *Theologie und Philosophie in Byzanz*. Byzantinisches Archiv 15 (Munich, 1977), pp. 64–87 and 107–124.

[90] There are no secure dates for the following events; however, Mauropous' extreme old age and the information of the synaxar that the settlement of the dispute took place during Alexios' reign, makes the dating of the events in the second year of his rule seem probable.

[91] Karpozilos, *Symbole*, pp. 46–50 and *id.*, 'The Biography', pp. 53–4.

[92] *Patrologia Graeca*, vol. 29, col. 391. Mauropous' interest in the three Hierarchs predates the events of 1082 as can be seen from a series of epigrams (nos. 14–17) praising the three Fathers separately and one joining them together (Bollig and de Lagarde, *Johannis Euchaitorum metropolitae*, pp. 9–10). On the feast in general, see P. E. Lamerand, 'La fête des trois Hiérarques dans l'Eglise Grecque', *Bessarione* 4 (1898–9) pp. 164–76.

to the individual feasts in honour of the three Church Fathers, all of which were celebrated in January.[93]

The patriarch and the Synod accepted the proposal. On 30 January, 1083 and in front of the State and Church authorities, Mauropous delivered from the pulpit of St Sophia – the capital's imperial cathedral – the first panegyrical oration on the three Hierarchs, entitled *To the Three Holy Fathers and Teachers, Basil the Great, Gregory the Theologian, and John Chrysostom.*[94] In numerous passages Mauropous underlines the sense of measure which the three hierarchs displayed. He praises the style of each one of them, stresses their similarities and points to their importance as pedagogues. The oration could have stopped there. But Mauropous, towards the end of the speech, turns his attention to Julian and the by now notorious problem of religion versus education. He accuses the Apostate for his arrogance and his usurpation of Greek culture, he accuses, moreover, all those who follow him.[95] However, he defends the importance of 'correct education' and presents the three Hierarchs, who preferred 'the middle and smooth course',[96] as models of the perfect union between Greek letters and Christian ethos. Through the insistent praise of measure and restrained eloquence, Ioannes attempts to offer a generally acceptable solution to the problem: the extremes should be smoothed away without, however, sacrificing the fruits of his and his pupils' efforts. This low-key suggestion found a positive response, for on one hand the dispute of the scholars ceased,[97] on the other the personal ban on Italos was lifted some time later and some of his pupils returned to their teaching posts.[98]

The affair then closed with an appeal for reconciliation and mutual toleration between the State and the intellectuals. The Feast of the Three Hierarchs was established not only because of some general spiritual needs of the faithful, but much more so out of the necessity to protect the role of the teacher and the fruits of knowledge. We recognise here the Byzantines' favourite device for defending innovations: resistance against repressive measures is expressed as the wish to revive

[93] January 1 (memory of Basil the Great), January 25 (memory of Gregory Nazianzenus), and January 27 (translation of the relics of John Chrysostom).
[94] Bollig and de Lagarde, *Iohannis Euchaitorum metropolitae*, pp. 106–119 (no. 178); on the oration in general see also Karpozilos, *Symbole*, pp. 162–6.
[95] Bollig and de Lagarde, *Iohannis Euchaitorum metropolitae*, pp. 116–7.
[96] Bollig and de Lagarde, *Iohannis Euchaitorum metropolitae*, p. 111.
[97] *Patrologia Graeca*, vol. 29, col. 393.
[98] This is what Anna Komnene indirectly suggests in the *Alexiad* v.9.7 (Leib II, p. 40.11–22); see Gouillard, 'Le procès', p. 168.

ancient and generally revered, but 'unfortunately' forgotten, ways of conduct. The protection of academic freedom is now to be guaranteed by the authority of the three Fathers; a new concept appears under the guise of an old model.

However, the end of the Italos affair did not stop the developments set in motion by the emperor's policy. Mauropous had proposed a more active role of the Church in the matters of education; a few years later, Patriarch Nikolaos III Grammatikos (1084–1111), following these suggestions, made some efforts to reorganise schools in the capital.[99] Alexios, in his function as protector of the Church, reacted on a grand scale; an imperial decree was issued in June of 1107 regulating in substantial detail questions of teaching within the Church.[100] The decree obviously attempted to control liberal education and set the tone for a more conservative policy.[101] As the ruling family of the Komnenoi systematically extended their power in the State's military and bureaucratic ruling class, the twelfth century witnessed a steady grow of imperial interference in matters of theology and education.[102] By the end of the century the innovative clashes of the previous century had been smoothed out in favour of the State.[103] It was not until after the fall of Constantinople to the Crusaders in 1204 that Byzantium was forced to substantially re-examine its policy of education and to redress the balance between pedagogical ideals and the ideology of power.[104]

---

[99] U. Criscuolo, 'Chiesa ed insegnamento a Bisanzio nel XII secolo: Sul problema della cosidetta «Accademia patriarcale»', *SicGymn* 26 (1973) 373–90, and V. Katsaros, *Ἰωάννης Κασταμονίτης. Συμβολὴ στὴ μελέτη τοῦ βίου, τοῦ ἔργου καὶ τῆς ἐποχῆς του.* Βυζαντινὰ Κείμενα καὶ Μελέται 22 (Thessaloniki, 1988), pp. 175–96.

[100] P. Gautier, 'L' édit d' Alexis Ier Comnène sur la réforme de clergé', *REB* 31 (1973) 165–201.

[101] This policy is briefly but clearly described in the *Alexiad* v.9.4 (Leib II, pp. 38.27–39.6).

[102] On the whole issue, see Browning, 'Enlightenment', *passim*.

[103] Recently P. Magdalino, 'Enlightenment and Repression in Twelfth-Century Byzantium: The Evidence of the Canonists', in N. Oikonomidis (ed.), *Byzantium in the Twelfth Century: Canon Law, State and Society.* Διπτύχων Παράφυλλα 3 (Athens, 1991), pp. 357–73 and 'The reform edict of 1107', in Mullett and Smythe, *Alexios*, pp. 199–218, has argued for a revision of this conservative image of the twelfth century. However, a conservative policy of the State in doctrinal questions does not preclude innovations in other areas; the Komnenian age is full of such examples in literature and art. What Alexios succeeded in stopping was the application of philosophy to theology, a method which could and did, as we have seen, endanger ecclesiastical or imperial 'authority'.

[104] See, for example, the radically different and highly individualistic attitude towards imperial power in questions of pedagogy as expressed by the thirteenth-century scholar Nikephoros Blemmydes in his *Autobiography* I.I–10 and I.49–73 (J. A. Munitiz, *Nicephori Blemmydae Autobiographia sive Curriculum Vitae.* Corpus Christianorum. Series Graeca 13 (Turnhout and Louvain, 1984), pp. 3–7 and 23–37; English translation by J. A. Munitiz, *Nikephoros Blemmydes. A Partial Account.* Spicilegium Sacrum Lovaniense. Etudes et Documents 48 (Louvain, 1988), pp. 43–8 and 71–85).

CHAPTER 9

Reading power in Roman Greece: the paideia of Dio Chrysostom

Tim Whitmarsh

I

Marrou's *Histoire de l'éducation dans l'antiquité*, still generally cited as the standard account of ancient pedagogy, omits any specific discussion of the values and functions of education in the Greek world under Roman occupation.[1] This silence is perhaps not at first sight surprising: the nineteenth century and its heirs, while embracing Classical Greek culture wholeheartedly, have been notoriously harsh upon later Greek literature.[2] Yet surprise it should, for if it is at all possible to quantify such things, the period of Greek history spanning the early centuries of the Roman empire (often known as the 'Second Sophistic'[3]) invested

[1] H. I. Marrou, *Histoire de l'éducation dans l'éntiquité* (Paris, 1948); English trans. by G. Lamb, *A History of Education in Antiquity* (Madison and London, 1956). I should like to thank Simon Goldhill, Christopher Kelly, Julie Lewis, and the editors for their astute comments on this chapter. Jonathan Hesk, Richard Hunter and Peter Stewart helped with their discussions of individual aspects. The text of Philostratus used is that of C. L. Kayser (Leipzig, 1870–1). *VA* means Philostratus' *Vita Apollonii* (for τὰ ἐς τὸν Τυανέα Ἀπολλώνιον), *VS* the same author's *Vitae Sophistarum*; the latter is cited by page and line number from Kayser, with the pagination of Olearius (more familiar from the Loeb edition) also supplied; translations are modified (where necessary) from the Loeb edition of W. C. Wright (London and Cambridge, MA, 1921 repr. 1968).

[2] The bibliography on the Victorian reception of Classical Greece is growing rapidly: especially useful are F. M. Turner, *The Greek Heritage in Victorian Britain* (New Haven and London, 1981) and the essays in G. W. Clarke ed., *Rediscovering Hellenism: The Hellenic Inheritance and the English Imagination* (Cambridge, 1989). For some references to Victorians' prejudices against Roman Greek culture, see M. W. Gleason, *Making Men. Sophists and Self-Presentation in Ancient Rome* (Princeton, 1995), pp. xvii–xviii.

[3] The term was coined by Philostratus (*VS* 2.27 = 481 O; 21.27 = 507 O) and is conventionally applied to the period from 50 to 250 CE (for a recent discussion with bibliography, see S. Swain, *Hellenism and Empire: Language, Classicism and Power in the Greek World, AD 50–250* (Oxford, 1996), pp. 1–7). I am extremely reluctant to use the label, and have avoided it as far as possible, finding it misleading: firstly, because Philostratus uses it not of a historical period but of a literary style (founded in the fourth century by Aeschines), but more importantly because it might be taken to convey a certain contempt for a culture deemed to be both parasitic and trivial. As Voltaire might have said, the Second Sophistic was neither (intrinsically) 'second' nor

192

more than any other in education.[4] Or, rather, in *paideia*, the Greek term which carries an altogether different range of meanings both sociological and semantic from the English 'education.'[5]

To possess *paideia* – that is, to be *pepaideumenos* – meant to be familiar with a set of canonical texts, mostly in prose, predominantly from the fifth and fourth centuries BCE. It often meant to be able to write or declaim in the archaising Attic dialect in which those texts were written.[6] At a semiotic level, it meant to be Greek, and to be a man. Recent studies have emphasised the distinctive importance of *paideia* for Greek cultural identity (among the élite, at any rate)[7] and for ideals of manhood (public contests of *paideia* were represented as trials of virility).[8] In certain circumstances, Greek *paideia* could even allow non-Greeks a (not uncontested) claim to Greek identity.[9] Education was a crucial medium for locating the (male, élite) self in relation to society. As the philosopher Iamblichus put it in the fourth century, in the context of a discussion of *paideia*, 'it is upbringing which distinguishes

(exclusively) 'sophistic.' Nevertheless, it has been necessary at times to use to phrase in order to obviate such cumbersome monstrosities as 'early imperial Roman Greece.' For some of the problems involved in the term, see the (rather overstated, to my mind) views of P. A. Brunt, 'The Bubble of the Second Sophistic', *BICS* 39 (1994), 25–52.

[4] On the importance of the notion of *paideia* to the literature of this period, see esp. B. P. Reardon, *Courants littéraires des IIe et IIIe siècles après J.-C.* (Paris, 1971), pp. 3–11. On the practice and social implications of *paideia*, there is much that is relevant in the useful study of R. A. Kaster, *Guardians of Language: the Grammarian and Society in Late Antiquity* (Berkeley, Los Angeles and London, 1988). A complete bibliography of studies of Greek literary culture and the Roman empire would be beyond the present scope. Among the most important publications are G. W. Bowersock, *Greek Sophists in the Roman Empire* (Oxford, 1969); *id.* ed., *Approaches to the Second Sophistic* (Pennsylvania, 1974); E. L. Bowie, 'Greeks and Their Past in the Second Sophistic', *PP* 46 (1970), 3–41, = M. I. Finley ed., *Studies in Ancient Society* (London, 1974), pp. 166–209; *id.*, 'The Importance of Sophists', *YCS* 27 (1982), 29–59; G. Anderson, *The Second Sophistic. A Cultural Phenomenon in the Roman Empire* (London, 1993); G. Woolf, 'Becoming Roman, Staying Greek. Culture, Identity and the Civilising Process in the Roman East', *PCPS* 40 (1994), 116–43; Swain, *Hellenism*, with an extensive and up-to-date bibliography.

[5] See e.g. T. J. Morgan, *Frames of Mind. Literate Education in the Hellenistic and Roman Worlds* (unpublished PhD thesis, University of Cambridge, 1995), p. 11, n. 19.

[6] On Atticism, see, most recently, Swain, *Hellenism*, chs. 1–2.

[7] Esp. Bowie, 'Greeks'; *id.* 'Importance'; Swain, *Hellenism*. The emphasis upon language and culture as primary markers of Hellenism seems to have had its roots in the fifth century BCE: see J. M. Hall, 'The Role of Language in Greek Ethnicities', *PCPS* 41 (1995), 83–100.

[8] Gleason, *Making*, *passim*.

[9] See esp. Gleason's discussion of Favorinus, who attempted to transcend his origins by means of *paideia*, so as 'to seem Greek, and to be Greek' (Fav. *Corinth.* [= ps.-Dio Chr. *Or.* 37] 25): *Making*, pp. 16–7; 167–8. Gleason's emphasis (pp. xx–xxvi) upon the processual elements of rhetorical education constitute an important corrective to the assumption (evident e.g. in the title of Woolf, 'Becoming Roman, staying Greek') that Greek culture was a tradition transmitted unproblematically from generation to generation. Greeks also needed to 'become' Greek.

humans from beasts, Greeks from foreigners, free men from household slaves, and philosophers from ordinary people.'[10]

Some modern scholars have tended to see *paideia* as discrete from political power, a purely 'cultural' system: a recent book devoted to Philostratus' (a writer of the third century to whom we shall return) conception of the relationship between power and *paideia* proceeds from the premise that Philostratus perceived 'sophistic as an autonomous cultural phenomenon.'[11] Whilst there have been more sophisticated formulations of this opposition between culture and politics,[12] the most common perception remains that *paideia* was only related to political power to the extent that it worked as an opiate to sedate the restless Greeks, that the focus upon the Greek past enabled them to come to terms with, and acquiesce in, their greatly reduced role in the present.[13]

The present chapter aims to show that *paideia* and pedagogical relations could be 'political' in a more immediate sense, although the multiple demands of the political situation required the articulation of political ideas to be complex and covert. I shall argue that the emphasis upon broad learning and the literature of the past provided a backdrop against which contemporary debates could be conducted, and detected by other *pepaideumenoi*. I shall also argue that *paideia* gave access to resources of rhetorical sophistication which could enable the speaker to generate nuances and subtexts which may have had different meanings for different readers. Although this argument has certain other implications (notably, a less monolithic view of 'power'), my central point concerns methodologies of reading: in order to read power in the writings of the Roman Greek world, we need to be alert to the potential, as well as the 'literal,' meanings of language.

To make a general argument to this effect would be beyond the scope of a chapter of this length. I have elected, instead, to focus narrowly upon the pedagogical relationship of the philosopher Dio Chrysostom with the emperor Trajan, which I consider from two perspectives, that of imperial propaganda and that of Philostratus, a Greek *pepaideumenos*

---

[10] Iambl. *De vit. pythag.* 44: σχεδὸν γὰρ ταῖς ἀγωγαῖς διαφέρειν τοὺς μὲν ἀνθρώπους τῶν θηρίων, τοὺς δὲ Ἕλληνας τῶν βαρβάρων, τοὺς δὲ ἐλευθέρους τῶν οἰκετῶν, τοὺς δὲ φιλοσόφους τῶν τυχόντων . . . (trans. G. Clark (Liverpool, 1989)). For more on the distinctiveness conferred by education, see Kaster, *Guardians*, pp. 15–17.

[11] J.-J. Flinterman, *Power*, Paideia *and Pythagoreanism. Greek Identity, Conceptions of the Relationship between Philosophers and Monarchs and Political Ideas in Philostratus'* Life of Apollonius (Amsterdam, 1995), p. 40.

[12] Esp. Swain, *Hellenism*, pp. 88–9.

[13] See esp. Bowie, 'Greeks,' pp. 35–41, the *fons et origo* of this notion.

who included a biography of Dio within his *Vitae Sophistarum* (*Lives of the Sophists*). This choice has been motivated by two factors. Firstly, Dio was more directly involved with Roman power than many other writers of the period, and the story Philostratus tells allows us to see in starker relief the problems involved in representing power and *paideia*. Dio (whose life spanned from 40–50 CE until some time after 110) was a citizen of the Bithynian town of Prusa, but also a Roman citizen. In addition to his political role as an intermediary between Prusa and Rome in the reign of Trajan (98–117), which will not be discussed here, Dio was also exiled by Domitian (81–96), recalled by his 'old friend' Nerva (96–8) and, apparently, warmly welcomed by Trajan.[14] The figure of Dio allows us to explore the issues at stake in the complex relations between Greek *pepaideumenoi* and Roman emperors.

Secondly, imperial-philosophical relations give us the opportunity to investigate pedagogy in a narrower sense, for the idealised paradigm for such relationships was educational: the good king heeds the sage words of the philosopher (Dio Chrysostom repeatedly evokes this paradigm when he addresses Trajan, and his interest in the relationship of Nestor to Agamemnon is a thinly disguised allegory for it[15]). But because of the very paradigmatic quality of this relationship, it becomes overdetermined: carefully disguised inflections allow the participants to emphasise subtle differences from the paradigm, to tell stories other than that of Nestor. The philosopher, whose presence in a pedagogical capacity is 'supposed' to help legitimise the emperor, might well subtly subvert his authority, for those who have the ears to hear. Power is not unilateral here: the equivocations and ambivalences of language allow the speaker or writer to open and close various alternative readings, to allow for multiple responses from different sources.[16]

My central point, then, concerns the need for sophisticated methodologies of reading in order to unpack the dense layers of multiple and sometimes conflicting meanings in the texts of the Second Sophistic. My approach clearly owes much to advances made in recent years in the criticism of Latin imperial literature. Frederick Ahl and Shadi

---

[14] For Dio's claim to friendship with Nerva, see Dio Chr. *Or.* 45.2.

[15] As noted by J. L. Moles, 'The *Kingship Orations* of Dio Chrysostom', *PLLS* 6 (1990), 297–375, esp. pp. 361–2. For Nestor and Agamemnon, see Dio Chr. *Or.* 49.4; 57 *passim*. For a discussion of Seneca's pedagogical relationship to Nero, see Y. L. Too, 'Educating Nero: a Reading of Seneca's *Moral Epistles*' (J. Elsner and J. Masters eds., *Reflections of Nero. Culture, History and Representation* (London, 1994), pp. 211–24).

[16] This is not the same thing as claiming that all texts are limitlessly readable, an opinion frequently (and unfairly) attributed to 'literary critics' (e.g. by Swain, *Hellenism*, 12).

Bartsch, in particular, have emphasised precisely the need for equivocation which was felt by those writing or performing under the gaze of
the emperor. Ahl focuses upon the rhetorical theories which inspire
and underpin such equivocation; Bartsch upon the possibilities for
multiple (politicised) readings in the Roman theatre and elsewhere.[17]
Scholars working on the Second Sophistic have in general been slow
to appreciate the potential which such approaches offer.[18] No doubt the
pervasive (and, I might add, inherently implausible) notion that Greek
paideia was abstracted from political power has led to an insensitivity to
the ruses and strategies involved in the negotiation of Roman power.

II

First of all, a few words on the socio-historical factors which helped to
form the new role of *paideia* in the Second Sophistic. I should stress
that these words are of the order of a sketch; moreover, this approach,
as we shall see particularly in the following section, can yield only a
rather inflexible model of power relations.

A new type of Greek élite emerged in the first century CE, consisting of those who managed to achieve power and authority within the
Roman system. Roman citizenship could be granted by a Roman holding *imperium*, that is to say, a general or an emperor, and was thus a
form of *beneficium*, a favour bestowed within a strictly hierarchical framework.[19] By the second century, the trickle of Greeks who gained mem-
bership of the senate had become a minor flood.[20] Such honours were
keenly sought after: this was the world of *philotimia*, of great competition between the élite for the privileges (both economic and prestigious)
conferred by the emperor and his agents.[21] And the competition for

[17] F. Ahl, 'The Art of Safe Criticism in Greece and Rome', *AJP* 105 (1984), 174–208; *id.* 'The Rider and the Horse: Politics and Power in Roman Poetry from Horace to Statius', *ANRW* 2.32.1 (1984), 40–110; S. Bartsch, *Actors in the Audience. Theatricality and Double-Speak From Nero to Hadrian* (Cambridge, MA, 1994), esp. ch. 3.
[18] See Moles, *Kingship*, 304–5 for a well-argued exception; his argument, however, that Dio 'made a sincere effort to teach Trajan true philosophy' (p. 364) ignores the very challenge to Victorian notions of 'sincerity' which is presented by such an approach.
[19] F. Millar, *The Emperor in the Roman World (31 BC–AD 337)* (London, 1977), pp. 477–90, esp. 479–81.
[20] The standard account is H. Halfmann, *Die Senatoren aus dem östlichen Teil des Imperium Romanum bis zum Ende des 2. Jh. n. Chr.* (Göttingen, 1979); see also K. Hopkins, *Death and Renewal* (Cambridge, 1983), ch. 3, esp. pp. 184–93, and particularly p. 188. The evidence available yields a rough percentage of Eastern senators as 17% under Vespasian, 16% under Domitian, 35% under Trajan, 37% under Hadrian, 47% under Pius, 54% under Marcus, 61% under Commodus, and a stable 57–8% in the third century (see Hopkins, *Death*, 200).
[21] On φιλοτιμία, see A. Wardman, *Plutarch's Lives* (London, 1974), pp. 115–24; P. Brown, *The Making of Late Antiquity* (Cambridge, MA, 1978), pp. 30–2.

status, as Gleason has recently emphasised, was bound up with the display of *paideia*.[22] At a basic level, *paideia* was its own message: 'most people,' the satirist Lucian tells us, 'thought that *paideia* required great labour, much time, considerable expense and conspicuous social position.'[23] The *pepaideumenoi* and the élite were practically synonymous. But at a deeper level, *paideia* was a locus for internal competition among the élites. The status and power so sought after were articulated and contested through the display of *paideia* (partly in writing, but primarily through rhetorical performances).

What prizes were at stake in this competition? As far as we can tell, the vast majority of Greek literary texts from this period were written by men who either acquired Roman citizenship themselves, or whose families had been granted it (although the predilection for archaism means that writers often omit any mention of citizenship[24]). Citizenship was originally only granted by Rome to those who distinguished themselves in battle, but as early as the late Republic we hear of one Theophanes, who won citizenship for his literary work, albeit work which benefited Pompey.[25] No imperial writers are known to have gained citizenship as a direct result of their writings, but the citizenship which was already held by Greek writers implies a certain complicity in the hierarchies and values of Roman power. Indeed, some Greek writers even achieved success in Roman government. Greek orators, philosophers, prose-writers, and poets were popular appointments to prominent roles, both official and semi-official (such as imperial friend [*amicus*] or adviser [*sumboulos*]).[26] The most spectacular example from

---

[22] Gleason, *Making*, pp. 159–68.

[23] *Somn. siu. uit. Luc.* 1: τοῖς πλείστοις οὖν ἔδοξεν παιδεία μὲν καὶ πόνου πολλοῦ καὶ χρόνου μακροῦ καὶ δαπάνης οὐ μικρᾶς καὶ τύχης δεῖσθαι λαμπρᾶς... (trans. A. M. Harmon (modified) (Cambridge, MA, 1921, repr. 1969)). Lucian represents himself as the exception to this rule. On the elitism of education, see further Swain, *Hellenism*, p. 64. On the three 'lower class' sophists referred to by Philostratus, see Bowie, 'Importance,' pp. 54–5.

[24] On the tendency of Roman Greek writers not to allude to Roman aspects of their nomenclature, see Bowie, 'Greeks', pp. 199–200, and Swain's comments on Pausanias: *Hellenism*, p. 332. Apollonius of Tyana is said to have castigated those who took Roman names: Philostr. *VA* 4.5; *Epist. Apoll.* 71.

[25] Cicero, *Pro Arch. poet.* 10/24: Theophanes recorded Pompey's campaigns. For more on Theophanes, see G. W. Bowersock, *Augustus and the Greek World* (Oxford, 1965), p. 4; L. Robert, 'Théophane de Mytilène à Constantinople' (*CRAI* 1969, 42–64); Millar, *Emperor*, p. 478.

[26] On imperial *amici*, see J. Crook, *Consilium Principis* (Cambridge, 1955), ch. 3; on σύμβουλοι, E. Rawson, 'Roman Rulers and the Philosophic Adviser' (M. T. Griffin and J. Barnes, eds., *Philosophia Togata* (Oxford, 1989), pp. 233–57); on the approximation of Dio Chrysostom to this role, see Moles, 'Kingship,' pp. 332–3. On Greek appointments to positions in the Roman government, see esp. F. Millar, *A Study of Cassius Dio* (Oxford, 1964), pp. 182–8; Bowersock, *Greek Sophists*, ch. 4; Bowersock, *Augustus*, ch. 3; G. Salmeri, *La politica e il potere. Saggio su Dione di Prusa*

our period is that of Arrian, best known as the author of the *Anabasis of Alexander* (as well as several other texts), but also a suffect consul in Rome (probably in 129) and governor of the important, armed frontier province of Cappadocia.[27] Arrian, whom modern scholars often like to see as straddling two separate worlds, was referred to even in antiquity as a man of two aspects, the literary and the political.[28] It is, of course, hard to show that any individual's political preferment might be due directly to his literary output (although Bosworth has asserted this in Arrian's case[29]), and some scholars have argued that literary activity was neither a guarantee of political success nor the sole route to it.[30] Be that as it may, it is hard to deny that *paideia* was both a sign of élite status and a highly charged locus within which the élite staked out their competing claims for status.

In the second century, as is well-known, the Roman empire began to recreate the Greek past for the present, a policy of *paideia* in action. Building in Athens resumed under Trajan after a lapse of almost one century; the province of Achaea (a deliberately archaic appellation) was created; Hadrian created the Panhellenion, an institution which conferred the status of 'Greek' upon cities; emperors sponsored the arts and even (in the case of Marcus Aurelius) wrote philosophy in Greek.[31] Why was post-Flavian Rome so keen to revive interest in the Greek

---

(Catania, 1982), pp. 5–9; R. Syme, 'Greeks invading the Roman government' (Brookline, MA, 1982 = A. Birley, ed., *Roman papers* IV (Oxford, 1988), pp. 1–20); V. A. Sirago, 'La seconda sofistica come espressione della classe dirigente del II sec.', *ANRW* 2.33.1 (1989), 36–78, esp. pp. 58–9.

[27] On the date of Arrian's consulship, see P. Stadter, *Arrian of Nicomedia* (Chapel Hill, 1980), pp. 10–11. For recent discussions of the career of Arrian, see G. Wirth, 'Anmerkungen zur Arrianbiographie', *Historia* 13 (1964), 209–45; A. B. Bosworth, 'Arrian's Literary Development', *CQ* 22 (1972), 163–85; Halfmann, *Senatoren*, pp. 146–7, no. 56; Stadter, *Arrian*, pp. 5–14; R. Syme, 'The Career of Arrian', *HSCP* 86 (1982), 171–211 = Birley, ed. *Roman papers* IV, pp. 21–49. Only marginally less impressive was the career of the sophist Herodes Atticus: see P. Graindor, *Un milliardaire antique: Hérode Attique et sa famille* (Cairo, 1930), ch. 4; Halfmann, *Senatoren*, pp. 55–60, no. 68.

[28] Luc. *Alex.* 2: καὶ Ἀρριανὸς γὰρ ὁ τοῦ Ἐπικτήτου μαθητὴς ἀνὴρ Ῥωμαίων ἐν τοῖς πρώτοις καὶ παιδείᾳ παρ' ὅλον τὸν βίον συγγενόμενος. For contemporary reactions to Arrian's (and others') combination of statesmanship and *paideia*, see Bosworth, 'Literary,' pp. 164–72.

[29] Bosworth, 'Literary', pp. 164–72.

[30] Bowie, 'Importance,' *passim*; N. Lewis, 'Literati in the Service of Roman Emperors: Politics before Culture', in L. Casson and M. Price, eds., *Coins, Culture and History in the Ancient World. Numismatic and Other Studies in Honor of Bluma L. Trell* (Detroit, 1981), pp. 149–66 = N. Lewis, *On Government and Law in Roman Egypt* (Atlanta, 1995), pp. 257–74.

[31] On building in Athens, see P. Graindor, *Athènes sous Hadrien* (Cairo, 1934), *passim*; T. L. Shear, 'Athens: From City-state to Provincial Town', *Hesperia* 50 (1981), 356–77, esp. pp. 368–77; S. E. Alcock, *Graecia Capta: the Landscapes of Roman Greece* (Cambridge, 1993), p. 93; pp. 181–2; 195–6. On the creation of the province of Achaea, see Alcock, *Graecia Capta*, pp. 14–16. On the Panhellenion, see A. J. Spawforth and S. Walker, 'The World of the Panhellenion. I: Athens and Eleusis', *JRS* 75 (1985), 78–104; *eid.*, 'The World of the Panhellenion. II: Three Dorian Cities', *JRS* 76 (1986), 88–105.

past? Traditionally, scholars have assumed that this was a strategy of domination: by appeasing and coopting the support of the élite, the Roman rulers could maintain peace in the East.[32] *Paideia* is thus considered as a vehicle for the fusion of Greek élite power with Roman imperial power, and the Greek texts written in this period are reckoned to aim towards the facilitation of Roman power.[33] Whatever the merits of this interpretation as an overarching theory of *paideia*, it is reckless to interpret specific texts and situations on the basis of generalising assumptions. As we shall see, this inflexible, monolithic model of power is belied by close attention to specific situations and texts. In the following two sections, I consider Dio firstly from the perspective of imperial propaganda, and then from the more ironic perspective of Philostratus, his *pepaideumenos* biographer in the early third century.

III

Cocceianus Dio, or Dio Chrysostom ('golden-mouth') as he was later known,[34] was born into a wealthy family in the Bithynian *prouincia* of Prusa, and he seems to have inherited Roman citizenship from both his father and mother.[35] He was, thus, certainly a member of the élite, and the seventy-seven extant orations attributed to him betray both the partisanship of his class and the results of an immersive education

[32] For the older scholarship, see C. P. Jones, *Plutarch and Rome* (Oxford, 1971), p. 43, n. 25; 110. For a more recent interpretation along these lines, using comparative material from British India, see Swain, *Hellenism*, pp. 71–2.

[33] For an interpretation of Dio and Plutarch along these lines, see M.-H. Quet, 'Rhétorique, culture et politique. Le fonctionnement du discours idéologique chez Dion de Pruse et dans les *Moralia* de Plutarque', *DHA* 4 1978, 51–117.

[34] For the details of Dio's name, and of its confusion with that of Cassius Dio the historian, see A. M. Gowing, 'Dio's Name', *CP* 85 (1990), 49–54.

[35] Dio's wealth: *Or.* 46.3; 5–6; see C. P. Jones, *The Roman World of Dio Chrysostom* (Cambridge, MA, 1978), p. 6 and Swain, *Hellenism*, pp. 190–1 for brief discussion and further references. The question of Dio's Roman citizenship is complex. He tells us himself (*Or.* 41.6) that his maternal grandfather received Roman and Apamean citizenship from 'the emperor then,' whilst his father received citizenship of Apamea. As A. N. Sherwin-White points out (*The Letters of Pliny. A Historical and Social Commentary* (Oxford, 1966), pp. 676–7), he would not have inherited citizenship from his mother alone in normal circumstances. Yet Apamea seems to have been a Roman *colonia*, and, if this is the case, then his father must have also held the Roman citizenship (see F. Millar reviewing, *JRS* 58 (1968), p. 222; on the status of Apamea, Salmeri, *Politica*, p. 15, n. 39 and Swain, *Hellenism*, pp. 207–8). Momigliano's non-committal suggestion that the name Cocceianus reflects the instrumental role of Nerva (M. Cocceius Nerva) in Dio's enfranchisement is thus unlikely: see A. Momigliano, 'Dio Chrysostomus' *Quarto contributo alla storia degli studi classici e del mondo antico* (Rome, 1969), pp. 257–69, esp. p. 257; elaborated upon by J. L. Moles, 'The Career and Conversion of Dio Chrysostom', *JHS* 98 (1978), 79–100, esp. p. 86. Sherwin-White's own suggestion that Dio received the citizenship under Domitian is equally, if not more, improbable.

available only to members of his class.[36] Dio travelled the Roman world,
and (as we might expect) his *paideia* earned him success and powerful
Roman friends.[37]

Yet in the first century CE, at any rate, Rome's relationship to Greek
culture still bore the traces of the ambivalence of earlier periods. The
second century BCE, for example, had seen both a series of expulsions
of Greek philosophers (and corresponding reassertions of Roman in-
digenous values) and the consolidation of the notion that upper-class
Romans required Greek philosophical education.[38] In the first century
CE, a large number of Roman senators counted themselves as Stoics.[39]
Now, while this philosophical background to Roman politics was to a
certain extent taken for granted, it was not uncontested: in the first
century, various emperors (notoriously, Nero) exiled and executed a
number of philosophers, and Vespasian and Domitian (the 'bald Nero'[40])
instituted exiles of all philosophers from Rome.[41] Not long into his reign
(but not in one of his 'blanket' banishments), Domitian exiled Dio from
Italy and Bithynia.[42]

---

[36] Of the eighty transmitted orations, 37 (*Corinthiacus*) is usually attributed to Favorinus, while
63 and 64 (both *De fortuna*) are reckoned to be the work of an unknown author. On Dio's
aristocratic perspective, see esp. Jones, *Roman world*, chs. 11–12 for the local political background; more generally, Salmeri, *Politica*, pp. 14–45.

[37] On Dio's early successes, see Moles, 'Career,' pp. 82–8.

[38] On Rome's ambivalent relationship to Greek philosophers in the second century BCE, see esp.
E. S. Gruen, *Studies on Greek Culture and Roman Policy* (Leiden, 1990), ch. 5; for more general
remarks on Rome's attitude to Greece in the period, see *id.*, *The Hellenistic World and the Coming
of Rome* (Berkeley and London, 1984), vol. 1, ch. 7.

[39] On the Stoic background, see esp. P. A. Brunt, 'Stoicism and the Principate', *PBSR* 30 (1975),
7–35, esp. p. 27.

[40] Juv. *Sat.* 4.38; for another equation of Nero and Domitian, see Mart. *Epig.* 11.33, and further,
S. Bartsch, *Actors*, p. 245, n. 66. Nero is contrasted positively to Domitian at Philostr. *VA* 7.12.

[41] Vespasian's ban in 71, intriguingly, exempted the philosopher Musonius Rufus (Cass. Dio
66.13.2); on the date, see Moles, 'Career,' p. 85, n. 56. Domitian re-enacted the decree: see
Suet. *Domit.* 10.5; Tac. *Agr.* 2.1–2; Plin. *Ep.* 3.11.2–3; Philostr. *VA* 7.11. The question of how
many expulsions Domitian enacted, and their dating, remain problematic: see B. W. Jones,
The Emperor Domitian (London, 1992), pp. 119–20. On clashes between emperors and philosophers in the first century generally, see J. M. C. Toynbee, 'Dictators and Philosophers in
the First Century AD', *G&R* 13 (1944), 43–58; R. MacMullen, *Enemies of the Roman Order. Treason,
Unrest and Alienation in the Empire* (London, 1992 (1966), chs. 1–2; Brunt, 'Stoicism'; E. Wistrand,
'The Stoic Opposition to the Principate', *SC* 18 (1979), 93–101. For an interpretation from a
purely political perspective, see C. Wirszubski, *Libertas as a Political Idea at Rome during the Late
Republic and Early Principate* (Cambridge, 1968), pp. 138–50. On the ambivalent position of
philosophers under the empire, see J. Hahn, *Der Philosoph und die Gesellschaft. Selbstverständnis,
öffentliches Auftreten und populäre Erwartungen in der hohen Kaiserzeit* (Stuttgart, 1989), p. 100.

[42] A ban from Bithynia and Italy is most likely (as Jones, *Roman*, p. 45). P. Desideri, *Dione di Prusa:
un intelletuale greco nell' impero Romano* (Messina and Florence, 1978), pp. 193–4 claims that the
ban was only from the territory of Prusa; not impossible, but perhaps implausible given the
great noise made by Dio. On the reasons for Dio's exile, see *infra* p. 202.

The problem which faced Nerva in his brief reign (subsequent to that of Domitian), and more particularly Trajan and his successors, was one of reinvention of the image of imperial power after the unpopular régime of Domitian.[43] Records of Domitian were erased from public places (the process which scholars call *damnatio memoriae*[44]), and Trajan proclaimed a 'new age.'[45] This new age was (according to its rhetoric) to be open and 'free.'[46] One means of constructing the new age in opposition to the previous one was to embrace the Greek arts, and to represent the Flavians (and especially Domitian) as having attacked them.[47] The younger Pliny, in his address to Trajan, knew what the emperor wanted to hear:

And the teachers of rhetoric and professors of philosophy – how you hold them in honour! Under you, the liberal arts are restored, to breathe and live in their own country – the learning which the barbarity of the past punished with exile, when an emperor acquainted with all the vices sought to banish everything hostile to vice, motivated less by hatred for learning than by fear for its authority.[48]

[43] The modern debate as to whether Domitian's rule was 'really' repressive (see e.g. Jones, *Emperor Domitian* and B. Levick, 'Domitian and the Provinces', *Latomus* 41 (1982), pp. 50–73 for opposing views) does not interest me here.

[44] For the *damnatio memoriae* of Domitian, see Suet. *Dom.* 23.2; Cass. Dio 68.1.1. On the erasure of Domitian's inscriptions in the East, see F. Grosso, 'Aspetti della politica orientale di Domiziano', *Epigraphica* 16 (1954), 117–79, esp. pp. 165–6; on the removal of his images, T. Pekáry, *Das römische Kaiserbildnis in Staat, Kult und Gesellschaft. Dargestellt Anhand der Schriftquellen* (Berlin, 1985), p. 138.

[45] Talk of a new *saeculum* under Trajan is widespread. Pliny's letters and panegyric to Trajan frequently refer to 'your *saeculum*' (*Ep.* 10.1.2; 10.3.2; 10.23.2; 10.37.3; *Panegyr.* 40.5; 46.7), and the word *saeculum* recurs on its own (*Ep.* 2.2–3; 10.97.2; *Panegyr.* 36.4; 46.4; 93.2). Florus captures a similar tone when he writes 'sub Traiano principe . . . senectus imperii quasi reddita iuventute revirescit' (*Epit. praef.* 8). Interestingly, Tacitus writes of the 'primo . . . beatissimi saeculi ortu' under Trajan's short-lived predecessor, Nerva (*Agr.* 3.1).

[46] On the rhetoric of *libertas* under Trajan, see Wirszubski, *Libertas*, pp. 167–71; and esp. Tac. *Hist.* 1.1 (the period under Trajan is a time 'ubi sentire quae uelis et quae sentias dicere licet').

[47] In fact, evidence suggests that Domitian was not as unequivocally hostile to Greek philosophy as subsequent writers made out: see Jones, *Emperor Domitian*, pp. 121–2. The emperor's reputation as a despiser of uncensored *paideia* was, partly at any rate, the result of attempts to contrast subsequent emperors' love of *paideia*. Domitian's self-presentation was, moreover, notably 'philhellenic,' but he does not seem to have attempted to present himself as a philosophical ruler in the manner in which Trajan and subsequent emperors did.

[48] *Panegyr.* 47.1–2: 'Quem honorem dicendi magistris, quam dignitationem sapientiae doctoribus habes! ut sub te spiritum and sanguinem et patriam receperunt studia! quae priorum temporum immanitas exsiliis puniebat, cum sibi uitiorum omnium conscius princeps inimicas uitiis artes non odio magis quam reuerentia relegaret' (trans. [modified] B. Radice [Cambridge MA, 1975]). In pointing to the 'propagandistic' element of the *Panegyricus*, however, I am inevitably underplaying the rhetorical polyphony of the speech (which I certainly do not wish to deny): for a sophisticated discussion of this aspect, see Bartsch, *Actors*, ch. 5. For Pliny's celebration of literature under Trajan, see also *Panegyr.* 49.5–8; *Ep.* 1.10.1; E. Cizek, 'La littérature et les cercles culturels et politiques à l'époque de Trajan', *ANRW* 2.33.1 (1989), 3–35, esp. p. 4, and *passim* on

Domitian's exiles here play a figurative as well as a literal role: the 'country' (*patriam*) which the arts have regained under Trajan is also a symbolic space in which kingship and wisdom are united. Significantly, learning is here represented as a form of power, inspiring not only hatred but also fear in the evil emperor. Domitian's expulsions were thus, according to Pliny, a display not of power but of weakness. Conversely, Trajan's positive attitude towards the arts is by implication represented as an index of his fitness to rule.

Trajan's interactions with Greek intellectuals of this period also reflect the image-making with which Pliny engages. Dio's contemporary Plutarch was apparently granted by Trajan the highest imperial award available to non-senators, the *ornamenta consularia*.[49] An inscription in Athens reveals the dedication of a library to Trajan by a certain T. Flavius Pantaenus, 'prince of the philosophical muses.'[50] Dio's role in all this is complex. His exile was the result not of Domitian's expulsion of philosophers, but of the philosopher's friendship with a notable Roman who incurred Domitian's displeasure.[51] Nevertheless, he was later associated with the philosophical exiles, and he himself encourages this association by claiming to have spoken out freely under Domitian.[52] The opposition between Trajan's openness to pedagogy and the Flavians' repression of philosophy could thus be articulated through the figure of Dio with only a minor sleight-of-hand. It was Nerva who in his brief reign included Dio in a general recall of Domitian's exiles,[53] but Trajan who capitalised upon the propagandistic value of Dio's return, which was to symbolise what Pliny might call the 'repatriation' of wise, prudent government.[54] Dio delivered before Trajan four orations on

Latin literature in the period. Note, however, that Pliny does not refer specifically to Greek *paideia*; indeed, *Panegyr.* 13.5 ('Graeculus magister adsistit') might be taken to perpetuate Roman contempt for Greeks. Pliny's superciliousness, however, does not seem to have restrained Trajan.

[49] *Suda*, Π 1793; Jones, *Plutarch*, p. 29. The information here given by the Suda, however, is not necessarily to be trusted: see D. Babut, 'ἱστορία οἷον ὕλη φιλοσοφίας: Histoire et réflexion morale dans l'oeuvre de Plutarque', *REG* 88 (1975), 206–19, esp. p. 207.

[50] For the inscription, see B. D. Merritt, 'Greek Inscriptions' (*Hesperia* 15 (1946) 169–263), esp. p. 233; see further, J. H. Oliver, 'Flavius Pantaenus, Prince of the Philosophical Muses', *HTR* 72 (1979), 157–60.

[51] Dio Chr. *Or.* 13.1. The friend is usually reckoned to have been T. Flavius Sabinus; for a recent reexamination of the issue, see B. W. Jones, 'Domitian and the Exile of Dio of Prusa', *PP* 45 (1990), 348–57.

[52] Luc. *De mort. Peregr.* 18 associates Dio with Musonius and Epictetus, as philosophers who were exiled διὰ τὴν παρρησίαν καὶ τὴν ἄγαν ἐλευθερίαν. At *Or.* 45.1, Dio claims to have confronted Domitian openly (ἐρεθίζων ἀντικρυς) with his speeches.

[53] Jones, *Roman*, p. 52, with p. 176, n. 61 for references.

[54] This point is made by Jones, *Roman*, p. 53 and, somewhat obliquely, by A. Charles-Saget, 'Un miroir-du-prince au 1er siècle après J. C. Dion Chrysostome, *Sur la royauté* 1' in B. Cassin ed., *Le plaisir du parler* (Paris, 1986), pp. 111–29, esp. pp. 128–9.

kingship, based upon a style which was popular in the Greek kingdoms of the Hellenistic period, and what the public saw was a new monarch who paid careful heed to the philosopher who had been banished by Domitian.[55] The soldier Trajan emerged, perhaps somewhat incongruously, as a kind of philosopher-king.[56]

According to this interpretation, Dio's *paideia* was co-opted by the emperor to validate the 'new age,' to construct a veneer of philosophical legitimation for his autocratic power. The continuation of this process can be observed in Marcus Aurelius' *Meditations*. Marcus claims to have been inspired by his brother Severus to know Thrasea, Helvidius, Cato, Dio, and Brutus, and to 'accept the notion of a democratic system which governs according to equality and freedom of speech.'[57] The emperor surprises not only with his arrant appropriation of the political rhetoric of democratic Athens – a feature of post-Flavian imperial rhetoric[58] – and his allusion to the republican heroes Cato and Brutus,[59] but also with his name-check of the famous philosophical victims of the first century, Helvidius, Thrasea and Dio himself.[60] Like Trajan, Marcus Aurelius uses Dio, Greek philosophy and the antityrannical tradition to reinforce his own authority.

Considered from the perspective of Roman propaganda, then, Dio's *paideia* was a vehicle for imperial power. Trajan's sponsorship of Greek learning was a form of co-optation, a means of masking the arrogance and brutality of totalitarian power behind a golden sheen of philosophical benevolence.

IV

But this interpretation, for all that it accords with the conventional view that *paideia* was a means of synthesising the interests of the Greek élite and the Roman government, is too monolithic. To assume the

---

[55] Christopher Kelly disagrees with me, suspecting that the picture of Trajan as a keen student of philosophy is a mirage fabricated by Dio. I stick to my account: there seems to me to be enough evidence that Trajan was encouraging a public perception of himself as a patron of the arts.

[56] A king who listens to philosophy is the next best thing to a philosopher-king: see Rawson, 'Roman rulers,' p. 230 and Flinterman, *Power*, p. 172.

[57] Marc. Aur. *Med.* 1.14: καὶ τὸ δι' αὐτὸν γνῶναι Θρασέαν, Ἑλβίδιον, Κάτωνα, Δίωνα, Βροῦτον καὶ φαντασίαν λαβεῖν πολιτείας ἰσονόμου κατ' ἰσότητα καὶ ἰσηγορίαν διοικουμένης καὶ βασιλείας τιμώσης πάντων μάλιστα τὴν ἐλευθερίαν τῶν ἀρχομένων.

[58] See Flinterman, *Power*, pp. 201–4.

[59] On the marked role of Cato and Brutus in republican rhetoric, see MacMullen, *Enemies*, ch. 1.

[60] Desideri, *Dione*, pp. 16–19 claims that the Dio referred to here is the Prusaean sophist; R. B. Rutherford, *The* Meditations *of Marcus Aurelius* (Oxford, 1989), p. 64, n. 51 argues that the reference is to the tyrannicide. I incline, with very fragile confidence, towards the former interpretation, which yields a list of men who fought for freedom in Rome.

perspective of Roman power is to simplify drastically the complex dissemination of power: what of the dissenters, what of the stumbling-
blocks which threaten to thwart the unproblematic dissemination of
power in this manner? More importantly for our purposes, it is crucial
to observe that the same event may be staged so as to have different
meanings for different audiences. Being *pepaideumenos* meant more than
simply adopting a style of life; it meant learning to present oneself with
a sophistication and canny allusiveness. Ambivalent self-presentation
could be a crucial strategy. We have considered Dio's return from
exile from the perspective of Trajan; might it have other implications
when considered from other angles?

Fortunately, we have an account of Dio's return by a *pepaideumenos*
of the Second Sophistic. Philostratus' *Lives of the Sophists* (in fact, the
origin of the term 'Second Sophistic'[61]), composed in the early third
century, is the work of an ingenious author, every bit as sophistic as
the subjects of his text.[62] I want to suggest that his account of Trajan's
'co-optation' of Dio presents a much more ambivalent, equivocal version
of relations between emperors and *pepaideumenoi*. I also want to argue
that Philostratus uses the story of Dio's return to present issues germane
to the reading of his own, equally equivocal text. As Frederick Ahl has
emphasised, the rhetorical tradition provided resources for 'figuring'
speech before monarchs, for implying more than it is safe to articulate.[63]
Philostratus himself was familiar with the complexities involved in
articulation under the shadow of the imperial household: before the
Lives of the Sophists, he wrote a biography of the philosopher Apollonius
of Tyana at the behest of the empress Julia Domna.[64] The *Lives of the
Sophists* places great emphasis upon relations between emperors and
Greek intellectuals, and this emphasis comports an interest in the prob-
lems of free and 'figured' expression in the Roman empire.[65]

---

[61] *Supra*, n. 3.

[62] For a recent bibliography on the *VS*, see S. Swain, 'The Reliability of Philostratus's *Lives of the Sophists*', *ClAnt* 10 (1991), 148–63, esp. p. 148, n. 1.

[63] *Supra*, n. 17. As will become clear, I am not as convinced as Ahl appears to be that we can recover in all cases a single, stable, unifying 'meaning' which might be uncovered underneath the various overlaid strata of 'figuring.'

[64] The *VA* was composed before the *VS* (see the reference to the earlier work at *VS* 77.6 = 570 O), although it has been argued that the times of composition may have overlapped: see E. L. Bowie, 'Apollonius of Tyana: Tradition and Reality', *ANRW* 2.16.2 (1978), 1652–99, esp. pp. 1669–70. For Julia's request, see *VA* 1.3.

[65] On the preoccupation of the *VS* with imperial/intellectual relations, see Flinterman, *Power*, pp. 38–45. For a striking example of Philostratus' interest in 'figured' speech, see the well-known story of Herodes Atticus in his grief neglecting to 'figure' his speech (οὐδὲ σχηματίσας τὸν λόγον) before Marcus Aurelius (*VS* 68.17–24 = 561 O), with the discussion of Ahl, 'Art,' pp. 201–2.

The account of Dio's life is longer than any of the preceding ones.[66] Dio lived, we are told, 'at the time when Apollonius of Tyana and Euphrates of Tyre were philosophising': this reference to Philostratus' earlier biography of Apollonius of Tyana orientates the reader towards imperial/philosophic relations, since a large part of the *Life of Apollonius* concerns Apollonius' meetings with emperors, and the relationships between Dio, Euphrates and Apollonius are played out in predominantly imperial contexts.[67] With this background in mind, the reader is expecting to hear of Dio's celebrated quarrels with emperors, and, sure enough, Philostratus alludes to his avoidance of Rome, 'for fear of tyrannies in the capital, by which all philosophy was being driven out.'[68]

Yet the biographer specifically denies that this was exile *stricto sensu*, in that 'exile was not forced upon him' (*VS* 7.25–6 = 488 O). And there is no frank, fearless criticism here: Dio, we are told, 'hid himself from sight and hearing' (*VS* 7.37 = 488 O). There is little consensus as to why Philostratus denies that Dio was exiled.[69] It has not been observed, however, that Philostratus may be playing upon his audience's awareness of Dio's writings, which cleverly manipulate the theme of exile in order to represent their author as a wandering philosopher, unconstrained by society and free-speaking before tyrants.[70] Philostratus' abnegation, then, deliberately undermines Dio's (rhetorical) self-representation. Elsewhere in this account (as we shall see), Philostratus underlines Dio's rhetorical trickiness (in the *Life of Apollonius*, too, Dio's philosophy is 'too

---

[66] Philostr. *VS* 6.30–8.22 = 486–8 O, 57 lines of Teubner text, more than the total devoted to all the previous biographies (54 lines); it is also the first biography to take place in identifiably Roman times. Of the 57 lines, 31 are concerned with Dio's imperial sojourn abroad and his return.

[67] Philostr. *VS* 7.20–2 = 487–8 O: Γενόμενος δὲ κατὰ τοὺς χρόνους, οὓς 'Απολλώνιός τε ὁ Τυανεὺς καὶ Εὐφράτης ὁ Τύριος ἐφιλοσόφουν . . . On Apollonius' relationship with emperors, see Flinterman, *Power*, ch. 4. Euphrates, Dio and Apollonius first meet in Alexandria, in the presence of Vespasian: *VA* 5.26ff. Euphrates goes on to be instrumental in the prosecution of Apollonius before Domitian: *VA* 7.9.

[68] Philostr. *VS* 7.28 = 488 O: . . . δέει τῶν κατὰ τὴν πόλιν τυραννίδων, ὑφ' ὧν ἠλαύνετο φιλοσοφία πᾶσα.

[69] Jones, *Roman*, p. 48 suggests that Philostratus conceals this 'blemish' in Dio's biography, comparing the denial that Favorinus was exiled (*VS* 9.2 = 489 O, perhaps a rash interpretation of οὐδὲν ἔπαθεν: see most recently S. Swain, 'Favorinus and Hadrian', *ZPE* 79 (1989), 150–8, esp. p. 154). He might have also mentioned Herodes Atticus: *VS* 69.19 = 562 O. Jones thus suggests that Philostratus regarded exile by Domitian as a reason for shame, which it surely would not be under later emperors. H. von Arnim, *Leben und Werke des Dion von Prusa* (Berlin, 1898), p. 225–6 and Desideri, *Dione*, p. 36 suggest that Philostratus denies exile to Dio in order to reserve all the *kudos* of confrontation with Domitian for his hero, Apollonius of Tyana. This seems a rather evasive explanation.

[70] Moles, 'Career,' pp. 96–100.

rhetorical'[71]). In other words, Philostratus is slyly suggesting what John Moles has argued influentially, that Dio's own version of his biography is economical with the truth, displays an ingenious facility with *personae*, and is designed to perpetuate a heavily loaded perception of him.[72]

Indeed, Philostratus' account of Dio's exile and return places a heavy emphasis upon Dio's role-playing. Describing Dio's travels, Philostratus tells us that he took two books with him, Plato's *Phaedo* and Demosthenes' *On the False Embassy*. Rather than considering these simply as reading-matter for the journey,[73] we should be alert to the connotations which both these texts carry. The *Phaedo* tells of Socrates', the greatest philosopher's, calm acceptance of his unjust fate, clearly a positive paradigm for Stoic philosophical resistance, while *On the False Embassy* tells of Demosthenes' opposition to a conspiracy with a tyrant who aims to subdue Greece. These texts are scripts for Dio's performance of the role of martyred champion of free Greece. Indeed, when news of Domitian's death reaches the military camp in which Philostratus' Dio happens to be, his performance reaches its peak:

. . . he leaped naked on to a high altar, and began his harangue with the verse:

Then Odysseus of many counsels stripped himself of his rags (Homer, *Odyssey* 22.1)

and having said this and thus revealed that he was no beggar, nor what they believed him to be, but Dio the wise (*sophos*), he delivered a spirited and energetic indictment of the tyrant.[74]

Has Dio really 'revealed himself'? Is he really 'naked'? As Philostratus tells it, it is precisely at the moment when Dio claims to be revealing himself that he is most masked, that the parallel with Odysseus comes to the fore (a parallel which the 'real' Dio encouraged when he spoke on the subject of his exile[75]). And in presenting himself under a guise,

---

[71] Philostr. *VA* 5.40: ἡ δὲ τοῦ Δίωνος φιλοσοφία ῥητορικωτέρα τῷ ᾽Απολλωνίῳ ἐφαίνετο. In the *VS*, Dio is treated (1.1 = 479 O; 11.17–18 = 492 O) as one of those who 'philosophise under the guise of sophistry' (τοὺς φιλοσοφήσαντας ἐν δόξῃ τοῦ σοφιστεῦσαι). Note also *Ep. Apoll.* 9.

[72] Moles, 'Career,' *passim*.   [73] Jones, *Roman*, p. 48.

[74] Philostr. *VS* 8.6–13 = 488 O (modified): ἀλλὰ γυμνὸς ἀναπηδήσας ἐπὶ βωμὸν ὑψηλὸν ἤρξατο τοῦ λόγου ὧδε: "αὐτὰρ ὁ γυμνώθη ῥακέων πολύμητις ᾽Οδυσσεύς," καὶ εἰπὼν ταῦτα καὶ δηλώσας ἑαυτόν, ὅτι μὴ πτωχός, μηδὲ ὃν ᾤοντο, Δίων δὲ εἴη ὁ σοφός, ἐπὶ μὲν τὴν κατηγορίαν τοῦ τυράννου πολὺς ἔπνευσεν, τοὺς δὲ στρατιώτας ἐδίδαξεν ἀμείνω φρονεῖν τὰ δοκοῦντα ᾽Ρωμαίοις πράττοντας.

[75] For Dio's use of the *persona* of Odysseus, see Moles, 'Career,' p. 97. Odysseus was often portrayed as the archetypal long-suffering exile: see W. B. Stanford, *The Ulysses Theme* (Oxford, 1954), p. 175.

Dio is of course emulating Odysseus, whose deceitful role-playing was legendary. Philostratus is again drawing attention to Dio's rhetorical manipulations. Indeed, it is not simply 'Dio' whom the soldiers see, but Dio 'the wise'; or is it Dio 'the clever,' or even Dio 'the crafty' (the Greek *sophos* can mean all of these)?

Once we have accepted that Philostratus' Dio is a player of roles, the next question to ask is how successful his role-playing is. The line he cites is from the beginning of *Odyssey* 21, where Odysseus leaps on to the 'great threshold' (compare Philostratus' 'high altar') and shoots Antinous, the leader of the suitors. So in Dio's script, as directed by Philostratus, Domitian is playing Antinous, a corrupt usurper of another's property. Dio's indictment of tyranny is a shaft aimed by Greece at the neck of the Roman oppressors. But Odysseus then proceeds to slaughter the remaining suitors, and reestablish his place as rightful ruler; Dio, by way of contrast, quells the mutiny and goes on to take his place beside Trajan on the emperor's chariot. Once again, Dio's 'hard line' philosophical credentials are stripped away to reveal a manipulator of masks.

But does he really side unequivocally with the Romans? Philostratus apparently tells us that Dio by his actions 'taught the soldiers to think better, and to act in accordance with the will of the Romans'; but the Greek is ambiguous, and could equally well mean 'taught the soldiers, who were doing what the Romans wanted, to think better of it.'[76] On this latter interpretation, Dio's actions would encourage not acquiescence to 'the Romans,' but an organised resistance. This Dio begins to resemble Odysseus much more closely: the soldiers represent not the suitors whom he must slaughter, but Philoetius and Eumaeus, his rustic allies in the battle against those who step in to take the place of the dead Antinous. This equivocation makes it unclear whether Dio's stance should be read as pro- or anti-Roman.

Philostratus' account of Dio on the chariot is also extremely suggestive. What sort of power-play is going on here?

For in fact the persuasion of the man was such as to charm even those who do not accurately understand Greek matters. An instance of this is that the Emperor Trajan set him in front of all Rome, by his side on the golden chariot in which the emperors ride in procession when they celebrate their

[76] Philostr. *VS* 8.11–13 = 488 O: ... τοὺς δὲ στρατιώτας ἐδίδαξεν ἀμείνω φρονεῖν τὰ δοκοῦντα Ῥωμαίοις πράττοντας. The traditional interpretation is the more immediately evident, given the separation of στρατιώτας and πράττοντας. Nevertheless, the sentence *can* be construed in the way I suggest, if the subversive will is there.

triumphs in war, and often he would turn to Dio and say: 'I do not understand what you are saying, but I love you as I love myself.'[77]

Once again, Dio's rhetorical side is stressed, that is to say his persuasion (*peitho*) and ability to charm (*thelgein*), notions which have been associated with rhetorical language since Gorgias,[78] and may even remind the reader of Odysseus: as well as the avenging father returned from exile, Odysseus is also the master of duplicity and advantageous manipulation.[79] The most striking aspect of this passage, however, is its emphasis upon non-comprehension. There are two points to make here. Firstly, it was traditional for a *triumphator* to process with a slave belonging to the state beside him in his chariot, reminding him, 'look behind you, remember that you are mortal.'[80] For Dio to take the place of this slave is an intriguing twist to the power-play in Philostratus' anecdote. Does Dio's assumption of the submissive role of the slave represent his passive role in the circuits of power? Yet the slave represents the voice of state duty: Trajan's non-comprehension, then, reflects his failure to recognise the limits of his power, his dangerous excess. Like Pentheus in Euripides' *Bacchae*, Philostratus' Trajan may be seen as a ruler dangerously close to ignorance of the boundaries of monarchical prerogative. Who is in control here?

My second point concerns Trajan's failure to understand 'Greek matters.' It is notoriously difficult to specify exactly what Philostratus means here: scholars usually assume that Philostratus means 'the Greek language,' and are content to note that Trajan did in fact receive a Greek education.[81] Yet in this context which stresses Dio's slipperiness and rhetorical manipulation, it is tempting to interpret Philostratus as referring not to Trajan's ignorance of the Greek language, or even of Greek culture, but to his ignorance of the *paideia*, the complex and

[77] Philostr. *VS* 8.13–19 = 488 O (modified): καὶ γὰρ ἡ πειθὼ τοῦ ἀνδρὸς οἷα καταθέλξαι καὶ τοὺς μὴ τὰ Ἑλλήνων ἀκριβοῦντας· Τραιανὸς γοῦν ὁ αὐτοκράτωρ ἀναθέμενος αὐτὸν ἐπὶ τῆς Ῥώμης ἐς τὴν χρυσῆν ἅμαξαν, ἐφ' ἧς οἱ βασιλεῖς τὰς ἐκ τῶν πολέμων πομπὰς πομπεύουσιν, ἔλεγε θαμὰ ἐπιστρεφόμενος ἐς τὸν Δίωνα "τί μὲν λέγεις, οὐκ οἶδα, φιλῶ δέ σε ὡς ἐμαυτόν."
[78] E.g. Gorgias fr.11.10 DK, συγγινομένη γὰρ τῇ δόξῃ τῆς ψυχῆς ἡ δύναμις τῆς ἐπῳδῆς ἔθελξε καὶ ἔπεισε καὶ μετέστησεν αὐτὴν γοητείᾳ.
[79] On the importance of θέλγειν to the *Odyssey*'s poetics, see G. B. Walsh, *The Varieties of Enchantment* (Chapel Hill, 1984), ch. 1, *passim*, esp. pp. 14–15. On Odysseus' deceptive faculties, the bibliography is large: see S. D. Goldhill, *The Poet's Voice. Essays on Poetics and Greek Literature* (Cambridge, 1991), p. 34, with the references cited there.
[80] 'Respice post te, hominem te esse memento.' See H. S. Versnel, *Triumphus. An Inquiry into the Origin, Development and Meaning of the Roman Triumph* (Leiden 1970), p. 57.
[81] Moles, 'Kingship,' p. 300, with references; P. Desideri, 'Dione di Prusa fra ellenismo e romanità', *ANRW* 2.33.5 (1991), 3882–902, esp. p. 3885, n. 9; Swain, *Hellenism*, p. 194, n. 32.

elaborate coding, of Greeks such as Dio.[82] Is Philostratus suggesting
that Trajan could not follow Dio's ingenious rhetorical sophistication?
That he did not understand that the devious Dio was *still* playing the
returning Odysseus, *still* denouncing tyranny? On this interpretation,
rhetorical *paideia* allows 'Dio the clever' to contest Roman power, for
those who *can* understand, in full view of the emperor, and to represent
an Odyssean threat to Trajan at the point at which he would appear
to be most 'co-opted.'

There is, however, yet another interpretation of this episode, one
which presents a Trajan closer to the shrewd propagandist of the previous section. It is possible to read Philostratus as suggesting that Trajan
is observing that comprehension is not at stake here, that it is the mere
display of solidarity which counts: Dio is a 'sophiste-ornement-du-
pouvoir . . . dont les paroles importent moins que leur éclat ou leur
chant.'[83] On this interpretation, Trajan's words must be read as a
cynical acknowledgement that the whole display is staged, and that
actual communication is unnecessary. Perhaps Philostratus' Trajan is
even shrewd enough to realise that comprehension of the full import of
Dio's role-playing *must not* occur if the propaganda is to be successful:
for the theatre of imperial propaganda, any 'tyrannicidal' connotations
must actively be ignored.

What is important, I suggest, is not to choose between these interpretations, but to allow Philostratus' scene its undecidability. The anecdote is interesting because it can be read in different ways, as a tacit
admission that Dio's *paideia* is staged as imperial propaganda and as an
assertion that anti-imperial messages subsist if you know where to look.
There are two conclusions to be drawn about the relationship between
paideia and power as presented in this episode. The first concerns the
paideia of Dio Chrysostom and its openness to co-optation as imperial propaganda. As Philostratus tells it, Dio cannot be read simply as
one who 'resisted' Domitian and 'supported' Trajan. As we have seen,
Dio's relationship with emperors is characterised by Philostratus as

---

[82] The phrase τοὺς μὴ τὰ Ἑλλήνων ἀκριβοῦντας, as well as referring forwards to Trajan (γοῦν
implies that the previous sentence is exemplified by what follows), is linked to the soldiers of
the previous sentence by καὶ γάρ. This does not, however, invalidate the interpretation of
τοὺς μὴ τὰ Ἑλλήνων ἀκριβοῦντας as referring to more than linguistic incompetence. Firstly,
there is no reason to assume that the soldiers are merely ignorant of the language: they may be
competent in Greek, but uneducated. Secondly, καὶ γάρ implies elaboration as well as gloss-
ing: I have taken it in the sense of 'and in fact,' for which see J. D. Denniston, *The Greek Particles*
(Oxford, 1934, 2nd ed. 1954, repr. 1966), pp. 108–9.
[83] Charles-Saget, 'Miroir-du-prince,' p. 112.

fundamentally 'rhetorical' (tricky and theatrical, as well as eloquent), and little of the image which he presents can be said to be certain. *Paideia*, in this instance, is the locus not for an uncontested display of imperial power, but for a confluence of competing modes of power, some consolidatory, some resistive. This is not to argue that Philostratus presents Dio as directly 'opposing' Roman power, but that the construction of this pedagogical relationship is an uneasy process of negotiation, rather than a simple expression of monarchical power. This negotiation involves threats of violence and coercion (on the emperor's side) and of tyrannicide (on the philosopher's side), which intermittently puncture the veil of intercultural harmony. The pedagogical instruction of the potentate, Philostratus tells us, is a complex business in which multiple positions are staked out and multiple roles are played.

My second point concerns the *paideia* of Philostratus himself. A complex scene such as the one presented here needs *reading*, and needs reading against the rich, sophisticated and complex backdrop of *paideia* as conceived in the Second Sophistic. The reader needs to be alert to nuances and ironies, to literary allusion, to theories of rhetorical strategy. Philostratus' prominent emphasis upon Trajan's non-comprehension might be interpreted as a self-referential moment, indicating the stratification of layers of interpretation, from the superficial through to the sophisticated. This constitutes a challenge to Philostratus' readers: can *you* read *this* text? How do you read power? How advanced is your *paideia*, your reading-power? The episode thus constitutes a lure to readers, whose reading-power sites them in their own relation to imperial power.

v

In conclusion, I should like to sum up the arguments presented so far, and point towards some implications for the interpretation of the politics of the Second Sophistic.

Traditionally, *paideia* has been perceived as instrumental in the integration of the Greek élites into the hierarchical structures of the Roman empire. By allowing the Greeks to continue to enjoy their rich cultural heritage, it is argued, the Roman government co-opted the support of the élite and defused any animosity. I suggested that this generalising view is too vague, and that close attention to specific cases will show a more complex picture. When we consider the return of Dio from exile, we see that the episode can be interpreted in different ways from different perspectives. From the perspective of imperial propaganda, Dio's return under Trajan represents the synthesis of the *paideia* of the Greek élite and the power of Rome, a 'new age' of philosopher-kingship visibly opposed to the reign of Domitian. But from the perspective of a Greek *pepaideumenos*, the episode is all about theatre. Dio, according to Philostratus, tries on a number of roles and gives off a number of sometimes conflicting signals. I made two points about this. Firstly, Philostratus presents the scene as more complex than a simple display of imperial power: the pedagogical relationship is, rather, the locus for multiple power strategies. Secondly, Philostratus issues a challenge to his *pepaideumenoi* readers, tempting them to read the text with wit and ingenuity. The text thus becomes a means for a reader to negotiate the relationship between power and *paideia* for him- or herself.

In pointing to the broader implications of these conclusions, I do not claim to have 'proven' any general claims about the relationship between Greek culture and Roman power: such a project would be beyond the scope of a chapter of this length. Nevertheless, the methodology I have adopted has ramifications beyond the narrow focus of this chapter. I confine myself to two observations, developed along the lines of the two conclusions to the previous section.

Firstly, the dominant view of Greek *paideia*, as an instrument of imperial power designed to facilitate the integration of the Greek East into the empire, must be qualified. As we recall, according to this view, *paideia* provided a means of coming to terms with Greece's reduced political role in the Empire, compensating the elite with the comfort of cultural hegemony. The image of Dio on Trajan's chariot has traditionally been read as a symbol of the cultural complementarity of the nascent Second Sophistic, of the perfect harmony of Roman power and Greek 'culture.' But, as we have seen, the pedagogical relationship between Greek teacher and Roman ruler should not be considered solely from the perspective of Roman power. If we read the episode with an eye to the oddities and irregularities of Philostratus' perspective, we see that the *pepaideumenos* stands in a more contested, and thus more immediately political, relationship with Roman power. At a more general level, we should consider *paideia* not as inherently and exclusively stabilising and conservative, but as a complex, prism-like space, in which power is refracted in different directions. Now it may well be objected that *paideia* could not construct real power, and represented no real threat to Rome. Such a discrimination between 'real' and 'imaginary' power is, however, highly problematic, especially for post-Foucauldian scholarship:

structures of language and thought provide some of the most fertile
ground for the construction and contestation of authority.[84] Moreover,
by closing down the possibilities that *paideia* provided a discursive negotiation of power, one runs the risk of presenting a unilateral, 'colonialist'
perspective upon the phenomenon of the Roman conquest of Greece.
To view *paideia* simply as a vehicle for Roman power, however com-
mendable may be one's intentions to expose that power, is ultimately
to reproduce the pattern of imperial dominance. We need a more plur-
alistic view of power in the Second Sophistic.

The second implication I wish to underline centres upon the status
of the Greek texts of the period as sophisticated and complex works
of literature. It is too often assumed that texts will give us direct access
to the 'opinions' of their authors about Roman power. 'Opinions' are
mutable and vague at the best of times, and the opaque relationship
between any literary text and its author makes them even more elusive.
But the problem becomes even more acute with the texts of the Second
Sophistic, since, as we have seen, *paideia* provided a set of resources
whereby to increase the complexity and depth of literary production.
As a result, the need is increased not only for close reading and attention to detail, but also for sensitivity to the deliberate equivocations
and ambiguities of self-consciously ironic and witty texts. In order to
understand the role of *paideia* in the society of the Second Sophistic,
we need to be alert to the fundamental importance of the *reader*. The
Greek novel is not the only product of the Second Sophistic which –
as recent critics have observed – is aware of the privileged position
of the interpreter.[85] The literature of this period is ever playing to the
most sophisticated audience, an audience willing to mull over minor
insinuations and pore over details. To neglect this element is to im-

---

[84] In his later works, as is well-known, Foucault considers power to be constructed, disseminated
and contested through 'discourse,' that is to say, he 'conceives of the space of language, culture
and society as an open, mobile and dynamic field of interrelations, in which power is everywhere and comes from everywhere' (E. T. Bannet, *Structuralism and the Logic of Dissent: Barthes,
Derrida, Foucault, Lacan* (London 1989), 168). The key text is M. Foucault, *La volonté de savoir*
(Paris, 1976); English trans. by R. Hurley, *The History of Sexuality. Volume 1: An Introduction*
(London, 1990 (1978)).

[85] For such narratological analyses, see J. J. Winkler, 'The Mendacity of Kalasiris and the Narrative
Strategy of Heliodoros' *Aithiopika*', YCS 27 (1982), 93–158; S. Bartsch, *Decoding the Ancient Novel:
the Reader and the Role of Description in Heliodorus and Achilles Tatius* (Princeton, 1989). The article
by Thomas Schmitz entitled 'Trajan und Dion von Prusa. Zu Philostrat, *Vit. Soph.* 1.7 (488)'
(*RhM* 139 (1996), 315–19) appeared too late for consideration in this chapter. I am glad,
however, to find support there for the notion that Trajan's non-comprehension of Dio is not
simply a case of difficulty with the Greek language.

poverish our understanding not only of the texts, but also of the social function of *paideia*.

This chapter has been about reading power, about interpreting its multiple, complex and covert forms. It has also been about reading-power, the faculty of interpreting texts which was only available to the highly resourced (in both senses) members of the Greek élite. What I hope has become clear is that these two senses are inseparable, that the power of sophisticated reading provided by *paideia* played a fundamental role in the negotiation of Roman power.

CHAPTER 10

Children, animals, slaves and grammar

Catherine Atherton

I

In the classical west the possession of language made an early appearance in lists of what were claimed as human prerogatives, and swiftly
became a fixture there, taking its place alongside such varied items as
reason; upright posture and gait; a face or countenance; a sense of
humour; sciences and skills; the ability to plan for the future; the capacity to form general concepts or beliefs; and morality.[1] The uniqueness
of our status as language users was often and powerfully challenged:
but at least some of the evidence in its favour must, one feels, have
been as obvious and as persuasive as it is today. Then, as now, human
infants (literally 'non-speakers') typically came to understand at least
one language, in contrast, it appears, to all other animals, including
even the chimpanzees reared by diligent 20th-century researchers. (The
Roman god *Uaticanus*, who presided over the beginnings of human
speech, took the initial syllable of his name from the first sound children utter: Aulus Gellius *noct. att.* XVI xvii 2.) Almost effortlessly, in a
predictable sequence, with only informal and haphazard instruction
and correction from speakers lacking special didactic skills and having at best only generalised didactic motivation, human offspring move
from a radically languageless state to mastery of their native tongue,
phonology, morphology, syntax, idioms, intonations, and all.

But that is how a linguist today might describe the situation. What
now pass for relatively innocuous claims about language development
would have seemed almost bizarre to most teachers of grammar in antiquity. These professionals were fully aware that children had normally
learned to talk and to understand what was said to them by the time

---

[1] An early example is in Sophocles' *Antigone*, l. 353. The sheer variety of characteristics allegedly
unique to humans is well illustrated by R. Sorabji, *Animal Minds and Human Morals* (London,
1993) ch. 7, esp. pp. 89–93.

214

their formal education began, if they were fortunate enough to receive one. But they would have thought of what all children learn from their parents, other adults, and other children – colloquial, untutored speech – as something intrinsically flawed, something of which knowledge in any strict sense is not even possible: for such language is subject, in particular, to the defects of formal irregularity (most conveniently referred to as 'anomaly'), the intrusion of non-native usages ('barbarisms'), syntactic errors ('solecisms'), and misuses of words.

Evidence of this attitude to ordinary language[2] is easy to find in grammatical texts. The introduction to Diomedes' *ars grammatica*, from the late 4th or early 5th century CE,[3] provides an outstanding instance of the grammarian's presentation of himself as creator of a refined language whose excellence lies precisely in its conformity to rule:

> It remains to commit individual points to your tenacious memory by re-reading, lest with the passage of time my industry sink uselessly into oblivion: the industry by which above all we are known to surpass the ignorant – who by the irregular nature of their rusticity, and arrangement of their uneducated discourse, wound – nay, disfigure, the precisely regulated soundness of discourse, and darken its refined splendour, product of our expertise – by fully as much as they themselves may seem to differ from the beasts.
>
> [superest ut singula recolendo memoriae tenaci mandentur, ne frustra cum tempore euanescat labor, quo tanto maxime rudibus praestare cognoscimur, qui rusticitatis enormitate inculteque sermonis ordine sauciant, immo deformant examussin normatam orationis integritatem politumque lumen eius infuscant ex arte prolatum, quanto ipsi a pecudibus differre uideantur.] *ars gr.* (*G.L.* I) *pr.* 299.18–24

Diomedes has already referred (ll. 1f.) to the 'brilliance of human skill' (*humanae sollertiae claritas*) which, with the help of literature, has 'fully refined' (*expolivit*) the 'expertise of genuine Latinity, instructress in pure discourse' (*artem merae Latinitatis puraeque eloquentiae magistram*). It is not just 'industry' which distinguishes grammarians from brutish humans, although discipline and dedication to the art are themselves signs of the good character, one capable of restraint and self-discipline, to which grammarians laid claim,[4] and to which their pupils could aspire: as Pliny remarks (*ep.* II xiv 2), the hardest things (in this case, Homer) come first at school – and Diomedes aimed his handbook at a school audience

---

[2] I have explored this topic more thoroughly in C. Atherton, 'What Every Grammarian Knows?' [= 'WEGK?'], *Classical Quarterly* (1996), 239–60.

[3] On Diomedes' dates: R. A. Kaster, *Guardians of Language: the Grammarian and Society in Late Antiquity* (Berkeley/Los Angeles/London, 1988), p. 271; also p. 15, on his approach to grammar.

[4] Cf. Kaster, *Guardians*, pp. 27ff.

(299.10). He presents himself as a specimen of a higher *humanitas* in part precisely because his regularisation of language has lifted him as far above 'the herd' as 'the herd' is above the beasts, while simultaneously, unsurprisingly, removing him from the country to the town. (Rusticity is, of course, commonly associated with 'lack of letters' in both a broad and a narrow sense in a wide variety of ancient texts.[5]) The glory could be shared. Priscian sees his dedicatee Julianus 'shining in every branch of learning, of the Greeks no less than the Romans', his 'intellect composed equally of the soul of Homer and of Virgil'; his worldly renown is no more splendid than the *decor* he derives from his immense cultivation (*inst. gr.*, *pr.* (*G.L.* II) 2.24ff.). Presumably grammar has the potential to elevate Diomedes' child-audience likewise. And this holds good even though the *ars* proper opens with a definition of speech, *oratio*, because it alone reveals humans as different from all the other animals (300.12–15): we already know that bare possession of language is *not* the end of humanity's struggle to raise itself above the level of the beasts.

Grammarians such as Diomedes are hardly the only people ever to have seen themselves as somehow privileged in relation to animal-like inferiors. Cicero's Crassus, for example (*de or.* I 33; cf. 31), treats oratory as permitting an individual to surpass his fellows in what first and foremost makes men, as a group, surpass animals – language – and as having raised men from the level of primitive society to 'this human culture and polity'; since he excels at what makes humans superior to the beasts, the successful speaker, we may infer, is *ipso facto* a successful human being. An orator who failed to speak proper Latin would not even be thought human by his audience (III 52). An orator or rhetorician might understandably want to represent his art as a symbol of, and a means to, peace and civilisation. But grammarians, too, could find the source of their superiority in their mastery of language. And they may have been unique – were certainly distinctive – in supporting their claims by appeal to their professional concern with linguistic correctness: in particular, with the construction and application of *rules*. Such rules, and the norms or notions of correctness they embody, appear to permit principled discrimination between the acceptable and the unacceptable in certain privileged areas of language use, above all in literary and formal public discourse. Connections can also be discerned between the grammarians' systems of basic linguistic

---

[5] See e.g. W. V. Harris, *Ancient Literacy* (Cambridge, MA, and London, 1989), p. 17. Rhetoricians in particular were sensitive to the need to distinguish urban(e) from rustic speech (e.g. Cicero *Br.* 170f., *de or.* III 42–4) – although some orators deliberately affected the latter (*Br.* 137).

regularities, subject to authorised departures from rule, and the secure and continuing pattern of distribution of social and political power under which professional educators functioned, and to the maintenance of which they contributed.

This paper has a modest aim: it sets out to sketch some of the parallels between the grammarian's world, a world of linguistic norms and rules and of authorised infringements of norms and rules, and the world of social norms and of supreme authorities above these norms in which his pupils had eventually to lead their lives. Further, it will suggest how education in the schools of grammar permitted, or forced, children to rehearse acquiescence in, and then full conformity with, the difficult and complex systems of norms which governed the world of adults.

II

To appreciate grammar's contribution to élite education, in both a broad and a narrow sense, it must be located within the rest of pedagogic theory and practice. I shall focus on the long period, from roughly the 1st century BCE to the end of antiquity, during which precepts and practices in the teaching of language and literature came to be sufficiently uniform in the Greek and Roman worlds for us to study them together, within the limits of the evidence.[6] I shall make due allowance for differences between them: physical and musical training, often neglected in Roman education, form a part of the old tradition of *paideia* in the Greek east, for example, and Roman children were likely to read comparatively modern Latin authors, while their Greek counterparts tended to be restricted to the ancient canon. In the grammarian's classes – which the child (a boy, in all probability) would begin to attend at about 7–10 years of age, after acquiring the more basic literacy skills[7]

[6] Kaster, *Guardians*, p. 99, has some salutary advice about the exegetical dangers inherent in evidence for grammarians' social and economic circumstances. Evidence for teaching practices often demands similar caution.

[7] The traditional trichotomy of schools into primary, grammar, and rhetorical has been recently and effectively challenged. In particular, many 'grammar' teachers probably gave instruction in the three Rs as well as in literary texts and in more advanced reading and writing skills; and at least some 'primary' teachers may have moved 'up' to grammar as their career developed, so that it would have been relatively easy for a hostile witness to blur whatever distinctions obtained. On all these points, see e.g. S. Bonner, *Education in Ancient Rome* (London, 1977) pp. 165ff.; A. D. Booth, 'Elementary and Secondary Education in the Roman Empire', *Florilegium* 1 (1979), 1–14; Kaster, *Guardians*, pp. 323ff.; Harris, *Literacy*, p. 238. It is also still debated how far schooling ever replaced teaching at home for the well-to-do: e.g. Harris, *Literacy*, pp. 96, 233; Booth, 'Education', pp. 3f.

– the content of literary, especially poetic, texts was analysed line by line, even word by word; and unusual words, phrases, meanings, and constructions, and historical, mythical, and geographical allusions were explained. The texts themselves often inspired the child's first exercises in composition, such as précis and paraphrase, of the sort Augustine remembered with horror (*conf.* I 17). Instruction in some of the apparatus of 'technical' grammar[8] was another requisite, since the concepts and categories of noun and verb, case and mood, and so on, were thought essential for both comprehension of literature and composition according to the canons of correct discourse.

The linguistic purity or correctness taught by the grammarians was one of the standard 'excellences', *virtutes*, of language in antiquity.[9] Correct Greek, or 'Hellenism' ('than which there is nothing fairer amongst the race of men', Scholia on Dionysius Thrax (D.T. Sch.) 160.1–3), might be defined as 'sound diction, and uncorrupt combination of the parts of speech which is congruent with regard to the various sound and legitimate usages'[10] (D.T. Sch. 446.12–14; note the conditions imposed on usage). The commonest offences against purity, whether in Greek or in Latin, are 'barbarism' and 'solecism' (e.g. *ad Her.* IV 17; Cicero *part. or.* 18, *opt. gen. or.* 4, 7; Quintilian VIII i 1),[11] and the definition of Hellenism just quoted captures the positive counterparts of these two negatives, as the scholiast's own explanation of it brings out (D.T. Sch. 446.14f., with 31ff.; cf. *ad Her.* IV 17).

A formal literary education thus came to be the almost invariable first step in the making of a member of the élite. How could grammatical instruction, especially in 'correct' or 'pure' language, be an essential part of that process?

It is easy to see why *rhetoricians*, and others with an interest in oratorical training, might find language learning a source of concern. Purity of speech was commonly a prerequisite for that mastery of public political and forensic discourse to which a rhetorical education was the normal route ('what is so essential as correct speech?', asks Quintilian (I vi 20 and cf. iv 5; see also Cicero *Br.* 258)). Instruction in correct discourse became part of the grammarian's special competence, and

---

[8] On this portion of ancient grammar, see e.g. C. Atherton, *The Stoics on Ambiguity* (Cambridge, 1993), pp. 487ff.

[9] On this well-known branch of stylistics, see e.g. Atherton, *Ambiguity*, p. 483.

[10] 'λέξις ὑγιὴς καὶ ἀδιάστροφος λόγου μερῶν πλοκὴ κατάλληλος κατὰ τὴν παρ' ἑκάστοις ὑγιῆ καὶ γνησίαν διάλεκτον.'

[11] Cf. E. Siebenborn, *Die Lehre von der Sprachrichtigkeit und ihren Kriterien. Studien zur antiken normativen Grammatik* (Amsterdam, 1976), p. 36.

to that extent grammar had an unshakeable grasp on the earlier stages of élite education. But the rhetoricians seem not to have regarded bare correctness as a source of prestige. No-one has ever admired an orator for speaking proper Latin (*quod Latine loqueretur*), says Cicero's Crassus: rather, people laugh at him if he fails to do so (*de or.* III 52).

One of the best surviving examples of the pedagogic genre is, significantly, the first book of Quintilian's *Education in oratory*, the *institutio oratoria*. Quintilian reveals a deep concern with correct speech: but, he says, this is something best learned at your mother's knee.[12] The single most important thing about nurses, Quintilian announces, is that their way of speaking should not be 'corrupt' (*uitiosus*), the context showing that purity of form rather than of content is in question – although, of course, their *mores* must be pure too, and Quintilian hastily corrects himself: good character is even more important (I i 4). Still, 'the child should not, even when a baby [*infans*], become accustomed to a way of talking [*sermo*] which will have to be unlearned' (§5) – 'unlearned', that is, when he is consigned to the *grammaticus*. Children's hold on pure Latin (and pure Greek) must be sure before rhetorical performance is even attempted: 'So when they are still grasping the outline of correct and pure language [*formam rectae atque emendatae orationis*], impromptu loquacity, with no time for reflection, and with hardly a pause before standing up <to speak>, is truly worthy of a street performer's display' (II iv 15). Other evidence confirms the high status conferred on precocity in the field of oratory which Quintilian finds so distasteful:[13] children were often judged by their capacity to exercise adult skills, the most important of which, to the élite, was oratory, especially, in this period, declamation.[14]

It has long been recognised that teachers both of basic literacy and numeracy and of broader literary culture tended to have humble, even unsavoury, reputations amongst the élite whom they served, most markedly under the early Empire.[15] W. V. Harris speculates that this attitude

---

[12] Or rather, Quintilian's audience being what it was, at your nurse's knee: little attention was paid by educationalists to the children of the poor, one exception being Ps.-Plutarch's *On the education of children* 5E.

[13] E.g. Tacitus *dial.* 30.1; Petr. [?] *sat.* 4, Ps.-Plutarch. *educ.* 6c, E; Pliny *ep.* II xiv 1ff.; for an example of adults encouraging literary display, see Herondas III 30f.

[14] Cf. T. Wiedemann, *Adults and Children in the Roman Empire* (London, 1989), pp. 167ff.

[15] E.g. Callimachus fr. 195 (a schoolteacher is given a veiled warning against continuing to abuse his pupils); Juvenal X 224 (more sexual abuse); Cicero *off.* 1 151. Dionysius the tyrant, expelled from Syracuse, supposedly ended up in Corinth as a primary-school teacher (γραμματίστης, e.g. Lucian *The dream, or the cock* 23); Lucian's *Symposium* is especially interesting not just for the charges of sexual and financial abuse made against a tutor and a philosopher in a private

may have sprung 'from some feeling among the educated that part of
their birthright was being sold in sordid circumstances',[16] and he contrasts the special status indicated by teachers' occasional exemptions
from taxes and civic duties under the Empire with the 'wretched . . .
physical conditions of schooling'.[17] It may have been precisely because
teachers, of grammar and of rhetoric alike, *sold* what the élite represented
to itself as a sign of its superiority that they fell so low in the opinion
of those they had helped to educate. Kaster has thoroughly explored
the peculiar social status of grammarians: their liminality between the
élite and the lower classes, their changing position as grammar teaching
became a more respectable métier in late antiquity, and their 'mastery
of the language' with its reward of 'conceptual power'.[18] We shall find
another possible reason for the lowly status of instruction in literacy
and in literature. The grammarian's hope of being recognised as a
master of Greek or Latin is of more immediate relevance.

Teaching the three Rs bore the further stigma of being merely the
inculcation of skills which were, supposedly, easier to acquire than (the
rest of) élite education,[19] and were certainly more widely available in
society, so that Tacitus, for example, can make it a species of reproach
to Iunius Otho that he began life running a 'school of letters', a *ludus
litterarius* (*Ann.* III lxvi 3). Yet, in comparison with rhetoric, lower status
was also assigned to the teaching of the literary canon, and this holds
good even if it is true that in the west *rhetores* too took time to win
respectability: they had themselves challenged tradition, that of learning the political ropes by personal contact with an established figure.[20]

---

household (26, cf. 32), but for the way Lucian reverses the standards of behaviour usually
associated with the educated and the vulgar (34f.). See further e.g. A. D. Booth, '*Litterator*',
Hermes 109 (1981), 371–8; Harris, *Literacy*, p. 234; Kaster, *Guardians*, pp. 50ff.

[16] Harris, *Literacy*, p. 96; cf. p. 237.

[17] Harris, *Literacy*, p. 236; cf. Kaster, *Guardians*, pp. 55f., 122f. On exemptions from taxes, etc.:
Harris, *Literacy*, p. 306, n. 103; Kaster, *Guardians*, pp. 223ff.

[18] Kaster, *Guardians*, pp. 54f.; cf. 51, 57ff.

[19] Fluent reading, at sight, was no mean achievement, given the scribal conventions common
throughout antiquity (e.g. Petronius [?] *sat.* 75), and the social spread of (the varieties of) literacy in antiquity is, of course, a hugely problematic area. Yet it was something of a commonplace that learning the alphabet was extremely easy (e.g. Isocrates *Against the sophists* 10, where
the advocates of what might be called 'alphabetic oratory' are made to make a comparison
between the two; Quintilian (I iv 1) argues that only memory is required to acquire these basic
skills, which are thus within the reach even of very small children). But all that is needed for
the present argument is recognition that such skills were certainly not entirely the prerogative
of the well-to-do.

[20] An attempt had reportedly been made to expel them legally from Rome as late as 92 BCE
(Suet. *gr.* xxv 1f.). Cicero had felt obliged to defend the comparatively novel practice of
rhetorical teaching (*or.* 140ff.), but had also distinguished teaching 'as if in a school', which in

Rhetoricians could at least be seen as passing on the skills required by the central social-cum-political activities of male adults in the élite; and teachers of oratory might double as performers in the public arena or its substitutes. Grammarians could not lay claim to status on either count. From the point of view of the rhetorician, their role, as we have seen, was limited to instruction in literature, which would provide boys with the appropriate cultural baggage, and to teaching, by means of exercises in composition, the most basic essentials of successful public speaking: correctness and, perhaps, clarity too.[21] The author of the *ad Herennium*, the earliest surviving Roman treatise on rhetoric, devotes only a few sentences to the stylistic excellence of *elegantia*, which comprises Latinity and clarity (IV 17), and he refers us to his treatise on grammar (not extant, but one of the first surviving references to such a thing in Latin)[22] for a fuller discussion of the former.

It is not surprising, then, to learn that Roman grammarians started expanding their repertoire to include everything bar declamation itself. Quintilian deplores this distinctively Roman error as imposing too great a burden on the *grammaticus* (I ix 6). Parental ambition no doubt had a part to play in this shift of responsibilities (we have already observed the praise heaped on adolescent orators), but so must the grammarians' own desire for more pupils, larger salaries,[23] and higher professional status. It is remarkable just how many of the grammarians whose careers

his view certainly does lack dignity, from personal, informal encouragement and advice, presumably along the lines of the traditional training by personal contact between elder stateman and youthful acolyte (the *tirocinium fori*). Under the early Empire we find in Pliny (*ep.* IV xi 1) a contrast between the past of the disgraced Valerius Licinianus, as a senator and an orator, with his present, as an exile and a rhetorician, or, to use the unfortunate man's own word, as a *professor*, and one dressed as a Greek at that: since exiles could not wear the toga, Licinianus was painfully denied even the appearance of a Roman statesman. (Juvenal's comment on the case (*sat.* VII 197f.) is that *consul* and *rhetor* metamorphose into one another at Fortune's whim.) In the same period, Quintilian, from whom we might expect particular sensitivity on the point, was well aware of the shortcomings of some orators-turned-teachers (XII xi 14; cf. I xii 17). Pliny also discusses (*ep.* III iii 3f.) the need to find a suitable teacher of rhetoric for a boy, hitherto educated safely at home, whose physical charms mean care must be taken in the choosing. This concern with morality will come up for us again later (§v). By the 4th century, however, a rhetorical career was so respectable that Libanius could complain about the way it could give a social lift to such unsavoury figures as the sons of sausage-sellers, bath-attendants, and labourers (*or.* XL 10, 25f.; from Harris, *Literacy*, p. 288).

[21] Cicero's characters frequently make just these assumptions: see e.g. Crassus at *de or.* III 38, 48, Atticus at *Br.* 252, 258f., 261 (cf. *or.* 161; also Quintilian XIII x 44).

[22] Surprisingly, it does not seem to be mentioned in the account of early Roman *artes grammaticae* by K. Barwick, *Remmius Palaemon und die römische ars grammatica* (= *Philologus* Suppl. 15:2, Leipzig, 1922; repr. Hildesheim, 1967), pp. 109ff., 229ff.

[23] Kaster's discussion of the grammarians' financial position (*Guardians*, pp. 112ff.) allows us to appreciate the extreme vulnerability to the vagaries of the market of workers in this particular service industry, especially if they were not in receipt of state or civic funding.

are described by Suetonius are former slaves, and Barclay, who does not see how charged the material is with the ideology of social distinctions, at least observes that quite a few of them have 'the oddest backgrounds'.[24] The outstanding case, of course, is that of Remmius Palaemon, supposedly author of the first Latin grammar, whose lowly origins – a slave originally trained as a weaver, he learned the rudiments of his profession when attending his mistress's child to school (Suet. *gr.* 23) – prove, unsurprisingly, to be wholly in keeping with his low character and lower tastes; and it is these, not his scholarly achievements, which are Suetonius' real interest.[25] Grammarians, it seems, were later to become somewhat more respectable.[26] They never achieved, however, the dignity accorded their elder brothers, the teachers of rhetoric; and upward social mobility seems to have required a change of profession.[27]

III

The low status of teachers notwithstanding, the social, political and economic benefits accessible to those who received the standard literary education (or some portion thereof) are central to most recent explanations of the nature and purpose of ancient education.[28] Children would be given this education because in practice it was a fairly reliable route to some degree of security, power and prestige. Reaching each successive level in the educational hierarchy would confer ever greater advantages on those seeking advancement and social success.[29] Despite the practical advantages their teaching could confer,

[24] W. Barclay, *Educational Ideals in the Ancient World* (London, 1959), p. 273.
[25] Cf. Kaster, *Guardians*, pp. 55ff.
[26] Cf. Kaster, *Guardians*, pp. 99ff. ('respectable if unprepossessing members of the local élites', p. 123).
[27] Cf. Kaster, *Guardians*, p. 130.
[28] Cf. e.g. P. Heather, 'Literacy and Power in the Roman World', in A. K. Bowman and G. Woolf, eds., *Literacy and Power in the Ancient World* (Cambridge, 1994), 181–97, at p. 182; Harris, *Literacy*, p. 202.
[29] This holds good even though the evidence indicates that there was never, even under the Empire, inside or outside Egypt, and not even in the Greek east, with its long tradition of public and private subventions at least for literacy teaching, anything like a publicly-funded education *system*. Both basic literacy instruction and more advanced literary education appear to have remained overwhelmingly private and unregulated, making all the more remarkable what the evidence suggests was a high degree of synchronic and diachronic stability in both content and methods: cf. e.g. Harris, *Literacy*, pp. 20f., 129ff., 235, 244–6, 306f. The great variation in nomenclature for pedagogic professionals may, however, reflect some variation in how teaching was structured and conducted: at least, there appears to have been no single, context-independent content associated with each of the different titles 'teacher', '(school)master', or even 'grammarian' (*didaskalos, grammatodidaskalos, grammatistēs, grammatikos, kathēgētēs; magister*

however, grammarians do not seem to have seen themselves merely as part of a service industry to the élite. It may seem remarkable how few sources speak of the material rewards awaiting the educated.[30] Quintilian feels only contempt for those who try to work out how much a course of liberal studies might earn them later as a public speaker (I xii 17, cf. 18), and in Petronius [?] *Sat.* 46.7 the attitude Quintilian disdains is favoured only by a boorish freedman. Lucian's personified Paideia does, admittedly, offer the worldly rewards of prestige, influence, and renown (*The dream, or Lucian's career*, 11–13), and Lucian concludes (§18) by presenting his 'dream' as an encouragement to the young not to be put off getting themselves an education by poverty – but here it is a career in rhetoric which is the goal. And on reflection, this silence makes perfect sense. Some *independent* value must have been attached to familiarity with literature, and to mastery of correct discourse, in order to explain their association with high social status, rather than *vice versa*. 'Education ['*paideia*'] alone is immortal and divine', says Pseudo-Plutarch (*educ.* 5E). What makes the neo-Pyrrhonist Sextus Empiricus' heterodox presentation of usage as the sole criterion of good Greek (*hellēnismos*) so striking is not just that it replaces purity with clarity, the other basic excellence of discourse, but also that it makes explicit the pragmatic attractions of speaking well: social acceptability is the name of the game, and what matters is that people understand what you say and do not laugh at the way you say it (*Against the professors* [*M.*] I 176ff.).[31]

One justification of grammar is readily enough available which *does* make appeal to its benefits, but which, on the surface at least, has nothing to do with social success. As a self-styled 'expertise' (*technē*), grammar was in fact required to boast some sort of practical goal or *telos*,[32] and the subject boasted of its usefulness in the interpretation of

---

(*ludi*), *litterator, grammaticus*). On terminology, see e.g. P. Collart, 'A l' école avec les petits Grecs d'Egypte', *Chronique d'Egypte* 11 (1936), 489–507, at pp. 493f.; E. W. Bower, 'Some Technical Terms in Roman Education', *Hermes* 89 (1961), 462–77; Booth, '*Litterator*'; Harris, *Literacy*, p. 96; Kaster, *Guardians*, Appendices 1–3, pp. 443ff. It is (to us) equally remarkable that the burden on parents and guardians to find suitable teachers for children led, not to a call for public regulation, but to sharp criticism from educational theorists of carers who failed to vet applicants thoroughly (e.g. Ps.-Plutarch *educ.* 4B–5A).

[30] As noted by Harris, *Literacy*, pp. 202f.

[31] Cf. Atherton, 'WEGK?', pp. 251ff. It is significant that the Dionysian scholiasts implicitly disagree about the relation between Hellenism and clarity: contrast 446.6ff. with 113.25f. In these and subsequent discussions of norms and rules, I am indebted to R. Bartsch, *Norms of Language* (London/New York, 1987).

[32] Thus Sextus can quite reasonably argue that grammar is not an expertise because it is not useful, unlike basic literacy teaching (*grammatistikē*): *M.* I 55f.

literature.[33] Yet this is simply to presuppose that familiarity with certain canonical texts is valuable in its own right. Again, social pressures in antiquity could explain the desirability of a 'good' accent, 'pure' diction, 'correct' grammar, and so on, just as easily as they do now, and there can be little doubt about the social impact of élite education: its restriction of mobility between classes. If being 'one of us' requires familiarity with the standard dialects of Greek and Latin, and with poetry composed in extinct or literary dialects (and of a foreign language at that, for Romans reading Homer or Hesiod), grammarians must be seen as contributing to the perpetuation of social divisions.[34] That they do not seem to have presented themselves expressly as purveyors of an arbitrarily privileged set òf skills whose value lies solely in its association with social rank is hardly surprising. But *was* that association merely arbitrary? Did nothing in the élite curriculum fit the children who benefited from it for their future functions as members of the traditional ruling classes, beyond mere possession of the right cultural baggage?

IV

To answer that question we must turn to what may seem an unrelated topic: the conditions under which teaching was given and received.

For the regular use of physical force on their pupils by grammarians (and by literacy teachers) there is overwhelming evidence, literary, subliterary, epistular, and graphic, from the Classical Greek and Hellenistic worlds and the Empire alike.[35] Such evidence prompted Carcopino famously to characterise Roman primary education as comprising

[33] The scholiasts on the Dionysian *ars grammatica*, for example, claim that grammar is useful for resolving ambiguities (2.14–18) or inclarities in old-fashioned texts, both prose and poetic (113.15–20): grammar is the medicine for difficult and obscure language (20–26; cf. 2.14–18 (orators and philosophers find it useful too), 113.25f.). This leads us to grammar's second function: instruction in linguistic correctness (see p. 218 above): e.g. 109.37f., 160.1–5, 170.21f., 446.6f. The goal (*telos*) of grammar is also defined as 'the understanding of discourse [ἡ κατάληψις τοῦ λόγου], that is, teaching what has meaning and how it has meaning, i.e. through which parts <of speech> discourse is signified [ὁ λόγος δηλοῦται]' (115.4–7). In this context we must ignore grammar's secondary purpose, as a stepping-stone to rhetoric (e.g. Quintilian 1 iv 5).
[34] Cf. Harris, *Literacy*, p. 333. Heather, 'Literacy', pp. 195f., suggests that this cultural hegemony gained importance with the loss of political and military power by the old élite.
[35] Plato's Protagoras alludes to the way a bad child is 'straightened like a bent piece of wood with threats and blows' (*Prt.* 325c). Horace reports that his teacher was known as 'plagosus Orbilius', 'Orbilius the Whacker' (*ep.* II i 70). Augustine recalls childhood beatings inflicted, to the amusement of his parents, simply because he preferred play to study (*conf.* 1 9f.; cf. *civ. dei* XXI 14). There is the well-known fresco (illustrated in e.g. Bonner, *Education*, p. 118) from the forum at Pompeii of a boy being beaten, on bare skin, in the 'catomus' ('over-the-shoulders') position,

'senseless, stumbling repetitions punctuated by savage punishments'.[36] Unusually, it seems, Quintilian took a stand against corporal punishment (1 iii 13ff.), and the considerations he advances are of great interest: it is an injustice (*iniuria*), he argues, fit only for slaves (*seruile*), not for free men, even if they are immature. If a child has a '*mens*' so '*illiberalis*', 'so unfree a spirit', that only force affects him, he will probably end up 'hardened to blows, like the worst sort of slave [*mancipia*]' (§14). Beating has bad effects on the character (§16; presumably timidity and low self-esteem are meant). There are always 'scoundrels' (*nefandi homines*) who will abuse their authority to punish; but children are weak and vulnerable, and no-one should have too much power over them (§17).

Pseudo-Plutarch expresses similar concerns: corporal punishment 'surely seems to be more fitting for slaves than for free men; for they become dull at and shy of their work', as a result of the pain and of the insults (*hubreis*) dealt them (8F). Praise and criticism are preferable, and if corporal punishment has to be meted out, parents must inflict it themselves, and never allow such a thing to depend 'on a hireling's character' (9D). Anger generally, and especially violence toward slaves, are not to be tolerated in the young (10B), nor lying, 'which is slavish' and inexcusable even in the middling sort of slaves (11C). Children's faults should be tolerated to some degree: even slaves can be forgiven for getting drunk (13E). Seneca too, if for very different reasons, disapproves of violence toward those weaker than oneself, including children, both one's own and pupils in class (*clem.* 1 xvi 2f.; cf. 1 xviii 1f., on slaves).

The use of force on children finds a place in the ancient tradition within educational theory, as well as in laws and social norms, of associating them with animals. Plato's well-known discussion of education in the *Laws* (VII 808de) opens with comparisons between children and sheep (d2f.), slaves (d4, 3e4), and wild animals, and of all these the child (*pais*) is the 'most intractable', since if 'the fountainhead of wisdom' ('πηγὴν τοῦ φρονεῖν') goes untrained, he is 'a treacherous, cunning and shameless thing' (d4–7). Just as to a horse, so too to a child, a bit

in class, apparently meeting semi-publicly in a colonnade: meant, perhaps, to amuse adults and terrify children; for more examples, see F. A. G. Beck, *Album of Greek Education* (Sydney, 1975), plates 49–53. In Egypt, a mother writing to her son's teacher encourages him to beat the boy regularly, as his father used to do, since 'he is a child and stupid' (see F. G. Bratton, *A History of Egyptian Archaeology* (London, 1967), p. 253); cf. Herondas III (a mother urges a schoolmaster to beat her lazy and ignorant son within an inch of his life).

[36] J. Carcopino, *Daily Life in Ancient Rome* (Harmondsworth, 1956, trs. E. O. Lorimer; first edn. 1941), p. 122, a vision largely shared by Barclay, *Ideals*, pp. 166, 169; Collart, 'A l'école', p. 495; also Bonner, *Education*, pp. 143–5; A. D. Booth, 'The Schooling of Slaves in First-Century Rome', *TAPA* 109 (1979), 11–19, at p. 12.

must be applied, or rather several bits: his *paidagogos*; his teacher; and the learning befitting a free man (e2–4).[37] As befits a slave, however, a child is liable to chastisement by any free man, as are his *paidagogos* and his teacher, if they too go astray (4–7).

More informative here, because at least presented as a practical guide, is the treatise *On the Education of Children* once attributed to Plutarch. It opens with the reassurance that all bad qualities can be overcome by training and effort, and one important illustration of this principle is that all animals, even the wildest, can be tamed if broken young enough (2F). Admittedly, the author is, unusually, opposed to much corporal punishment, as we have seen: the 'taming' is to be done gently, and sharp distinctions observed between the treatment suitable for slaves, and that appropriate for free-born children. But his anxious protestations against the (over-)use of force suggest the practice of treating children in much the same way as slaves was widespread.

The relationships between the categories of child, slave, and animal would bear far more investigation, and attitudes to these groups were more diverse and complicated than I have perhaps suggested. The point I wish to make is simply that the consignment of children, not just to literacy instructors, but also to teachers of literature, the grammar teachers, would typically involve their prolonged exposure to physical punishment, from adults whose social standing might well be lower than their own (or rather than that of their parents or guardians), but against whom they had, as a rule, little power of appeal or redress (leaving aside such episodes as Plautus *Bacchides* 440ff., which is, after all, a piece of fiction; cf. *Rudens* 1000 for a similar flogging – inflicted on a slave). Further, such treatment was applied, supposedly, to further their mastery of the skills and learning which would allow them to take their place amongst the adult élite. Hence, bizarrely, grammarians could also represent themselves as loving nurses and carers, giving the milk of culture to their charges, with their use of force justified by the great rewards in store.

Horace famously observed that children are given tidbits, *crustula*, to coax them into learning their ABC (*sat.* 1 i 25): but the grammarians' own descriptions of their role are what interest us here. Ausonius, for example, relates his own teaching experience in the following terms:

---

[37] For the image, compare the passage from Ausonius, quoted below. One of the Dionysian scholiasts remarks that 'the better sort of people' tend to have even their slaves taught their letters, as they are taught the laws and religion, so they may be 'tamed' by them and 'be educated with a view to ordinary usages' (159.20ff.).

I myself nurtured many 'children' from their milk-drinking years; cherishing them on my lap, articulating their mumblings, I snatched their tender age away from their gentle nurses. Soon I enticed them, as boys, with gentle admonishment and a tingle of fear, into the harsh pursuit of mellow advances, to pluck the sweet fruit of a bitter root. It was I again who led them forward, wearing their first beards, with the change to adolescence already upon them, to achieve good characters and goodness in the arts, and to forcefulness in speaking, although they declined to bear my rule on their necks or to offer their mouths to the curbs placed in them.

> [. . . multos lactantibus annis
> ipse alui gremioque fouens et murmura soluens
> eripui tenerum blandis nutricibus aeuum.
> mox pueros molli monitu et formidine leni
> pellexi, ut mites peterent per acerba profectus,
> carpturi dulcem fructum radicis amarae.
> idem uesticipes motu iam puberis aeui
> ad mores artesque bonas fandique uigorem
> produxi, quamquam imperium ceruice negarent
> ferre, nec insertis praeberent ora lupatis.] (*ep.* xxii 63V.)

The standard pedagogic hierarchy[38] can be discerned beneath the carefully-chosen oxymorons: boys begin with basic reading and writing, move on to literature, and finally to the *progymnasmata*, with the emphasis on composition, before rhetorical training proper begins. Education emerges as a judicious mix of coercion and enticement, violence and gentleness, as Ausonius implicitly justifies his severity as moderate, well-intentioned and ultimately beneficial. Booth is surely right to see exaggeration in the reference to suckling babes.[39] It is just as surely wrong to see this as an example of the *father*-image cultivated by many teachers in antiquity:[40] Ausonius substitutes the milk of learning for real milk, and his gentleness is that of a wet-nurse.

We can see a fuller version of such self-advertisement in Sidonius Apollinaris' account of the education of Consentius (born c. 410 CE) (*c.* xxiii 204ff.). Consentius is told that as a new-born baby he was

---

[38] Martianus Capella speaks (iii 230) of grammar itself as coming of age, maturing from simple literacy instruction for children (what was probably called *grammatistikē/litteratio*) into grammar proper (*grammatikē/litteratura*): cf. Bower, 'Some technical terms', pp. 468f.; for the distinction, see e.g. Sextus *M.* i 44, D.T. Sch., 114.23ff.; and cf. Kaster, *Guardians*, pp. 447ff.

[39] Booth, 'Education', pp. 5–7 and n. 18. Paulinus, in a letter to one of the pupils Augustine had as a *grammaticus* in Thagaste, does describe Augustine as he 'who carried you in his own bosom when you were just a little thing, filled from childhood with the first milk of a man of worldly wisdom' (*ep.* viii 1). The female, nutritive imagery of this Christian exhortation is strikingly similar to that found in the grammarians.

[40] As assumed by Kaster, *Guardians*, p. 68; cf. Booth, 'Education', p. 7 and p. 12, n. 21.

immediately given over into the care of the Muses, a very fine set of nurses, who steeped him in the Hippocrene spring of 'speaking water' (*loquacis undae*), so that 'you drank in your letters' (*litteras bibisti*); then he was handed over to the *magister*, who trained him in grammar, rhetoric, and gymnastic: 'just as, still a tender child, you had already drained <the one>, so you devoured <the other> (*sicut iam tener hauseras, uorasti*). Elite education is presented as a progression from liquid to solid food, and one by implication just as natural and beneficial.

Educationalists often emphasise the importance of female carers, and especially of mothers, to the correct development of the young. It is not just that mothers should breast-feed their children themselves wherever possible (as urged by Favorinus, Aulus Gellius *noct. att.* XII 1; Ps.-Plutarch *educ.* 3D) to strengthen the bond between them. Women (if aristocratic) could also be good linguistic models for their children (Cicero *de or.* III 45 (Crassus), *Br.* 211 (Cicero), 252 (Atticus); Quintilian I i 6), and, as we have seen, nurses should be chosen in part because they speak properly. Here the motherly, caring, tender image is being borrowed by purveyors of formal education. Quintilian had recommended that teachers in the early stages of rhetorical training should 'like nurses, nourish minds still tender with a softer kind of food, and allow them to get their fill of, so to say, the milk of a more pleasurable learning regime' (*ut teneras adhuc mentes more nutricum mollius alant et satiari uelut quodam iucundioris disciplinae lacte patiantur*, II iv 5). Nurses, although they too were slaves, or hired servants, bring with them associations of gentleness and tenderness toward children at their youngest and most vulnerable, and the grammarian is softening his own, less comfortable, relationship with his pupils by identifying himself with another paid, but loving, and perhaps beloved, personage.

When reflecting on his relations with his own students, therefore, the grammarian finds himself, curiously, in a position to exploit to his own advantage what in other, social, contexts is actually a serious weakness. We noted earlier (§II) that the grammarian, while enjoying higher status amongst the élite he served than did mere teachers of basic literacy and numeracy, suffered in comparison with teachers of rhetoric. The source of the grammarian's low social position, I would suggest, was the very fact that he exercised his skills and his authority on children.[41] The rhetorician, in contrast, not only instructed 'pre-adults',

---

[41] See Aulus Gellius *noct. att.* XVIII iv 1, and Suet. *gr.* XXIV 2 (on Valerius Probus), for examples of grammarians deliberately distancing themselves from the orthodox adult/child relationship with their 'students'. (Both references from Kaster, *Guardians*, pp. 54, 59.)

but instructed them in activities shared with adult males in the élite. In these passages we see how – if only when he is addressing fellow-grammarians and those they educate – the grammarian can make his principal liability over into an asset: a traditionally female, and thus less valuable, nurturing role, is appropriated, and then cleverly adapted. Ultimately, control of the young 'animal' is to be won only through force and the threat of force.

v

Even when they were trying to present themselves in an attractive light, then, teachers of literacy and of literature did not deny their reliance on force: rather, they justified it by reference to the good effects education could bring. Such behaviour, and the condoning of it, may to us seem at odds with the grammarians' lofty sense of their own mission and position. In the light of the evidence for an apparently paradoxical relationship between the two, can we now assess the grammarian's contribution to the education of the child? On the cusp between animal and human, slave and free, children of the élite were expected to achieve in a few short years some degree of mastery over long-dead literary dialects and idiolects, and were most probably beaten into learning first their letters, and then canonical literature and the fundamentals of correct composition. What in this education could justify its status as a prerogative of the rightfully ruling classes?

The first step to take in retracing grammar's path to that lofty position is to see that it was *moral* training and instruction which educationalists usually counted as the good parent's supreme concern.[42] This is the main thrust of Messalla's account of the Roman way of bringing up children, with its contrasts between carers past and present, native and Greek, free and slave, blood-related and hired, morally upright and 'utterly worthless' (*vilissimus*) (Tacitus *dial.* 28f.). What can almost be called an obsession amongst pedagogic theorists with the character of the child's nurses, tutors and educators, is familiar enough to modern scholarship. Ancient writings on education, Greek and Roman, early and late, whatever their other differences, are crammed with advice on discipline and with dire warnings against neglect of morals and manners. The lavish flattery heaped by Plato's Protagoras on (Athenian? democratic? all?) parents and carers is most plausibly interpreted as

---

[42] Cf. Heather, 'Literacy'; Kaster, *Guardians*, pp. 27ff.

part of Plato's own comprehensive indictment of sophistic pandering
to any potential client (325c4ff.). More orthodox are the criticisms of
parental laxity in the *Alcibiades I* 122ab and *Lysis* 223ab, or in Pseudo-
Plutarch *educ.* 4D. Juvenal devotes an entire satire (XIV) to the bad
examples which parents set their children, and he is thinking of moral
examples, not ignorance of geography or literature. 'The beginning,
middle, and end in all these matters [*sc.* to do with children] is good
upbringing and customary education [ἀγωγὴ σπουδαία καὶ παιδεία
νόμιμος]' (Ps.-Plutarch *educ.* 5C). Even proper dress and table manners,
it is (flatteringly?) assumed, are carefully taught (Plut. *fort.* 99D; this
work, incidentally, is one of the many in which it is claimed that our
capacity for reason, *logismos*, explains our dominance over the beasts
(98c)). Marcus Aurelius thanks his mother for her blood, his father for
his seed, his nurse for her milk, and his *tropheus*[43] for breaking him of a
fanatical devotion to spectator sports,[44] and for getting him 'to endure
hard work, to be limited in my desires, to look after my own needs, to
mind my own affairs, and to be unwilling to listen to people slander-
ing one another' (*med.* V 4). Although he may well be untypical in his
ungrudging gratitude for what education has done for him, Marcus
at least confirms that moral improvement was the goal of education,
broadly conceived. Eumenius' public call for state support for schools
(298 CE), while chiefly concerned with rhetoric, bases its case partly on
the claim that 'literature is the foundation of all the virtues', which, if
instilled early, improve performance of all public offices, even military
ones (*inst. sch.* 8). Lucian's personified Paideia, in the dream which
(so his story goes) persuaded him to a career in rhetoric rather than
sculpture, holds out before him the rewards of, *inter alia*, those glorious
adornments of the soul, the virtues (§10); here again, the immediate
context perhaps suggests that the literary portion of education will play
this educative role.[45]

Contact with slaves, and even with freedmen, was often criticised
by educationalists as a peculiarly acute *moral*, as well as linguistic,
danger for the young. Thus Quintilian warns that 'bad slaves' are as
much a danger as free-born companions with too little modesty (I ii 4),
and advises parents to employ a 'serious-minded gentleman or faithful freedman' (§5) to watch over their child. The tirade against the lax

---

[43] Presumably his *paidagogos*: see Bonner, *Education*, p. 41.   [44] Contrast Suetonius *Nero* 22.1f.
[45] The promise is that Lucian will learn everything there is to know about matters both human
and divine, a description which fits more neatly the literary stage of education (cf. e.g. D.T. Sch.
180.6f., and note the Stoic definition of poetry at Diogenes Laertius VII 60) than the rhetorical.

and over-indulgent upbringing of the day (§§6–8) includes an allusion to 'words which are not allowed even from Alexandrian favourites', yet seem charming if one's own child utters them. Because of their peculiar position, at once dependent and uncontrolled,[46] such 'pet' slaves (*deliciae*) had licence to speak in a way which ought to be unacceptable in freeborn children: here, sadly, bad parents reverse their positions. Cato Censor was famous for having taken the education of his son into his own hands, although he had a trained slave, Chilon, available for the purpose, and for doing so on the grounds that he did not want a slave to mistreat his child physically or verbally, nor his child to owe his education to a slave (Plutarch *Cato maior* xx). But this was unusual, just as it was a reversal of normal owner/slave roles for Cato's wife to suckle their slaves' children herself, so that they would regard their young master as a brother (that he might equally come to regard the slaves as his siblings is not a possibility Plutarch mentions: this is dangerous ground). The story is told of the philosopher Aristippus that a man asked his advice as to how much he should spend on his son's education: a thousand drachmas, came the reply. I can buy a slave for that much, the man objected. Well then, said Aristippus, you will have two slaves: your son, and the one you buy (Ps.-Plutarch *educ.* 4F–5A). Pseudo-Plutarch himself advises association between children and only such slaves as have 'good habits . . . , speak good Greek, and speak it with great distinctness'; from the wicked and the barbarian they might carry off 'something of their lowness [φαυλότητος]' (*educ.* 3DE).

It was above all in their long-standing role as *paidagogoi* that slaves and freedmen were feared and scorned by the educationalists. The poor reputation of the *paidagogos* in antiquity is well-known: Quintilian, for example, could describe the inferior sort of private teacher who prefers one pupil at a time as little better than a *paidagogos* (I ii 10). Tacitus' Messalla is incensed by the 'new' Roman fashion of abandoning their children to a Greek nurse and one or two worthless slaves chosen at random (*dial.* 32). Pseudo-Plutarch urges particular care in the selection of *paidagogoi*: war captives, foreigners, and the unstable are to be avoided (4AB). It is unclear whether it speaks volumes about attitudes to children, including children of persons wealthy enough to have a *paidagogos*, that even venal or vicious slaves were regularly given positions of responsibility and influence over them; or speaks volumes about attitudes to

---

[46] Special treatment for favourites might extend to a liberal education of sorts: e.g. Petronius [?] *sat.* 75.4; and see Booth, 'Schooling'; Harris, *Literacy*, pp. 255ff.

slaves that they were regularly given such positions, yet became a by-word for laziness and insolence, dishonesty and lechery.

Children's special vulnerability to physical violence (sketched in §IV) was to some extent shared with those (slaves) who could be their carers and companions, at least when very young. (Plutarch offers as one explanation of the origin of the *bulla* worn by a free-born child that it signalled its wearer's sexual unavailability even when naked (*Q.R.* no.101, 287F–288B).) Hard work (as noted in §I), formed part of the grammarians' self-image, but neither this, nor the practical demands of control, should be allowed to conceal the broader social conditions and associated ideologies which made children available for and liable to physical correction, and permitted, even promoted, it on the grounds that children were likely to benefit thereby.

The opportunities for loose behaviour provided by schools evoked particular anxiety amongst educationalists and, it seems, amongst parents too. Aeschines speaks of strict regulation by ancient legislators of contact between the teacher (*didaskalos*), the trainer (*paidotribēs*), the *paedagogos*, and their charges (I 9–11). Quintilian would reject schooling altogether were it shown to be, as many believe, detrimental to *mores*, however beneficial to *studia*: he is himself convinced, however, that 'the foundation of an honourable life' (*ratio uiuendi honeste*) and 'the foundation of great oratory' (*optime dicendi <ratio>*) are in fact inseparable, given that no man but a good one can be an orator (I ii 3; cf. I iii 2). He also regarded as one of the advantages of sending children to school its fostering of the *sensus communis*, a sense of community with one's fellow-creatures, which is found even amongst dumb animals (I ii 20).

Linguistic deterioration in particular could be represented as one component in a broader cultural and moral decline (the theme of a famous letter of Seneca's, *ep.* CXIV). Tacitus' Messalla, for example, very much a *laudator temporis acti*, claims that, whereas orators used to be given a grounding in literary studies (*grammatica*), as well as in music and geometry, today they are innocent of such general cultural attainments, 'so that in their court-cases the disgusting and shameful defects of this everyday speech are to be found as well', not to mention ignorance of the laws and a horror of philosophy (*dial.* 32). Children seem even to have played at speech-making: Seneca speaks of their pretending to conduct public business and to hold trials, his point, of course, being that grown-ups play at the same games (*const. sap.* XII 2); and Plutarch mentions a game in which older boys acted as *iudices* (*Cato minor* II 5). If so, there would have been ample opportunity for influence, good or bad, from playmates even on the crucial quasi-formal use of language with which rhetoricians were concerned, in addition to more ordinary linguistic contact between children, and between children and adults, which professionals in the field of education also sought to regulate. Many grammar teachers would find that their vulnerable charges had already been exposed to what they saw as bad, impure, incorrect language, the usual discourse of the uneducated masses; and their task was, in part, as we have seen, to correct such deficiencies.

So closely associated were linguistic norms with cultural ones that Zeno of Citium, founder of the Stoa, regarded rusticity in dress, eating, and walking as a kind of practical solecism (*S.V.F.* I 82, with Diogenes Laertius VII 22, and cf. Theophrastus *Characters* IV 4).[47] Orthodox solecising, of course, is a syntactic defect. Two of the kinds of barbarism which Quintilian lists are familiar enough: importing foreign words (he is even aware of the possibility of 'corruption' resulting from bilingualism in childhood, §§13f., cf. I v 22–4); and addition, removal, or misplacement of letters or syllables,[48] 'of which very many examples are current' (§§8, 10). But he accepts as a third variety that 'which has its origin in character [*animi natura*], so that the person by whom something is said in an arrogant or threatening or brutal manner is thought to have spoken barbarously [*barbare*]' (I v 9). Here, moderns would tend to say, not barbarism, but barbarity, is in play: lack of culture, not (merely) a linguistic defect, just as Zeno was thinking of boorishness, not (just) of non-standard dialects.[49] But the association of bad (subor non-standard) speech habits with bad (low, vulgar, even immoral) habits generally was strong and influential in antiquity. It is significant that Quintilian elsewhere draws an explicit parallel between usage, *consuetudo*, and *mores* (I vi 44f.). 'Usage' is not simply what most people do, which would constitute 'a most dangerous rule', since some 'usages' are open to grave criticism: we do not copy bad habits of dress or deportment, even if we do do some things on the basis of usage; likewise 'in speaking, if something corrupt [*vitiose*] has taken a grip on many people, it is not to be accepted as a rule of language [*pro regula sermonis*]'. Pseudo-Plutarch is emphatic that nurses must be Greek, but this is

---

[47] Ironically, Zeno was himself criticised for imposing neologisms on the Greek tongue, *S.V.F.* I 33–35; and see Atherton, *Ambiguity*, p. 94, n. 61.

[48] On the *quadripertita ratio*, 'fourfold scheme', alluded to here, see e.g. Atherton, *Ambiguity*, p. 329n.

[49] It became usual for 'barbarian' aristocratic youths to be given a Greco-Roman education in local cultural capitals (see Harris, *Literacy*, pp. 250f.), where they could, I take it, function as hostages whilst shedding some of their 'barbarian' status.

(also) because they must be of good character, competent to shape correctly children's characters (*ēthē*) as much as their limbs (*educ.* 3E).

So one source of value for the grammar teacher's wares could be explicitly moral (cf. e.g. D.T. Sch. 159.11–160.1, 5ff., 163.8ff.). Ethical training was so important that children were even given moralising tags to copy when learning their letters.[50] But another link can be forged between grammar teaching and ancient ideals of education in the broadest sense: the process of making children into adults. It is hardly surprising, given the uncertainty and insecurity attending their professional lives and status, that grammarians constructed elaborately flattering metaphors for their function in society: as gymnastic trainers (at least in the Greek east), as initiators into the mysteries, as guardians of language against the barbarians within and without.[51] We have already seen Diomedes' self-presentation as regulator of the language, into which the uneducated introduce irregularities and distortions (§1). We must now take a closer look at what grammarians had to say about their special fields of competence, Hellenism and Latinity, and compare it with what a child might learn about them.

Over the centuries a number of criteria had been proposed by which texts could be constructed and emended, and language in general judged good or bad simply as language, apparently regardless of its communicative, persuasive, expressive, or aesthetic properties.[52] The principal standards were: analogy (of word forms); etymology (for the basic shape and pronunciation of words, as well as their meaning); authority (of literary authors); and usage (provided it was 'good'). The first two stand a

---

[50] Primary teachers had a reputation for retailing tired proverbs and precepts (such as those in the collection attributed to Cato) and backing them up with nothing more than brute force. Seneca presents the schoolmaster as an example of those who in effect teach us to 'do as I say, not as I do': 'These <precepts> are passed on by the *paedagogus* to the boy, by the grandmother to her grandson, and the schoolmaster [*magister*], most irascible of men, contends that one must not get angry. If you go into any school of letters [*ludum litterarum*], you will learn that what heavy-browed philosophers produce with a flourish are models for children learning their letters to copy' (*ep.* XCIV 9). Chrysippus (3rd c. BCE) had anticipated as a criticism of his method of compiling poetic quotations in support of one of his theories that it '. . . is perhaps the garrulity of a teacher of letters [γραμμάτων διδασκάλου] who wants to list as many lines as possible under the same thought [διανόημα]'; our source, in the 2nd c. CE, agrees: 'what could be more appropriate to a schoolteacher [γραμματιστῇ]?' (Galen *P.H.P.* III iv 16, p. 196.1–3, 5f. De Lacy, quoting Chrysippus' *On the soul* I).

[51] See Kaster, *Guardians*, pp. 16, 30.

[52] See e.g. Barwick, *Remmius Palaemon*, pp. 183f., 203–215, 228f.; Siebenborn, *Lehre*, pp. 30f., 53–5; M. Frede, 'Principles of Stoic Grammar', in his *Essays in Ancient Philosophy* (Oxford, 1987), pp. 303–37, at p. 311; K. Versteegh, 'Latinitas, Hellenismos, "Arabiyya"', in D. J. Taylor, ed., *The History of Linguistics in the Classical Period* (Amsterdam/Philadelphia, 1987), pp. 251–274, at p. 265.

little apart from the others in virtue of being, to some extent, text- and user-independent. In judging, say, a word-form as correct, a grammarian would not only rule on this particular instance, but would also rule, explicitly or implicitly, that in this and similar cases such-and-such a principle is to be authoritative. The impression should not be given, of course, of consensus in rulings of either sort. Disagreement was rife, particularly regarding the rival claims of analogy and of (ordinary) usage,[53] and the various theories of correctness or purity would be too complex and difficult a topic for a child to be taught in all their polemical detail. A typical pupil would not have been a budding textual or literary critic, and would not have been exposed to more theory than was necessary to get him to read, speak and write well by whatever standard his teacher chose to set. Quintilian observes that as language users we must assent to 'the consensus of the learned' (*consensum eruditorum*), just as is in life we follow 'the consensus of the good' (§45), a sure indication that Quintilian is employed in instructing the young, not in joining the complexities of grammatical debate.[54] We can thus construct at least a broad description of what a child would learn, both explicitly and implicitly.

He would need to appreciate, above all, that what was correct in a poem – an unusual word form, say, or the omission of a preposition – would not necessarily be correct in his own compositions; and reading and interpreting poets require some modest understanding of their

---

[53] A brief survey of the Roman tradition may be helpful. Analogy was apparently given precedence by such theorists as L. Cornelius Sisenna (Cicero *Br.* 260; Varro *ling. lat.* VIII 73; Aulus Gellius *noct. att.* II xxv 9f.), while both Varro and Quintilian saw the analogy/usage opposition as artificial (*ling. lat.* IX 3; *inst. or.* I vi 16f.). Varro listed four criteria of Latinity (fr. 268 Fun. = Diomedes (*G.L.* I) 439.15ff., cf. Charisius 62.15ff. ed. Barwick): 'nature', the basic shapes of words; 'analogy', which is natural to language, and abstracted therefrom by the technical grammarians, who use it to distinguish 'learned' from barbaric language, as silver from lead; 'usage', the power of which comes from people, not from language, and to which the 'system of the art' of grammar, the *artis ratio*, makes concessions; and 'authority', the criterion of last resort. If the rules (*praecepta*) of analogy are derived from usage (*consuetudo*), Varro's anomalist argues, then usage is actually our only guide: if not, we run the risk of being thought mad (*ling. lat.* VIII 33). Quintilian offers reason (that is, analogy and etymology), antiquity, authority, and usage (I vi 1). Cicero (e.g. *or.* 157, 159f., 162; *de or.* III 150 (Crassus)), Quintilian (I v 4), Pliny the Elder (fr. 83 della Casa, p. 151), and many others, wanted to take into account the sound of the language, as orators naturally would (and cf. Charisius *ars gr.* 63.10f. ed. Barwick). Where usage was granted authoritative, prescriptive status – as it commonly was by rhetoricians – it was 'approved' usage, that of respected authors, which was in question (e.g. Charisius *ars gr.* 63.9f. ed. Barwick). The language of the period (if ever there was one) when there was little or no contact with foreigners might be 'pure' Greek or Latin (e.g. Cicero *Br.* 258), but such undiluted *antiquitas* was not to everyone's taste (e.g. *or.* 155).

[54] On Quintilian's procedure here, see K. von Fritz, 'Ancient Instruction in "Grammar" According to Quintilian', *AJP* 70 (1949), 337–66.

idiolects. Thus the pupil would begin to see that different texts and types of text bring with them different standards of correctness: woe to the boy who thought that what was good enough for Virgil was good enough for him (e.g. Augustine *contra Faust.* XXII 25; Pompeius (*G.L.* v) 269.22ff.). Many of Servius' comments on Virgil's 'misuse' of Latin were 'directed more at the student than at the text'.[55] The child would not merely learn the rules of analogy (governing the various patterns of inflection), but also absorb, not necessarily from express instruction, that such regularities have normative force,[56] and, further, come to appreciate that that force can be overridden by other norms, other conceptions of correctness. And he will recognise that normativeness resides not merely in the regularities, but in the correct ways of settling competition between norms, of assigning privilege, in different contexts, to already privileged norms. It is overwhelmingly likely that no true system of such norms existed,[57] but this defect may very well have been hidden from the grammarians themselves, let alone from their pupils.

Diomedes' preface reminds us that formal irregularity or anomaly had long been associated with ordinary usage, which was held to have distorted the 'correct', more regular, patterns of inflection that (it was often claimed) naturally characterised Greek and Latin; and various 'remedies' for this malaise had been recommended.[58] Of course, the opposition between (impure, irregular) usage and (pure, regular) nature was not clear-cut, and grammatical texts can be found in which the Greek and Latin languages are themselves criticised as prey to defects which usage had made good.[59] Further, there was no single, authoritative, explicit doctrine on the extent to which regularity should be given precedence over usage or over other sources of correctness. Yet

---

[55] Kaster, *Guardians*, p. 180.

[56] Of course, such regularities *do* have normative force: see further Atherton, 'WEGK?', p. 254. Nor is my point merely that pupils became aware of their normativeness through formal grammatical instruction, for it is just as significant that assigning normative force to them was one of the privileges appropriated by the grammarian. The naturalness to language of (say) analogy does not necessarily render it *supremely* authoritative; thus that some grammarians rested their claim to authority partly on the 'naturalness' of the phenomena they were classifying (cf. e.g. C. Atherton, 'Apollonius Dyscolus and the ambiguity of ambiguity', *CQ* 45 (1995), 441–73, at pp. 462f.) does not justify their claim.

[57] See Kaster, *Guardians*, pp. 137ff., on the internal inconsistencies in the grammarians' treatment of texts.

[58] For more discussion, see Atherton, 'WEGK?', pp. 243ff.

[59] See e.g. Priscian (*G.L.* II) II 565.21–24; Varro fr. 268 Fun., on the unchanging 'nature' of words; Pompeius (*G.L.* v) 264.17–19.

reducibility to rule was regarded as something good and valuable in language.[60] Common usage and individual authors' idiosyncrasies alike may make inroads into the basic regularities of language, the laws governing, not just inflection, but also pronunciation, spelling, syntax, and meaning; but regularity remains (more or less) intact, and the felt need for principled judgements as to where regularity can be *properly* infringed allowed grammarians to assume the privilege of assigning normative force to these regularities and to infringements thereof.[61]

The pupil would also learn that in some contexts, notably in poetry, apparent 'misuse' could be transformed into stylistic ornament: confusingly, but significantly, barbarisms[62] and solecisms are not always barbarisms and solecisms. When used by a writer in the canon, especially a poet, they could be tansformed into stylistic ornaments, into tropes and figures (e.g. Quintilian I viii 14ff.; Servius *Comm. in Don.* 447.5ff.).[63] Metaphor in particular was also justified as a way of making up for a language's natural lexical deficiencies (Cicero *de or.* III 155), and it was permissible, too, to use foreign words when there were no good Latin ones available (Quintilian I v 57). As Quintilian remarks, almost everything we say nowadays, compared with the way the ancients used to talk, is a figure of speech, and such figures keep changing as ordinary usage, *consuetudo*, constantly changes too (IX iii 1; the view that ordinary

---

[60] Herodian, for example, speaks of analogy as 'containing, as it were in a net, by means of expertise, the multifold nature of human speech' ('ὥσπερ εἰ ἐν δικτύῳ συνέχουσα τὸ πολυσχιδὲς τῆς ἀνθρώπων γλώσσης φθέγμα τῇ τέχνῃ', *verb. sing.* 909.18). Inflectional regularity is even associated by Varro with the learnability of language (*ling. lat.* VIII 3): but this seems to be unique.

[61] Thus Aulus Gellius' most powerful attack on the grammarians he tends to despise takes the form of an 'invented rule' (*finitio ficta*) which they are unable to prove false (*noct. att.* XV ix 6ff.).

[62] Further, what counted as 'barbaric' shifted over time. Plato's Prodicus could already, it seems, joke that the Lesbian Greek dialect was a 'barbaric tongue' (*Prt.* 341c8f.; cf. 346d8f.; to take this, rather than Pittacus' Thracian origins, as responsible for his supposedly imperfect grasp of Greek, squares better with a rivalry between Lesbos and Prodicus' own island, Cos). Quintilian admits Sabine and Tuscan words as Roman (I v 55f., cf. 8 and VIII i 2f.): Cicero's Crassus does not (*de or.* III 42–4). Cicero's Atticus raises the possibility of native speakers' talk being corrupted by some 'household barbarism' (*barbaries domestica*, *Br.* 258). It became a matter of debate as to how Greek words should be declined in Latin and *vice versa* (e.g. Varro *ling. lat.* VIII 65, 72, X 70), and which Greek words could be used in Latin or translated into it (e.g. Aulus Gellius *noct. att.* XVI viii 5) – important questions for those equally at home in both languages. At this juncture moderns might say, simply, that the Latin and Greek languages had changed so much over time that a literary education was needed just to be able to read the canon, even if the great Roman authors, such as Virgil, were less remote than Homer and the 5th-century tragedians. But it is far from clear that grammarians had so sharp a concept of diachronic variation: cf. esp. Kaster, *Guardians*, pp. 181ff.

[63] See further M. Baratin and F. Desbordes, '"La troisième partie" de l'ars grammatica', in Taylor, *History*, pp. 41–66; Kaster, *Guardians*, pp. 151f.; Atherton, *Ambiguity*, p. 485.

language is 'figured' is shared by *ad Her.* iv 43 and by Apollonius Dyscolus, *Syntax* (*G.G.* ii ii) ii 77, pp. 183.14–184.1). And he criticises teachers who show off their learning by claiming to detect 'barbarisms' in literary texts, when poets, in particular, are allowed far more licence with the language, and so cannot provide straightforward models for composition (i v 11; cf. xii x 14). If reliable, the criticism reveals how anxious grammarians were to wield their authority over the authors whose usage they judged (for an example of what Quintilian means, see Pompeius (*G.L.* v) 283.37f.).

Failure to use words in their 'proper' sense constituted another potential defect: tropes (acceptable) would have to be distinguished from catachrestic usages (unacceptable: e.g. Quintilian viii vi 34ff.). Ancient grammarians accordingly constructed a genre, or sub-genre, specifically 'On distinctions between words', *de differentiis verborum*: basically, lists of words, of similar form, having different meanings which had to be kept distinct, there being ample evidence from texts in the *differentiae verborum* genre that word use was not being described, but, rather, prescribed, ignoring, in many cases, lexical changes in ordinary language.[64]

So, from the range of theoretical views available, one area of broad consensus does emerge: that different criteria operate in different (con)-texts, according to the type of text, the status of its author, and the date of its composition (especially important for Latin literature, with its relatively recent coming-of-age). Prose and poetry constituted the main dichotomy, but oratory too was distinctively subject to the demands of audience acceptability, and so to those of usage and euphony. And it is vital for understanding the role of grammar teaching in ancient education that we appreciate that children would be introduced, admittedly in a simplified and not wholly systematic way, to this array of standards and the principles underlying them. The use of literary texts as models for good Latin or Greek caused grave pedagogic difficulties in practice; and their confused and confusing theoretical status can be inferred from the commentaries standardly employed. What is important here is that language, particularly the language of the canon and the associated standard dialects, was assumed to be open to judgement by experts – by the grammarians, that is, the 'rulers [*moderatoribus*] of

---

[64] For example, §83 in Uhlfelder's selection (M. L. Uhlfelder, *De proprietate sermonum vel rerum (Papers and Monographs of the American Academy in Rome*, vol. 15 (1954)), distinguishes *externus* 'external' from *hesternus* 'yesterday's' and adds: 'for many ignorant people say *externa dies* [literally "external day", instead of *hesterna dies*, "yesterday"], which is not allowed'.

each of the two tongues' (Priscian *inst. gr., pr. (G.L.* II) 2.7). And grammatical expertise consisted precisely in constructing and defending the nice, and normative, balance between strict regularity, in all its manifestations, and permissible variation. Children would already have learned rules for the writing and pronunciation of letters and for their formation into syllables (of immense importance for correct scansion of poetry). Now, under the grammarian, they would learn both rules (in a fairly straighforward sense) for word-formation, the inflectional paradigms, which were subject to the laws of analogy, and, just as important, the far more complex and subtle norms which control the use of language, in all its richness and diversity, grounded on the basic *differentiae* of the nature and status of the text. In class, when reading a text, a standard procedure which the child saw repeated, and had to master himself, was identification of passages where the appropriate questions would be: is this usage barbaric (solecistic, catachrestic), or not? and then: how do I decide? what authority do I appeal to here: ideal patterns of inflection in a language, or use of that language, whether the author's usage or that of his genre or his age?

Kaster has characterised grammar as 'at once niggling and necessary',[65] and cites Valerius Probus' disgust[66] at 'those rotten rules [*finitiones*] and cesspits of grammar' (Aulus Gellius *noct. att.* XIII ii 1). In similar vein, Quintilian (I v 14) expresses contempt for the grammarians who insist that of two variant verb forms one *must* be correct: either *adsentio* 'assent' is formed by *detractio* from *adsentior*, or the latter is formed from the former by *adiectio*. His objection is to the grammarians' pedantic obsession with the construction of precise rules comprehensively governing all aspects of word formation, as well as other features of language, such as prosody or orthography.[67] But this is only half the story of rules in ancient grammatical education. What is being learned is not only the rules governing form, function, meaning, and so on, but also the *merits* of regularity – since it is rules which allow language to be categorised, classified, mastered as the grammarian masters it; and, furthermore, one learns the principle that there are norms governing the acceptable use of variants: variants in spelling, pronunciation, inflectional form, derivation, meaning, syntax. Acceptability in such

---

[65] Kaster, *Guardians*, p. 54.   [66] On Probus, see Booth, 'Education', n. 39.
[67] He has more patience with a prosodic innovation of 'certain learned men, and some grammarians too', which, if the new usage (*consuetudo*) prevails, will oust the 'old law' (*uetus lex*) (§§25ff.).

cases is itself regulated, usually by factors we moderns would class as quite independent of 'the language': the decision is made by appeal to 'permissive norms', the age or authority of the text, or to the status of its creator.[68] 'Good' authors must, as a rule, take precedence, even if grammarians could criticise Thucydides, Plato, Demosthenes (Sextus Empiricus *M.* 1 98), or Cicero (Aulus Gellius *noct. att.* XVII 1), and even if Kaster is right to emphasise the authority to which grammarians laid claim by such judgements.[69] But the basic distinction between, or rather hierarchy of, types of text of different status remains unchallenged. The grammarian's role in exposing children to a normative hierarchy may help explain the close association of 'good' grammarians with the virtue of *uerecundia*, 'modesty': precisely the capacity to know your place in a hierarchy, and act accordingly.[70] Teaching the text, ancient style, is grounded in the implicit assumption that infringements of regularity are allowed, but only for those users whose status – whose authority, that is – is so great that they can be allowed certain limited, circum-scribed, and therefore acceptable, transgressions of the law.

This 'truth' is as pervasive, as invisible, and as significant, as the 'fact' all students of rhetoric would have learned, that words and their complexes have detachable, communicable 'contents', to be tricked out in the most suitable verbal dress (as at Quintilian VIII *pr.* 15, 32).[71] Similarly, the programme of constructing the *de differentiis verborum* was possible only on the premise that a more or less fixed stock of words do, or should, have one or more sharply demarcated signification(s). These assumptions (comparable to the two components of Roy Harris' 'lan-guage myth'[72]) were never made explicit, let alone justified. They are vital, nonetheless, to understanding ancient stylistics. In a similar way, the hierarchy of texts and users, implicit in the way linguistic correct-ness was taught, is essential for understanding the nature and purpose of ancient élite education.

[68] It may seem strange to ignore the distinction, vital to modern linguistics, between 'system' and 'text', but that distinction was unknown to ancient grammar. Instead, a stylistic distinction was drawn amongst the excellences, and thus the properties, of a single thing, viz., discourse or language, the 'virtue' of most relevance to grammar being (as we have seen) purity or correct-ness, as determined by several rival criteria; of these, analogy appeals to properties of word-forms, but that is not the same as appealing to properties of a linguistic system. For a defence of this view, see Atherton, 'WEGK?', p. 251.

[69] E.g. *Guardians*, p. 183.   [70] As argued by Kaster, *Guardians*, pp. 60–2.

[71] See further D. A. Russell, *Criticism in Antiquity* (London, 1981), p. 4; and cf. Atherton, 'Apollonius Dyscolus'.

[72] The 'telementational' and 'deterministic' fallacies: R. Harris, *The Language Myth* (London, 1981), p. 9.

Learning the language(s) of a community was and is a fundamental and necessary part of a child's socialisation within that community. Some linguists today see their task as reconstructing whatever it is that children acquire in the course of this learning process, something conceived of as (roughly speaking) a set of rules generating the sentences of a language. In contrast, the rules constructed by ancient grammarians and passed on, in simplified form, to the children they taught bear no such conceptual relation to native-speaker knowledge, which was denied any (direct) role in the grammarians' professional activities; and the socialisation which this sort of 'language learning' helped constitute is not to be seen as the informal, relatively painless, universal experience to which all children are exposed in human societies. But these differences only make more plausible the existence of a broad parallel between exposure to the sorts of sophisticated and complex rule- and norm-governed uses of language which dominated public discourse, and acquisition of social habits relating to the role of laws and norms in Greco-Roman society under the late Republic and especially the Empire.

I do not want to suggest that the later standard practice amongst the élite of instruction in a literary canon and associated reading and compositional skills is to be contrasted with an earlier, 'pure', oral culture. An early example of a perceived similarity between rule-following in the linguistic sphere and law-abidingness generally can be found in Plato's *Protagoras*, and here basic literacy instruction is already being used alongside language 'teaching' by native speakers as a parallel for the inculcation of laws and social norms. Thus the sophist is made to compare the way children are given letters to copy, drawn for them by their teachers, with the provision of laws for citizens as models of good conduct (326c6ff.).[73] Similarly, the handing on of basic ethical norms is presented as comparable to the way members of a society instruct childen in their first language (327e1ff.). Whatever the historical evidence may be about the actual spread of literacy in classical Greece, the relevant point here is the assumption that some, perhaps rudimentary, level of literacy will be one of the things citizens typically have in common. Even if this assumption is a deliberately flattering one, and even if the sophist's association of formal literacy instruction with learning one's

---

[73] The exact relation beween the exemplars and the child's copies of them has been disputed: see Quintilian's description of the method, I i 27, and cf. E. G. Turner, 'Athenians Learn to Write: Plato *Protagoras* 326d', *BICS* 12 (1965), 67–9.

first language is problematic and intended to be felt as such, these passages at least indicate not merely the status attached to the ability to read and write, but also some familiarity with the rule-governed nature of this sort of activity.

My contention is rather that mastering the intricacies of correct written and spoken Greek or Latin is to be seen as practice for life under social and political conditions essentially very different from those prevalent in the Athens of the 5th- or 4th-century BCE: a life in which the authority vested in rules and norms, in laws and conventions, could always be subordinated to the authority of privileged groups or individuals, whose 'infringements' may turn out to be, quite precisely, marks of a superiority itself sanctioned by higher norms. Thus 'partial' social norms, those privileging certain 'parts' of society, would be introduced to children in the guise of the partial linguistic norms which both favour certain users, texts, or dialects, and help identify the élite whose language, itself in part the product of literary discourse, has to be mastered. Not all users of language share the same status: some are privileged to extend or change the forms, meanings, and sounds of words or their combinations. A boy would be told, time and time again, that this or that word, word-form, construction, or sound was as a rule 'not correct', yet 'correct' in this or that context: the (broadly) educative power of that information was far greater than this simple description might suggest.

Grammarians and those they educated thus moved from the 'natural' state, not of the languageless, but of those whose linguistic activities are intrinsically flawed and irregular. They progressed to control both of the 'nature' of language, that is, its internal regularities, formal, semantic, and so on, and also of the multiform, diverse departures from rules which were legitimised by the authority of literary status, age, or 'good' usage, and classified by the grammarian's expertise. (The perilously conventional status of the orthographic rules invoked by Plato's Protagoras – arguably another nail in the coffin which Plato is busy building for sophistic pretensions – is thus not shared by the 'natural' patterns of inflection and derivation.) What has been changed in children thus taught is not merely their linguistic habits, but their understanding of the role of norms and the rules they support in determining what is and is not correct, and why.

It is therefore wholly unsurprising that children were subject to the grammarian's authority in a straightforward physical sense, as a slave or an animal might be subject to a master, as well as in the pedagogic sense I have been describing. For some considerable portion of their childhood, and perhaps of their adolescence too, correct speech would have been the product, not of immanent norms, unreflectingly determining acceptable linguistic performance, but of *prescriptions*. These prescribed norms and associated rules were not only unfamiliar, but also, at least at first, unjustified, even unintelligible, and imposed, typically, by unpopular and socially inferior adults with everything to lose from their pupils' failure. In these circumstances the use of force by teachers makes perfect sense. On top of gargantuan amounts of rote-learning of difficult and obscure texts, children were being forced – literally – to alter their old speech habits with little or nothing by way of immediate reward: certainly nothing as attractive as the promise of self-expression and communication with one's fellows which so powerfully motivates primary language learning. The long-term rewards, visible to parents and teachers, were real enough, but only the precocious or the truly gifted could hope to share their elders' vision; and, in any case, it was oratory, not literature, which held the real prizes, as Lucian's Paideia implies (*The dream, or Lucian's career*, 9–12).

Somehow children had to move from mere, enforced, conformity to rule, to genuine, 'exclusionary', rule-following, where citing the relevant rule excludes all other justifications for following it. In much of classical antiquity, learning the standard dialects constituted both a part of, and a rehearsal for, the broader social learning processes essential to children's absorption into adult life. The grammarian's true lesson was applicable far outside the sphere of language: all infringements of rules are classifiable; some of them are permissible; others are not, and appeals to higher authority are justified only when the infringements belong to one or other of the accepted groupings. These groupings and their authority are *given*, beyond questioning or appeal, at least by children.[74]

---

[74] Of course, educated *adults* could, and did, challenge the grammarians' authority: I refer not so much to professional disputes about the weight to be assigned to different norms, whether generally or in particular cases, as to questioning of the assumption that grammarians could or should function as 'guardians of language'. Complaints were directed at the uselessness of their activities (e.g. Sextus *M.* 1; Augustine *doct. christ.* II xiii 19), as well as their lack of intellectual rigour (e.g. Quintilian 1 iv 5ff.) or gentlemanly cultivation (Aulus Gellius *noct. att.* xv ix 6ff.). By continuing to use, and require the use of, the standard dialects of Greek and Latin, the élite of course made it possible for grammarians to issue and apply linguistic norms: this will not, however, explain why they alone took that role – that is, why social norms gave grammarians a virtual monopoly on issuing explicit linguistic norms. In particular, it remains unclear why public institutional regulation (by academies or comparable bodies) played no part in preserving and propagating correct language. The (general) absence of public regulation of literacy, grammar, and rhetoric teaching and teachers has already been remarked on (n. 28). The emergence of linguistic academies has been plausibly linked historically with the rise of nation-states: perhaps these same political and social forces can explain the development of publicly funded and regulated school systems.

And (the real point) this *is* authority, not power: unlike the beast or slave, the child will, it is assumed, come to appreciate the value and rightness of the system under which he lives.

The aim was to make of certain privileged children expert users of language, as speakers and writers, composers and interpreters. Children stand halfway between animals and adults, and must be treated in a way which combines the methods of instruction appropriate to both these groups – physical force, gentle encouragement, threats and rewards – but never rational persuasion, the supreme goal of élite education, and the reserve of adults alone. The subtle hierarchy of linguistic authority thus emerges as a superb preparation for the complex hierarchies of social authority under which the child would eventually exercise the *artes liberales* he had so painfully acquired. Famously, Tiberius was advised that he could grant citizenship to people, but not to words (Suet. *gr.* XXII). The grammarian, in contrast, had the power to construct the norms which legitimised, or outlawed, words and uses of them, as well as to grant children a passport to élite status.

CHAPTER 11

A good man skilled in politics: Quintilian's political theory

Teresa Morgan

There are, broadly speaking, two ways of reading Quintilian. One can see him as a type of likeable pedagogue: conscientious and agreeable; perhaps, among the major writers of the first century, not quite first class. This approach is favoured by historians of education and educationalists, some of whom have praised him as 'doubtless the ideal schoolmaster . . .',[1] dwelling on his 'native good sense',[2] his 'prevailing sanity',[3] even his 'simple sincere soul'.[4] Alternatively, one can mine him for the information he contains rather than the opinions he expresses. This method has a rather different history, being preferred by a long line of distinguished historians of rhetoric and literary theory.

If the first is largely a diversion, in the double sense that it at once entertains and distracts us from more serious considerations, the second approach is the measure of Quintilian's status as a source for ancient education and particularly for rhetoric. The *Institutio Oratoria* or 'Education of the Orator' is the longest and most detailed educational work to survive from the classical world. In twelve books it takes a learner through every stage of the training of an orator, incorporating on the way a long and detailed rhetorical handbook which matches in importance anything to survive elsewhere in Greek or Latin. If anything, though, Quintilian's descriptions of the pre-rhetorical stages of education are even more to be treasured than the later material. They provide the fullest systematic description we have of the content and organisation of *enkyklios paideia*, the 'common' or 'general' (though not encyclopaedic) education which is found throughout the Hellenistic and Roman worlds and which is attested by a number of Greek and Latin authors and

[1] E. C. Reinke, 'Quintilian Lighted the Way', *Classical Bulletin*, 51 (1975), 65–71.
[2] H. J. Rose, *Handbook of Latin Literature* (London, 1949), 400.
[3] J. W. Duff, *A Literary History of Rome in the Silver Age* (New York, 1930), 407.
[4] C. E. Bennett, 'An Ancient Schoolmaster's Message to Present-Day Teachers', *Classical Journal*, 4 (1909), 149–64.

hundreds of papyri and other documents. The components of this general education included learning to read, write and calculate, reading literature, and learning grammar, arithmetic and geometry, rhetoric, astronomy, music and philosophy.[5] The first seven subjects, which were taught wherever literacy existed, seem to have gone together and to have been taught in a regular order and with a regular repertoire of texts and exercises. The last four were alternatives of which any or all might be studied according to the taste and opportunities of the pupil or his elders or teachers. That we can be fairly sure both that the order and content of these subjects was highly standardised and that standardisation persisted right across literate society is in large measure due to the fact that we have the prescriptions of Quintilian to compare with the more fragmentary accounts of other authors and the evidence of the papyri.

If there is a snag in all this, it is that the 'mining' approach to the *Institutio* has been so successful that it has distracted attention from the overall structure of the work. In particular it has tended to obscure the obvious but important fact that the *Institutio* presents itself as a work of educational theory, not merely as a handbook of rhetoric or a sourcebook of literary criticism. The distinction is substantial. If the *Institutio* were a rhetorical handbook we should not expect it to discuss what rhetoric is for, whether it is a good thing or what its putative product is equipped to do with his life.[6] But if it is a work of educational theory, then it stands in a different tradition in ancient literature and such questions are highly relevant.[7]

In the ancient world educational theory regularly occurred in the context of political theory.[8] Education, whether of an orator, a philosopher,

---

[5] H.-I. Marrou, *Histoire de l'Education dans l'Antiquité*, 6th edn. (Paris, 1965), 266ff., 356ff.; T. J. Morgan, *Frames of Mind: Literate Education in the Hellenistic and Roman Worlds* (Cambridge University PhD thesis, 1995), ch. 1.

[6] The masculine pronoun is used throughout: Quintilian makes no indication that he expects women to be taught like this.

[7] This distinction is inevitably not hard and fast, but there is a distinction between technical works such as *Peri Hypsous* (*On the Sublime*), the *Progymnasmata* and the *Techne Grammatike* and writers such as Plato, Aristotle, Isocrates, Cicero, and Tacitus who discuss wider issues as well.

[8] So, for instance, in Plato, *Republic* and *Laws*, Aristotle, *Politics*, Isocrates, *Panegyric*, Xenophon, *Cyropaedia*, Ps.-Aristotle, *Rhetorica ad Alexandrum*, Zeno, *Republic* (and discussion in M. Schofield, *The Stoic Idea of the City* (Cambridge, 1992)), Diogenes, *On Piety* (and discussion in E. Goodenough, 'The Political Philosophy of Hellenistic Kingship.' Yale Classical Studies, 1 (1928) 55–102), Nicolaus, *Life of Augustus*, Philo, *On Mating with the Preliminary Studies, et passim*, Plutarch, *On How the Young Man Should Listen to Poetry, On Listening to Lectures*, Cicero, *Republic, Orator, On Oratory*. See also G. J. D. Aalders, *Political Thought in Hellenistic Times*, (Amsterdam, 1975); N. Wood, *Cicero's Social and Political Thought* (Berkeley, 1988).

a general, or a smith, was examined in its social and political context on the understanding that the function of education was to produce people suited to bring about or maintain whatever political organisation the author proposed for a particular state. From the beginning of the *Institutio* Quintilian places himself unambiguously in this tradition. He says that for a long time he refused to write about the art of speaking, knowing that the most distinguished authors in both Latin and Greek had dealt with it. There are good reasons not to suppose that he meant the writers of rhetorical handbooks by the phrase 'the most brilliant authors in both languages.[9] The natural assumption should be that he means Cicero in Latin and Plato, Aristotle and Isocrates in Greek. His references throughout the work bear this out: he cites Cicero constantly and Plato more often than any other prose writer apart from Cicero; his citations of Aristotle and Isocrates are only just behind those of Plato, numerically.[10] He therefore aligns himself from the start with a group of authors all of whom discuss rhetoric alongside or as part of philosophy, and for whom the relationship between rhetoric and politics was a central concern.

Since Quintilian identifies the *Institutio* as a work about education, rather than a rhetorical handbook or anything else, we should therefore ask what political theory underlies it, or at least we should consider whether such a question can reasonably be asked of it. My aim in what follows is a limited one: to try to show that the question of the political context and purpose of education is one which we can properly put to Quintilian, and that he has an answer which is both cogent and original.

From what we know of Quintilian's career it should not surprise us that he wrote as he did. He had flourished in Rome (and earlier in Spain) as an orator and teacher under every emperor from Nero to Domitian.[11] Vespasian gave him a state salary in 71 CE for teaching rhetoric.[12] Domitian awarded him consular insignia in 94/5, a rare honour for a man who was neither a soldier nor a senator. At the time of writing the *Institutio* he was tutor to Domitian's great-nephews and heirs.[13] He was prominent, successful and close to the imperial court.

[9] *auctores utriusque linguae clarissimos*, 1 pr. 1.
[10] M. Odgers, 'Quintilian's use of earlier literature', *Classical Philology*, 28 (1933), 182–8.
[11] Juvenal *Sat.* 7. 188–9; Martial *Ep.* 2.90; G. A. Kennedy, *Quintilian* (New York, 1969), 15–30; W. C. McDermott, 'Quintilian and Domitian', *Athenaeum*, 57 (1979), 9–26.
[12] M. Woodside, 'Vespasian's Patronage of Education', *TAPA*, 73 (1942), 123–9.
[13] S. Giet, 'Quintilien et les jeunes Flaviens', *Revue des Sciences Religieuses*, 32 (1958), 321–34; 33 (1959), 1–17; S. J. Simon, 'Domitian, Patron of Letters', *CB*, 51 (1975), 58–9.

We should expect him to be politically informed and we should not be surprised to find politics in his work.

And once we begin to look for it, it is not hard to see. In the four books which frame the work (two at each end), and scattered throughout the others, Quintilian has a good deal to say about the nature and expectations of the ideal orator whom he aims to create and the sort of world in which he expects him to live. The orator's expectations are clear: he is educated to rule. If we look closely at the passages in which his political activities are described, however, we find that the orator's world is a rather curious one. It is not quite the Rome of Quintilian's own day. Neither is it the political landscape of earlier theorists like Cicero, though it owes something to them. It is Quintilian's own vision of how Roman society might be if his educational programme were carried out.

A GOOD MAN SKILLED IN SPEAKING

The nature of the orator's power and the qualities which equip him to exercise it are summed up in the definition of the orator borrowed by Quintilian from the elder Cato, alluded to throughout the *Institutio* and quoted repeatedly in its culminating book: 'a good man, skilled in speaking'.[14] Quintilian's project is to show that the orator can be neither good nor skilled without education and it is worth examining in some detail how he establishes the connection.

The good man, in Quintilian's analysis, is the product of education acting on nature.[15] In books one and two he claims that all human beings have an inherent tendency to virtue. Virtue, in his view, is natural and nature virtuous,[16] a double principle which is put forward as a statement of faith. But virtue is not the product of nature unaided; it requires education to bring it to fruition.[17] 'Virtue, though it uses some natural impulses, must be perfected by learning . . . Will he who does not know what abstinence is, be abstinent? Will he be brave, who has not overcome the fear of pain, death and superstition by reason? . . . What a small thing they think [virtue] is, if they think it comes so easily! But

---

[14] *Vir bonus dicendi peritus*, 12.1.1, 31, 44; 12.2.1; 12.11.19; cf. 1 pr. 9; 12.1.27; Seneca the Elder, *Contr.* 1 pr. 9.

[15] A commonplace in educational theory: cf. Isoc. *Soph.* 10, 17; Plato *Phaedr.* 276d–7a; Protagoras DK 80B3; Ps.-Plutarch *De lib. educ.* 4a–c.

[16] 1.12.19: *dedit . . . hoc providentia hominibus munus, ut honesta magis iuvarent*; 12.1.1–2; 12.2.1.

[17] 1.1.1–2; 2.19.1–3; 10.3.2.

I pass over this, because I believe that no-one who has even tasted education, as they say, could doubt it . . .'[18]

All the disciplines of *enkyklios paideia* are described as contributing not only to the pupil's intellectual development but also, both individually and cumulatively, to the development of virtue. Quintilian recommends the teacher of letters to set his pupil to copy gnomic sayings from literature on the grounds that, 'the memory of them will follow him into old age and, because it has been impressed on his mind when raw, will inform his morals'.[19] Reading the Greek and Latin authors is a highly complex process with many functions, but Quintilian repeatedly emphasises it as a source of ethical precepts, role models and attitudes to life.[20] Grammar is important because the speaker's authority, including his moral authority, is linked with his linguistic accuracy.[21] Geometry and astronomy are not only practically useful; they also lead one to understand the world: 'When the calculations [of geometry] show us the regular and ordained courses of the stars, we learn that nothing [in the universe] is random or accidental . . .'[22] Ethics and dialectic aid the development of character and present the pupil with rational justifications for his moral beliefs.[23] Physics illustrates the correspondence between providence and the orator: 'If the world is governed by providence, the state should certainly be run by good men'.[24]

The constituents of education act on the pupil's inherent tendency to virtue to produce a good man. What is more, Quintilian asserts that good and bad cannot coexist in the same person, which means that the well-educated man will be not just good but wholly good.[25] This condition of total virtue will prove essential to the political status of the orator.

The second half of Cato's definition, skill in speaking, has an even more complex exegesis. Like virtue it is the result of nature and education acting together and is both a natural virtue and an acquirable art. The first quality on which it depends is reason. Quintilian claims that reason is native to most men, though not quite all: 'Precepts and methods are useless unless nature helps. These writings will be no more use to him who is lacking in ability than writings on agriculture are

---

[18] 12.2.1–4. [19] 1.1.36; cf. 1.8.6–7.
[20] 1.8.67; 10.1.86ff. A longstanding concern of Greek literary education: cf. Plato *Rp.* 376dff. (against); Plutarch *Quomodo adulescens, passim* (in favour).
[21] 1.4.1–1.7.35; 1.5.1; 1.6.1ff. For full discussion see Morgan *Frames of Mind* ch. 2.
[22] 1.10.34, 46; probably from Plato; on the reception of this idea from Plato to the second century CE see L. Taub, *Ptolemy's Universe* (Chicago, 1993), 135–53.
[23] 12.2.10–20. On music see 1.10.9–15. [24] 12.2.20–1. [25] 12.1.4.

to barren soil'.[26] Reason is one of the things which in general distinguish men from animals (and also from women, barbarians and slaves). '[Reason] is natural to men, as birds are born to fly, horses to run and wild beasts to be savage; our native agility of mind and wisdom are such that our minds are believed to derive from heaven'.[27] If reason is natural, however, it must be a virtue, because nature in general is 'a mother, not a stepmother',[28] and would not give men gifts which lead to evil.[29] If reason is a virtue, then according to Quintilian's theory of virtue it needs education to perfect it.

The second precondition of skill in speaking is the ability to speak at all. This ability too, Quintilian claims, is natural to men and distinguishes them from animals. By that token speech is also a virtue and, as a virtue, dependent on education to bring it to fruition.[30] Quintilian goes on to claim that rhetoric is a form of speech and that the ability to speak *well* (that is, rhetorically) is natural to some people.[31] If that is the case then rhetoric too must be a virtue and also dependent on education for its fulfilment.

The importance of this move is that skill in speaking, which forms half of Cato's definition of the orator, is now seen to be part of the other half, the good man. They go together: the skilled speaker is bound to be a good man and *vice versa*.[32] And both are seen to depend on education for their fulfilment. Quintilian's status as an educationalist will now depend on his ability to devise a more complete and effective education in speaking and virtue than anyone else, and in the prologue to book one he sets out to do just that. He criticises other rhetoricians for ignoring the early stages of education, comparing them to architects who are so concerned with the showy exterior of a building that they neglect the foundations.[33] He, in contrast, holds that, 'nothing without which it would be impossible to be called an orator, is irrelevant to the art of oratory, nor can one reach the summit of anything without passing through its earlier stages . . .'[34] The 'earlier stages' take up most of the rest of the twelve books and include the whole of rhetorical theory.

---

[26] 1 pr. 26. Quintilian is equivocating here, conflating the fundamental human quality of reason with the ability *to* reason in a specifically rhetorical way. He is also referring to the 'nature/nurture' debate endemic in philosophy, rhetoric and education theory since the fifth century BCE. His image leaves open the interesting question whether clods of earth are expected to read agricultural treatises or, more to the point, whether pupils are ever expected to read the *Institutio*. The work begins as if addressed to a teacher but by the end it seems to address the pupil directly.

[27] 1.1.1; 2.16.12–5.   [28] 12.1.2.   [29] 12.1.2.   [30] 2.20.6–7, 9.   [31] 2.19.1–3, 20.9–10.

[32] Implied at 2.20.1ff; 12.1.3ff.   [33] 1 pr. 4.   [34] 1 pr. 5.

Quintilian's contribution to the history of rhetoric has received its share of attention elsewhere.[35] The only point I want to make here is that the connection he makes between skilled speech and virtue is central to his political theory, and if we examine the activities of the finished orator it becomes clear why.

ROME RECONSTITUTED

The great majority of descriptions of the orator in the *Institutio* show him engaging in politics, in a state ruled above all by the word and institutions in which words are the medium of government. He is by definition a political animal[36] who takes on all manner of political offices[37] and every duty of a good citizen:[38] 'the man who is a true citizen and fitted to administer both public and private business, the man who can rule cities with his counsels, give them a foundation with his laws and regulate them with his judgements, is indeed none other than the orator'.[39] The orator is expected to 'defend his friends, rule the senate and the people by his advice and lead an army wherever he wants it to go . . .'[40] He directs 'the debates of the senate and leads the foolish people to better things. . . .'[41] He must be prepared to speak in 'public meetings and all councils'.[42]

When he is not directing the senate or the people the orator is often to be found in the lawcourts. 'The laws themselves would be useless if they were not reinforced by the voice of a suitable authority . . . the orator will not allow the complaints of allies nor the death of a friend or neighbour nor conspiracies against the state to go unpunished – not because he enjoys punishing the guilty but because he desires to correct vice and improve morals . . .'[43] Forensic oratory is one of the

---

[35] Especially G. Boissier, 'The Schools of Declamation at Rome', in *Tacitus and Other Roman Studies* (London, 1906), 163–94; D. L. Clark, 'Imitation: Theory and Practice in Roman Rhetoric', *Quarterly Journal of Speech*, 37 (1951), 11–22; *Rhetoric in Graeco-Roman Education*, (New York, 1957); M. L. Clarke, *Rhetoric at Rome* (London, 1953), 109ff.; J. Cousin, *Etudes sur Quintilien*, (Paris, 1936); *Recherches sur Quintilien*, (Paris, 1975); G. A. Kennedy, 'An Estimate of Quintilian', *American Journal of Philology*, 83 (1962), 130–46; *The Art of Rhetoric in the Roman World* (Princeton, 1972), 487ff.; E. P. Parks, *Roman Rhetorical Schools as a Preparation for the Courts under the Early Empire*, *Johns Hopkins University Studies*, 63.2 (Baltimore, 1945), *passim*; O Seel, *Quintilian – oder die Kunst des Redens und Schweigens* (Stuttgart, 1977); M. Winterbottom, 'Quintilian and the *vir bonus*', *JRS*, 54 (1964), 90–7; *Problems in Quintilian* BICS suppl. 25 (1970); 'Quintilian and Rhetoric', in T. A. Dorey ed. *Empire and Aftermath: Silver Latin II* (London, 1975), 79–97.
[36] *Vir civilis* 12.2.21.　　[37] *Civilibus officiis* 12.2.6.　　[38] *Omni . . . officio boni civis* 12.11.1.
[39] 1 pr. 10.　　[40] 2.16.19; 2.16.19; 12.9.13.　　[41] 12.1.26–8; 2.20.8.
[42] 2.27.8, again reflecting a long tradition of debate about the function of rhetoric in public life.
[43] 12.7.1–7, 11.1; 2.4.33–4, 16.19, 17.23ff., 20.8ff.

many means by which the orator makes and maintains friends and clients, as well as doing justice and keeping order in the state.[44]

At first sight there is nothing very remarkable about all this: it is all the sort of behaviour which typifies Roman public life. But on closer inspection it proves to be an odd mixture of activities, some of which we associate with the Republic and others with the Principate. Quintilian's language of oratorical power and influence is strikingly regal, bringing to mind the politics of his own day. The orator is described repeatedly as ruling (*regere*) both the senate and the people and several passages make clear how sharp the imbalance of power between orator and audience is conceived to be. Quintilian quotes with approval, for instance, a description in Virgil's *Aeneid* (1 151ff.) of a statesman quelling a riot which ends: 'He *controls* their minds with his words and soothes their breasts'.[45] On the other hand, explicit references to the emperor and imperial forms of government are very rare. The emperor is addressed honorifically in prefaces but never referred to in any functional capacity.[46] There are no references to the private councils or the groups of 'friends of the emperor' whose informal influence was so important in the making of imperial policy, nor to the imperial freedmen who held so many administrative positions, to the fury of aristocratic families, nor to the imperial system of appointments.[47] Quintilian writes as though government were carried out mainly by means of the spoken word, which we associate rather with the republican than the imperial administration.

If he does not give us a straightforward account of politics under the Principate, however, neither does Quintilian present the reader with a systematic picture of the Republic. Public meetings, which were abolished after the death of the emperor Augustus in 14 CE, are alluded to as though they were still a functional element of government. On the other hand, the major magistracies, the motor of the republican administration, are never mentioned and Quintilian is vague about the

---

[44] 2.16.19; R. Saller, 'Patronage and friendship in early imperial Rome', in A. Wallace-Hadrill ed. *Patronage in Ancient Society* (London, 1989), 49–62.
[45] 12.1.27; 10.1.16ff. (my italics). In passages like these Quintilian's language recalls that of earlier writers describing the emperor's absolute power – notably Seneca in *De Clementia* but also Virgil and Horace. M. Griffin, *Seneca: A Philosopher in Politics* (Oxford, 1976), 141ff.; G. Brugnoli, 'Quintiliano, Seneca e il *De causis corruptae eloquentiae*', *Orpheus*, 6 (1959), 29–41.
[46] Except as a poet (10.1.91).
[47] F. Millar, *The Emperor in the Roman World* (London, 1977), chs. 3, 6; J. A. Crook, *Consilium Principis* (Cambridge, 1955), chs. 2–3, 48ff.; K. Hopkins, *Death and Renewal* (Cambridge, 1983), ch. 3.

everyday details of his orator's political life. And he makes very few references to anything outside the internal government of the city state – which, given Rome's long history of power abroad, is equally surprising whether he has a republican or an imperial *scena* in mind.

The picture is surely intended to represent Rome, or a city modelled on Rome. We could explain its inconsistencies by assuming that Quintilian was stupid or escapist – that he did not notice the problems or deliberately blurred his account to avoid saying anything provocative. It would be hasty, however, to dismiss him so lightly. He had prospered under a string of emperors; he was a survivor and a success; it is implausible that he was either politically naive or unintelligent. Since he was involved with the imperial household anything he published was likely to be politically visible and might have been regarded as significant, so it is unlikely that he wrote in a spirit of irresponsibility or naïveté. Before we jump to any such pessimistic conclusion there are other possibilities to explore.

Quintilian was writing at a time of much discussion about the purpose and future of oratory under the Principate. Some writers claimed a role for public, political speech even under a monarchy; others argued that where power was invested in one man, debate was meaningless and oratory was nothing if not the vehicle of debate.[48] The obvious question, therefore, is whether Quintilian can be interpreted as an apologist for either of these positions, or, more to the point, the political interests they represented, namely the emperor and his senatorial adversaries. The idea that he is acting as an apologist for the emperor is superficially attractive, given his professional position and his use of the vocabulary of political control, but the picture does not fit well enough to be convincing. For one thing, Quintilian describes the orator doing a great many things which Domitian in practice did rarely or not at all, like attending the lawcourts and the senate, addressing public meetings and leading the army.[49] To have been seen to describe the ideal emperor doing things which the emperor in practice did not do would surely have been to invite trouble. Worse, Quintilian makes very little

---

[48] Cf. Tacitus *Dialogus*; [Longinus] *On Sublimity* 44.1ff.; Seneca the Elder *Contr.* 1 pr. 6ff.; Seneca the Younger *Panegyricus*, *De Ira*; F. Ahl, 'The Art of Safe Criticism in Greece and Rome', *AJP*, 105 (1984), 174–208; S. Bartsch, *Actors in the Audience: Theatricality and Double-Speak from Nero to Hadrian* (Cambridge, MA, and London, 1994), chs. 4–5.

[49] B. Jones, 'Domitian's Attitude to the Senate', *AJP*, 94 (1973), 79–91; *The Emperor Domitian* (London, 1992), chs. 8–9; P. M. Rogers. 'Domitian and the Finances of State', *Historia*, 33 (1984), 60–78; cf. R. Syme, 'Domitian: the last years', *Chiron* 13 (1983), 121–46.

of the one area in which Domitian did intervene often and successfully: the administration of provinces.[50] To have refused to give the emperor credit for what he did do would have been dangerously to compound the folly of praising him for things he did not do. Worst of all, if the perfect orator were synonymous with the emperor, Quintilian would be placing himself in the position of kingmaker, since he insists throughout the work that the orator can only be created by means of his educational curriculum. That would have been dangerous enough had he been teaching only Domitian's great-nephews, but he had also taught many of the wider Roman elite (including we know not how many potential claimants to the purple) and in the *Institutio* itself he recommends his curriculum to his own children and the son of the dedicatee. He could not have done so if the perfect orator of his prescriptions had been intended to be identified solely with the emperor.

If he is not himself the emperor, neither does Quintilian's orator apparently live under an emperor. In this connection one aspect of Quintilian's rhetorical analysis has received less attention than it deserves: the fact that he has very little to say about epideictic oratory in general and panegyric in particular. Panegyric forms no part of his orator's public or political duties, in stark contrast with the political realities of his own day in which, in the form of the public address to the emperor, it was perhaps the only remaining form of oratory with direct access to the hub of power.[51] The *Institutio* treats epideictic at any length only in one chapter of book three, and Quintilian's language in that passage invites a brief comment. He observes that Aristotle and Theophrastus divorce epideictic from the business side of rhetoric, but that Romans do use epideictic for political purposes – in funeral orations, in the courts and in elections.[52] In addition, of course, they use it for show, including for panegyrics of gods and great men of the past – and, startlingly, animals and inanimate objects.[53] Only at the very end of the passage does he make the briefest acknowledgement that we sometimes praise individuals during their lifetimes, and he immediately

[50] B. M. Levick, 'Domitian and the Provinces', *Latomus*, 41 (1982), 50–73; H. W. Pleket, 'Domitian, the Senate and the Provinces', *Mnemosyne*, 4a ser. 14 (1961), 296–315.
[51] Though not the only form of literature with access to the emperor; cf. Kennedy, *Art of Rhetoric*, 428ff.; S. MacCormack, 'Latin prose panegyrics', in T. Dorey ed. *Empire and Aftermath*, 143–205; F. Millar *Emperor*, 341ff., 366ff., 368ff., 497ff.; C. E. Nixon and B. S. Rodgers, *In Praise of Later Roman Emperors* (Berkeley, 1994), 1–35; J. Sullivan, *Literature and Politics in the Age of Nero*, (London, 1985).
[52] 3.7.1; 3.7.2–3; Arist. *Rhet.* 1358b2ff. cf. W. Grimaldi, *Aristotle, Rhetoric I: A Commentary* (New York, 1980), *ad loc.*
[53] 3.7.3–18.

adds that we rarely have the opportunity to celebrate divine honours, votes of thanks or the setting up of statues. There is no mention of the emperor among either political or non-political occasions of epideictic – at best he is barely alluded to by implication in the comments on praise of the living. It is all so brazenly inappropriate to contemporary politics that it is hard not to suspect that Quintilian is inviting us to share a joke. If so, the joke makes a serious point. It corroborates what we have seen elsewhere, that Quintilian is interested only in functional forms of speech, and that he defines such speech as that performed by the orator in his capacity as ruler in the traditional fora of public life: the law and the commonly acknowledged political institutions. The sort of speech associated with emperors, which takes place outside the framework of political institutions (whether in public or in private), he declines to acknowledge, and by implication he ignores, if he does not explicitly repudiate, the role of the orator in the Principate of his own day.

The idea that the *Institutio* is a pro-senatorial, anti-imperial work also has its attractions, the more so since the descriptions of the orator engaged in politics owe a great deal to Cicero.[54] An example from *De oratore* makes the point:

> There is to my mind no more excellent thing than the power, by means of oratory, to get a hold on assemblies of men, win over their minds, direct their will wherever the speaker wishes, or divert them from whatever he wishes. In every free nation . . . this one art has always flourished above the rest . . . for what is so marvellous as that, out of the innumerable company of mankind, a single being should arise who either alone or with a few others can make effective a faculty bestowed by nature on every man? . . . What achievement is so mighty and glorious as that the impulses of the crowd, the conscience of the judges, the austerity of the senate should suffer transformation through the eloquence of one man . . . ? What function is so kingly (*regium*), so worthy of the free, so generous . . . ?[55]

Cicero goes on to discuss how the ability to speak distinguishes men from animals: 'This is our greatest advantage over beasts: we can talk among ourselves and express what we feel in speech'.[56] The parallels with Quintilian are clear enough. The difference, when it comes to

---

[54] Especially *De Or.*; also *Orator, De Rep., De Leg.*; Wood, *Cicero's Social and Political Theory*, pp. 120ff; 176ff. On the comparison between Cicero and Quintilian see A.-M. Guillemin, 'Cicéron et Quintilien', *Revue des Etudes Latines*, 37 (1959), 184–94.

[55] 1.30–32 trans. E. W. Sutton and H. Rackham. *Regere* occurs not infrequently of the orator's effect in the works of rhetorical theory, especially *De Or.* 1.

[56] 1.32.

assessing the political implications of their language, is that Cicero's republican sympathies are not in doubt. Though many opinions are expressed in the course of the *De republica*, and though his oratorical and philosophical works span the whole of his working life, Cicero never wavered in his allegiance to a form of republican mixed constitution in which political eminence was always contested and at best temporary. Moreover in his rhetorical works, at least, Cicero does not demand moral perfection of his orator – he must be good enough to rule effectively, but he need not be perfect.[57] Quintilian does demand perfection of his orator, which makes him a political idealist, and that, coupled with the fact that we have no external information about his political sympathies, makes it much harder to gauge what he means when he uses the language of rule and control.

There are a few signs that he is unlikely to have been a republican. There is no indication that his credit with the emperor suffered with the publication of the *Institutio*: he may even have received the consular insignia as a result.[58] It is noticeable that he does not discuss the possibility of competition between his orator and others, nor does he refer to orators in the plural. He does talk as though anyone might have access to his educational programme but there is no real indication that he imagined training a whole generation of equally matched, competing speakers and politicians. It looks rather as though however many orators may be trained, only one is expected to arrive at the degree of authoritative perfection which is its aim. All these somewhat slender indications may incline us to doubt that the *Institutio* is intended to be read as pro-republican political theory, though they fall short of a conclusive case.

QUINTILIAN'S CONTRIBUTION TO ROMAN POLITICAL THOUGHT

However, there may be good reasons for thinking that Quintilian does not intend us to prove the case either way – that in fact the search for clear-cut, traditional political affiliations in the *Institutio* cannot do other than draw a blank. Our confusion about Quintilian's political programme drives us back to seek enlightenment in the educational material. If anything, this strategy succeeds rather too well and many readers have overlooked the work's political frame altogether. But if

[57] *De Officiis* 3.13–17; *De Leg.* 1.30; G. M. Grube, 'Educational and Literary Theory in Cicero', *Phoenix*, 16 (1962), 234–57.
[58] Kennedy, *Quintilian*, p. 28.

we keep it in mind, and return to the programmatic statements at the opening of the work, we can begin to see Quintilian's individual contribution to Roman political theory more clearly.

He defines his project as the creation of, 'that perfect orator, who can be nothing other than a good man . . .'[59] In the past, he says, the study of virtue has been seen as the business of philosophy. He has several objections to this. First, virtue is essential to the man in public life – 'the proper citizen.' Second, he claims that oratory and philosophy are really, as Cicero shows, part of the same subject, and that in the past the same men were orators and philosophers. More recently the two professions have split apart with bad results all round: the philosophers have withdrawn from public life and the orators have lost their ethical guidelines. His aim is to reunite the two disciplines to produce a statesman who is both eloquent and virtuous.

The stage is therefore set for a drama familiar from earlier political theory: the production of a model statesman by means of a model education. And that is what Quintilian provides – but in such peculiar proportions that it is as if the genre has been turned inside out. Its educational element, instead of being one scene in the action, seems to have taken over the plot, while the political *dénouement* is all but eclipsed.

The effect of this inversion of what we might expect to be the normal relationship between education and politics, is that what is achieved through education appears to justify what happens in politics, rather than vice versa. Instead of devising a political structure and then working out an education to produce suitable people to maintain it, Quintilian implies that the state can be run well through any and all institutions but only by a man or men properly educated in wisdom and the means by which to impose wisdom on others. Brushing constitutional theory aside, he envisages a state of affairs which can be brought about by nothing more radical than his version of conventional contemporary educational practices. The effectiveness of Quintilian's programme as a theory of government is based on the idea that the pupil acquires, at each successive stage of education, a higher degree both of technical competence and authority, and of the virtue which justifies that authority. The man most skilled in speaking, in other words, will always be both the effective ruler and the man most fitted to rule, while those who are slightly less competent will be fitted to a slightly lesser degree of power, and so on down the scale. The offices which such men occupy in the state, in this

---

[59] I pr. 9.

construction, is a matter of secondary importance. The crucial thing is their status as good men skilled in speaking. If we were to put this re-evaluation of the relative importance of political structures and educa-tion in more conventional 'republican *versus* imperial' terms, we might say that Quintilian is delivering a rebuke to emperor and senate alike for behaving as though it were the forms of government, rather than the qualities of individuals, that enable the state to run well.

SPEECH AND WRITING

One of the ways in which Quintilian effectively blurs the difference between forms of government is by treating speech and writing as barely divergent aspects of the same discipline. We see it in the earlier stages of education where the pupil is prepared to study rhetoric by means of a literate education in which the single most important element is *reading*. Quintilian's orator-to-be learns almost everything by read-ing, from morals, role models and style to the construction of a speech, forms of argument and how to flatter a judge.[60] Quintilian emphasises repeatedly that the very language used by the orator is different from the ordinary language of the uneducated and that it is acquired above all by reading the great authors.[61]

There is, in other words, a particular language associated with power and authority and it is based on writing. This is true both on linguistic and cognitive levels. On the cognitive level, the construction and analysis of every aspect of a speech, from its language to the proportions of its parts, is performed in a manner characteristic of literate discourse.[62] On the linguistic level, the language which the pupil learns to recognise, appreciate and ultimately to use under the supervision of the *grammaticus* and *rhetor* is based on that of poets, orators of the past and historians.[63] As Quintilian puts it, right language is based on reason, authority,

---

[60] 1.4.6ff., 6.1; 3.2.1 and see J. Adamietz, *M. F. Quintiliani Institutiones Oratoriae Liber III* (Munich, 1966) *ad loc.*, 10 pr. 1, 1.8–13, 3.13–15, 7.1ff. (cf. R. J. Lewis, 'A crux in Quintilian', *Classical Review*, 11 (1961), 204–5).

[61] 1.5.1ff.; 1.6.1; 10.1.27ff.

[62] On the intellectual consequences of literacy see, among a vast number of studies, M. T. Clanchy, *From Memory to Written Record*, 2nd edn. (Oxford, 1993); J. Goody, *The Logic of Writing and the Organization of Society* (Cambridge, 1986); E. Havelock, *The Literate Revolution in Greece and its Cultural Consequences* (Princeton, 1982); A. R. Luria, *Cognitive Development* (Cambridge, Mass, 1976); W. Ong, *Orality and Literacy: The Technologising of the Word* (London, 1982); K. Robb, *Literacy and Paideia in Ancient Greece* (Oxford, 1994).

[63] Though not all authors are regarded as equally appropriate models for every type of discourse.

antiquity, and usage.[64] 'Reason' means formal grammar, which is based on written forms of language. 'Authority' is that of the most respected writers. 'Antiquity' is explained only as the qualities of 'majesty' and 'sanctity',[65] but in practice, reference to ancient forms of language is likely to have been made largely to texts. Only in appeals to usage might education have paid significant attention to non-literary elements of the language, but even here the role of orality is strictly limited. Having introduced the idea of usage Quintilian goes back to discussing grammar for forty-two paragraphs, only to finish with a definition of usage as the agreed practice of *educated* men – that is, highly literate men who have learned their grammar and rhetoric.[66]

In all this Quintilian is following the normal principles of grammatical and rhetorical theory, of both of which, in Latin and Greek, the written word is at once the medium and the material. But Quintilian goes further by attributing the use of literate language to the politically powerful, and by claiming that the orator's power and authority, and even his virtue, are actually generated by his education in, among other things, grammar and rhetoric. Two claims follow from this. The larger and more important, which we cannot pursue here, is that if in some sense the product of an education in a certain type of language is political power and virtue, then the use of that language comes close in itself to guaranteeing the virtue and authority of the man who uses it. The second, which is relevant here, is that that educated language which is the accompaniment of power and virtue is substantially the same language, whether it is written or spoken. The spoken form is a version of the written form and they are learnt in the same process. So the good orator and the good administrator through the written word are indistinguishable and the language of each is equally authoritative. Readers need not worry about which areas of government are conducted orally or through the written word (one of the defining differences between the republican and imperial administrations); the important distinction is between those communications which are authoritative and educated – and those which are not.

This is not to claim that Quintilian recognises no difference between a speech read and a speech heard. It is rather that the differences are not linguistic: they depend on the extra-linguistic effects of the orator's presence on the crowd. This is how he describes them:

---

[64] 1.6.1.   [65] *maiestas quaedam et, ut sic dixerim, religio commendat.*   [66] 1.6.45.

The advantages conferred by reading and listening are not identical. The speaker stimulates us by the animation of his delivery, and kindles the imagination, not by presenting us with an elaborate picture but by bringing us into touch with the things themselves. Then all is life and movement, and we receive the new-born offspring of his imagination with enthusiastic approval. We are moved not merely by the actual issue of the trial, but by all that the orator himself has at stake. Moreover his voice, the grace of his gestures, the adaptation of his delivery . . . have their educative effect. In reading, on the other hand, the critical faculty is a surer guide, inasmuch as the listener's judgement is often swept away . . . Reading, however . . . does not hurry us past with the speed of oral delivery: we can reread a passage again and again if we are in doubt about it or wish to fix it in the memory.[67]

Though presented as a distinction between reading and hearing, this is really a distinction between linguistic and non-linguistic means of communication. There is no suggestion that the orator's language or argument would be any different in written form: indeed, the comparison depends on their being the same. What vary are the other things: the orator's passion, his grace and his voice.[68] In some passages Quintilian goes further and denies that the illiterate can make effective use even of non-linguistic means of persuasion. Gestures and tone, for instance, must be appropriate to the words they accompany, so even they depend on the formal rhetorical education.

We have already observed the power which Quintilian gives the orator over his audience. Nowhere is it more evident than in passages where the audience consists of the uneducated and illiterates. Throughout the *Institutio* illiterates are described as dumb: they cannot speak, or if they do, their speech is described as ephemeral, accidental, ignorant, subjective, even a different language, meaningless to the educated.[69] Exaggerated as these descriptions sound, they prove to be yet another way of claiming that education and power, skill in speaking and skill in politics, go together. Quintilian identifies the uneducated variously as barbarians, peasants, slaves, children, and women.[70] These categories are oddly anomalous: they do not quite coincide with what we know about education and literacy in the ancient world, where we know of quite a number of literate women, literate slaves, and, of course, literate

---

[67] 10.1.16–7 trans. H. E. Butler. On earlier rhetorical influences on Quintilian in this and other areas see Kennedy, 'An estimate of Quintilian'; P. Mackendrick, *The Philosophical Books of Cicero* (London, 1989).

[68] 10.1.48; though even these factors can be learnt to some extent from literature. Literacy also seems to improve one's control of them.

[69] 2.16.19; 2.17.16; 2.20.6; 2.21.16; 10.1.16ff; 10.7.12–16; 12.1.27; 12.10.40.

[70] 2.17.6; 2.20.6–7; 2.21.16; 10.3.16; 12.10.40, 53.

children, not least Quintilian's own pupils.[71] Nor do they sound like a typical political audience. But they do coincide with those who lacked political freedom in Quintilian's Rome. Drawing them together in a picture of an imaginary audience therefore makes a vivid statement about the nature and degree of the orator's political authority. By the power of his words he rules the city as justifiably and absolutely as the Roman male rules barbarians, women or slaves.

As a successful rhetor and teacher, an associate of the imperial household, the holder of consular ornaments, and the friend of senators, Quintilian must have known how fruitless and how dangerous the feud between the emperor and the aristocracy could be. In the *Institutio* he offers Romans his prescription, the prescription of a lifelong educationalist, for settling it without revolution or bloodshed. If they concentrate on the education of good men skilled in speaking and worry less about political institutions, Rome might be a more peaceful and a juster state.

At the same time, Quintilian is anxious to reassure the reader that his ideas do not represent a radical departure from all that is best in Roman tradition. And he is lucky enough to have a definition of the orator coined by the elder Cato, that paradigmatic Roman of the old school. It is notable how well Quintilian's many references to Cato fit the picture of Quintilian's ideal orator. Like Cato the wise, he says, the good man must choose carefully what cases to defend, prosecuting only when it is his duty to the state or to an individual.[72] Like Quintilian's orator Cato is described as at once a great philosopher, orator, historian, and general, an expert in law and agriculture, the model Roman who took up Greek culture in old age (Quintilian's orator has progressed further down this line and is brought up to speak Greek before he speaks Latin).[73] Quintilian even observes that Cato was the first Roman to write on rhetoric – perhaps a discreet advertisement for the pristine virtue of rhetoricians, who sometimes had a rather bad reputation in Quintilian's day.[74] The testimony of the elder Cato is that the best modern ideas have the blessing of history.

---

[71] A. D. Booth, 'The Schooling of Slaves in First Century Rome', *TAPA*, 109 (1979), 11–19; A. K. Bowman, 'Literacy in the Roman Empire: Mass and Mode', in M. Beard, A. K. Bowman, M. Corbier, T. J. Cornell, J. L. Franklin Jr., A. Hanson, K. Hopkins, N. Horsfall *Literacy in the Roman World*, *Journal of Roman Archaeology*, suppl 3 (Ann Arbor, 1991), 119–31; C. A. Forbes, 'The Education and Training of Slaves in Antiquity', *TAPA*, 86 (1955), 321–60; A. E. Hanson, 'Ancient Illiteracy', in Beard et al, *Literacy*, 159–97; W. V. Harris *Ancient Literacy* (Cambridge, MA, and London, 1989), 196ff, 248ff.
[72] 12.7.4.   [73] 12.3.9; 12.11.23; on learning Greek before Latin see 1.1.12.   [74] 3.1.19.

There is no evidence that Quintilian's ideas had any effect on the emperor Domitian, nor on his enemies in the senate, nor on those among his household who finally murdered him. But in the second century there was to be a period in which emperors saw themselves as philosopher kings and their subjects as the citizens of a single, idealised world state whose city walls were contiguous with the ends of the earth itself.[75] Is it too much to speculate whether Quintilian's idea of the orator king influenced the beliefs of Antoninus or Marcus Aurelius?[76] There is no direct evidence for it but Quintilian would have recognised and approved of a world in which education was seen as a source of virtue and right speech, and those qualities valued in tandem as the proper criteria of a well-run state.

---

[75] Aelius Aristides *To Rome*, cf. Marcus Aurelius *Meditations*; L. S. Mazzolani, *The Idea of the City in Roman Thought* (Indiana, 1970), 173ff.

[76] There is plenty of evidence that Quintilian was remembered and that later rhetoricians throughout antiquity, and at least one Christian apologist (Jerome *Ep.* 107), made use of the *Institutio*. Cf. Kennedy, *Quintilian*, 139–41; R. Rutherford, *Marcus Aurelius: A Study* (Oxford, 1989), 41–2, 97–8; also M. L. Clarke, 'Quintilian, a Biographical Sketch', *Greece and Rome* ser. 214 (1967), 24–37; 'Quintilian on Education', in T. Dorey ed. *Empire and Aftermath*, 98–118; G. Downey, 'Education and Public Problems as Seen by Themistius', *TAPA*, 86 (1955), 291–307.

CHAPTER 12

The voice of Isocrates and the dissemination of cultural power

Niall Livingstone

Twentieth-century reading of Isocrates has tended to concentrate on his achievements or shortcomings as a 'thinker' rather than on his pedagogy,[1] but he has a long-established image as one of antiquity's supreme pedagogues. In Cicero's dialogue *De Oratore*, Antonius speaks of Isocrates' school 'from which, as from the Trojan horse, all who emerged were leaders'.[2] In the Italian Renaissance, Isocrates' works were popular objects of translation, especially the speech *To Nicocles* which instructs Isocrates' pupil, the young King Nicocles, on the ideals of kingship. The passage from *De Oratore* was echoed in a funeral oration for Guarino Guarini, revered as the 'father of humanists': Guarino was to be seen as a new Isocrates.[3] The self-proclaimed arch-pedagogue Erasmus presented a translation of *To Nicocles*, along with his own *Panegyricus* and *Institutio christiani principis*, to his royal patron Emperor Charles V.[4] And if Isocrates is invoked as a model by the humanists, humanism in turn provides a paradigm for incorporating Isocrates into a continuous narrative of Western culture: H.-I. Marrou's history of ancient education discusses Isocrates' 'ethical rhetoric' in a section entitled 'Le humanisme d' Isocrate', and a famous essay by the historian

[1] E.g. E. Mikkola, *Isokrates: seine Anschauungen im Lichte seiner Schriften* (Helsinki 1954); C. Eucken, *Isokrates: seine Positionen in der Aufeinandersetzung mit den zeitgenössischen Philosophen* (Berlin and New York, 1983). The subject of Isocratean pedagogy has been re-opened by Yun Lee Too's book *The Rhetoric of Identity in Isocrates: Text, Power, Pedagogy* (Cambridge, 1995); see also H.-I. Marrou, *Histoire de l'éducation dans l'antiquité* (Paris, 1948), pp. 121–136.
[2] *De Oratore* II.94: *cuius e ludo tamquam ex equo Troiano meri principes exierunt.*
[3] L. Carbone 'Oratio Habita in Funere Praestantissimi Oratoris et Poetae Guarini Veronensis' in E. Garin (ed.), *Prosatori latini del quattrocento* (Milan and Naples, 1952), pp. 382–427, esp. p. 392. Cf. L. Jardine and A. Grafton, *From Humanism to the Humanities: Education and the Liberal Arts in Fifteenth- and Sixteenth-Century Europe* (London, 1986), p. 1: Guarino as 'the modern equal of Theophrastus and Isocrates'.
[4] In Erasmus's dealings with Charles V and his father Philip – discussed by Rundle in this volume, p. 157 – there seems to be a deliberate imitation of Isocrates' dealings with Nicocles and Evagoras. I am grateful to David Rundle for discussions of Isocrates' Renaissance readers and translators.

Moses Finley calls Isocrates to account for the whole tradition of *belles lettres* in education.[5] In short, Isocrates has been an important link in attempted genealogies of classical pedagogy.

This chapter has two objectives: to identify, so far as possible, the character and stated aims of Isocrates' pedagogical work, without the benefit of later paradigms or assumptions about its place in an imagined continuum of Western education; and in particular to examine the theory and practice of Isocrates' claim to provide a *political* education: an education which fits pupils for leadership within their city or state.

Some of the most obvious questions to pose to a pedagogical programme – 'what was taught?', 'how was it taught?', and 'who was it taught to?' – do not have straightforward answers in the case of Isocrates. To begin with the pupils: what we can say, first of all, is that they were men – not women (references of any kind to the female sex are extremely sparse in Isocrates' pedagogical writings),[6] and not children, but young men about to enter adult careers. It seems likely that the number of pupils at any one time was quite small,[7] which is significant because it implies direct and reasonably intimate contact between teacher and pupil.[8] Our information as to the narrower definition of the group is extremely unreliable, and consists largely on the one hand of Isocrates' self-publicity and on the other of the assertions of ancient scholars, who are notoriously promiscuous in creating teacher-pupil relationships between eminent men of (roughly) succeeding generations;[9]

---

[5] Marrou, *Histoire*, pp. 131–3, and cf. p. 133: 'Isocrate apparaît bien comme la source de tout le grand courant de l'humanisme scolaire'; M. I. Finley, 'The Heritage of Isocrates', in his *The Use and Abuse of History* (London, 1975).

[6] The exception is the *Helen*, a lavish rhetorical display cast in the form of praise of Helen of Troy. Elsewhere a characteristic context in which women appear is as victims in catalogues of the atrocities of war.

[7] Calculations of the number of pupils at any one time are attempted by Marrou and by Johnson, but their precision is illusory (Marrou, *Histoire*, p. 129 and p. 491, n. 11: five to six pupils on average; R. Johnson, 'A Note on the Number of Isocrates' Pupils', *AJP* 105 (1957) 297–300: 'about six at any one time' (p. 299)). For the intimacy of association, see *Antidosis* 87–88: they may spend 3–4 years with Isocrates, and they leave with 'tears and yearning' (οὕτως ἠγάπων τὴν διατριβὴν ὥστε μετὰ πόθου καὶ δακρύων ποιεῖσθαι τὴν ἀπαλλαγήν, 88).

[8] Isocrates prefers to describe his students as 'companions' or 'associates' (συνόντες, πλησιάζοντες) rather than as pupils or disciples (μαθηταί), a preference which will also reflect class-consciousness: Greek aristocrats tended to look down on paid work, and Isocrates would wish to avoid any suggestion that his professional activity as a teacher amounts to paid employment on a par with that of the artisanal classes.

[9] A particularly colourful, and unlikely, story has the orator Demosthenes seeking a cut-price version of Isocrates' instruction: 'They say that Demosthenes approached him eagerly when he was still teaching rhetoric, and said that, while he could not come up with the demanded 1000

but some general observations are possible. Isocrates prides himself on the fact that he draws pupils from the far ends of the Greek world, from Sicily and the Black Sea (*Antidosis* 224). But above all he takes pride in pupils who become leaders in politics and in war. At *Antidosis* 93 he lists ten, all of whom, he says, the city (of Athens) has crowned with crowns of gold. His two especial favourites – not included in this list – are the Athenian general Timotheus, son of Conon, and the Cypriot king, Nicocles, son of Evagoras. The picture Isocrates presents is certainly a onesided one: many of the pupils ascribed to him in the ancient tradition are not politicians but *littérateurs*, including, for instance, the historians Theopompus and Ephorus and the orators Hyperides and Lycurgus.[10] While individual cases are debatable, we can be sure that at least some of Isocrates' pupils did go on to be writers and rhetoricians. In the passage from *De Oratore* cited above, Antonius goes on to say that of the 'leaders' who emerged from Isocrates' school, 'some sought to distinguish themselves in the battle-line, others in the festive procession', i.e. in literary art;[11] Isocrates' bias against mentioning the latter is significant.

For Isocrates' pedagogical practice – what he and his pupils actually did together – we have little concrete evidence.[12] (Modern analogies – scholars have spoken, for instance, of 'seminars'[13] – are dangerous.) What we do know is that Isocrates emphatically denies the possibility of teaching eloquence by rule, or reducing it to a system:

I am amazed to see that there are some people who are thought fit to teach students, although – without realising it – they present an inflexible technique as a model for an activity which is creative. Surely none but them is unaware that, whereas letters of the alphabet are fixed and stay in the same order, so that we always keep using the same ones for the same words, speeches (*logoi*) have quite the opposite characteristic; what one person has said is not equally effective for a subsequent speaker. The best technician is the speaker

---

drachmae, he would pay 200 drachmae to learn one-fifth of the course. But Isocrates replied "Demosthenes, we do not sell this profession in slices. Quality fish are sold whole; and similarly, if you want to be my pupil, I will sell you the expertise complete" ' (Pseudo-Plutarch, *Lives of the Ten Orators* 837de).

[10] For a fuller list, with references, see Marrou, *Histoire*, p. 130.

[11] '. . . meri principes exierunt; sed eorum partim in pompa, partim in acie inlustres esse voluerunt.'

[12] Marrou's account (*Histoire*, pp. 126–8) is over-systematic and goes well beyond the evidence: a symptom of this scholar's inclination to show unbroken continuity in education from late antiquity, if not from twentieth-century universities, back to classical Greece.

[13] Marrou, *Histoire*, p. 128; Johnson, 'A note on the number', p. 297, n. 2; F. A. G. Beck and R. Thomas in *OCD*[3], s.v. 'education, Greek' ('a seminar technique of group discussion and criticism').

who, while doing justice to the subject-matter, can find words quite unlike anyone else's.[14]

Rules are useful for spelling, but not for eloquence. It is fair to conclude that Isocrates himself taught primarily by example, not by precept;[15] in this respect his teaching will have resembled that of fifth-century teachers of rhetoric who gave their pupils 'example speeches' to study and copy.[16]

Isocrates' last work, the *Panathenaicus*, offers a *mise-en-scène* of Isocrates among his pupils, and perhaps gives us a glimpse of what his teaching was like. He describes himself presenting a draft of the *Panathenaicus* itself to his pupils for comment and criticism:

I was correcting a written version of this speech, consisting of all that has been read so far, together with three or four of the young men who regularly study with me.[17]

They agree that what he has written is good and needs only a conclusion; but Isocrates decides to expose his work – which, as its title suggests, is a eulogy on Athens, a speech suitable for delivery at the Athenian patriotic festival of the Panathenaia – to a more exacting critic, namely a former pupil of oligarchic and pro-Spartan tendencies. The pro-Spartan pupil duly arrives, and admires what Isocrates has written, but suggests that Sparta too deserves praise. Isocrates replies fiercely, to applause from the other pupils present; but he is left in doubt about the merit of his work, and decides to summon a larger gathering of former pupils – including the pro-Spartan – to seek their advice. This

---

[14] θαυμάζω δ' ὅταν ἴδω τούτους μαθητῶν ἀξιουμένους, οἳ ποιητικοῦ πράγματος τεταγμένην τέχνην φέροντες λελήθασιν σφᾶς αὐτούς. τίς γὰρ οὐκ οἶδεν πλὴν τούτων ὅτι τὸ μὲν τῶν γραμμάτων ἀκινήτως ἔχει καὶ μένει κατὰ ταὐτὸν ὥστε τοῖς αὐτοῖς ἀεὶ περὶ τῶν αὐτῶν χρώμενοι διατελοῦμεν, τὸ δὲ τῶν λόγων πᾶν τοὐναντίον πέπονθεν· τὸ γὰρ ὑφ' ἑτέρου ῥηθὲν τῷ λέγοντι μετ' ἐκεῖνον οὐχ ὁμοίως χρήσιμόν ἐστιν, ἀλλ' οὗτος εἶναι δοκεῖ τεχνικώτατος ὅστις ἂν ἀξίως μὲν λέγῃ τῶν πραγμάτων, μηδὲν δὲ τῶν αὐτῶν τοῖς ἄλλοις εὑρίσκειν δύνηται (*Against the Sophists* 12). (All quotations from Isocrates follow the text in G. Mathieu and E. Brémond (eds.), *Isocrate* (4 vols.: Paris, 1929–1962); translations are my own unless otherwise stated.)

[15] Some explicit rhetorical precepts were attributed to Isocrates in later antiquity (see Mathieu and Brémond (eds.), *Isocrate* IV 228–234), but of these some are simply extrapolated from his practice in the published works, while others may stem from a later 'handbook' of rhetoric which was either a *pseudepigraphon* or the work of another Isocrates. See K. Barwick, 'Das Problem der isokrateischen Techne', *Philologus* 107 (1963) 43–60.

[16] See T. Cole, *The Origins of Rhetoric in Ancient Greece* (Baltimore and London, 1991), esp. Chapter 5, 'Technē and Text'. In a well-known passage of the *Sophistical Refutations* (183b36–184a8) Aristotle associates this type of teaching particularly with Gorgias, and objects that it is no better than if one were to try to teach shoe-making by handing out examples of different kinds of shoes.

[17] ἐπηνόρθουν μὲν τὸν λόγον τὸν μέχρι τῶν ἀναγνωσθέντων γεγραμμένον μετὰ μειρακίων τριῶν ἢ τεττάρων τῶν εἰθισμένων μοι συνδιατρίβειν (*Panath.* 200).

episode will be discussed further below; at this point I wish only to note an observation put in the mouth of the pro-Spartan on the occasion of the second gathering of Isocrates' pupils: 'I am surprised', he says,

> that you called us together in order to seek our advice on your speech, when you know for certain that we praise everything you say or do. On questions of importance sensible people usually consult those who know better than themselves, or failing that people who will express an independent opinion: but you have done the opposite.[18]

The tone is clearly polemical, appropriate to the shadow-boxing that is being constructed between 'Isocrates' and his pupil. But the criticism attributed to the latter is interesting in two respects. First, its assumptions – that the pupils normally praise everything their master says or does and cannot be expected to express, perhaps not even to have, opinions of their own – point to a method of teaching which does not consist of debate or mutual critique (as the 'seminar' analogy might suggest), but is more hierarchical, with demonstration from the master, adulation from the pupils. This, of course, accords well with the idea of 'teaching by example': praise is a step towards imitation, as Isocrates explains to the young King Nicocles when presenting him with an encomium of his father Evagoras (*Evagoras* 73–79). Secondly, the pupil's criticism of Isocrates' choice of advisers has a wider significance. The giving of practical, especially political, advice (*sumbouleuein*) is a key theme in Isocrates' writings; it is one of the primary skills which education is to impart.[19] Elsewhere Isocrates has drawn attention to a group of people for whom finding advisers is a particularly serious problem, namely kings: their subjects are likely to be deterred by fear or distracted by the hope of favour from giving honest advice; so the king must turn to the pedagogue, and a work like Isocrates' *To Nicocles* (which became a model for Renaissance 'mirrors for princes') is a uniquely valuable gift to a king (§ 1–8). As emerges from the *Panathenaicus*, the pedagogue faces similar difficulties when seeking advice, but for a more fundamental reason: no-one knows better than him; he is at the top of the pyramid of advisers and advised.[20] It will be seen that Isocrates' works

---

[18] [θαυμάζω . . . εἴτε] συμβούλοις περὶ τοῦ λόγου χρήσασθαι βουλόμενος ἡμᾶς συνήγαγες, οὓς οἶσθ' ἀκριβῶς ἅπαν ὅ τι ἂν σὺ λέγῃς ἢ πράττῃς ἐπαινοῦντας. εἰθισμένοι δ' εἰσὶν οἱ νοῦν ἔχοντες ἀνακοινοῦσθαι περὶ ὧν ἂν σπουδάζωσιν μάλιστα μὲν τοῖς ἄμεινον αὐτῶν φρονοῦσιν, εἰ δὲ μή, τοῖς μέλλουσιν ἀποφαίνεσθαι τὴν αὑτῶν γνώμην· ὧν τἀναντία σὺ πεποίηκας (*Panath.* 235).

[19] See e.g. *Antid.* 204 (cited below). For the pedagogue as advisor, cf. also *To Nicocles* 50–53; *Antid.* 104.

[20] In fact Isocrates' position is closely parallel to that of the *ideal* king as presented in Isocrates' encomium of Evagoras: 'he had no need of advisers, but still sought his friends' advice' (*Evag.* 44).

often point to an analogy between what may be called the hegemony of the pedagogue and the temporal hegemony of the king or leader, with a tendency to give priority to the former.

Thus the *Panathenaicus* may give some indication of what a meeting between Isocrates and his pupils was like, except that the situation is subverted because Isocrates himself takes the role of a pupil and seeks his pupils' advice – to their embarrassment, since they know that he knows best. The outspoken pro-Spartan pupil is given, partly and temporarily, the role of the pedagogue. The effect of this role-reversal will be discussed further below.

I turn now to the question of what was to be imparted by this pedagogy – what were the pupils actually to get from it? In the speech *Against the Sophists*, which is signalled within the corpus as 'launching' Isocrates' teaching career, he is careful to clear himself in advance of any charge that he claims to 'teach virtue': this work states emphatically that *dikaiosunē*, moral rectitude, cannot be taught; but it leaves a loophole: the practice of *logoi politikoi* is the best 'incitement and preparation' for virtue.[21] Much later, in his semiautobiographical self-defence *Antidosis*, Isocrates congratulates himself for never having exaggerated the power of education: he has always given natural ability its proper importance (194–195). In a long, abstract defence of intellectual education *(logōn paideia)*, he explains that it exercises the soul as gymnastics exercises the body, and produces improvement, but cannot succeed where natural ability is lacking (181–185); that someone of great ability can succeed even with mediocre education (189–190); and finally, and most specifically, that some at least of those who have received an advanced education have emerged

some rounded-off as competent participants in debate, some having acquired the ability to educate others; while those who chose not to enter public life were more agreeable in conversation than they had been before, and had become better than most people at evaluating speeches and at giving advice.[22]

In *Panathenaicus* we find a slightly more detailed account of what characterises 'educated people' (*pepaideumenoi*):

---

[21] συμπαρακελεύσασθαί γε καὶ συνασκῆσαι μάλιστ' ἂν οἶμαι τὴν τῶν λόγων τῶν πολιτικῶν ἐπιμέλειαν (*Soph.* 21).

[22] τοὺς μὲν αὐτῶν ἱκανοὺς ἀγωνιστὰς ἀποτελεσθέντας, τοὺς δὲ παιδεύειν ἑτέρους δυνηθέντας, ὅσοι δ' αὐτῶν ἰδιωτεύειν ἐβουλήθησαν, ἔν τε ταῖς ὁμιλίαις χαριεστέρους ὄντας ἢ πρότερον ἦσαν, τῶν τε λόγων κριτὰς καὶ συμβούλους ἀκριβεστέρους τῶν πλείστων γεγενημένους (*Antid.* 204). The word ἀποτελεσθέντας, 'finished' or 'rounded off', is deliberately vague – it does not commit Isocrates to a particular assessment of how much of their debating skill is actually due to their education.

First of all [I regard as educated] those who can deal successfully with affairs that arise from day to day, and have a mind able to respond to what the situation demands and to form a fair estimate of what is expedient. Secondly, those who are respectable and honest in their dealings with all they meet, who respond with good humour to other people's boorishness and bad temper and are not aggravated by it, and who are themselves as refined and restrained as possible in their dealings with others. Thirdly, those who always stay in control of their own pleasures, and do not let themselves be worn down too much by misfortunes, but respond to them robustly and in a way which does justice to human dignity. Fourthly, and most important, those who are not corrupted by good fortune and do not get above themselves or become proud, but stick to their place among people of good sense and take no more pleasure in benefits conferred by fortune than in the innate benefits of ability and intelligence. Anyone with a soul well-ordered not just in one, but in all of these respects is, in my opinion, a wise man, a perfect man, a possessor of all virtues.[23]

The truly educated man, then, possesses perfect civic virtue. But most of the qualities described here will, as Isocrates elsewhere insists, depend more on nature than on education; and the passage does not bring us very much closer to understanding what *specifically* Isocrates' pupils were expected to derive from their education.

One answer to the question, '*what* did Isocrates teach?' – an accurate, but uninformative answer – would be '*logoi*'. Isocrates regularly describes his pedagogy as 'education in *logoi*' or 'concerning *logoi*' (*logōn paideia* or *paideusis peri logōn*), and characterises his own activity as 'professional concern with *logoi*' (*peri logous diatribein*). The Greek word *logos* (plural *logoi*) can encompass 'word', 'argument', 'reason', 'account', 'explanation', 'narrative', and many of these senses may be latent to a certain extent in the formulations just cited, but the primary sense here is certainly 'speech' or 'discourse': the reference is to *logoi* in the sense in which Isocrates' own writings are *logoi*. Doubtless some of the *logoi* which served as instructive examples in Isocrates' teaching were not

---

[23] [πεπαιδευμένους καλῶ] πρῶτον μὲν τοὺς καλῶς χρωμένους τοῖς πράγμασι τοῖς κατὰ τὴν ἡμέραν ἑκάστην προσπίπτουσι, καὶ τὴν δόξαν ἐπιτυχῆ τῶν καιρῶν ἔχοντας καὶ δυναμένην ὡς ἐπὶ τὸ πολὺ στοχάζεσθαι τοῦ συμφέροντος· ἔπειτα τοὺς πρεπόντως καὶ δικαίως ὁμιλοῦντας τοῖς ἀεὶ πλησιάζουσι, καὶ τὰς μὲν τῶν ἄλλων ἀηδίας καὶ βαρύτητας εὐκόλως καὶ ῥᾳδίως φέροντας, σφᾶς δ᾽ αὐτοὺς ὡς δυνατὸν ἐλαφροτάτους καὶ μετριωτάτους τοῖς συνοῦσιν παρέχοντας· ἔτι τοὺς τῶν μὲν ἡδονῶν ἀεὶ κρατοῦντας, τῶν δὲ συμφορῶν μὴ λίαν ἡττωμένους, ἀλλ᾽ ἀνδρωδῶς ἐν αὐταῖς διακειμένους καὶ τῆς φύσεως ἀξίως ἧς μετέχοντες τυγχάνομεν· τέταρτον, ὅπερ μέγιστον, τοὺς μὴ διαφθειρομένους ὑπὸ τῶν εὐπραγιῶν μηδ᾽ ἐξισταμένους αὑτῶν μηδ᾽ ὑπερηφάνους γιγνομένους, ἀλλ᾽ ἐμμένοντας τῇ τάξει τῇ τῶν εὖ φρονούντων καὶ μὴ μᾶλλον χαίροντας τοῖς διὰ τύχην ὑπάρξασιν ἀγαθοῖς ἢ τοῖς διὰ τὴν αὑτῶν φύσιν καὶ φρόνησιν ἐξ ἀρχῆς γιγνομένοις. τοὺς δὲ μὴ μόνον πρὸς ἓν τούτων, ἀλλὰ καὶ πρὸς ἅπαντα ταῦτα τὴν ἕξιν τῆς ψυχῆς εὐάρμοστον ἔχοντας, τούτους φημὶ καὶ φρονίμους εἶναι καὶ τελέους ἄνδρας καὶ πάσας ἔχειν τὰς ἀρετάς (*Panath.* 32).

copied or preserved, and are lost to us; but it is plausible, if not probable, that Isocrates' surviving works were themselves used in this way during the long process of their composition (ancient sources speak of ten to fifteen years spent on the *Panegyricus*).[24]

Isocrates' pupils learn by imitating him and his work. But this leaves us with the question, what *exactly* are they to imitate? What is the goal of the imitation? For other contemporary pedagogies which work by example and imitation, a clearer answer may be available: someone who studied with a practical forensic rhetorician such as Lysias would aim to make a living as a speech-writer; an associate of Socrates or a student of Plato might aim to follow where the master has led in dispelling false beliefs and progressing towards true knowledge. But Isocrates characterises his typical pupil as a political leader, whereas he himself takes no active part in politics, lacking, as he tells us, the necessary powerful voice and confidence.[25] As Yun Lee Too has argued, the 'small voice' can paradoxically be a powerful rhetorical tool, allowing Isocrates to adopt the stance of a dispassionate and reflective observer;[26] yet it inevitably makes him problematic as a direct object of imitation: to 'become' an Isocrates is not a relevant goal for a pupil bent on a political career. To see how, if at all, Isocrates' imitative pedagogy could work, it is necessary to look more closely at the medium of imitation – at the *logoi* which are at the centre of the *paideia*.

Isocrates, like the older rhetorician Gorgias (who was certainly an influence on Isocrates, if not, as some ancient sources claim, his teacher), insists on the versatility and power of *logos*:

since the nature of *logoi* is such that it is possible to narrate the same things in many different ways; to diminish great subjects, and to impart grandeur to small subjects; to tell old stories in a fresh style, and to speak of recent events in an archaic style – therefore there is no more need to avoid subjects on which others have spoken before; rather one must try to speak better than them.[27]

---

[24] Cf. Marrou, *Histoire*, p. 128: 'dans l'école d'Isocrate, les textes de base ne sont autres que les chefs-d'oeuvres mêmes du maître.' On the composition of *Panegyricus*, see for instance Timaeus' joke that it took Alexander less long to conquer the whole of Asia than Isocrates to write this speech (Pseudo-Longinus *On the Sublime* 4.2); cf. Dionysius of Halicarnassus, *On Literary Composition* 25.

[25] *Phil.* 81; *Panath.* 9–10.

[26] Too, *Rhetoric of Identity*, Chapter 3: 'The Politics of the Small Voice'.

[27] ἐπειδὴ δ' οἱ λόγοι τοιαύτην ἔχουσι τὴν φύσιν ὥσθ' οἷόν τ' εἶναι περὶ τῶν αὐτῶν πολλαχῶς ἐξηγήσασθαι καὶ τά τε μεγάλα ταπεινὰ ποιῆσαι καὶ τοῖς μικροῖς μέγεθος περιθεῖναι, καὶ τά τε παλαιὰ καινῶς διελθεῖν καὶ περὶ τῶν νεωστὶ γεγενημένων ἀρχαίως εἰπεῖν, οὐκέτι φευκτέον ταῦτ' ἐστὶ περὶ ὧν ἕτεροι πρότερον εἰρήκασιν, ἀλλ' ἄμεινον ἐκείνων εἰπεῖν πειρατέον (*Paneg.* 8). Cf. Plato, *Phaedrus* 267a (on 'Teisias and Gorgias', who 'make what is small seem great, and what is great seem small, by the power of *logos*'), and the excursus on the power of *logos* in Gorgias' *Encomium of Helen*, 8–14.

Isocrates, again like Gorgias, aims to make prose rival poetry, and he suggests that there are as many varieties of prose *logoi* as of poems:

there are no fewer kinds of *logoi* than of poetry . . . It would be no small task, if one were to try to enumerate all the types of *logoi*.[28]

And yet the overwhelming effect of Isocrates' writings is one of homogeneity. This homogeneity is partly one of style; Isocrates' prose is very distinctive, and uniform both in the sense that it varies remarkably little over his long career and in the sense that it aims for, and achieves, a high degree of smoothness and polish, with little to interrupt the flow.[29] It is not purely a matter of style, however; the speeches also have a distinctive, and consistent, moral and intellectual tone, and a distinctive sense of purpose, which create a strong impression of unity. Isocrates repeatedly sets out the features which distinguish his works from all others. For instance, the passage just quoted from *Antidosis* continues

but I shall mention the one [sc. the type of *logoi*] which is my own, leaving the others aside. There are some, who are not without experience of the genres I have mentioned, but who have chosen to write speeches not about your [i.e. individual Athenian citizens'] private business, but about the affairs of Greece and of the city, speeches for great civic gatherings ([*logous*] *Hellēnikous kai politikous kai panēgurikous*): all would admit that these bear more resemblance to compositions set to music and in metre than to what is said in a court of law. They describe their subjects using a poetic and varied style, they seek to employ weighty and original arguments, and they organise the whole *logos* with many brilliant formal devices. All are gladdened when they hear them, no less than when they hear poetry, and many wish to become students of them, in the belief that those who achieve pre-eminence in these *logoi* are much wiser and better and have much more power to do good than those who plead legal cases well.[30]

---

[28] πρῶτον μὲν οὖν ἐκεῖνο δεῖ μαθεῖν ὑμᾶς, ὅτι τρόποι τῶν λόγων εἰσὶν οὐκ ἐλάττους ἢ τῶν μετὰ μέτρου ποιημάτων . . . εἴη δ' ἂν οὐ μικρὸν ἔργον, εἰ πάσας τις τὰς ἰδέας τὰς τῶν λόγων ἐξαριθμεῖν ἐπιχειρήσειεν (*Antid.* 46).

[29] In particular, Isocrates' style goes to great lengths in the avoidance of hiatus (the 'clash' of two vowels at the end of one word and the beginning of the next). The subjective impression that Isocrates' style is distinctive and homogeneous is confirmed by a set of computerised stylometric tests conducted by Gerard Ledger. A range of variables are used to assign passages of Greek to their authors. With the other authors tested, there are always at least a small number of misassignations; with Isocrates there are none (G. R. Ledger, *Recounting Plato: A Computer Analysis of Plato's Style* (Oxford, 1989)).

[30] ἧς δ' οὖν ἐμοὶ προσήκει, ταύτης μνησθεὶς ἐάσω τοὺς ἄλλους. εἰσὶν γάρ τινες οἳ τῶν μὲν προειρημένων οὐκ ἀπείρως ἔχουσιν, γράφειν δὲ προῄρηνται λόγους, οὐ περὶ τῶν ὑμετέρων συμβολαίων, ἀλλ' Ἑλληνικοὺς καὶ πολιτικοὺς καὶ πανηγυρικούς, οὓς ἅπαντες ἂν φήσειαν ὁμοιοτέρους εἶναι τοῖς μετὰ μουσικῆς καὶ ῥυθμῶν πεποιημένους ἢ τοῖς ἐν δικαστηρίῳ λεγομένοις. καὶ γὰρ τῇ λέξει ποιητικωτέρᾳ καὶ ποικιλωτέρᾳ τὰς πράξεις δηλοῦσιν, καὶ τοῖς ἐνθυμήμασιν ὀγκωδεστέροις καὶ καινοτέροις χρῆσθαι ζητοῦσιν, ἔτι δὲ ταῖς ἄλλαις ἰδέαις ἐπιφανεστέραις καὶ πλείοσιν ὅλον τὸν λόγον διοικοῦσιν. ὧν ἅπαντες μὲν ἀκούοντες χαίρουσιν οὐδὲν ἧττον ἢ τῶν ἐν τοῖς μέτροις πεποιημένων, πολλοὶ δὲ καὶ μαθηταὶ γίγνεσθαι βούλονται, νομίζοντες τοὺς ἐν τούτοις πρωτεύοντας πολὺ σοφωτέρους καὶ βελτίους καὶ μᾶλλον ὠφελεῖν δυναμένους εἶναι τῶν τὰς δίκας εὖ λεγόντων (*Antid.* 46–47).

Compare this with another antithetical characterisation of Isocrates' own speeches, at the end of his last work, *Panathenaicus:* Isocrates wishes to commend those members of his audience who have appreciated this speech, and who in general

regard as more serious and more educational *logoi* which are instructive and display art, rather than those written for show or for disputes; *logoi* which aim at the truth, rather than those which seek to give a shock to their listeners' opinions; and *logoi* which reproach and criticise wrongdoing, rather than those spoken in order to gratify and win favour.[31]

Such programmatic statements serve to create the impression that, in the end, there are only two fundamental categories of *logoi*: good ones and bad ones. The good ones, not surprisingly, are Isocrates' own; bad ones are the ones which he rejects, but which, so it is implied, other writers do choose to compose. A whole moral and aesthetic vocabulary accumulates around this dichotomy. Isocrates' themes are grand, public, serious, not petty, selfish, or frivolous; his aims are to help, to advise, to criticise constructively, to speak his mind, rather than to attack, slander, or flatter; his speeches are polished, ordered, embellished, not random and unconsidered. None of these claims are very surprising, indeed it would be surprising for any pedagogical writer to claim the opposite; but the sheer repetition of these evaluative terms serves to create the impression that in these texts one is within a cultured, civilised discourse, outside which – carefully, but precariously, excluded from it – is a chaos of amoral, unrestrained, barbarous voices.[32]

Isocrates' *logoi*, then, identify themselves as forming a special category, and a category which is both morally and artistically superior. Collectively they construct a very recognisable, 'Isocratean' voice, which emphatically lays claim to moral and rhetorical authority. There are other respects, however, in which the corpus is less overtly unified.

One of these is the 'voice' of the speeches in a more literal sense: the identity of the imagined speaker. Sometimes the speaker is strongly identified as being Isocrates 'himself': this is obviously the case in the self-justifying *Antidosis*, where the writer addresses his readers or audience directly before entering into the fiction of the court-case. In the preface

---

[31] σπουδαιοτέρους καὶ φιλοσοφωτέρους εἶναι νομίζοντας τοὺς διδασκαλικοὺς καὶ τεχνικοὺς τῶν πρὸς τὰς ἐπιδείξεις καὶ τοὺς ἀγῶνας γεγραμμένων, καὶ τοὺς τῆς ἀληθείας στοχαζομένους τῶν τὰς δόξας τῶν ἀκροωμένων παρακρούεσθαι ζητούντων, καὶ τοὺς ἐπιπλήττοντας τοῖς ἁμαρτανομένοις καὶ νουθετοῦντας τῶν πρὸς ἡδονὴν καὶ χάριν λεγομένων (*Panath.* 272).

[32] Cf. Too's discussion of unifying elements in the Isocratean corpus (Too, *Rhetoric of Identity*, pp. 10–73), esp. p. 35: (Isocrates) 'establishes the claim to his authority in "otherness", in a discrimination against all other authors and their discourse.'

(1–12) he complains of the way he has been misunderstood, explains the fictional basis of the speech, and adds a personal touch by mentioning his advanced age ('I wrote this speech, not in my prime, but at the age of eighty-two; so you must forgive me if it seems less robust than those I have published before,' *Antid.* 9), something which he does also in *On the Peace* (145), in *Philip* (18), and in the *Panathenaicus*. In the last the personal reference is made still more concrete: he began the speech, he tells us, at the age of ninety-four, but he was stopped half-way by a disease 'which it would be indelicate to name, but which can kill not just old men, but many in the prime of life, in three or four days', and at the time of completion he is ninety-seven (*Panath.* 3, 266–270).[33]

These speeches, then, 'attach' themselves firmly to their author, but in others the imagined speaker is someone else: *Nicocles* is ostensibly spoken by Isocrates' pupil King Nicocles, *Archidamus* by the Spartan prince Archidamus, and *Plataicus* by an unnamed former citizen of the destroyed city of Plataea. It is nothing unusual for a Greek writer to put (written) words 'in someone else's mouth' – historians regularly write their characters' 'own words', and, at a different level, Isocrates himself began his career writing speeches which his clients would deliver as their own in a court of law. But it is interesting that none of these three works carries any authorial introduction or explanation, though *Nicocles* is made to refer to the companion-speech *To Nicocles* ('you have heard from Isocrates about the duties of a king: now hear from me about the duties of a subject'[34]). Different voices are introduced in a less striking way through Isocrates' occasional practice of presenting the direct speech of a friend, adviser or pupil; this has been seen in the case of the pro-Spartan pupil in *Panathenaicus*, and occurs also in *Antidosis*, *Areopagiticus*, and *Philip*.[35]

Another feature which might seem to divide the speeches is their range of political viewpoint. *Panegyricus* claims for democratic Athens the right to the hegemony of all the Greeks, and urges the city of Athens to lead the Greeks against the barbarians. *Antidosis* refers back to the *Panegyricus* and again embraces its political programme, and *Panathenaicus* returns to the theme of Athens' claim to hegemony. But *Philip* 'offers' the leadership of the Greeks to Philip of Macedon, while *Evagoras* and *To Nicocles* are concerned with defining, and indeed creating, an ideal monarch. *Nicocles*, the speech 'spoken' by the Cypriot king himself, explicitly asserts that

[33] On Isocrates' use of references to his age, see also Too, *Rhetoric of Identity*, pp. 43–44.
[34] Paraphrasing *Nicocles* 10–11.   [35] *Antid.* 142–149; *Phil.* 18–21.

monarchy is better than democracy or oligarchy (15). Again, *Panegyricus* and *Panathenaicus* contain sharp attacks on Sparta, whereas *Archidamus* is a robust articulation of traditional Spartan values, and the praise of Sparta is taken up by the voice of Isocrates' pupil in *Panathenaicus* itself (253–259). This is, of course, a schematic and simplifying account: the speeches were written over a period of very complex political developments, a time of shifting power-balances and alliances among the Greek states. I am concernd here not with the specific contemporary significance of the positions adopted in Isocrates' writings, but with their cumulative effect: the texts incorporate a diversity of political perspectives, including some which are diametrically opposed to each other.

Taking the speeches as a group, then, I suggest that they present, on the one hand, a distinctive authorial identity which remains the same; and, on the other hand, a sense of shifting voices and perspectives. The effect is one of ventriloquism: the voice can emanate from different positions and different personae, but the reader remains aware that it is the *same* voice.

Before returning to the question of how these *logoi* relate to Isocrates' pedagogy, I wish to consider once again one of the ways in which they are characterised, and to look at this in relation to the most ambitious claim Isocrates makes for *paideia*. At *Antidosis* 46 Isocrates speaks of *Hellēnikoi kai politikoi kai panēgurikoi logoi*, which I have translated above as 'speeches about the affairs of Greece and of the city, speeches for great civic gatherings'. At *Panathenaicus* 11, looking back on his whole career, he says that he chose to write, not about petty or private matters, but 'about the affairs of Greece, of kings and cities'.[36] Thus the scope of Isocratean *logoi* is Panhellenic. But pedagogy, *paideia*, looks even beyond this: at *Panegyricus* 50, at a climactic point in his praise of the city of Athens, Isocrates writes:

so much has our city surpassed the rest of humanity in thought and speech, that her pupils have become the teachers of the rest, and she has made the name of 'Greeks' seem to belong, no longer to the race, but to the cast of mind, and it is rather those who share our education who are called Greeks than those who share the common nature/ birth (*tēs koinēs phuseōs*).[37]

---

[36] περὶ τῶν Ἑλληνικῶν καὶ βασιλικῶν καὶ πολιτικῶν πραγμάτων (*Panath.* 11).

[37] τοσοῦτον δ᾽ ἀπολέλοιπεν ἡ πόλις ἡμῶν περὶ τὸ φρονεῖν καὶ λέγειν τοὺς ἄλλους ἀνθρώπους, ὥσθ᾽ οἱ ταύτης μαθηταὶ τῶν ἄλλων διδάσκαλοι γεγόνασιν, καὶ τὸ τῶν Ἑλλήνων ὄνομα πεποίηκεν μηκέτι τοῦ γένους, ἀλλὰ τῆς διανοίας δοκεῖν εἶναι, καὶ μᾶλλον Ἕλληνας καλεῖσθαι τοὺς τῆς παιδεύσεως τῆς ἡμετέρας ἢ τοὺς τῆς κοινῆς φύσεως μετέχοντας (*Paneg.* 50). Cf. Thuc. II.41.1 (Pericles' speech): ξυνελών τε λέγω τήν τε πᾶσαν πόλιν τῆς Ἑλλάδος παίδευσιν εἶναι . . .

On the face of it this means that being Greek depends more on Greek education than on Greek birth, and implies that a non-Greek could become Greek by receiving education, an idea which certainly was not commonplace in fourth-century Athens, though it was to become so with the expansion of the Greek world through Alexander's conquests. Indeed there is some resistance among classicists to the idea that Isocrates is really questioning the ethnic basis of Greek identity: thus the most recent commentator on the *Panegyricus*, Stephen Usher, asserts in his note on this passage that 'Isocrates is narrowing the idea of "Greekness" within the national boundaries, using the test of intellectual excellence, rather than extending it to include foreigners.'[38] Such an interpretation is certainly possible, but there is no good reason to reject the more straightforward alternative. (The view that Isocrates *does* allow for the possibility of non-Greeks becoming Greek derives support from *Evagoras* 66, where Evagoras is said to have turned his Cypriot subjects 'from barbarians into Greeks'.[39]) It is possible that Usher thinks it inappropriate for barbarians to be spoken of as potential Greeks in a work whose main thesis is that the Greeks should unite to make war on the barbarians: surely the theme requires a firm antithesis between barbarian and Greek? But this seems to me to be a misreading: the central point at *Panegyricus* 50 is not about the potential of barbarians, but about the potential of *paideia*. Isocrates urges the Athenians to extend the limits of the Greek world by war; at the same time, he claims for his own profession of *paideia* the ability not merely to define Greekness, but also to extend it.

This puts Isocrates' *Hellēnikoi logoi*, and his whole pedagogical programme, in a new perspective. A direct analogy can be drawn between his political ideal of a pan-Hellenic crusade and his pedagogical programme of *logoi*. The unifying authorial voice – the voice of the pedagogue – corresponds to the individual city or ruler endowed with hegemony of the Greeks; it is a voice which is able to encompass and include the whole Greek world, with its different political systems (democracy, oligarchy, monarchy) and its geographical range (Athens, Sparta, Sicily, Macedon, and Cyprus); a voice which claims for its own discourse the ability to define what is Greek and to extend further the

---

[38] S. Usher, *Greek Orators III: Isocrates* (Warminster, 1990), p. 161. Usher rather slyly makes his translation of the Greek text support his interpretation, rendering the last clause 'men are called "Greeks" when they share our education rather than *merely* our common blood' (emphasis added): 'merely' has no equivalent in the Greek.

[39] τοὺς δὲ πολίτας ἐκ βαρβάρων μὲν Ἕλληνας ἐποίησεν . . . (*Evag.* 66).

limits of Greekness. What the pupils learn, if they imitate the pedagogue
well and acquire his voice, is a way of speaking with authority for Greece
as a whole – adopting a central position within the field of 'Greekness';
by becoming the mouthpiece for this Panhellenic discourse, the pupil
becomes identified with the power to define and extend the civilised
world.

Before concluding, I wish to turn to two passages where individual
pupils of Isocrates are presented at some length. First, the ending of
the *Panathenaicus*, already referred to above. The main body of this text
consists of praise of the city Athens, in which Sparta is used for unfa-
vourable comparison. But then, as was described above, the authorial
voice breaks off in order to tell the reader how Isocrates sought advice
about this speech, first from his current pupils, then from a known
'Spartan sympathiser' among his former pupils. The pro-Spartan praises
the speech – thereby appearing to accept its criticism of Sparta – but
suggests that Sparta can be praised on one ground at least, namely the
excellence of her institutions (202). Isocrates vehemently rejects this
suggestion, even though it is a response which he has already explicitly
anticipated (111); by doing so he wins the applause of his other pupils.
But he remains troubled about the speech, and decides to read it to a
larger gathering. Here once again it is received with enthusiasm by all
except the Spartan sympathiser, who, after a pause, presents his views
at some length (235–263). Once again he praises what Isocrates has
written, but he now presents a radical re-interpretation of it: in his
view it is a masterpiece of deliberate rhetorical ambiguity, containing
one message for the Athenian public, another for the *cognoscenti*; Isocrates,
he claims, has deployed conventional criticisms of Sparta in such a way
as to expose their conventional quality, and to allow a 'real' message of
approval to shine out from underneath them. The pupil allows his interpretation of Isocrates' speech to develop rhetorically into a brief praise
of Sparta, followed by praise of Isocrates himself.

In response, Isocrates congratulates the pupil on his 'ability and
diligence', but makes no comment at all on the substance of what has
been said; and the speech ends with the comments already quoted
on Isocrates' age and health and a final exhortation to his audience.
How far the pupil's interpretation of Isocrates' speech can be seen as
'right' – i.e. as being tacitly endorsed by the principal authorial voice
– has been much debated, and is, I think, a question which the text
determinedly does not resolve. I describe this episode because in it the
Panathenaicus – which, as has been seen, dramatises the process of its own

composition – also dramatises the transmission of authority from ped-agogue to pupil. We are shown the pupil's skill as a 'judge of speeches' (whether or not his judgement is *correct* in this particular instance), and his ability to speak on a grand theme – the praise of one of the great Greek cities; finally Isocrates falls silent and the pupil is given the last word. And yet the text continues, and this reminds us that the pupil is speaking in Isocrates' own voice.

This drama representing a pupil who takes on and immortalises his master's voice may be contrasted with another vignette of Isocra-tean pedagogy and its results, namely the defence of the memory of Timotheus, son of Conon, in *Antidosis* 101–139. Timotheus' otherwise successful military career came to a bad end with prosecution and exile after the Athenian defeat at Embata in 356; he died not long after-wards. Here it is imagined that the (fictitious) prosecutor has dwelt on Timotheus as an example of the negative effect of Isocrates' teaching; Isocrates responds at corresponding length. He praises Timotheus' military achievements (107–113), and his brilliance as a general, with an emphasis on intellectual qualities (114–128);[40] but he must then go on to explain how such a paragon came to be condemned by the people. Apparently Timotheus' downfall was that his sense of dignity[41] – appro-priate in military command, but less useful in other departments of life – prevented him from justifying himself; he lacked the natural ability to deal with people and win their support. Isocrates had often warned him about this: and we are presented with what are ostensibly the actual words of the pedagogue to his pupil, teaching him that it is human nature to respond better to charm and flattery than to genuine merit, and advising him to ingratiate himself with the leaders of the demos. Timotheus, we are told, admitted the truth of his master's words, but was unable to change his natural disposition (138).

The rhetorical strategy which this story represents is a simple one: Isocrates is imagined to be accused of 'corrupting the young'; the conventional implications of such a charge, going back to the accusation of Socrates and other attacks on 'sophists', include inciting young men to neglect practical business in favour of idle talk, and turning them

---

[40] Thought-processes and reasonings are emphasised, and the vocabulary too is chosen in such a way as to highlight the intellectual component of generalship: thus in relation to Timotheus' ban on indiscriminate devastation of enemy land it is said that 'his philosophical object in this was' (τοῦτ' ἐφιλοσόφει . . . ὅπως, 121) to avoid instilling terror in potential subject cities.
[41] Or 'pride' (Gk. μεγαλοφροσύνη, 131); Isocrates insists that he was not 'arrogant' (ὑπερήφανος) or anti-democratic.

into clever, devious, unprincipled rhetoricians. Isocrates' Timotheus is the antitype of such a 'corrupted' pupil: his mind was so firmly fixed on affairs of state – on acting to further the interests of the city – that he had no time even for the little eloquence, the little pandering to the masses, that would have justified him and saved his reputation. Isocrates turns the failing of his friend and pupil to his own advantage, incidently exonerating himself (he warned Timotheus of the danger) and appropriating the whole episode as a stick with which to beat the Athenian public: it is too late to show gratitude to the pupil, but they can at least show gratitude to his master.

But if we pose a different question to this story – not 'did Isocrates corrupt the young?' but 'what skills, or what knowledge, did Isocrates impart to this pupil?' – it reads rather differently. What does Timotheus owe to Isocrates? The emphasis on the intellectual side of generalship is clearly intended to maximise his debt in this area; Timotheus' prudent decision-making, his *euboulia*, may be attributed in part to his education, as may his tact towards neutral cities and his gentleness towards the conquered (121–126). But when it comes to the exercise of persuasive power and the use of *logoi*, he is a failure. He is unable, or unwilling, to advise the people and influence them to do what is after all for their own good, namely to continue to place their confidence in him. It is significant that, while Isocrates' past advice to his pupil is presented as direct speech, Timotheus' response is merely reported, and in the briefest possible form: 'he said that I was right'.[42] Timotheus is tongue-tied, even within the text: he has not acquired the Isocratean voice.

That Timotheus will not, and cannot be expected to, acquire full mastery of *logoi* is implicitly acknowledged in the fragment of instruction at *Antidosis* 133–137: he is advised, not to take on the task of persuading the people himself, but to ingratiate himself with popular orators who can provide this service for him. This advice threatens to expose the limitations not just of Timotheus' education but of Isocratean pedagogy itself – it seems that Isocrates' pose of detachment from active life, and the high moral tone of his rhetorical discourse, made him unable to supply the attractive public image his friend needed, so that he was actually forced to refer him to unprincipled demagogues.[43] But Isocrates

---

[42] ὀρθῶς ... ἔφασκέν με λέγειν, 138.

[43] Isocrates frequently contrasts his own determination to give honest advice with the predilection of the demos, or of 'most people', to listen only to what they want to hear; the idea is developed most extensively in the opening of *On the Peace*, a fictional address to the Athenian assembly, in which the emphasis on the anticipated hostility of the audience is so extreme that

evades this inference by switching attention from popularity in life to
fame after death: posthumous reputations have always depended less
on merit than on the luck of being celebrated in literature; for this
reason Timotheus should cultivate rhetoricians, 'in order to gain high
repute in both ways: through your own actions and through their *logoi*'
(137). Thus the passage becomes nicely self-referential: *here*, in *Antidosis*,
is the timeless praise of Timotheus, the fruits of his association with Isocrates. This mirrors an observation at the start of this section of *Antidosis*,
where Isocrates expresses surprise at the prosecutor's (imagined) use of
Timotheus' name against him: 'I would have thought that, even if I
were shown quite clearly to be guilty of wrongdoing, I ought to be protected by my friendship with him'.[44] The impression is of a relationship
of reciprocity, a case more of mutual patronage than of pedagogy. We
may recall at this point the ancient tradition (of uncertain authenticity)
that Isocrates wrote for Timotheus a series of *Letters to the Athenians*,
while Timotheus set up a bronze statue of Isocrates at Eleusis.[45] Isocrates writes *for* Timotheus, rather than teaching Timotheus to write;
Timotheus reciprocates with a concrete, rather than a verbal, 'imitation'
of his master. Each man remains in his separate sphere; nothing tangible
is *transmitted*; to put it another way, Isocrates cannot change Timotheus'
phusis, his essential nature. But each stands to gain glory from association with the other.

The same dynamic of an exchange of patronage, an exchange of
glory, can be seen in the relationship between Isocrates and his other
most politically eminent pupil, King Nicocles. Through the speeches
Isocrates writes for him, Nicocles gains lasting glory (and publicity at
Athens) for himself and his father Evagoras; Isocrates, besides financial
remuneration, gains the ability to promote himself as a teacher of kings,
and above all associates himself with a ruler at the eastern limit of the
Greek world, actively engaged in fighting the Persians and hellenising
his subjects: a perfect symbol for the Panhellenic idea. I quote just one

---

it draws attention to the speech's fictional character: the Athenian demos, it is implied, would
never really listen to such plain speaking. The antithesis between unpalatable truth on the one
hand, and pleasant but unwholesome confections on the other, is of course commonplace; compare in particular the image in Plato's *Gorgias* of the philosopher as doctor and the demagogue
as pastrycook competing for influence over a demos of children (464de, 521e–522a).

[44] ἐγὼ δ' ᾤμην μέν, εἰ καὶ φανερῶς ἐξηλεγχόμην ἀδικῶν, διὰ τὴν πρὸς ἐκεῖνον φιλίαν
σῴζεσθαί μοι προσήκειν . . . (102).

[45] Pseudo-Plutarch, *Lives of the Ten Orators* 837c (letters), 838d (statue). For the letters see also
Mathieu and Brémond (eds.), *Isocrate* IV.163; in relation to the statue, note Isocrates' characterisation at *Evagoras* 73–75 of written praise as a superior alternative to carved or painted
likenesses.

example of the explicit articulation of this relationship, at the opening of the speech *To Nicocles*. Isocrates finds fault with people who offer rulers material gifts of clothing, bronze, gold, and such like. The rulers, after all, have more of these things than they do, and therefore less need of them. What they are really doing is not making gifts but engaging in commerce (*emporia*), in a subtle kind of trade: they hope to get back more of the same in return. Isocrates, by contrast, in sending Nicocles a speech of moral advice, is offering the finest possible gift: he is giving Nicocles precisely what kings characteristically lack (*To Nicocles* 1–4). Isocrates is not 'trading' like the others because what he gives is something which Nicocles cannot directly return, and which cannot be reduced to a particular monetary price; but that is not to say that he does not anticipate *anything* in return; indeed by stressing the exceptional quality, the pricelessness, of his gift, he hints at the opposite. The parallel with the case of Timotheus is clear: Nicocles, by his very position in life, lacks the benefit of pedagogic *logoi*, which Isocrates can supply; in return, we may infer, Isocrates receives what to him is otherwise inaccessible, namely an (indirect) involvement in the exercise of political rule.

The cases of Timotheus and of the anonymous pupil in *Panathenaicus* present two distinct models for the relationship between Isocrates and his pupil. One is a self-contained, binary relationship of exchange, mutually beneficial – even now Isocrates gains authority with readers from his association with figures like Timotheus and Nicocles, while in turn we read about them in Isocrates' texts – but essentially static. The other, more authentically pedagogical relationship is reproductive in character: the pupil is his master's true successor, he acquires mastery of Isocratean *logoi*, and will go on speaking – or rather writing – in Isocrates' voice.

In conclusion, Isocrates' pedagogy of Panhellenic *logoi* mirrors his political ideal of a Panhellenic crusade. It embraces the characteristic types of political system (kingship, oligarchy, democracy); it addresses itself to the existing boundaries of the Greek world, and it claims for itself the potential to extend those boundaries. This textual, pedagogic Panhellenism perhaps threatens to displace military and diplomatic Panhellenism: producing Panhellenic speeches may come to appear more important than realising concrete Panhellenic aims. This conflict is represented in the two images of the pupil: on the one hand, there is the pupil who is a king or general, a prime mover in political events; this figure is idealised in Isocrates' writings, but is ultimately unable to appropriate Isocratean *paideia*, and remains in a state of interdependence with the pedagogue; on the other hand, more in the shadows (and never identified with a specific individual), there is the inheritor of Isocratean discourse: the pupil who is like his master, who can speak with Isocrates' voice (which is a textual voice, a voice that exists in writing), and who can continue where Isocrates left off.

Isocrates' commitment to the instruction and glorification of rulers is undercut by the self-contained and self-referential nature of the world of *logoi* which his pedagogy constructs. Isocratean pedagogy has the potential to honour the ruler as pre-eminently Greek, pre-eminently civilised, the leader of the civilised world, but this civilisation is not ultimately in the ruler's possession: it is reserved by the pedagogue, and passed on by him to his successors in pedagogy. This relationship continues in the uneasy symbiosis between *paideia* and political power in the Greek and Greco-Roman world.[46] It also has a counterpart in modern universities, which face pressure to create the type of élite that a particular government demands, but where pedagogues often see their greatest success in the creation of more pedagogues.

---

[46] Well illustrated by Whitmarsh, in this volume.

CHAPTER 13

Xenophon's Cyropaedia: *disfiguring the pedagogical state*

Yun Lee Too

I

The Persia of Xenophon's *Cyropaedia* is an important site of political pedagogy, providing a historical scenario for a ruler's education and then a reference point for subsequent sites of instruction in power. Cicero informs us that Scipio Africanus kept the *Cyropaedia* by his side to supply himself with an image (*effigies*) of just empire (*Ep. Quintum* 1.1.23; also *Ep. ad Fam.* 9.25 and *De Senectute* 79–81).[1] Later, Renaissance scholars regarded Xenophon's work as a prescriptive account of how to produce an ideal ruler of an ideal state, and prior to Machiavelli, as the most influential 'mirror for princes'.[2] Modern readers add their voices to this regard for the work, continuing to find in Xenophon's portrayal of Cyrus the Great and his career a paradigm of ancient kingship and the system that produced it. In this chapter, I want to suggest, however, that this is not the only narrative provided by the *Cyropaedia*. If the work as a whole affirms the link between education and political authority, it also qualifies it. Xenophon's text presents a system of education which precipitates the collapse of a kingdom, not least because it tolerates a series of discontinuities between the knowledge Cyrus requires to be a good leader and the knowledge he actually possesses.

II

In the first book of the *Cyropaedia* Xenophon provides the idealising image of a pedagogical Persia whose authority is to be called into

[1] For the work's influence on historical kingships, see J. J. Faber, 'The *Cyropaedia* and Hellenistic Kingship', *AJP* 100 (1979), 497–514.
[2] J. Tatum, *Xenophon's Imperial Fiction. On The Education of Cyrus* (Princeton, 1989), p. xiii.

question. Power, most simply the capacity to rule oneself and others,[3] is predicated on knowledge, specifically the knowledge of how to rule. Persia is a state where knowledge and political status are conceived as inseparable from one another and where the figures of didactic and political authority, namely the teacher and the ruler, refer to, and are elided, into one another. In pedagogical Persia adult citizens are required to accord the same respect to those in charge of the state, particularly the leader (*archōn*), and to those who oversee the *paideia* of their children (1.2.12). The pedagogue is endowed with a privileged political identity, which the author goes to some length to reinforce and elaborate. In book 1 Xenophon reveals that the task of the pedagogue is to rehearse his pupil in obedience to and in reverence for the state's rulers. The teacher instructs his young charges to 'obey (*peithesthai*) their leaders (*tois archousi*)' (1.2.8, cf. 1.6.20). His role is to mediate the ruler's power with the assistance of other individuals whose authority also refers and defers to that of king. When the teacher trains his young pupils to control their appetites for food and drink, he permits them to eat only after receiving a signal from individuals named 'leaders (*archontes*)' (1.2.8). As ephebes the youths are again watched over by other individuals also designated *archontes* (1.2.5; 1.2.9; 1.5.1).[4] Chrysantas, a figure commended for his acumen (cf. 2.3.5 and 4.1.4[5]), stresses the continuity between pedagogical and political authority when he assigns to both teachers (*didaskaloi*) and rulers (*archontes*) the task of giving good directions and habituating those under their authority to act reputably (3.3.53). The training of the youth comes to an end with a hunt led by the overall 'leader' of the state, the king. The hunt is presented as a rehearsal for war (1.2.10[6]) but also implicitly as a climax affirming the goal of Persian education to be the training of the subject.

Persian education is far more than a temporary intervention in an individual's life if only because it entails the inception of a social identity which continues to be enacted and sustained by an individual throughout his life as a member of a community. It is a process of socialisation coterminous with a citizen's life, spanning childhood and

[3] Cf. Aristotle *Politics* 1277a25–9, who says that it is a virtue of the respectable (δόκιμος) citizen to rule and to be ruled.
[4] In the *Constitution of the Lacedaimonians* Xenophon tells his reader that the παιδονόμος is referred to as an ἄρχων (2.10.11; cf. Plato *Republic* 479d).
[5] B. Due, *The Cyropaedia. Xenophon's Aims and Methods* (Aarhus and Copenhagen, 1989), p. 71.
[6] καὶ βασιλεὺς ὥσπερ καὶ ἐν πολέμῳ ἡγεμών ἐστιν αὐτοῖς, 1.2.10.

old age (cf. Aristotle *Pol.* 1337b4–5; 1337b36).[7] Both Due and Tatum observe that when Xenophon writes of Cyrus being 'educated in the Persian laws'[8] the author points to a blurring of the distinction between citizenship and education. As the state's ruler and leader, the king continues, or rather completes, the work of the teacher, 'instructing' his subjects as if they were his pupils. Accordingly, Xenophon later figures the exercise and articulation of the Persian king's power as a form of 'instruction'. Cyrus 'teaches' his army and subjects when he addresses them: the verb *didaskein* recurs throughout the work as a description of the leader's speech act.[9]

Barry Strauss has drawn attention to what he understands to be the 'intrinsically *political* nature of the father-son relationship' in Greek thought, where the father stands for the lord (*kurios*) of the household (*oikos*) and the son is his successor.[10] It is the father's obligation and a sign of his authority that he instructs his 'children' in virtue, particularly moderation, as the taxiarch Aglaitadas highlights at 2.2.14. According to Xenophon, the king's pedagogy is also the teaching of the 'father' of the state. He observes that the Persian leader regards his subjects as if they were his children, while they in turn revere him as a 'father' (8.8.1; cf. 8.1.44; 8.2.9).[11] In book 8 the sagacious Chrysantas declares the good leader (*archōn*) to be similar to the good father, as both concern themselves with the well-being of those under their authority and care (8.1.1). The ruler-father serves as a source of knowledge and a

---

[7] R. Nickel, *Xenophon, Erträge der Forschung*, Bd. III (Darmstadt 1979), p. 57; W. E. Higgins, *Xenophon the Athenian. The Problem of the Individual and the Society of the Polis* (Albany, NY, 1977), p. 54; Due, *The Cyropaedia*, p. 15; Tatum, *Xenophon's Imperial Fiction*, p. 90.

On the understanding that the Persian teacher has a limited function and that Persian education has this preparatory status, R. Breitenbach regards the work's title, 'The Education of Cyrus', as being appropriate as a description only for book 1, which relates the strict training and regimen of the Persian youth; R. Breitenbach *RE* IX, A 2, col. 1707a. Also see H. Arendt, 'What Was Authority?' in C. J. Friedrich (ed.) *Authority*. Nomos 1 (Cambridge, MA, 1958), pp. 96–7. Arendt insists on a distinction between political and pedagogical authorities, assuming that in antiquity once the pupil assumes his position as a full subject in the state he ceases to have to answer to pedagogical authority.

[8] ἐπαιδεύθη γε μὴν ἐν Περσῶν νόμοις.

[9] e.g. διδάσκειν, 2.1.20; 2.2.6; διδασκέτω, 6.2.24; ἐδίδαξε, 8.1.15; διδάσκω . . . αὕτη γὰρ ἀρίστη διδασκαλία, 8.7.24.

[10] Discussions of the analogy between the οἶκος and the πόλις may be found in B. S. Strauss, '*Oikos/Polis*: Towards a Theory of Athenian Paternal Ideology 450–399 BC' in W. R. Connor, M. H. Hansen, K. A. Raaflaub, B. S. Strauss, with a preface by J. R. Fears, *Aspects of Athenian Democracy*, Classica et Mediaevalia Dissertationes XI (Copenhagen, 1990), 101–27 at p. 108, and B. Strauss, *Fathers and Sons in Athens: Ideology and Society in the Era of the Peloponnesian War* (London, 1993), pp. 32ff.

[11] Due, *The Cyropaedia*, p. 17, for other comparisons of a political leader to a 'father' in Greek literature.

paradigm for imitation by his 'offspring' (cf. 7.5.85–6; 8.7.24). Cyrus' own father, Cambyses, provides the work's ideal example of the paternal king as teacher. In the second half of book 1, in the most obvious of Cambyses' *paideutic* interventions in the work (also cf. 1.6.20 and 8.5.22–7), Cambyses, significantly designated 'father (*patēr*)', instructs his heir and son (*pais*) in the art of warfare (1.5.14).[12] Later Tigranes, the son of the Armenian king, corroborates the pedagogical obligations of Cyrus' royal father, echoing what seem to be banalities regarding paternal authority.[13] Tigranes advises the youth to imitate (*mimeisthai*) his father if he admires the latter's plans and actions (3.1.15).

Cyrus at least ostensibly follows this advice when he inherits the role of civic educator from his father Cambyses. He instructs his subjects to educate their children (*kai tous paidas . . . paideuōmen*, 7.5.85–6), while in the final book he is depicted as telling his own sons, Cambyses and Tanaoxares, that he educated (cf. *epaideuon*) them to honour those above them in rank and to be honoured by those beneath them (8.7.10). Cyrus reinforces the ideal of *paideia* as a lesson in the structure of social rank and its obligations.

III

Plato proposes that there was a discrepancy between the ideal pedagogical state and the real Persia. In *Alcibiades I* Socrates praises Persia for ensuring that its future kings are educated by the most wise, just, moderate, and courageous individuals (121e). In this dialogue Plato portrays the barbarian state as one in which the leader has been prepared for his position of political authority and responsibility by a rigorous training in virtue. In the *Laws*, however, the author offers a critique of Persian education. Here Plato's Athenian Stranger pronounces the education of Cyrus the Great 'incorrect' and finds fault with the king for not educating his children properly (3.694c). The Stranger declares that the sons of Cyrus have been 'educated' into corruption and luxury, and not into virtue (3.695b). For Plato, the historical Persia of Cyrus and his heirs is an example of the improperly enacted pedagogical state.

Ancient and modern scholars locate the critique of the education of Cyrus in the *Laws* within a larger narrative about the relationship of

---

[12] Tatum, *Xenophon's Imperial Fiction*, p. 87.

[13] See Tatum, *Xenophon's Imperial Fiction*, p. 139 on the characterisation of Tigranes as a 'bright young man armed with a little learning from study with a sophist'.

Plato to Xenophon. Aulus Gellius observes that some people regard
the *Cyropaedia* as a response to the *Republic* (14.3), while Diogenes Laertius
regards both as works which depict ideal constitutions (3.34). Athenaeus,
followed by modern readers, perceives the *Laws* to be Plato's response
to the *paideia* of Cyrus as portrayed in the *Cyropaedia* (504e–505a).[14]
However, this narrative, which attempts to give Plato the last word
over his contemporary, ignores the polemical conclusion of Xenophon's
work which supplies the reader with a catalogue of problems following
the death of Cyrus and thus seems to assent to the verdict of the *Laws*.
Here the author points to strife amongst the king's sons, the empire's
cities and peoples (8.8.2), a decay of religious piety (8.8.3–5), a relaxation of morality, demonstrated in the Persians' now indulgent attitudes
towards food and drink (8.8.6–12), abandonment of the rigorous out-
door training of children (8.8.13–14), and an ensuing decline in military
standards (8.8.19–26). Perhaps most significant of these problems is the
easing of the formerly strict system of education, which constitutes the
removal of one of the crucial supports of the pedagogical state.[15]

Because this concluding passage calls into question the ideal deline-
ated in the first book, individuals attempt either to deny Xenophon's
authorship or else to downplay, by qualifying, its obviously critical tone.
As Tatum notes, until the nineteenth century, the work's epilogue was
regarded as authentic and seen to be an instance of the 'decline of
empire' motif.[16] Later critics turned their attention to it, often to treat
it as a textual problem rather than as one of sense. Bizos and Hirsch,
for instance, argued that the apparent inconsistencies and contradictions between it and earlier parts of the work meant that it must be
apocryphal.[17] Others, such as Eichler, who produced a dissertation on
the problem of the *Cyropaedia*'s ending, and Miller, the editor of the Loeb
text, were either puzzled by it or coped by ignoring it.[18] Weathers
maintained the authenticity of these chapters but saw them as affirming
the greatness of Cyrus in that they report political difficulties only *after*

[14] E.g. Tatum, *Xenophon's Imperial Fiction*, p. 234. Also see D. Gera, *Xenophon's* Cyropaedia: *Style, Genre and Literary Technique* (Oxford, 1993), p. 12.

[15] Note that Herodotus blames the introduction of luxury into Persia on the influence of the conquered Lydians (*Histories* 1.71.2).

[16] Tatum, *Xenophon's Imperial Fiction*, pp. 220ff. The 'decline' motif perhaps begs a question as to whether, and how, it should be seen in relation to the Greeks' perceptions of themselves and of the decline of their own institutions (see, for instance, the nostalgia of Isocrates' *On the Peace* and the *Areopagiticus*).

[17] Cf. M. Bizos, *Xénophon. Cyropédie* I (Paris, 1971), pp. xxviff., and S. W. Hirsch, *The Friendship of the Barbarians. Xenophon and the Persian Empire* (Hanover and London, 1985), pp. 92f. and 181.

[18] Tatum, *Xenophon's Imperial Fiction*, pp. 220ff.

the leader's death,[19] while Delebecque, regarding them as genuine, accorded them the status of afterthought.[20] Due insists that they were an integral part of the author's plan, though he perceives the critique to be limited to the Persia of Artaxerxes II rather than to the Persia depicted in the work as a whole.[21] He justifies his position by insisting that Xenophon is providing a picture only of Persia's leader, Cyrus, and not the state's overall system, despite the fact that Wood has shown that for the author good leadership proceeds from good organisation of society.[22] For Due, Persia's more ideal period under the leadership of Cyrus the Great signals the possibility that the present and future can be better again. Tatum and Gera, prepared to tolerate the explanations of pre-nineteenth century critics, seem to accept the epilogue at face value. Tatum suggests that Xenophon's work turns at the end into a 'novel of disillusionment',[23] while Gera sees the last section as pointing to a decline of moral standards in Persia after the conquest of Babylon, implicitly rehearsing the truism that 'power corrupts' and 'absolute power corrupts absolutely'.[24]

If the reader is uncomfortable in accepting the implications of what the final chapters of the *Cyropaedia* seem to be saying, this is due above all to the apparent contradiction with the preceding narrative and its image of an ideal Persia. The instinct to suppress any discourse which might qualify the image of the pedagogical state and of its leader is strong. Thus in the *Oeconomicus* readers assume that the conflation of the portrait of Cyrus the Great with that of the much less impressive Cyrus the Younger must be to the credit of the latter.[25] A Straussian 'reading between the lines' is the mode of reception which currently and notoriously tolerates apparent discrepancies in Xenophon's texts.[26]

[19] W. Weathers has proposed that the account of the decline of the Persian empire after the death of Cyrus affirms the greatness of Cyrus in that it suggests that it is the force of the king's personality which holds together his kingdom; see 'Xenophon's Political Idealism', *CJ* 41 (1954), p. 317. Also J. Luccioni, *Les idées politiques et sociales de Xénophon* (Paris, 1947), pp. 250–1.
[20] E. Delebecque, 'Xénophon, Athènes et Lacédémone' *REG* 59–60 (1946–7), pp. 101f.
[21] Due, *The Cyropaedia*, pp. 18–19.
[22] Due, *The Cyropaedia*, p. 25 and N. Wood, 'Xenophon's Theory of Leadership' *ClMed* 25 (1964), pp. 33–66, esp. pp. 55ff.
[23] Tatum, *Xenophon's Imperial Fiction*, p. 237.   [24] Gera, *Xenophon's* Cyropaedia, pp. 299–300.
[25] See A. Cizek, 'From the historical truth to the literary convention: the life of Cyrus the Great viewed by Herodotus, Ctesias and Xenophon', *L'Antiquité Classique* 44 (1975) 531–52; Hirsch, *The Friendship of the Barbarians*, pp. 61–74; and more recently, S. B. Pomeroy, *Xenophon Oeconomicus: A Social and Historical Commentary* (Oxford, 1994), pp. 248–50.
[26] For 'reading between the lines' as a strategy for reclaiming an esoteric and subversive text intended for an elite as distinct from the face value message intended for the generality, see A. Patterson, *Reading Between the Lines* (London, 1993), pp. 11–35, esp. p. 22.

So in this vein of reading, Higgins proposes that Xenophon produces a gap between what is apparently being said and what is in reality the case, with an effect which the former terms an 'ironic humour', regarding the *Cyropaedia* as a representation of an ideal government which shows up the failure of contemporary political structures.[27]

Yet 'reading between the lines' is a mode of interpretation which takes enormous liberties, and I would argue that the discrepancies in the *Cyropaedia* are sufficiently explicit to demand that we read the lines themselves, that we take the epilogue as an integral and necessarily disturbing element of this work. The critique of contemporary Persia at the end of book 8 is a rupture only inasmuch as it is far more obvious in its point than the narrative which precedes it: the conclusion makes clear the consequences of the youth and subsequent actions of Cyrus. Against previous attempts to present the work as a eulogy of Cyrus, I maintain that Xenophon displays his subject's deficiencies, first as a student and then as a ruler-teacher, to account for the non-fulfilment and collapse of the pedagogical state. The work is evidence of the point that the author makes in the text's very first chapter, namely that all constitutions – whether they are democracies, oligarchies or tyrannies – are bound to disintegrate unless those who rule them (*archontes*) are wise and fortunate (1.1.1).

IV

Xenophon informs the reader that Cyrus is educated in the conventional Persian manner until the age of twelve or so (1.3.1). After this, Cyrus is taken by his mother, Mandane, away from Cambyses, the father-king who can best provide him with the knowledge of how to rule (cf. 1.5.14), and to the Median court of his grandfather Astyages (1.3.1). Due asserts that Cyrus is not compromised by his time in Media,[28] while Tatum, adhering to the Herodotean characterisation of the Persian leader as someone who cannot be tempted by luxury (cf. Herodotus 9.122), optimistically argues that the youth resists the bad model offered to him by Astyages.[29] Because they are bound to the idealised image of the mature king, these scholars actually disjoin Cyrus' youth and adulthood in a

---

[27] Higgins, *Xenophon the Athenian*, pp. 12 and 44.   [28] Due, *The Cyropaedia*, p. 152.

[29] Tatum must invest in such a reading because he regards the *Cyropaedia* as a precursor of the *Bildungsroman*, or narrative which relates the development of an adolescent into maturity, in this case, of the uninhibited child Cyrus into restrained leader at e.g. 1.4.11–12. Tatum, *Xenophon's Imperial Fiction*, pp. 97–8; also see pp. 37 (for the comparison of the *Cyropaedia* to a *Bildungsroman*) and 107.

manner that is questionable. They ignore both unfortunate influences upon the boy and aspects of his behaviour which must call into question his subsequent authority as Persian leader.

Immediately troubling for the idealising reading are the young Cyrus' interactions with his grandfather's beloved attendant favourite, Sakas.[30] When the prince first arrives at Astyages' court, he finds access to his grandfather hindered by Sakas. Sakas maliciously prevents the youth from running up to Astyages, deliberately inventing excuses to keep him away from the Median monarch (1.3.11). Although initially critical of the servant, Cyrus himself later assumes the roles of favourite and of 'gatekeeper' within the palace. First, the prince takes over Sakas' duties as wine-pourer in jest (1.3.9); then and more importantly, he adopts Sakas' role as the individual who controls and impedes access to the king. Cyrus finds himself needing to convince Astyages of his maturity when he wishes to go on a hunt with the king. He realises that he can no longer beg as if he were a child (*hōsper pais ōn*) or ask permission spontaneously (cf. 1.3.8) and that he must make cautious overtures to his grandfather. Cyrus adopts the posture of the syco-phantic courtier, as he learns to anticipate the rhetorically privileged moment of opportunity (*kairos*) for his request to be heard and acquires knowledge of how to fawn (cf. *hupoptēssōn*, 1.3.8). The prince controls and regulates access to his own grandfather, as Xenophon wryly observes, outgrowing childhood to become his own Sakas (1.4.6[31]; 1.3.8).

Markedly unlike the sober and virtuous Cambyses, Astyages is a figure who, in Xenophon's characterisation of him, makes us acutely aware of the absence of paternal and pedagogical authority at the Median court. As leader of Media, he comes to represent his state as a deeply feminised land of luxury and laxity, and so as a land which stands in marked contrast to the ideal of a moral, temperate Persia. As Tatum notes, even Astyages' own daughter Mandane is adamant that Cyrus will be unable to learn about justice (*dikaiosunē*) in the tyrant state of Media (1.3.16–18). When the Median king first appears, he does so in oriental finery which prompts Cyrus to declare him 'beautiful (*kalos*)' and 'most beautiful (*kallistos*)' (1.3.2). It is, perhaps, significant that the only other individuals described by this adjective are the slave

---

[30] Due regards Cyrus' interaction with his grandfather's favourite, Sakas, as evidence for a devel-opment of the youth's character for the better. Due, *The Cyropaedia*, p. 154, and S. Erasmus, 'Der Gedanke der Entwicklung eines Menschen in Xenophons Kyroupaedie' in *Festschrift für Fr. Zucker* (Berlin, 1954), pp. 111–125, esp. p. 115.

[31] αὐτὸς ἤδη Σάκας ἑαυτῷ ἐγίγνετο, 1.4.6.

Sakas (1.3.8) and Abradatas' gorgeous wife, Pantheia, that is figures
who are other than the free-born male and who are subordinate within
the structure of Median tyranny (4.6.11; cf. 5.1.4ff.).

Astyages is a poor example for his subjects and for his grandson
because he continually contradicts his words by his actions. As Cyrus
perceptively charges, the king and his companions do precisely what
they do not permit their children to do, with the result that those
around him have forgotten that Astyages is the state's king and ruler
(1.3.10[32]). The king's political position is compromised by his inability
to offer himself as a paradigm of virtue to others. On the one occasion
that the Median king is depicted as assuming the discourse of the
teacher-ruler, it is hardly as the benevolent father-teacher of his subjects idealised in the initial chapters of the work. In response to his
mother's, Mandane's, observation that he would be severely punished
if he showed signs of Median softness in Persia, Cyrus ventures that
Astyages 'instructs (*didaskein*)' his subjects to be content with the wealth
that they have. But even in Cyrus' account, it becomes clear that the
Median leader uses pedagogical discourse to articulate his own superiority as he 'teaches' his subjects that they should own less by virtue of
their inferior position with respect to their king (1.3.18). Cyrus' reference to his grandfather as Mandane's *patēr*, as father of a daughter (not
a son), at this moment in the narrative draws attention to the fact that
the ideal of the father as a locus of pedagogical and political authority
has been undermined (cf. 7.5.86; 8.7.24): to his children-subjects, the
Median king is a father who fails to justify his position of responsibility
by his behaviour.

Cyrus may criticise Astyages for undermining his own 'teaching', and
consequently his political position at 1.3.10; however, the prince takes
his grandfather as an implicit role model for his own actions. Media
also trains Cyrus in an extravagance which will manifest itself at later
points in his life. Astyages organises for his grandson a grand feast which
he hopes will whet the youth's appetite for the Median way of life. The
youth initially appears to resist luxury. He questions the need for such
excess, and draws a contrast between the numerous delicacies which the
diner has to go to great trouble (*pragmata*) to reach and the simplicity of
the Persian meal (1.3.4–5). Cyrus ostensibly espouses the Persian attitude

---

[32] 'First of all, you yourselves were doing what you did not allow us [your] children to do'
(πρῶτον μὲν γὰρ ἃ οὐκ ἐᾶτε ἡμᾶς τοὺς παῖδας ποιεῖν, ταῦτα αὐτοὶ ἐποιεῖτε, 1.3.10) and
'You had completely forgotten that you were the king; the others, that you were their ruler'
(ἐπελέλησθε δὲ παντάπασι σύ τε ὅτι βασιλεὺς ἦσθα, οἵ τε ἄλλοι ὅτι σὺ ἄρχων, 1.3.10).

of parsimony towards food and drink, which Xenophon describes else-where in the work. The author informs the reader in book 1 that the Persian citizen is educated to endure a diet of bread and water: the only delicacy permitted the Persian is cress (*kardamon*, 1.2.8; 1.2.11–12; 1.5.12; cf. Herodotus 1.71). Later Gobryas, the Babylonian general, affirms that no educated Persian would be caught snatching food while on campaign nor allow his meal to become an overriding passion (5.2.17). At 4.2.45 Cyrus reveals what appears to be his commitment to self-control.[33] He encourages his men to make a display of their education (cf. *epideixaimeth' an tēn paideian*) by restraining their appetites and reaffirms the educated Persian's view that self-denial is a form of gratification. The verb *epideixaimeth'* invokes the *epideixis*, the sophist's self-advertising performance of his skill and wisdom. Repeating the teaching of his father Cambyses (cf. 1.5.12), he tells his army that hunger is a delicacy (*opson*) and that they should enjoy drinking water from a flowing river (4.5.4). The Persian leader attributes carousing and drunkenness to the defeated Babylonians, tacitly characterising them as undisciplined and therefore susceptible opponents (7.5.15–21).

Due astutely observes of the feast episode at 1.3.4–5 that narrative compression has occurred despite the reader's impression that Cyrus is newly arrived in Media: the youth's familiarity with the palace servants, especially Sakas, discloses that he has already spent some time at the oriental court.[34] I suggest that this narrative economy helps to emphasise the discrepancy between Cyrus' critique and his subsequent actions, for Cyrus' own later practice with food is radically different from his 'teaching' on moderation. The Persian prince relaxes the strict dietary regimen for his Persian army. Although it is customary for a Persian to eat only after he has worked up a sweat (2.1.29 and 2.4.6), the leader summons his taxiarchs to a meal after only gentle instruction (*tēs te praotētos tēs didaskalias*, 2.3.21). Even the exhortation that Cyrus gives on the virtues of drinking water and eating bread while on campaign at 6.2.26ff. suggests that the leader has undermined the ideal of Persian moderation. Cyrus tells his men to accustom themselves to drinking water as they will not be able to carry sufficient wine with them (6.2.29). The implications of this directive are that wine is the preferred drink, and perhaps even that the Persian army has become used to drinking wine under Cyrus' command. Disregard for dietary restraint is more

---

[33] Gera, *Xenophon's* Cyropaedia, p. 26, deems self-control to be one of Cyrus' Socratic qualities.
[34] Due, *The Cyropaedia*, pp. 44–5.

obviously revealed elsewhere in the work. In book 4 we learn that the
Median army under Cyrus' command indulges itself on plundered food
and drink during victory celebrations, while his uncle Cyaxares gets
drunk with his men (4.5.8). If on this occasion Cyrus can be excused
by his absence from the festivities as he sets out to catch looters with
his Persian retinue, the reader is given the impression that Cyrus'
army later marches ultimately and above all on its stomach rather than
on virtue and restraint. Xenophon implies that an enormous retinue
attends the army in order to supply its meals when he draws an analogy between the military outfit and the different individuals needed to
prepare meals in a household at 8.2.6.

The youthful Cyrus undermines his subsequent identity as a reliable
spokesperson for Persian morality and virtue in other respects. According to the account of a Persian child's education given in book 1, the
hunt has a pedagogical function, offering the king an opportunity to
exercise his authority and his youthful subjects an opportunity to obey
it in rehearsal for war (1.2.10; cf. 8.1.34). But Cyrus' conduct on his
first hunt is troubling. The prince had previously accused Astyages of
forgetting (cf. *epelelēsthe*) his position and obligations as a king (1.3.1), but
as soon as the prince sees his prey, he forgets everything (cf. *pantōn
epilathomenos*) he has learned in order to follow the creature wherever
its leads him. In response to this indiscipline, his uncle Cyaxares tells
him to do as he wishes (cf. *poiei hopōs boulei*) since he now seems to be
the king (*basileus*) of the hunt, implying the youth has improperly and
prematurely assumed the position of leadership in the expedition (1.4.9–
10). That the youth disregards the instructions of his elders signals a
refusal to be ruled by others and to rule himself, both of which are
necessary prerequisites for good leadership (cf. *sautōi peithesthai*, 1.6.20;
2.2.11). Accordingly, Xenophon undercuts Cyrus' achievement in spear-
ing a deer with an exaggerated description of the creature as 'a fine
and great thing (*kalon ti chrēma kai mega*)' (1.4.8). The author shows up
Cyrus as the killer of a harmless animal, perhaps misappropriating to
the slain creature Herodotus' description of the menacing Mysian boar
as a 'great thing (*chrēma . . . mega*)' (*Histories* 1.36.1).

Because the hunt is a military rehearsal, Cyrus' behaviour determines
subsequent shortcomings on campaign. The lapse of memory which
Cyrus suffers at 1.4.8 is reenacted at 3.3.62 when, as the general of his
army, he forgets (*epilathomenos*) a military formation. Later, as the leader
of the Persian army, he reveals himself willing to tolerate similar carelessness in his subjects. The reader is told that Cyrus makes allowances

for his soldiers *forgetting* their provisions while on campaign. He decides to establish his camps close to one another with the intention of making retrieval of neglected items easy (6.3.1[35]; cf. 8.8.11). But the hunt also marks Cyrus' more worrying tendency to act prematurely. In the assault on the Assyrians that is narrated later in book 1 Cyrus again acts precipitously, rushing at the enemy as soon as he sees them and prompting his men to act similarly (cf. *apronoētōs*, 1.4.22). Xenophon compares the impetuous youth to an inexperienced dog who tracks a boar without foresight (*apronoētōs*, 1.4.21), and the metaphor proposes an analogy between the present military manoeuvre and the earlier hunt. The adverb *apronoētōs* highlights the absence of *pronoia*, the quality which, together with *philoponia*, distinguish the leader from those he leads (1.6.8; cf. 4.5.10; 8.1.13; 8.2.2.). Thus the otherwise doting and anti-authoritarian grandfather uncharacteristically intervenes to restore order to the hunt situation in book 1, blaming his grandson (cf. *aition men onta*) for the fiasco (1.4.24).

v

Shortly after his return to Persia from Media, Cyrus is named general (*archonta*) of the Median army by Cyaxares (1.5.5). It is at this point that Cyrus receives a Persian education. He invokes Cambyses' identity as father-teacher *par excellence* in order to learn *(mathōn)* about the art of war (1.5.14). What he receives from the king is an important lesson on how to possess and justify actual political authority rather than merely to appear to have authority. Cyrus' inquiries about how a leader should appear to be wiser than the individuals he leads (*phronimōteron dokein einai*, 1.6.22; cf. 1.6.21) prompts from Cambyses a disquisition on the value of virtue. Apart from demonstrating forethought (*pronoia*) and love of labour (*philoponia*) (1.6.8), actual authority requires that one must manifest real virtue. Cambyses declares that the most effective way of appearing to be wise (*dokein phronimos einai*) is actually *to be* wise (*to genesthai . . . phronimon*). Reality is privileged over appearance to such a degree that the good Persian leader will employ deceit (*exapatan*) only when he deals with enemies rather than with his friends: deceit operates in terms of a dichotomy between appearance and reality, undermining true power as far as Cambyses is concerned (1.6.29; 1.6.33).

---

[35] καὶ τῇ μὲν πρώτῃ ἡμέρᾳ ἐξεστρατοπεδεύσατο ὡς δυνατὸν ἐγγύτατα, ὅπως εἴ τίς τι ἐπιλελησμένος εἴη, μετέλθοι . . . 6.3.1.

Cambyses' 'lesson' on political leadership is intended to serve as a standard for Cyrus' subsequent conduct as general and king, and Tatum notes that the youth shows himself mindful of the teachings articulated by his father (cf. 1.6.3; 1.6.5; 1.6.6.; 1.6.8).[36] Yet if we accept that character development is a concept alien to antiquity, any apparent change in an individual is to be explained as the character *revealing* him- or herself for the person he or she really is.[37] Accordingly, Cambyses' pedagogical interventions are of little effect: the child in Media is essentially the same as and prefigures the mature adult and his subsequent moral condition. There is a sense in which the son invites his father's teaching only ultimately to reject it. The prince establishes his political identity and position above all through the very strategies of display and empty gesture which he had learned in Media and which Cambyses rejects as the basis for true authority.

The extravagant and beautiful garments of Astyages, which delight the child and grasp his attention when he initially arrives at his grandfather's court (1.3.3), become the whole foundation of Cyrus' power as the youth holds on to and develops the politics of display as the basis of his subsequent power. Astyages gives Cyrus his own set of Median clothing before the latter returns to Persia. In retrospect it will appear that he gives the latter the apparatus of apparent authority, a 'fashion system', through which to construct the basis of totalitarian power in his fatherland (1.4.26).[38] That the young prince already understands the significance of this gift is made clear when he proposes to Cambyses that a leader should distinguish himself from his subjects by a demonstration of privilege: he should dine more sumptuously than his subordinates, display his greater wealth, and be seen to lead a more leisurely life (1.6.8). Cyrus, as teacher-leader, gives a new twist to the notion of 'nutritionist' pedagogy, providing bodily rather than intellectual sustenance.

Cyrus first invokes the politics of appearance when he asserts his superiority over his Median uncle Cyaxares during the Assyrian campaign. In book 2 Cyrus fails to attire himself to impress the Indian leader as Cyaxares had commanded (2.4.1–8); however, in book 5 the prince takes a cohort of allies, including Medians, Armenians, Hyrcanians, and

[36] Tatum, *Xenophon's Imperial Fiction*, p. 88.
[37] See C. Gill, 'The Question of Character-Development: Plutarch and Tacitus' *CQ* 33 (1983), pp. 469–87, esp. p. 469 and n. 2.
[38] 'We could say that the institution of the linguistic sign is a contractual act (at the level of entire community and of history), while the institution of the Fashion sign is a tyrannical act: there are *mistakes* in language and *faults* in Fashion'; see R. Barthes, *The Fashion System*, tr. M. Ward and R. Howard (Berkeley and Los Angeles, 1990), p. 216 (= *Système de la mode* (Paris, 1967)).

others, to impress and in this way to disclose his power (*tēn dunamin*) to his uncle when he meets him (5.5.5). So effective is this display of power that when Cyaxares observes his nephew's army, he considers himself dishonoured (*atimon*) by his own motley retinue (cf. *oligēn te kai oligou axian therapeian*) (5.5.6). The uncle affirms the potency of appearance, proclaiming himself ready to die ten times over to avoid being seen to be worthless (*tapeinos*) and to avoid being mocked by his relatives. It is no coincidence that, where Cyaxares had previously competed with Cyrus, following this episode Xenophon makes it clear that the uncle now defers to his Persian nephew (cf. 5.5.39).[39]

The narrative of book 8 establishes even more securely the politics of theatricality. Wood understands clothing as supplementing and signifying actual ability; however, I would argue that the Persian leader encourages his state officials to articulate their position and influence wholly through a rhetoric of dress: attire is what fundamentally distinguishes the rulers from those they rule (8.1.40).[40] Cyrus' leaders are made to wear shoes which make them seem taller than they really are (*hōste dokein meizous einai ē eisi*); they wear make-up which causes their eyes to appear more handsome than they actually are (*hōs euophthalmoteroi phainointo ē eisi*); in short, they are dressed so as to seem more impressive than their true natures (cf. *hōs euchrōteroi horōnto ē pephukasin*, 8.1.41).[41] The contrast between appearance and actuality, sign and reality, marks the arbitrariness of the rhetoric of fashion and its politics. Cyrus requires the leaders of his empire to be able to 'charm (*katagoēteuein*)' their subjects. The verb *katagoēteuein* suggests deception and it identifies Cyrus' rulers with the stereotype of the fifth- and fourth-century sorcerer-rhetorician, the figure who charms, deceives and overpowers his audience through his skill at deploying a cultural language, above all words.[42] In this Persia the privileged cultural language is cosmetic appearance.

As Cyrus devises an empire in which the only recognised power is apparent power, he abandons the pedagogical state with its foundation of power on knowledge. Later in book 8 the Persian leader plans a public procession which employs the appearance of solemnity (*semnotēs*) to reinforce respect for his government (*archēn*, 8.3.1). Xenophon tells

[39] Due, *The Cyropaedia*, p. 59.
[40] Wood, 'Xenophon's Theory of Leadership', pp. 64–5. Gera, *Xenophon's* Cyropaedia, p. 291, notes that most editors delete 8.1.40–2.
[41] Also cf. 1.2.16 for Cyrus' training of his men in the appearance of good manners and virtue.
[42] For the association between magic and persuasion, see J. de Romilly, *Magic and Rhetoric in Ancient Greece* (Cambridge, MA and London, 1975), pp. 13ff., 28–35 and passim.

us that the Persian leader hands out extravagant Median attire, red and purple cloaks, to the Persians and to those allies who hold positions of authority (*archas*), both to wear and in turn to distribute to their friends to wear (8.3.5). These gifts of clothing are the means by which Cyrus now bestows honour and status upon his subjects (8.2.10) so that they in turn can purchase the goodwill and deference of their subordinates (cf. *tōi dōreisthai kai timan*; 8.2.10; cf. 8.3.7; 8.4.36). This whole episode is a significant turning point, for it is the first occasion on which Persians en masse assume Median clothing (8.3.1[43]) – later the army will also be dressed in Median fashion (8.5.17; cf. 8.8.15). Xenophon marks this moment as a betrayal of the Persian way of life, contradicting Isocrates' observation that it is Cyrus' Persia which conquers Media (*Evagoras* 37). In the *Oeconomicus* Ischomachus proposes that, if he or his wife were to use make-up, it would constitute a deception between intimates (10.2–8). The author's implication is that Cyrus resorts to the very deceptive devices which Cambyses insists should only be used against one's enemies and never against one's own people on his subjects (cf. *tōn technōn . . . tōn memēchanēmenōn*, 8.3.1; *hai technai . . . hai memēchanēmenai*, 7.5.37; also see 1.6.38–39). Cyrus' emphasis on the clothing of his officials implies that the prince has succeeded in alienating his subjects, perhaps just as one might expect of a tyranny such as that portrayed in the *Hiero*.[44]

In the theatre of power Cyrus gives the starring role to himself. The Persian leader designates the status of his officials through splendid dress, but he employs even more extravagant attire to construct his own pre-eminent position. At the beginning of book 7 Cyrus appears arrayed for war as a latter-day Achilles with gold armour gleaming like a mirror and surrounded by a retinue clad in purple cloaks and bronze armour (7.1.2; cf. *Iliad* 19.364–99). At 7.5.37 Cyrus is said to desire to dress himself as he deems appropriate for a king (cf. *hōs basilei hēgeito prepein*). What this entails becomes evident from the grand procession described in the following book. Here Cyrus processes on a chariot with a crown and purple cloak which signify his kingly status. Xenophon declares that 'Cyrus appeared much larger (*meizōn d' ephanē polu Kuros*)' than his charioteer and goes on to qualify this statement with the words, 'whether in reality (*tōi onti*)' or 'by some means (*hopōsoun*)' (8.3.13–14). While the author's comments make the point that physical appearance

---

[43] Cf. καὶ τότε πρῶτον Πέρσαι Μηδικὴν στολὴν ἐνέδυσαν . . .
[44] Wood, 'Xenophon's Theory of Leadership', p. 63.

creates political status by dramatising it – Cyrus appears, and so is, greater than his lowly driver – his uncertainty as to whether the king is actually greater in stature than those around him or whether he has devised and fabricated his superior size also suggests the impossibility of distinguishing between true and apparent power in the theatrical state.

Michel Foucault has discussed the role of observation and the use of technologies of observation as a means of exercising one's own power and constraining the power of others.[45] In Cyrus' Persia, power is consolidated and realised when the external trappings of position are displayed by the leaders of the state and viewed by their subordinates. To ensure that such is the case, the Persian leader purchases through gifts and honours the loyalty of spies and eavesdroppers, his 'eyes' and 'ears' (8.2.10). The numerous 'eyes' and 'ears' watch for insubordination (*ta mē sumphora basilei*) and unrest amongst Cyrus' subjects, with the result that the subjects live in constant wariness and apprehension (8.2.12). Xenophon takes pains to insist that the king has numerous 'eyes', and not just one as some people think, since one individual would not be able to see or hear as much as many 'eyes' (8.2.11). The king's 'eyes' and 'ears' enable him to watch the watchers and, in so doing, to disseminate his authority throughout the kingdom. Cyrus creates a 'panoptic' state, one in which power is maintained through surveillance rather than through more overt violence or force. He contrives observation as a means of exercising his own power and constraining the power of others. The point is that the king's informers, in keeping with the metaphorical description of them as 'eyes' and 'ears', extend the physical presence of the monarch's body politic, perhaps just as clothing augments the corporality of Cyrus' favoured Persian officials.

The power of Cyrus' whole visual apparatus is affirmed by the response that his subjects give to the procession described in the final book. Xenophon identifies this as the first occasion that any Persian prostrates himself (cf. *prosekunēsan*) before his leader (8.3.15). He speculates that the response is such either because some of the onlookers had been ordered to do so, or else because they were so overawed by their leader's splendid appearance (8.3.14[46]). The author seems to be offering alternative explanations for the Persians' response to their

---

[45] See M. Foucault, 'The Eye of Power' in *Power/Knowledge: Selected Interviews and Other Writings, 1972–77*, Colin Gordon, ed. (New York, 1980), pp. 146–65.
[46] τῷ δόξαι μέγαν τε καὶ καλὸν φανῆναι τὸν Κῦρον, 8.3.14.

leader's appearance, but it can also be argued that he implicitly points to the assimilation of drama to an act of will, for the apparatus of theatre now has the same effect as command. The custom of prostration identifies power with the degradation of one's inferiors. Arrian characterises *proskunēsis* as a barbarian act of self-humiliation and -degradation which emphatically stands in contrast to the Greek ideal of freedom. In the *Anabasis* he observes that Cyrus was the first person to be honoured in this fashion and that this custom remained amongst the Persians and Medians until the Scythians, who are significantly described as a poor but free (*autonomoi*) people in his narrative, brought them to their senses (*Anabasis* 4.11.8–9).

It is no accident that until the final book of the *Cyropaedia* the only person to bow down before Cyrus was the Assyrian eunuch Gadatas, who, as the Persian leader's captive and subject, greets the ruler according to the fashion of his people (5.3.18). Gadatas is a significant figure because he draws attention to the way in which Cyrus subverts and redefines the traditional roles of authority in the pedagogical state. Like Gobryas, the Assyrian captive who has lost his son (4.6.5), the Assyrian eunuch is also childless, if for quite different reasons.[47] After grovelling before Cyrus, Gadatas offers the Persian leader gifts from his estate and livestock and proceeds to make the Persian leader his son and heir (5.4.30). This act is poignantly inappropriate. For one thing, as Gera notes, both Gadatas and Cyrus are roughly the same age and therefore should be figured as contemporaries rather than as father and son (5.3.19).[48] For another thing, and more importantly, the conquered subject Gadatas becomes a paternal figure to Cyrus patently without the prerogatives of the Persian father. Gadatas turns on its head the ideal of *patēr* as the locus of political authority, transforming the father instead into a figure of abasement. This recognition of what 'father' might also signify reveals the extent to which Persia has departed from the pedagogical ideal when Xenophon observes that Cyrus later takes his castrated 'father' as a paradigm for the loyal *subject* of imperial Persia. The ruler surrounds himself with a bodyguard composed of eunuchs (7.5.65), and he appoints the archetypal eunuch, Gadatas, to be the commander of his bodyguard and the head of the royal *oikos* (8.4.2ff).[49] The Persian leader declares that, because eunuchs possess

---

[47] Due, *The Cyropaedia*, p. 87.   [48] Gera, *Xenophon's* Cyropaedia, p. 255.

[49] The majority of critics deny that Cyrus actually castrated his servants, believing that he merely selected eunuchs for his households. This is a crucial move for those who wish to maintain that the Persian leader is an ideal monarch. See Gera, *Xenophon's* Cyropaedia, p. 287, n. 32.

no familial ties, having neither wives nor children on whom they can bestow their love, they are inclined to respect and revere their masters as the individuals who can most enrich and support them (7.5.60–61). Later at 8.2.9 he identifies the eunuch as the individual who can best exemplify a loyalty which surpasses even kinship ties. The three eunuchs who kill themselves following Abradatas' death in battle and the suicide of the latter's wife Panthea provide evidence of the fidelity of the castrated servant (7.3.15).

At 8.2.9 Xenophon observes that through the magnitude of his gifts the Persian king, that is, Cyrus makes his subjects prefer their leader to their own brothers, fathers and sons. It is in the light of this statement that the eunuch is to be regarded less as the faithful servant than as an individual who emblematises the alienation of familial relationships and affections which are the basis of Cyrus' authority. This alienation calls into question the identity of Cyrus' Persia as an ideal pedagogical state on the terms set out at the beginning of the work. The eunuch and the eunuch's creator resemble a figure presented to the reader earlier in the work as a *bad* teacher. In book 3, Xenophon recounts the case of a sophist, who was known to both the Persian king and his friend Tigranes, and who had since been executed by the Armenian king for corrupting (*diaphtheirein*) his son. The familiar charge against professional teachers and sometimes against philosophers (as in the case of Socrates) is specifically inflected so that this instance of didactic corruption has to do with the teacher's claim on an obedience that rightly belongs to the student's parents.[50] The sophist is other than, and so in competition with, the *Cyropaedia*'s ideal of the didactic father. To justify the execution of the pedagogue, the Armenian king draws an analogy between this individual and adulterers, who destroy the *philia* between husbands and wives (3.1.39[51]). Like sophists and adulterers, eunuchs corrupt the pedagogical state because they bring the process of political filiation to an end. Eunuchs, whether they are understood as desexualised or, for the Greeks, as feminised by the loss of their sexual organs,[52] cannot have sons or in turn become fathers to their sons. Cyrus' household of eunuchs is the demise of the father-teacher-king

[50] See Gera, *Xenophon's Cyropaedia*, p. 92, who cites Xen. *Apol.* 19–20; *Mem.* 1.2.49.

[51] Cf. νομίζοντες ἀφαιρεῖσθαι αὐτοὺς τὴν πρὸς αὐτοὺς φιλίαν, διὰ τοῦτο ὡς πολεμίοις αὐτοῖς χρῶνται, 3.1.39.

[52] E. Hall, *Inventing the Barbarian: Greek Self-Definition through Tragedy* (Oxford, 1989), p. 209, observes that eunuchs represent Eastern effeminacy in Greek tragedy. Also see P. Guyot, *Eunuchen als Sklaven und Freigelassene in der griechisch-römischen Antike* (Stuttgart, 1980), pp. 77–81, and K. Hopkins, 'Eunuchs in Politics in the Later Roman Empire', *PCPS* 9 (1963), pp. 72–80.

precisely as the household (*oikos*) is a microcosm of the state (1.1.1; cf. 8.1.9).[53] The Persian pedagogical ideal is one which can only tolerate the masculine figure as pupil and teacher.

By denying to pedagogy the possibility of reproduction, both literally and metaphorically, Cyrus has not only displaced the role and figure of the father-teacher-ruler; he has also radically redefined it. The figure of the eunuch rearticulates the degradation emblematised by the Persians' *proskunēsis* in the final book. As Luccioni observes, Xenophon's Greek audience would have seen castration as a barbaric custom, which would have contradicted even the Persian ideal of physical prowess presented in an earlier part of the work.[54] But the author does not rely on his reader's anthropological sensitivity in making the indignity of castration incontrovertible. He reports Cyrus' belief that men deprived of their sexual organs are no less courageous than others, a belief based on the analogy of gelded animals, which are not deprived of their strength and ability to work (7.5.62–3). Although Xenophon has valorised the comparison of political subjects to animals when he proposes that a herd of beasts is easier to control than men at 1.1.2–3, this subsequent analogy begins from quite a different assumption. Unlike the author, the Persian leader regards beasts as creatures to be exploited and mishandled by those who own and control them: they are the wretched beasts of burden (*hupozugia*) to whom Xenophon poignantly compares the unfortunate slaves on Cyrus' military campaign (8.1.44). Indeed, Herodotus mentions eunuchs, along with pack-animals, as part of the auxiliary of Xerxes' campaign at *Histories* 7.187. Castration is a trope for the grotesque disfigurement of an implied body politic at the hands of Cyrus.[55]

The reappearance of Cyrus' father, Cambyses, in the narrative presents a subtle but nevertheless powerful critique of the prince's relationship with his subjects. At 8.5.22–6 Cambyses offers his final speech in which he warns Cyrus against using his political position to take advantage of his subjects (8.5.24). Tatum regards Cambyses' advice as a merely symbolic nod to the topos of warnings about the dangers of tyranny and as one which has no bearing on a virtuous leader like

[53] Tatum, *Xenophon's Imperial Fiction*, pp. 59–60; also see Wood, 'Xenophon's Theory of Leadership', p. 57, and Strauss, 'Oikos/Polis'.

[54] See Luccioni, *Les idées politiques et sociales de Xénophon*, p. 238.

[55] P. Carlier, 'L' idée de monarchie impériale dans la Cyropédie de Xénophon', *Ktema* 3 (1978), pp. 133–65, esp. pp. 155ff. suggests that Cyrus' eunuchs signify the ruler's aspirations to complete domination over his subjects.

Cyrus.[56] I prefer to regard this interaction as suggesting how far the Persian prince has departed from the ideal of pedagogical 'rule of the father', such that Cambyses has to reassert his identity as father and king of the state (8.5.26) and Cyrus' as his son ('you, Cyrus, are my child (*pais*)', 8.5.22). Cambyses' reappearance makes the reader aware that in the preceding narrative Cyrus has claimed leadership without the due reference and deference to his father-teacher, apart from the brief exchange with him in the first book. Xenophon points out to his reader in the final book that now nobles (*hoi aristoi*) and slaves alike call Cyrus 'father (*patera*)' (cf. 8.1.44) so that the word *pais* now denotes the Persian subject as both, and as simultaneously, 'son' and 'slave'. The characterisation of the Persian king as a 'father' always figures the citizen as a *pais*, as a child, and then inevitably, in the case of a corrupt leader, as a slave. Cyrus reconstructs the Persian 'father' as a figure who not only rules but also dominates, such that any possibility of an Oedipal struggle between father and son is abrogated.[57]

VI

Scholars have conventionally articulated what they perceive to be Cyrus' fulfilment of the ideals set out at the beginning of the work in terms of his Socratic qualities. So Cyrus displays self-control, moderation, physical stamina, engages in dialogue and elenchus: in short, he is what Socrates would have been if he were the philosopher-king of the ideal state.[58] Yet it is doubtful whether Socratic pedagogy can be transferred in this manner into Xenophon's Persia. The *Cyropaedia* is a narrative about the failure of Cyrus' Persia to live up to the ideal of the pedagogical state. It is an account of how the inadequate education of a future leader, Cyrus, leads to the vitiation and perversion of the political structure, particularly as regards the relationship of the ruler to those he rules. The Persian leader achieves the complete and utter enslavement of his subjects and in doing so he can only call into question his own authority as the state's father-teacher.

---

[56] Tatum, *Xenophon's Imperial Fiction*, p. 78.

[57] Note that in classical Athens the individual is only properly a citizen once he ceases to be a child and is formally recognised as an adult male, in a public ceremony called the *dokimasia*. See S. Goldhill, 'The Great Dionysia and Civic Ideology' in J. Winkler and C. Zeitlin, *Nothing to Do with Dionysos? Athenian Drama in Its Social Context* (Princeton, 1990), p. 113; on the *dokimasia*, the ceremony of adult initiation, see D. Whitehead, *The Demes of Attica* (Princeton, 1986), pp. 97–109.

[58] E.g. Gera, *Xenophon's Cyropaedia*, pp. 26ff.

In depicting the disintegration of one ideal of the pedagogical state, the *Cyropaedia* perhaps implicitly provides the opportunity for a reinscription with a more familiar literal and metaphorical pedagogical *topos*, namely Athens. Indeed, at the moment that the work's epilogue discloses the collapse of Persia as a state in which knowledge and virtue have failed to construct power, Xenophon significantly steps into the narrative to recast himself, the Athenian author, as the text's privileged teacher. He now portrays himself as offering in the final chapters of the work his lesson about the consequences of pursuing political power without knowledge, 'To speak in truth, I shall begin to teach (*didaskein*) . . .' (8.8.2); in turn, the work's reader is characterised as Xenophon's pupil by the verbs 'to learn (*katamathein*)' (8.1.40) and 'we learned (*katemathomen*)' (8.2.10). The author designates himself as teacher and his audience as his pupils, as it would appear, in order to affirm a particular mode of questioning and unsettling pedagogy represented in the Socratic dialogues, the *Memorabilia* and the *Oeconomicus*, and invoked only by default in the *Cyropaedia*. In this model the Greek *polis*, above all Athens, is the realised pedagogical state, while the philosopher, most obviously Socrates – perhaps together with the philosopher's biographer, Xenophon – is its ideal citizen and leader. Pedagogy is thus the trope which articulates the political and cultural superiority of the Attic democratic state by inviting the replacement of Persia by Athens and of Cyrus by Socrates.

Select bibliography

ABBREVIATIONS

AJP	*American Journal of Philology*
ANRW	*Aufstieg und Niedergang der Römischen Welt*
BICS	*Bulletin of the Institute of Classical Studies*
BZ	*Byzantinische Zeitschrift*
CB	*Classical Bulletin*
CJ	*Classical Journal*
ClAnt	*Classical Antiquity*
ClMed	*Classica et Medievalia*
CP	*Classical Philology*
CQ	*Classical Quarterly*
DHA	*Dialogues d'Histoire Ancienne*
ΕΕΒΣ	*Ἐπετηρὶς Ἑταιρείας Βυζαντινῶν Σπουδῶν*
GG	*Grammatici Graeci*
GL	*Grammatici Latini*
G&R	*Greece and Rome*
HSCP	*Harvard Studies in Classical Philology*
HTR	*Harvard Theological Review*
JHI	*Journal of the History of Ideas*
JÖB	*Jahrbuch der Österreichische Byzantinistik*
OCD	*Oxford Classical Dictionary*
PBSR	*Papers of the British School at Rome*
PCPS	*Proceedings of the Cambridge Philological Society*
PLLS	*Papers from the Leeds Latin Seminar*
PP	*Past and Present*
RA	*Realencyclopädie der classischen Altertumswissenschaft*
REB	*Revue des Etudes Byzantines*
REG	*Revue des Etudes Grecques*
SC	*Studii Clasice*
SicGymn	*Siculorum Gymnasium*
TAPA	*Transactions and Proceedings of the American Philological Association*
THES	*Times Higher Education Supplement*
TM	*Travaux et Mémoires*

YCS   Yale Classical Studies
ŽPE   Ẕeitschrift für Papyrologie und Epigraphik

Adams, R. M., *The Better Part of Valor: More, Erasmus, Colet and Vives* (Seattle, 1962).
Ahl, F., 'The Art of Safe Criticism in Greece and Rome', *AJP* 105 (1984) 174–208.
Ahrweiler, H., *L'idéologie politique de l'Empire byzantin* (Paris, 1975).
Albisetti, J. C., *Schooling German Girls and Women: Secondary and Higher Education in the Nineteenth Century* (New York, 1988).
Anderson, G., *The Second Sophistic: a Cultural Phenomenon in the Roman Empire* (London, 1993).
Angold, M., *The Byzantine Empire 1025–1204. A Political History* (London, 1984).
Apple, M. W., *Education and Power* (Boston, London, etc., 1982).
Appleby, J., Hunt, L. and Jacob, M., *Telling the Truth about History* (New York, 1994).
Archer, M. S., 'Process without System', *European Journal of Sociology* 24 (1983) 196–221.
    Culture and Agency. The Place of Culture in Social Theory (Cambridge, 1988).
Arendt, H., 'What Was Authority?' in C. J. Friedrich (ed.) *Authority.* Nomos 1 (Cambridge, MA, 1958), pp. 96–7.
Athanassiadi-Fowden, P., 'The Idea of Hellenism', *Philosophia* 7 (1977), 323–56.
    Julian and Hellenism. An Intellectual Biography (London, 1992, 2nd edition).
Atherton, C., *The Stoics on Ambiguity* (Cambridge, 1993).
    'Apollonius Dyscolus and the Ambiguity of Ambiguity', *CQ* (1995), 441–73.
    'What Every Grammarian Knows?', *CQ* (1996), 239–60.
Bardon, H., 'Dialogue des Orateurs et Institution Oratoire', *REL* 19 (1941) 113–31.
Barth, S., *Jungfrauenzucht: Literaturwissenschaftliche und pädagogische Studien zur Mädchenerziehungsliteratur zwischen 1200 und 1600* (Stuttgart, 1994).
Barthes, R., *The Fashion System*, tr. M. Ward and R. Howard (Berkeley and Los Angeles, 1990) = *Système de la mode* (Paris, 1967).
Bartsch, R., *Norms of Language* (London and New York, 1987).
Bartsch, S., *Actors in the Audience: Theatricality and Double-Speak from Nero to Hadrian* (Cambridge, MA, and London, 1994).
Barwick, K., *Remmius Palaemon und die römische ars grammatica* (= *Philologus* Suppl. 15: 2) (Leipzig, 1922; repr. Hildesheim, 1967).
Beard, M., Bowman, A. K., Corbier, M., Cornell, T. J., Franklin, J. L., Hanson, A., Hopkins, K., Horsfall, N., *Literacy in the Roman World. Journal of Roman Archaeology*, suppl. 3 (Ann Arbor, 1991).
Beard, M. and Henderson, J., *Classics. A Very Short Introduction* (Oxford, 1995).
Beck, F. A. G., *Album of Greek Education* (Sydney, 1975).
Beck, H.-G., *Geschichte der orthodoxen Kirche im byzantinischen Reiche* (Die Kirche in ihrer Geschichte I, D1) (Göttingen, 1980).
Becker-Cantarino, B., *Der lange Weg zur Mündigkeit: Frauen und Literatur in Deutschland von 1500 bis 1800* (Munich, 1989).

Benjamin, A. (ed.), *Poststructuralist Classics* (London, 1988).

Ben-Rafael, E., *Language, Identity and Social Division. The Case of Israel* (Oxford, 1994).

Bernal, M., *Black Athena. The Afroasiatic Roots of Classical Civilization*, 2 vols. (London and New Brunswick, 1987–91).

Bloom, A., *The Closing of the American Mind. How Higher Education Has Failed Democracy and Impoverished the Souls of Today's Students* (New York, 1987).

Bloom, H., *The Western Canon. The Books and School of the Ages* (New York, 1984).

Bonner, S., *Education in Ancient Rome* (London, 1977).

Booth, A. D., 'Elementary and Secondary Education in the Roman Empire', *Florilegium* 1 (1979), 1–14.

'The Schooling of Slaves in First-Century Rome', *TAPA* 109 (1979) 11–19.

'Some Suspect Schoolmasters', *Florilegium* 3 (1981) 1–20.

Bourdieu, P. and Passeron, J.-C., *Reproduction in Education, Society and Culture* (London and Beverley Hills, 1977 [1970]).

Homo Academicus (Oxford, 1988).

Bower, E. W., 'Some Technical Terms in Roman Education', *Hermes* 89 (1961), 462–77.

Bowersock, G. W., *Greek Sophists in the Roman Empire* (Oxford, 1969).

Julian the Apostate (London, 1978).

Bowie, E. L., 'Greeks and Their Past in the Second Sophistic', *PP* 46 (1970), 3–41; reprinted in M. I. Finley (ed.), *Studies in Ancient Society* (London, 1974). Pp. 166–209.

'The Importance of Sophists', YCS 27 (1982), 29–59.

Bowman, A. K. and Woolf, G. (eds.), *Literacy and Power in the Ancient World* (Cambridge, 1994).

Brennan, M., *Literary Patronage in the English Renaissance: the Pembroke Family* (London, 1988).

Briggs, W. W. and Calder, W. M. III (eds.) *Classical Scholarship. A Biographical Encyclopaedia* (New York, 1990).

Brink, J. R., 'Bathsua Rainolds Makin: "Most Learned Matron"', *Harvard Language Quarterly* 54 (1991) 313–26.

Bromwich, D., *Politics by Other Means. Higher Education and Group Thinking* (New Haven, 1992).

Brown, P., *The Making of Late Antiquity* (Cambridge, MA, 1978).

Browning, R., 'Enlightenment and Repression in Byzantium in the Eleventh and Twelfth Centuries', *PP* 69 (1975), 3–23, reprinted in his *Studies on Byzantine History, Literature and Education* (London, 1977) no. 15.

Brugnoli, G., 'Quintiliano, Seneca e il *De causis corruptae eloquentiae*', *Orpheus* 6 (1959) 29–41.

Brunt, P. A., 'Stoicism and the Principate', *PBSR* 30 (1975), 7–35.

'The Bubble of the Second Sophistic', *BICS* 39 (1994), 25–52.

Burke, P., *The Art of Conversation* (Cambridge, 1993).

Carcopino, J., *Daily Life in Ancient Rome*, tr. E. O. Lorimer (Harmondsworth, 1956; first published 1941).

Carey, J., *The Intellectuals and the Masses. Pride and Prejudice among the Literary Intelligentsia, 1880–1939* (London, 1992).

Carlier, P., 'L'idée de monarchie impériale dans la Cyropédie de Xénophon', *Ktema* 3 (1978) 133–63.

Carnochan, W. B., *The Battleground of the Curriculum. Liberal Education and American Experience* (Stanford, 1993).

Cartledge, P., *The Greeks. A Portrait of Self and Others* (Oxford, 1993).

Clark, T. and Royle, N. (eds.) *The University in Ruins* (special issue of *The Oxford Literary Review*, 1995).

Clucas, L., *The Trial of John Italos and the Crisis of Intellectual Values in Byzantium in the Eleventh Century*, Miscellanea Byzantina Monacensia 26 (Munich, 1981).

Cohen, S., *Academia and the Luster of Capital* (Minneapolis, 1993).

Cole, T., *The Origins of Rhetoric in Ancient Greece* (Baltimore and London, 1991).

Collart, P., 'A l'école avec les petits Grecs d'Egypte', *Chronique d'Egypte* 11 (1936) 489–507.

Collini, S., 'The Passionate Intensity of Cultural Studies', *Victorian Studies* 36 (1993) 455–60.

Colls, R. and Dodd, P. (eds.), *Englishness. Politics and Culture 1880–1920* (London, 1986).

Connor, S., *Theory and Cultural Value* (Oxford, 1992).

Connor, W. R., Hansen, M. H., Raaflaub, K. A. and B. S. Strauss, *Aspects of Athenian Democracy*, Classica et Medievalia Dissertationes XI (Copenhagen, 1990).

Cousin, J., *Etudes sur Quintilien* (Paris, 1936).

Recherches sur Quintilien (Paris, 1975).

Criscuolo, U., 'Πολιτικὸς ἀνήρ. Contributo al pensiero politico di Michele Psello', *Atti della Società Nazionale di Scienze, Lettere e Belle Arti di Napoli* 93 (1982) 95–130.

Michele Psello: Epistola a Giovanni Xifilino, Byzantina et Neo-hellenica Neapolitana 14 (Naples, 1990, 2nd edition).

Michele Psello: Epistola a Giovanni Cerulario, Byzantina et Neo-hellenica Neapolitana 15 (Naples, 1990, 2nd edition).

Culham, P. and Edmunds, L. (eds.), *Classics: a Discipline and a Profession in Crisis?* (Lanham, MD and London, 1989).

Damrosch, D., *We Scholars: Changing the Culture of the University* (Cambridge, MA, 1995).

Davidson, P., *Poetry of the English Civil War* (Oxford, 1997).

Davis, L., and Mirabella, M. B., *Left Politics and the Literary Profession* (New York and Oxford, 1990).

De Baar, M., Löwensteyn, M., Monteiro, M., Sneller, A. A. (eds.), Richards, L. (tr.), *Choosing the Better Part: Anna Maria van Schurman (1607–1678)* (Dordrecht, Boston and London, 1996).

Desideri, P., *Dione di Prusa: un intelletuale greco nell'impero Romano* (Messina and Florence, 1978).

Dorey, T. A. (ed.), *Empire and Aftermath: Silver Latin II* (London, 1975).

Dowling, L., *Hellenism and Homosexuality in Victorian Oxford* (Ithaca and London, 1994).

Downey, G., 'Education and Public Problems as Seen by Themistius', *TAPA* 86 (1955) 291–307.

D'Souza, D., *Illiberal Education. The Politics of Race and Sex on Campus* (New York, 1991).

Due, B., *The Cyropaedia. Xenophon's Aims and Methods* (Aarhus and Copenhagen, 1989).

Dunant, S. (ed.), *The War of the Words. The Political Correctness Debate* (London, 1994).

Durkheim, E., *L'Evolution Pédagogique en France* (Paris, 1938).

Euben, J. P., Wallach, J. R. and Ober, J. (eds.), *Athenian Political Thought and the Reconstruction of American Democracy* (Princeton, 1994).

Evans, J. A. S., 'The Classics in English Canada', *Cahiers des études anciennes* 32 (1995) 33–43.

Ezell, M., *The Patriarch's Wife: Literary Evidence and the History of the Family* (Chapel Hill and London, 1987).

Writing Women's Literary History (Baltimore, 1993).

Ferguson, M. W. et al. (eds.), *Rewriting the Renaissance: the Discourses of Sexual Difference in Early Modern Europe* (Chicago and London, 1986).

Feugère, L., *Les femme poètes au xvi⁰ siècle* (Paris, 1860).

Finley, M. I., 'The Heritage of Isocrates', in his *The Use and Abuse of History* (London, 1975), pp. 193–214.

Flintermann, J.-J., *Power, Paideia and Pythagoreanism. Greek Identity, Conceptions of the Relationship between Philosophers and Monarchs and Political Ideas in Philostratus' Life of Apollonius* (Amsterdam, 1995).

Foucault, M., *Power/Knowledge: Selected Interviews and Other Writings, 1972–77*, ed. C. Gordon (New York, 1980).

Frede, M., 'Principles of Stoic Grammar', in *Essays in Ancient Philosophy* (Oxford, 1987), pp. 303–37.

Frevert, U., *Women in German History: from Bourgeois Emancipation to Sexual Liberation* (Oxford, 1989).

Fritz, K. von, 'Ancient Instruction in "Grammar" According to Quintilian', *AJP* 70 (1949), 337–66.

Galinsky, G. K., *Classical and Modern Interactions. Postmodern Architecture, Multiculturalism, Decline, and Other Issues* (Austin, TX, 1992).

Gallop, J. (ed.), *Pedagogy: the Question of Impersonation* (Bloomington and Indianapolis, 1995).

Gardiner, D., *English Girlhood at School: a Study of Women's Education through Twelve Centuries* (London, 1929).

Garrison, J. D., *Dryden and the Tradition of Panegyric* (Berkeley, 1975).

Gera, D., *Xenophon's Cyropaedia: Style, Genre and Literary Technique* (Oxford, 1993).

Gill, C., 'The Question of Character-Development: Plutarch and Tacitus', *CQ* 33 (1983) 469–87.

Gleason, M. W., *Making Men. Sophists and Self-Presentation in Ancient Rome* (Princeton, 1995).

Gless, D. J. and Herrnstein Smith, B., *The Politics of Liberal Education* (Durham, NC, 1992).

Goodman, A. and MacKay, A. (eds.), *The Impact of Humanism on Western Europe* (London, 1990).

Gouillard, J., *La vie religieuse à Byzance* (London, 1981).

'Le procès officiel de Jean l'Italien: Les actes et leurs sous-entedus', *TM* 9 (1985) 133–74.

Graff, G., *Beyond the Culture Wars: How Teaching the Conflicts Can Revitalize American Education* (New York, 1993).

Grafton, A. and Jardine, L., *From Humanism to the Humanities: Education and the Liberal Arts in Fifteenth- and Sixteenth-Century Europe* (London, 1986).

Green, A., *Education and State Formation. The Rise of Education Systems in England, France and the USA* (London, 1990).

Griffin, M., *Seneca: a Philosopher in Politics* (Oxford, 1976).

Grube, G., 'Educational and Literary Theory in Cicero', *Phoenix* 16 (1962) 234–57.

Gruen, E. S., 'Cultural Fictions and Cultural Identity', *TAPA* 123 (1993) 1–14.

Gubar, S. and Kamholtz, J. (eds.), *English Inside and Out: the Places of Literary Criticism* (New York and London, 1993).

Guengerich, R., 'Der *Dialogus* des Tacitus und Quintilians *Institutio Oratoria*', *CP* 46 (1951) 159–61.

Hall, E., *Inventing the Barbarian: Greek Self-Definition through Tragedy* (Oxford, 1989).

Hardison, O. B., *The Enduring Monument: a Study of the Idea of Praise in Renaissance Literary Theory and Practice* (Chapel Hill, 1962).

Harris, R., *The Language Myth* (London, 1981).

Harris, W. V., *Ancient Literacy* (Cambridge, MA, and London, 1989).

Hermann, L., 'Quintilien et le Dialogue des Orateurs', *Latomus* 14 (1955) 349–69.

Hermann, U., 'Erziehung und Schulunterricht für Mädchen im 18. Jahrhundert', *Wolfenbütteler Studien zur Aufklärung* 3 (1976), 101–27.

Higgins, W. E., *Xenophon the Athenian. The Problem of the Individual and the Society of the Polis* (Albany, NY, 1977).

Himmelfarb, G., *On Looking into the Abyss. Untimely Thoughts on Culture and Society* (New York, 1995).

Hirsch, S. W., *The Friendship of the Barbarians. Xenophon and the Persian Empire* (Hanover and London, 1985).

Hollinger, D. A., *Postethnic America. Beyond Multiculturalism* (New York, 1995).

Hopkins, K., *Death and Renewal* (Cambridge, 1983).

Hoskin, K., 'The Examination, Disciplinary Power and Rational Schooling', *History of Education* 8 (1979) 135–46.

Hussey, J. M., *Church and Learning in the Byzantine Empire 867–1185* (London, 1937).

Jaeger, W., *Paideia: the Ideals of Greek Culture*, vol. 1, tr. Gilbert Highet (Oxford, 1939).

Early Christianity and Greek Paideia (Cambridge, MA, 1961).

Jardine, L., 'Isotta Nogarola: Women Humanists – Education for What?', *History of Education* 12 (1983) 231–44.

'"O decus Italiae virgo", or the Myth of the Learned Lady in the Renaissance', *Historical Journal* 28 (1985) 799–819.

Erasmus, Man of Letters (Princeton, 1993).

Johnson, B., *The Pedagogical Imperative. Teaching as a Literary Genre*, Yale French Studies 63 (1983).

Johnson, G., *F. M. Cornford's Cambridge and his Advice to the Young Academic Politician* (Cambridge, 1994).

Jones, C. P., *The Roman World of Dio Chrysostom* (Cambridge, MA, 1978).

Karant-Nunn, S., 'Continuity and Change: Some Effects of the Reformation on the Women of Zwickau', *Sixteenth-Century Journal* 13 (1982) 18–24.

Karpozilos, A., Συμβολὴ στὴ μελέτη τοῦ βίου καὶ τοῦ ἔργου τοῦ Ἰωάννη Μαυρόποδος (Δωδώνη, Παράρτημα 18) (Ioannina, 1982).

The Letters of Ioannes Mauropous Metropolitan of Euchaita: Greek text, translation and commentary, Corpus Fontium Historiae Byzantinae 34 (Thessaloniki, 1990).

Kaster, R. A., *Guardians of Language: the Grammarian and Society in Late Antiquity* (Berkeley, Los Angeles and London, 1988).

Kazhdan, A., 'Some Problems in the Biography of John Mauropous', *JÖB* 43 (1993) 87–111.

Kazhdan, A. P. and Franklin, S., *Studies on Byzantine Literature of the Eleventh and Twelfth Centuries* (Cambridge and Paris, 1984).

Kazhdan, A. P. and Wharton Epstein, A., *Change in Byzantine Culture in the Eleventh and Twelfth Centuries*, The Transformation of the Classical Heritage 7 (Berkeley, Los Angeles and London, 1985).

Kennedy, G. A., *Quintilian* (New York, 1969).

The Art of Rhetoric in the Roman World (Princeton, 1972).

Greek Rhetoric under Christian Emperors (Princeton, 1983).

(ed.), *The Cambridge History of Literary Criticism. Volume I: Classical Criticism* (Cambridge, 1989).

Kermode, F., *The Classics. Literary Images of Permanence and Change* (Cambridge, 1977).

King, M. L., 'Thwarted Ambitions: Six Learned Women of the Italian Renaissance', *Soundings* 59 (1976) 276–304.

'The Religious Retreat of Isotta Nogarola', *Signs* 3 (1978) 807–22.

King, M. L. and Rabil, A., *Her Immaculate Hand: Selected Works By and About the Woman Humanists of the Quattrocentro* (Binghamton, NY, 1983).

Knox, B. M. W., *The Oldest Dead White European Males and Other Reflections on the Classics* (New York, 1993).

Backing into the Future. The Classical Tradition and Its Renewal (New York, 1994).

Kraye, J. (ed.), *The Cambridge Companion to Renaissance Humanism* (Cambridge, 1996).

Lamb, M. E., 'The Cooke Sisters: Attitudes towards Learned Women', in M. P. Hannay (ed.), *Silent but for the Word: Tudor Women as Patrons, Translators and Writers of Religious Works* (Kent, OH, 1985), pp. 107–25.

Lanham, R. A., *The Electronic Word: Democracy, Technology and the Arts* (Chicago, 1995) [on floppy disk].

Le Doeuff, M., *Hipparchia's Choice: an Essay Concerning Women, Philosophy, etc.* (Oxford, 1991) [=*L'Etude et le rouet* (Paris, 1989)].

Leach, A. F., *A History of Winchester College* (London, 1899).

Lefkowitz, M., *Not Out of Africa: How Afrocentrism Become an Excuse to Teach Myth as History* (New York, 1996).

Lemerle, P., *Byzantine Humanism: the First Phase. Notes and Remarks on Education and Culture in Byzantium from its Origins to the Tenth Century*, tr. H. Lindsay and A. Moffatt, Byzantina Australiensia 3 (Canberra, 1986).

Levin, M. M. (ed.), *The Challenge of 'Black Athena'* (*Arethusa* special issue, 1989).

Lewalski, B. K., *Writing Women in Jacobean England* (Cambridge, MA and London, 1993).

Liedke, M. and Hohenzollern, J. G. Prinz von (eds.), *Der weite Schulweg der Mädchen: Die Geschichte der Mädchengildung als Beispiel der Geschichte anthropologische Vorurteile* (Bad Heilbrunn, 1990).

Loeb, P. R., *Generation at the Crossroads. Apathy and Action on the American Campus* (New Brunswick, 1994).

Lorti, D. C., *Schoolteacher* (Chicago, 1975).

Luccioni, J., *Les idées politiques et sociales de Xénophon* (Paris, 1947).

Magdalino, P., *Tradition and Transformation in Medieval Byzantium* (London, 1991).

Maier, H., 'Eine Kultur oder viele? Die Zukunft der Kulturen', *Gymnasium* 102 (1995) 1–30.

Mangan, J. A., *Athleticism in the Victorian and Edwardian Public School* (Cambridge, 1986).

Mango, C., *Byzantium and Its Image* (London, 1984).

Markopoulos, A. (ed.), *Constantine VII Porphyrogenitus and his Age. Second International Byzantine Conference (Delphi, July 1987)* (Athens, 1989), pp. 155–64.

Marrou, H. I., *A History of Education in Antiquity*, tr. G. Lamb (Madison and London, 1956) = *Histoire de l'éducation dans l'antiquité* (Paris, 1948).

Martindale, C., 'Professing Latin', *CUCD Bulletin* 23 (1994) 3–21.

Mathieu, G. and Brémond, E. (eds.), *Isocrate*, 4 vols. (Paris, 1929–62).

McConica, J. (ed.), *The History of the University of Oxford vol. III. The Collegiate University* (Oxford, 1986).

Erasmus (Oxford, 1991).

Mikkola, E., *Isokrates: seine Anschauungen im Lichte seiner Schriften* (Helsinki, 1954).

Milner, A., *Contemporary Cultural Theory. An Introduction* (London, 1993).

Mitchell, T. N., 'The Classics in an Age of Innovation and Technology', *Classics Ireland* 1 (1994) 1–17.

Moles, J. L., 'The Career and Conversion of Dio Chrysostom', *JHS* 98 (1978) 79–100.

'The *Kingship Orations* of Dio Chrysostom', *PLLS* 6 (1990) 297–375.

Morgan, T. J., *Frames of Mind: Literate Education in the Hellenistic and Roman Worlds*, unpublished PhD thesis, University of Cambridge, 1995.

Morrill, J. (ed.), *The Oxford Illustrated History of Tudor and Stuart Britain* (Oxford, 1996).

Morris, I. M. (ed.), *Classical Greece. Ancient Histories and Modern Archaeologies* (Cambridge, 1994).

Morrison, J. S., 'An Introductory Chapter in the History of Greek Education', *Durham University Journal* (1940) 55–63.

Nelson, C., *Repression and Recovery. Modern American Poetry and the Politics of Cultural Memory 1910–1945* (Madison, 1989).

Niekus Moore, C., *The Maiden's Mirror: Reading Material for German Girls in the Sixteenth and Seventh Centuries* (Wiesbaden, 1987).

Oakley, F., *Community of Learning. The American College and the Liberal Arts Tradition* (New York, 1993).

Oettel, T., 'Una cathedrática en el siglo xvi, Lucia de Medrano', *Boletín de la Real Academia de la Historia* (1935) 310.

Ong, W. J., 'Latin Language Study as a Renaissance Puberty Rite', *Studies in Philology* 56 (1959) 103–24.

Parks, E. P., *Roman Rhetorical Schools as a Preparation for the Courts under the Early Empire*, Johns Hopkins University Studies 63.2 (Baltimore, 1945).

Patterson, A., *Reading Between the Lines* (London, 1993).

Peck, L. L., *Court Patronage and Corruption in Early Stuart England* (London, 1993).

Peradotto, J. and Hansen, H. (eds.), *Rethinking the Classical Canon* (=*Arethusa* 27.1, 1994).

Perry, R., *The Celebrated Mary Astell: an Early English Feminist* (Chicago and London, 1986).

Petschauer, P., *The Education of Women in Eighteenth-Century Germany: New Directions from the German Female Perspective* (Lewiston, NY, 1989).

Phillips, C. R. III, 'Classical Scholarship Against its History', *AJP* 110 (1989) 636–57.

Plumb, J. H. (ed.), *Crisis in the Humanities* (Harmondsworth, 1964).

Podskalsky, G., *Theologie und Philosophie in Byzanz*, Byzantisches Archiv 15 (Munich, 1977).

Pomeroy, S. B., *Xenophon Oeconomicus* (Oxford, 1994).

Rabinowitz, N. S. and Richlin, A. (eds.), *Feminist Theory and the Classics* (London and New York, 1993).

Rand, R. (ed.), *Logomachia. The Conflict of the Faculties* (Lincoln, NB, 1993).

Rawson, E., 'Roman Rulers and the Philosophic Adviser', in M. T. Griffin and J. Barnes (eds.), *Philosophia Togata* (Oxford, 1989), pp. 233–57.

Reardon, B. P., *Courants littéraires des IIe et IIIe siècles après J.-C.* (Paris, 1971).

Reble, A. (ed.), *Zur Geschichte der höheren Schule* (Bad Heilbrunn, 1975).

Reverdin, O. (ed.). *Les études classiques aux XIXe et XXe siècles: leur place dans l'histoire des idées. Entretiens Hardt* 26 (Vandoeuvres-Geneva, 1980).

Riensch, D. R., 'Zur Identität einer Gestalt im *Timarion*', *BZ* 86–87 (1993–4) 383–5.

Ringer, F. K., *Education and Society in Modern Europe* (Bloomington and London, 1979).

Rudd, W. J. N., *Schoolmaster Extraordinary* (Bristol, 1980).

Rundle, D., 'A New Golden Age? More, Skelton and the Accession Verses of 1509', *Renaissance Studies* 9 (1995) 58–76.

Russell, D. A., *Criticism in Antiquity* (London, 1981).

Schleiner, L., *Tudor and Stuart Women Writers* (Bloomington and Indianapolis, 1994).

Schmeller, A., Halm, C., Meyer, W., et. al., *Catalogus Codicum Latinorum Bibliothecae Regiae Monacensis*, 4 vols. (Munich, 1866–74).

Schotel, G. D. J., *Letter- en oudheidkundige avondstonden* (Dordrecht, 1841).

Searle, G. R., *The Quest for National Efficiency* (Oxford, 1971).

Seel, O., *Quintilian – oder die Kunst des Redens und Schweigens* (Stuttgart, 1977).

Segal, C., 'Classical criticism and the canon, or, why read the ancient critics?', in S. Lawall (ed.), *Reading World Literature. Theory, History, Practice* (Austin, 1994), pp. 87–112.

Sellers, M. N. S. (ed.), *An Ethical Education: Community and Morality in the Multicultural University* (Oxford, 1994).

Siebenborn, E., *Die Lehre von der Sprachrichtigkeit und ihren Kriterien. Studien zur antiken normativen Grammatik* (Amsterdam, 1976).

Simmel, M., *Erziehung zum Weibe: Mädchenbildung im 19. Jahrhundert* (Frankfurt a. M., 1980).

Simon, S. J., 'Domitian, Patron of Letters', *CB* 51 (1975) 58–9.

Skinner, Q., *Foundations of Modern Political Thought*, 2 vols. (Cambridge, 1978).

Sorabji, R., *Animal Minds and Human Morals* (London, 1993).

Speck, P., *Die kaiserliche Universität von Konstantinopel*, Byzantinisches Archiv 14 (Munich, 1974).

Steiner, W., *The Scandal of Pleasure. Art in an Age of Fundamentalism* (Chicago and London, 1995).

Stephanou, P. E., *Jean Italos philosophe et humaniste* (Rome, 1949).

Steward, A., *Close Readers: Humanism and Sodomy in Early Modern England* (Princeton, 1997).

Stock, P., *Better than Rubies: a History of Women's Education* (New York, 1978).

Stone, L. (ed.), *The University in Society*, 2 vols. (Princeton, 1974).

Strauss, B. S., *Fathers and Sons in Athens: Ideology and Society in the Era of the Peloponnesian War* (London, 1993).

Stray, C. A., 'Paradigms of Social Order. The Politics of Latin Grammar in 19th-century England', *Henry Sweet Society Newsletter* 13 (1989) 13–23.

   'The Smell of Latin Grammar: Contrary Imaginings in English Classrooms', *Bulletin of the John Rylands University Library of Manchester* 76/3 (1994) 201–20.

   Grinders and Grammars. A Victorian Controversy (Reading, 1995).

   The Mushri-English Pronouncing Dictionary. A Chapter in 19th-century English Public School Lexicography (Berkeley, Swansea, Wellington, 1996). [privately printed]

Stray, C. A. and Kaster, R. A. (eds.), *Reinterpreting the Classics* (=*Annals of Scholarship* 10.1, 1993).

Swain, S., *Hellenism and Empire: Language, Classicism and Power in the Greek World, AD 50–250* (Oxford, 1996).

Tatakis, B., *La philosophie byzantine* (Paris, 1959, 2nd edition).

Tatum, J., *Xenophon's Imperial Fiction. On The Education of Cyrus* (Princeton, 1989).

Taylor, C., *Multiculturalism and 'the Politics of Recognition'*, ed. A. Gutmann (Princeton, 1992).

Taylor, D. J. (ed.), *The History of Linguistics in the Classical Period* (Amsterdam and Philadelphia, 1987).

Too, Y. L., *The Rhetoric of Identity in Isocrates: Text, Power, Pedagogy* (Cambridge, 1995).

Turner, E. G., 'Athenians Learn to Write: Plato *Protagoras* 326d', *BICS* 12 (1965) 67–9.

Uhlfelder, M. L., *De proprietate sermonum vel rerum* (*Papers and Monographs of the American Academy in Rome*), vol. 15 (1954)).

Weathers, W., 'Xenophon's Political Idealism', *CJ* 41 (1954) 317–21, 330.

Weiss, J. H., 'Interpreting Cultural Crisis: Social History Confronts Humanities Education', *JHI* 26.3 (1996) 459–74.

Whigham, F., *Ambition and Privilege: the Social Tropes of Elizabethan Courtesy Theory* (Berkeley, 1984).

Wiedemann, T., *Adults and Children in the Roman Empire* (London, 1989).

Wilson, J. K., *The Myth of Political Correctness. The Conservative Attack on Higher Education* (Durham, NC, 1995).

Wilson, K. M., *Encyclopedia of Continental Women Writers*, 2 vols. (New York and London, 1991).

Wilson, N. G., *Scholars of Byzantium* (London, 1983).

Winterbottom, M., 'Quintilian and the *vir bonus*', *JRS* 54 (1964) 90–7.

Wood, N., 'Xenophon's Theory of Leadership' *ClMed* 24 (1964) 33–66.

Cicero's Social and Political Thought (Berkeley, 1988).

Woods, J. M. and Fürstenwald, M., *Schriftstellerinnen, Künstlerinnen und gelehrte Frauen des deutschen Barock*, 2 vols. (Stuttgart, 1984).

Woodside, M., 'Vespasian's Patronage of Education', *TAPA* 73 (1942) 123–9.

Woolf, G., 'Becoming Roman, Staying Greek. Culture, Identity and the Civilising Process in the Roman East', *PCPS* 40 (1994) 116–43.

Wormser, G., 'Le Dialogue des Orateurs et l'Institution Oratoire', *RP* 36 (1912) 179–89.

Wright, F. A. and Sinclair, T. A., *A History of Latin Literature from the Middle of the Fourth to the End of the Seventeenth Century* (London, 1931).

Wrightson, K. and Levine, D., *The Making of an Industrial Society: Whickham 1560–1765* (Oxford, 1991).

Yates, F., *The French Academies of the Sixteenth Century* (London and New York, 1947).

Zeller, K., *Pädagogik und Drama: Untersuchungen zur Schulkomödie Christian Weises* (Tübingen, 1980).

Index

IDEAS IN CONTEXT

Edited by QUENTIN SKINNER (*General Editor*), LORRAINE DASTON
WOLF LEPENIES, J. B. SCHNEEWIND and JAMES TULLY

Titles marked with an asterisk are also available in paperback